Springer Proceedings in Business and Economics

More information about this series at http://www.springer.com/series/11960

Kesra Nermend · Małgorzata Łatuszyńska
Editors

Problems, Methods and Tools in Experimental and Behavioral Economics

Computational Methods in Experimental Economics (CMEE) 2017 Conference

Springer

Editors
Kesra Nermend
Faculty of Economics
and Management
University of Szczecin
Szczecin, Poland

Małgorzata Łatuszyńska
Faculty of Economics
and Management
University of Szczecin
Szczecin, Poland

ISSN 2198-7246 ISSN 2198-7254 (electronic)
Springer Proceedings in Business and Economics
ISBN 978-3-030-07573-6 ISBN 978-3-319-99187-0 (eBook)
https://doi.org/10.1007/978-3-319-99187-0

This Springer imprint is published by the registered company Springer Nature Switzerland AG
The registered company address is: Gewerbestrasse 11, 6330 Cham, Switzerland

Preface

Experimental and behavioral economics are essential part of modern economics. Experimental economy adapts methods developed in the natural sciences to study economic behavior. The latest research includes experiments both in the laboratory and in the field, and the results are used to test and better understand economic theories. Behavioral economics tries to make economics a more appropriate and powerful science about human behavior, integrating insight into psychology and social sciences into economics.

Experimental and behavioral economics are dynamic fields of economic research that shed new light on many known and important economic issues. Being young, these fields have gained wide recognition in the twenty-first century, for example, by awarding the 2002 Nobel Prize in Economics to Daniel Kahneman and Vernon Smith. Other Nobel Prize winners—Elinor Ostrom in 2009, Alvin Roth in 2012, and Richard Thaler in 2017, also significantly contributed to the development of these areas.

Experimental and behavioral economics are rapidly evolving. This book cannot therefore provide a comprehensive overview, but focuses on selected topics. It includes the papers of researchers who are interested in experimental and behavioral economics and represent a certain level of experience in these fields. Its main purpose is to illustrate the links between various fields of knowledge that are part of experimental and behavioral economics.

The book is divided into three parts:

I Theoretical Aspects of Contemporary Economics.
II Methods and Tools of Contemporary Economics.
III Practical Issues—Case Studies.

As the title suggests, the first part of the book presents the theoretical foundations of contemporary economics with particular emphasis on behavioral economics. It outlines the differences between the mainstream economics and behavioral economics, indicates the directions of using behavioral economics achievements in creating public policy, and presents the areas of behavioral factors' impact on the possibility of effective cost management. It also discusses theoretical aspects related to the problem of equilibrium in behavioral economics as well as several other issues referring to the contemporary economics.

The second part of the book contains a general outline of methods and tools that support scientists in the field of experimental and behavioral economics. The outline presents both methods commonly used by scientists (such as statistical ones), as well as those usually less associated with economics (e.g., artificial intelligence, computer simulation, cognitive neuroscience techniques, or multicriteria decision support methods), indicating their potential application in behavioral economics and economic experiments.

The last part of the volume presents examples of behavioral and experimental research in the field of economics. They use various methods and tools described in the methodological chapters of the book. There are shown only selected case studies, but they outline a wide range of topics connected to experimental and behavioral economics.

Issues raised in the monograph do not exhaust the subject of experimental and behavioral economics. Yet, in the opinion of the editors, it shows well the diversity of areas, problems, methods, techniques, and domains concerning this subject.

Szczecin, Poland

Małgorzata Łatuszyńska
Kesra Nermend

Contents

Part I
Theoretical Aspects of Experimental and Behavioral Economics

Chapter 1
Mainstream Economics Versus Behavioral Economics—A Contribution to Reflection

Ewa Mazur-Wierzbicka

Abstract The aim of the chapter is to show the differences between mainstream economics and behavioral economics. This allowed showing weaknesses of economics resulting from the shortcomings of the mainstream economics paradigm. The assumed goal was achieved by means of a critical analysis of the national and foreign subject literature in the field of economic sciences. The text presents the issues of mainstream economics and behavioral economics. Then, a critical view of mainstream economics from the perspective of behaviorists was presented and so was the view of behavioral economics from the point of view of mainstream economists. In the following parts, aspects that differentiate mainstream economics and behavioral economics were highlighted.

Keywords Mainstream economics · Behavioral economics · Rationality

1.1 Introduction

The recent global economic crisis has highlighted the shortcomings of economics in terms of prediction. It turned out that the forecasting models created in economics, despite the elegant, ordered form preserved—did not predict the future well. In turn, the possibility of an extended analysis including, i.a., bounded rationality or heuristics is created by behavioral economics, whose intensive development has been observed since the end of the twentieth century.

This was a premise to reflect on the differences between mainstream economics and behavioral economics (underestimated by some), which was adopted as the main goal of the chapter. It was also an impulse to draw attention to the weakness of economics resulting from the shortcomings of the mainstream economics paradigm.

E. Mazur-Wierzbicka (✉)
Department of Human Capital Management Faculty of Economics and Management, University of Szczecin, Mickiewicza 64, 71-101 Szczecin, Poland
e-mail: ewa.mazur-wierzbicka@wp.pl

K. Nermend and M. Łatuszyńska (eds.), *Problems, Methods and Tools in Experimental and Behavioral Economics*, Springer Proceedings in Business and Economics, https://doi.org/10.1007/978-3-319-99187-0_1

A broader view of economic issues including, i.a, bounded rationality or heuristics will certainly foster prediction in economic theory.

Its layout was subordinated to the implementation of the goal of the work. At the beginning, the issues of mainstream economics and behavioral economics were brought out. Then, a critical view of mainstream economics from the perspective of behaviorists was presented and a view of behavioral economics from the point of view of mainstream economists. In the following part, aspects that differentiate mainstream economics and behavioral economics were highlighted.

1.2 Mainstream Economics—Introductory Issues

The term mainstream economics defines schools and trends in modern economics, which, i.a., use deductive and abstract methods in research, analyze economic phenomena in a static and dynamic approach, take into account innovations in created models, develop microeconomic foundations for macroeconomic analysis ensuring internal consistency of the theory. The development of the theory makes the scope of mainstream economics change. Nowadays, it includes the neoclassical school, monetarism, the theory of rational expectations, the real business cycle theory and Keynesism (Kundera 2004).

It should be noted that characteristic especially for economists associated with the so-called mainstream economics is to emphasize the special position of economics among social sciences.

The subject of economics was perceived in various ways in the history of the development of this science. This was also true of mainstream economists. For example, Nassau W. Senior believed that the object of economic interest is to maximize wealth at a minimum cost. In turn, for L. C. Robbins it was the achievement of the assumed goals with limited resources. According to J. B. Say, it was a way and principles of creation, division and consumption of wealth that satisfy the needs of society. J. S. Mill, on the other hand, believed that these were the rights to create and divide wealth. M. Friedman took it up in a different way. He believed that the subject of interest in economics is a verifiable prediction based on hypotheses. In general, it can be said that the subject of mainstream economics is capital management, especially management of limited natural, human, and financial resources (Stankiewicz 2000).

Mainstream economics generally refers to the paradigm reaching with its roots the tradition of classical and especially neoclassical economics. The ideas that are particularly important for mainstream economics can be reduced to the following words: market, transaction, competition, producer, consumer, rationality, self-regulation (Ratajczak 2008). It applies a particular importance to the methodological tradition of model building and their empirical testing.

Economics is a social science. For this reason, it requires the recognition of human behavior in the field of management and therefore a specific and rather narrow view of the human being, defining its characteristics shaping economic activity (Sora 2006). Views on the concept of the economic man, otherwise known as homo oeconomicus, are the subject of a fundamental dispute in the theory of economics. This model constituted economics as a separate scientific discipline (Stępień and Szarzec 2007).

According to the definition of Stępień and Szarzec (2007), the economic man "is an entity that has a specific economic goal and on the basis of his knowledge of the available means and circumstances of the action selects the most effective ways to achieve this goal. At the same time, he is attributed rationality, but he is also characterized by volitionality and intentionality. Rational action therefore consists in such a selection of means by the subject, using his knowledge, to achieve a given goal". Swacha-Lech (2010) includes in the main features of the homo oeconomicus model approach the following:

- maximizing usability,
- optimal operation in an arbitrary environment,
- stability and continuity of preferences,
- independence from the context of general preferences,
- analytical information processing,
- unrestricted administration of information,
- a universal and homogeneous decision-making mechanism,
- the primary role of cognitive processes,
- unlimited willpower,
- unlimited selfishness.

The abstract assumption of homo oeconomicus states that specific human behavior in the sphere of management can be explained in terms of strictly rational choices (Wach 2010). To this day, this axiom is still the main assumption of mainstream economics. As Stiglitz writes (2010), analyzing the weaknesses of mainstream economics: "in science, quite often certain assumptions are so strongly held or so rooted in thinking that no one realizes that these are just assumptions."

Czaja very aptly captures the main aspects of mainstream economics. He argues that "(…) it can be concluded that the four basic structural elements of the neoclassical school dominant in modern economics—the idea of perfect competition, the Saya model, the assumption of rational behavior of economic entities and cognitive and methodological individualism—are derived directly from the mechanistic understanding of reality and carry all the important cognitive and methodological aspects of the Cartesian-Newtonian paradigm. Thus, they contain a conviction of a strictly deterministic, cause-and-effect nature of socioeconomic phenomena, their stability and propensity to achieve balance, which guarantees high predictivity, reversibility and stationarity, and the possibility of reductionist reduction to quantitative kinetic changes. At the same time, it can be said that the main trend in the theory of economics is based on anthropocentrism … (…)" (2011).

1.3 Behavioral Economics—Introductory Issues

Behavioral economics is one of the most intensively developing trends in modern economics. A rapidly developing field, it owes its success to the belief in the growing importance of psychological foundations in economic analyses, both theoretical and practical (Camerer and Loewenstein 2004).

The name behavioral economics was first used by Boulding (cf. Boulding 1961). He wrote in 1958 about the need to turn to behavioral economics, which is supposed to study hose aspects of human imaginations or cognitive and emotional structures that have an impact on economic decisions (Angner and Loewenstein 2012). However, the use of such a term is misleading. It suggests a strong link between this trend and the behavioral trend in psychology, whereas behavioral economists base primarily on the achievements of cognitive psychology, which is opposed to behaviorism. Therefore, it would be appropriate to use the name cognitive economics, as it was emphasized by E. Wanner, president of the Russell Sage Foundation, who contributed to the separation of behavioral economics as a scientific subdiscipline.

He described behavioral economics as the application of cognitive science from the sphere of taking economic decisions. He claimed that: "The field is misnamed—it should have been called cognitive economics" "We weren't brave enough" (Lambert 2006).

In the subject literature, however, the term behavioral economics is used, which was also maintained in this chapter.

It is worth emphasizing that the foundations of the behavioral school in economics were created by Smith (The Theory of Moral Sentiments) (1989), J. Bentham, and W. Jevons. The concept of bounded rationality proposed in 1956 by H. Simon and the X-efficiency theory created by H. Leibenstein in 1966 became the foundations of research in behavioral economics.

An important moment for the new trend in economics was publishing in 1979 of the work of D. Kahneman and A. Tversky Prospect Theory: An Analysis of Decisions under Risk. It is then that its creation is dated to. A year later, a paper titled Toward a Positive Theory of Consumer Choice by R. H. Thaler was published which is generally considered to be fundamental for explaining the assumptions and methods of behavioral economics.

Since the second half of the 1990s, behavioral economics has gone beyond its early phase of development focusing on collecting and documenting deviations from the assumptions of mainstream theories and the development of theory (see more in: Heukelom 2009). It was recognized by way of honoring its outstanding representatives with, i.a., the Nobel Prize: G. Akerlof in 2001, D. Kahnemann in 2002 (A. Tversky died in 1996), R. Shiller in 2013. J. Tirole—Nobel Prize laureate from 2014—in some of his works he also used behavioral models.

Behavioral economics, mainly due to its interdisciplinary nature, is defined in many ways. For example, it is referred to as:

- a joint research program of economics and psychology (Brzeziński et al. 2008),
- a synthesis of economics and psychology, which fills the existing gap in traditional economics (Buczek 2005),
- proof of restoring importance to the theoretical and methodological foundations of psychology in explaining economic phenomena (Polowczyk 2009).
- a field of economic analysis that verifies the assumptions of neoclassical economics based on the results of sociological and psychological research (Kirkpatrick and Dahlquist 2010),
- an attempt to build a bridge between economics and psychology (Waerneryd 2004), thanks to which there is a chance to enrich traditional economic theories with psychological realism.

According to Wilkinson (2008), behavioral economics is a science broadening the standard theory of economics by providing it with more realistic psychological foundations; using the behavioral model of behavior, it clarifies and explains the anomalies of the classical model of behavior—using both observation and experiment, it explains human behavior. In turn, E. Cartwright describes behavioral economics as the science of application of the conclusions of laboratory experiments, psychology, and other social sciences in economics (2011). As C. F. Camerer and G. Loewenstein write: "Behavioral economics increases the explanatory power of economics by providing it with more realistic psychological foundations" (2004).

Taking into account the definitions quoted above, one can assume that the essence of behavioral economics is the use of achievements of psychology, sociology or neurobiology to explain behaviors and phenomena in which neoclassical economics fails.

According to C. F. Camerer and G. Loewenstein: "At the core of behavioral economics is the conviction that increasing the realism of the psychological underpinnings of economic analysis will improve economics on its own terms …. This conviction does not imply a wholesale rejection of the neoclassical approach to economics.… The neoclassical approach is useful because it provides economists with a theoretical framework that can be applied to almost any form of economic (and even non-economic) behavior, and it makes refutable predictions (Camerer and Loewenstein 2004)".

Thus, it can be concluded that behavioral economics does not so much question the homo oeconomicus dogma, which broadens the perspective of perceiving and interpreting economic behavior. It makes an effort to investigate the real, realistic behavior of people using inductive knowledge for this purpose. Its theories take into account the social and psychological aspects of people's functioning, including culture, value systems, personality, and the specificity of cognitive processes.

Angner and Loewenstein (2012) stress that behavioral economics is characterized by methodological eclecticism. In contrast to mainstream economics, scientists working within behavioral economics in defining their field do not use the research method, but base on the inclusion in economics of knowledge, intuition, perception, and analysis of issues originating, i.a., from psychology. Behavioral economics is therefore not associated with any particular research method, but tries to match the method to the specifics of the currently examined problem.

Additionally, it should be emphasized that behavioral economics is treated more as a broad research project consisting of various hypotheses, tools, and techniques rather than a coherent scientific theory. It is created by many different directions related to each other in a more or less precise way (Polowczyk 2009).

Over several decades of development of behavioral economics, behavioral economists have found quite different ways of describing and analyzing economic events. Thus, behavioral economics consists of several "strands" (as defined by J. Tomer), as well as individual practitioners. For the purposes of this chapter, these strands should be called trends that have certain common features and are interrelated, and therefore, they can be assigned to the whole, which behavioral economics is. A summary of the main trends is presented in Table 1.1.

Within the framework of behavioral economics, over time, its two basic groups have evolved, i.e., the old and new behavioral economics. Mainly research traditions and trends in the development of modern psychology had impact on the internal division of behavioral economics. Naturally, the boundaries of both approaches are quite fluid.

Representatives of the old behavioral economics do not completely reject the neoclassical model of individual behavior, but treat it as a normative ideal (Heukelom 2009). Old behavioral economics developed on the basis of behavioral science. It combined methodologies of psychological research on behavior and theoretical knowledge in the field of economics.

Clear references to behavioral economics began to appear in the 1960s when efforts were made to incorporate psychological insights into economics. In early behavioral actions, computer simulations were used that allowed exploration and analysis of previously inaccessible phenomena. As part of the old behavioral economics, four groups of its contributors can be identified. The first included the Carnegie researchers: R. Cyert, J. March, and H. Simon. They focused on issues related to bounded rationality, satisficing, and simulations. Their observations were later extended at Yale University by other researchers, i.e., S. R. Nelson and S. Winter. The second group comprised scientists from Michigan. It was led by G. Katona. Its interests included studies of attitudes and psychological economics. While the Carnegie group focused mainly on company behavior, Katona's investigators were interested in consumer behavior and macroeconomic issues.

The third group included W. S. Andrews, D. M. Lamberton, H. Malmgren, J. Marschak, G. B. Richardson, G. L. S. Shackle. In their research, they emphasized the importance of case studies, uncertainty, and coordination.

The fourth group comprised the Stirling researchers. In their research, eclecticism and integration were emphasized, in accordance with the recommendations of N. Kay, B. Loasby, R. Shaw, J. Sutton, A. Tylecote, and P. Earl—rejection of the main trend to maximize profits, utility, and balance, and making an effort to develop an alternative (Esther-Mirjam 2004).

Representatives of the new behavioral economics (advocates of the teachings of C. Camerer and G. Loewensteien) completely reject the neoclassical model at the

Table 1.1 Main trends developed within behavioral economics

Trend of behavioral economics	Main representatives and creators	Assumptions
	H. Simon and the Carnegie School	– questions the key assumptions of neoclassical economics such as rationality and interest – has a pragmatic attitude toward mathematics
	G. Katona and the Michigan School	– puts great emphasis on psychological observations – takes into account the widespread use of social research, which makes the trend broad and open to cooperation with other disciplines
Psychological economics	C. Camerer, E. Fehr, D. Kahneman, D. Laibson, G. Loewenstein, M. Rabin, R. Thaler	– its foundation is largely based on the assumptions of cognitive psychology – is concerned with psychological processes that underlie consumer behavior – examines the influence of psychological factors on the behavior of decision makers and the consequences of their decisions – uses empirical methods, laboratory experiments, field studies, computer simulation, brain scanning, mathematics – practitioners of this field allow external factors and collective behaviors in the constructed models
	H. Leibenstein and X-Efficiency Theory	– involves questioning the rationality postulate, particularly the idea that is maximized by people – has an element of positivism but it is not strict positivism of mainstream economics
Behavioral macroeconomics	G. Akerlof	– does not use mathematical models – is interdisciplinary – explains the differences between real economy and the general equilibrium model – includes in the analysis psychological and sociological concepts such as reciprocity, honesty, identity, monetary illusion, avoidance of losses, herd behavior or procrastination as reasons for deviations from the general equilibrium model

(continued)

Table 1.1 (continued)

Trend of behavioral economics	Main representatives and creators	Assumptions
Evolutionary theory	R. Nelson, S. Winter	– focuses on the processes of economic progress and development, seeking inspiration in biology, – compares the ongoing economic processes in a similar way to the evolution process that takes place in the natural environment, – assumes that in the economic realities entities that change behavior patterns, adjusting to the prevailing conditions, will manage better over time, while weaker entities do not have a chance to survive, – searches for permanent behavior patterns in enterprises, which it calls routines and treats them in analogy to genes; better types of routines win with weaker ones, and the entities that use them survive and push others out of the market
Behavioral finance	R. Thaler, R. Shiller, A. Shleifer, H. Shefrin	– examines how rational the behavior of financial market participants is – takes into account the behavior of investors with the admission of human weaknesses – applies mathematical models, quantitative methods – subject of research: an answer to the questions of what company managers, other institutions and stock market players can do to take advantage of market inefficiencies (arbitrary behavior)? Why do investors and managers, borrowers and lenders make systematic errors and how do they affect prices and returns on financial assets?
Experimental economics	V. Smith	– uses laboratory experiments – is a method of empirical research – focuses on the behavior of people – main areas of research: game theory, functioning of various markets, individual preferences and choices

(continued)

Table 1.1 (continued)

Trend of behavioral economics	Main representatives and creators	Assumptions
Neuroeconomics	C. F. Camerer, V. S. Ramachandran, S. McClure, M. Platt, P. Glimcher, K. McCabe	– a multidisciplinary approach to the study of neurophysiological basis of economic choices made by man, – uses specific measurement methods, such as magnetic resonance, computed tomography, electroencephalography (EEG)
Complexity economics	W. B. Athur, E. D. Beinhocker	– brings together all opposing trends of economics – inductive, common-sense principles are used in making decisions

Source Author's own summary based on Polowczyk (2010), Smith (2013), Zielonka (2008), Tomer (2007), Zaleśkiewicz (2011)

descriptive and normative level, believing that the traditional ideal of economic rationality should not even be used as a recommendation as to how individuals should behave (Brzeziński et al. 2008). New behavioral economics mainly uses experiments. It employs, among others, field data, computer simulations, brain scanning. According to Mullainathan and Thaler, standard economic models (of mainstream economics) are based on three unrealistic assumptions: unbounded rationality, unlimited willpower, and unlimited egoism, which they believe are an excellent area for changes introduced by the new behavioral economics (2000). They believe that, firstly, in limited conditions of rationality, people have limited cognitive abilities. This limits their ability to solve problems. Secondly, the limited willpower shows that people sometimes make choices that are not beneficial for them in the long term. Thirdly, the limited self-interest shows that people are often willing to sacrifice their own interest to help others.

It is also worth mentioning the theory of unified behavioral science, the creator of which is H. Gintis, which in the future can include behavioral economics, built on the assumptions of rationality and supplemented by evolutionary and behavioral theory of games. H. Gintis rejects anomalies in individuals' behavior and choices, as is the case with traditional assumptions. His proposal is greeted with great reservations due to institutional or conceptual reasons, but in the future it is possible to think about it (Brzeziński et al. 2008).

In the context of the above division, in a sense, the so-called behavioral economics "prescription" can be brought in here as a conclusion:

"First, identify normative assumptions or models that are ubiquitously used by economists, such as Bayesian updating, expected utility and discounted utility. Second, identify anomalies, i.e., demonstrate clear violations of the assumption or model and painstakingly rule out alternative explanations (such as subjects' confusion or transactions costs). And third, use the anomalies as inspiration to create alternative theories that generalize existing models. A fourth step is to construct economic models of behavior using the behavioral assumptions from the third step, derive fresh implications, and test them" (Camerer and Loewenstein 2004).

1.4 Mainstream Economics from the Perspective of Behaviorists

Behavioral economics brings together researchers critical of mainstream economics (similarly to institutional economics). Fundamental criticism is focused on several areas included below.

Behaviorists question one of the main assumptions of mainstream economics, namely that economic entities are characterized by the so-called instrumental rationality understood as people aiming to optimally use their resources based on their appropriate knowledge and logical reasoning skills. Criticism includes traditionalists not taking into account obstacles (in theories concerning the company, the consumer) that could prevent the calculation and implementation of the objectives intended by the rational individual.

As a consequence, mainstream economics creates normative models of solving economic problems by adopting an idealized model of human action. Therefore, it does not take into account the real possibilities and behaviors of people in order to explain the course of decision-making processes.

Another important objection concerns the not taking into account by entities in decision making of social interest, pro-ecological activities and non-monetary benefits. According to representatives of mainstream economics, the decision maker always acts unemotionally and rationally, has full information, does not make mistakes in pursuit of maximum material benefits. It involves the matter of exclusion from the analysis of social issues, which results in a typical mathematical and formalized approach to the undertaken analyses.

The traditional approach to the concept of homo oeconomicus, which is an essential element of mainstream economics, is criticized by behaviorists as an inadequate approach to explaining the phenomena related to making real choices by decision makers in the modern economy. This is mainly due to the fact that the homo oeconomicus model is poor in the analysis of dynamic external factors and psychological and social features of market participants. It assumes that "specific human behavior in the sphere of management can be explained in terms of ideal, strictly rational choices (because economic man is perceived as a rational man)" (Wach 2010). However, it does not take into account individual traits and behaviors of individuals or conditions that can bring about in the participants of economic processes emotions (anger, fear, joy) related to the decisions made. Thus, according to critics, it does not provide accurate data that can be attributed to any market situation, because the features of the model "economic man" which include, among others: maximizing usability, constancy, continuity and independence of preferences, analytical processing of information or the original role of cognitive processes are not useful for describing the actual behavior of individuals (cf. Swacha-Lech 2010). Behaviorists base the above-mentioned views mainly on the results of research in the field of psychology and sociology, according to which in reality the assumptions of a rational man are practically never fulfilled. It was claimed by, among others, H. Simon, the creator of the concept of bounded rationality according to which man never has the information necessary to make a fully rational decision, and even if he had it, he would not have the cognitive abilities to process it (Simon 1955, 1976). He drew attention to several important limitations concerning the rationality of the decision-making process, e.g., achieving many, often incompatible goals in pursuit of maximum benefits (in order to optimize a particular decision, man neglects the implementation of other activities), insufficient knowledge of decision-making alternatives, searching for such a solution, which will be good and meet the expected requirements (not all options are examined, but the first good enough is chosen) (Czerwonka and Gorlewski 2008).[1]

Another argument against the homo oeconomicus paradigm is the perspective theory formulated by A. Tversky and D. Kahneman, according to which emotions and instinct lie behind human decisions. They distort the correct assessment of the situation and cause that decisions made by him from an economic point of view are not always beneficial (Kahneman and Tversky 1979). According to these behaviorists, man making economic choices is not guided by rules of logic and the theory of probability, but stops at the so-called heuristics, which on the one hand allows quick decision making, on the other, however, involves the risk of frequent errors.

Opponents of mainstream economics also point to an excessive level of formalization of economic models and a strongly mathematical approach to economic research, which is related to the previously mentioned issue of excluding social issues from the analyses. According to behaviorists, this forces the necessity of adopting simplified, rigid assumptions, which makes them unrealistic and limiting the usefulness of conducted research. In turn, the consequence of such actions is the lack of adaptability of the employed models to the economic reality of a given country or region, characteristic of a given period.

The object of research as well as the applied research methods became the subject of unfavorable assessments in relation to mainstream economics. It was also pointed to a significant restriction of competition between different methodological approaches, which was implied by the fact that mainstream economics is defined by the research method, not by the area of conducted research.

---

[1]H. Simon's concept of bounded rationality was then explored deeper in the work of, among others: Cyert and March (1963), Kahneman and Tversky, or D. C. North, O. E. Williamson—creators of the behavioral uncertainty hypothesis.

A concept similar to bounded rationality is one proposed by Akerlof and Yellen (1985): the concept of near rational behavior, resulting in relatively small individual losses for economic entities in comparison with optimal decisions.

Behaviorists criticized mainstream economics for underestimating previous experiences, i.e., disregarding historical experience, which made it impossible to avoid or minimize the consequences of certain negative phenomena that have already occurred in history.

All the above objections according to behavioral economists result in low prognostic capabilities of economic models.

In conclusion, we can assume that the increase in the level of realism in explaining, describing and predicting economic processes, obtained in the framework of behavioral economics, should improve the economy, broaden its perspective, allow going beyond the boundaries drawn by assumptions about rational choice, maximizing usability functions, balance and efficiency (cf. Ariely 2009).

1.5 Behavioral Economics from the Perspective of Mainstream Economists

Behavioral economics challenges some standard views that have been dominant in economics for many years. Its critics—mainstream economists address a number of objections against it.

One of the essential objections concerns the selective treatment of the neoclassical economy assumptions by behaviorists. According to mainstream economists, the removal of certain elements from the overall economic structure may lead to inconsistencies with other principles and, consequently, to the collapse of the entire structure which a given theory constitutes. They mean mainly adopting assumptions about greater psychological realism with which we are dealing when the conducted experiment involves the respondent and prompts him to make informed decisions. In behavioral economics, financial stimuli are used as a tool to ensure psychological realism (Solek 2010). Critics also accuse behavioral economics of not being a unified theory but a collection of a number of ideas and tools (Camerer and Loewenstein 2004). Another argument put forward by the opponents is behavioral economics taking into account additional variables omitted in the classical analysis (e.g., the function of the decision maker's usability should take into account variables related to social impact). While this can be observed in economic experiments, it is difficult to include it in the analysis of real events. Critics also say that the cognitive errors described in the behavioral economics regarding statistical concluding in reality do not exist, because there is controversy about the very notion of probability—whether to apply it on the basis of the Bayesian approach as a subjective measure for individual events, or a quantitative approach, describing the frequency of occurrence against a large sample (criticism of G. Gigerenzer) (Kahneman and Tversky 1996). Objections against behavioral economics also concern the fact that it deviates from the model of rational expectations and tries to formalize its conclusions by means of mechanical principles and models that serve to create prognostic conclusions. However, they are not a description of a departure from full rationality, but they present different characteristics of clearly irrational behavior [criticism of Frydman and Goldberg (2013)].[2] Representatives of mainstream economics are also very skeptical about the research techniques used in behavioral economics, based on experiments and surveys. They argue that the model decision maker, who is determined based on experiments, is unrealistic. He is either too simplistic (naïve) and does not allow learning that occurs in reality or too sophisticated: super-rational in the sense that he predicts perfectly the behavior of his future dual personality and brings about a balance between them. They also believe that the behaviors observed in experiments have no reference to real market situations, mainly due to taking into account or basing on limited, insufficient empirical data. In addition, they note that the subjects may deliberately follow the hypothesis postulated by the researcher. Therefore, the problem of the non-transferability of experiments from artificial experiments to the analysis of events outside the laboratory is also signaled. According to the critics, the experimental method itself raises objections, because the situations created in the laboratory are artificial and cannot be the basis for general conclusions. The stimuli that persons are subject to during experiments are different than in natural conditions. At this point, one should also refer to a critical view of the use of mainly neurobiology techniques in economic sciences (within the so-called neuroeconomics, which according to mainstream economists is an artificial science due to the fact that neurobiology and economics are two separate areas that cannot affect each other) (cf. Gul and Pesendorfer 2008). Critics of behavioral economics point to the low realism of research carried out or the lack of understanding of the experiment by the respondents. They claim that recording the activity of particular areas of the brain responding to the delivery of economic stimuli gives very general indications, which, with the interdependence of the action of many elements of the brain in each activity, does not allow the creation of models for events of a regular nature. This is so even regardless of the fact that the imaging technique is still on too low a level to give sufficiently accurate readings. Thus, the basic criticism of the use of neurobiology techniques in economic sciences focuses mainly on the method of obtaining neurobiological data and potential benefits for economic sciences (Harrison 2008). Such a view results in traditionalists negating the analysis of empirical data performed by behaviorists. However, it is worth remembering that the task of researchers is, above all, to take up polemics with the results of specific research, with their methodology and interpretation, not their complete rejection or the adoption of an ignorant attitude.

The deficiencies described above may result from the relatively young age of the discipline of behavioral economics, and the excessive tendency with which mainstream economists are willing to respect the division between individual scientific disciplines, separating economics from other sciences.

[2]Authors consider the work of R. Shiller and G. Akerlof, who perform analysis in a narrative way without building mathematical models, as the only trend in behavioral economics which, as they believe, avoids the mechanistic problem.

1.6 Mainstream Economics and Behavioral Economics—Differentiating Aspects

The objections made against both behavioral economics and mainstream economics raised by the opponents of particular disciplines fit largely in the aspects presented by J. Tomer, which allow, according to him, indicating significant differences between behavioral economics and mainstream economics (Table 1.2).

Assuming J. Tomer's classification criteria (aspects), behavioral economics in comparison to the mainstream economics is wider, more flexible, more tolerant, definitely less mechanical, separate or individualistic.

Frydman and Goldberg formulated the differences between mainstream economics and the behavioral approach to economics in another way. According to them (…) "There are two main approaches to modeling individual decisions. Almost all economists refer to a set of a priori theorems that characterize the behavior of rational individuals always and in all circumstances". In contrast, behavioral economists refer to the abundant evidence discovered by them showing that individuals make decisions in a way that is inconsistent with conventional standards of rationality. Their research turned out to be fundamental to opening economics to alternative explanations of individual decision making and its market effects. These studies led to the creation of new models in which some or all of the a priori assumptions were replaced by formalizations of empirical conclusions. (…)" (2013).

It can be assumed that the discussion, the polemic between supporters and opponents of both mainstream economics and behavioral economics, will continue for a long time. However, more and more often, under the influence of profound changes taking place in the global economy (starting from the 1990s, and especially after the outbreak of the global economic crisis), the issue of the need to introduce some changes in the neoclassical economy's perception of phenomena is raised. The increasing level of complexity (globalization, enormous technological progress, especially in the field of information and media technologies), which affects almost all areas of the economy, causes a lack of transparency of economic connections, increases the level of uncertainty and risk. This results, among others, in more and more often observed states of market imbalance, the emergence of which is certainly affected by irrational behavior of market participants.

The introduction of changes is also fostered by the growing awareness of the necessity of psychological knowledge for a fuller than to date explanation of, among others, the decision-making process and the behavior of market operators and the mechanism of financial crises. It should be noted that the foundation of the works of the first economists (A. Smith, The Theory of Moral Sentiments) were, among others, reflections on the psychological basis of human behavior (Solek 2010).

Table 1.2 Aspects differentiating behavioral economics and mainstream economics

Aspect	Description
Narrowness	It determines how much a given discipline narrows the methods of analysis, the scope of tasks, i.e., restricts the research area
Rigidity	It determines to what extent a given discipline is attached to a given research area, to specific forms used, research methods, to what extent there is flexibility in this respect. In economic sciences rigidity defines a strong attachment (it can even be irrational) to a specific form of narrowness. High rigidity results in a lack of flexibility with regard to the research methods that the discipline uses
Intolerance	It determines to what degree alternative research methods are accepted in order to refer to research problems represented by other sciences. In the case of intolerance, we are dealing with dismissive attitudes to scientific work that does not meet the expectations and assumptions of one's own discipline or one's own mainstream and a skeptical approach to other methods of studying the same phenomena
Mechanicalness	It determines to what degree a discipline is viewed as a machine-like system, in a mechanical way. Disciplines high on mechanicalness, in other words, those in which practitioners conceive of the economy as a complex machine, use descriptions derived from mechanics, also take the state of equilibrium as the most desirable situation (this is the case with the mainstream economics). The opposite of mechanicalness is an organic, holistic and evolving approach, where the individual is viewed in all his complexity (example: behavioral economics)
Separateness	It determines the degree to which economics is linked with other fields of science (e.g. sociology, social psychology). The greater the degree of interdisciplinarity, the smaller the separateness of a given scientific discipline. A high degree of separateness determines self-containedness and thus separation of a scientific discipline. A low degree of separateness characterizes domains that derive from the achievements of other sciences
Individualism	It defines the approach to economic problems in an individualistic way (i.e. all assumptions and events can be explained on the basis of individual's characteristics and behaviors), negating group, social and system rationality. The individual approach to economics does not include the analysis of the behaviors of an individual being part of collectivities and the behavior of the collective resulting from decisions relating to the individual

Source Author's own summary based on Tomer (2007)

1.7 Conclusion

Behavioral economics is a relatively new trend in economics that uses the achievements of psychology, sociology, and other social sciences to give the economy a more realistic basis for explaining economic phenomena. Its aim is to find the reasons for economic choices. Experiments using psychology carried out as part of it make it possible to better understand human behavior. Its foundation is that the correct picture of economic reality is broader than that based on the concept of homo economicus and therefore a rational, calculating, and egoistic individual, because it is extended with the results of behavioral research.

Bearing in mind contemporary, dynamically occurring changes both in the macro- and the microscale, it can be assumed that the behavioral approach can be a source of inspiration for the modification of the concept of homo oeconomicus. It should be strongly emphasized that the definitions of behavioral economics cited in the chapter stress the need to extend and not replace the mainstream economics paradigm. At the same time, one can observe a trend of departing from the classical axiom of a rational human being toward an emotional man. Therefore, behavioral economics adopts the assumption of bounded rationality. It is worth emphasizing that behavioral economics does not intend to replace classical economics, but only to supplement it—especially in the field of microeconomics and decision making.

When comparing behavioral economics to mainstream economics, a distinct position of both trends is clearly drawn. Mainstream economics is read as highly formalized, inflexible, intolerant, and separate from the achievements and methods of other social sciences. It appears as a science that believes in the closed balance system and unlimited individuality of the individual. Therefore, it would be important then, taking into account, for example, the dynamics of changes taking place in the economy, for mainstream economics to consider thoughtfully extending mainstream economics with the behavioral approach to the investigated issues. This will allow it to develop in the desired direction and will certainly contribute to reducing the negative dimension of each of these features. Mainstream economics should "make real" the adopted assumptions, for example by taking into account the process of profound changes and their impact on the behavior of individuals, the functioning of markets, departure from a heavily mathematic approach to economic research, extending the time horizon of research, and taking into account the achievements of social sciences (this would allow the inclusion of the social factor in the performed analyses).

Also, behavioral economics as a new trend has many imperfections and areas not yet explained, which is criticized. These deficiencies, however, can be reduced as a result of ongoing research and the development of related fields. A big advantage of behavioral economics is its flexibility and openness to information coming from outside. This gives a chance for a better, more contemporary approach to socioeconomic problems.

References

Akerlof G, Yellen JL (1985) A near-rational model of the business cycle, with wage and price inertia. Q J Econ 100:823–838

Angner E, Loewenstein G (2012) Behavioral economics. In: Mäki U (ed) Philosophy of economics. Handbook of the philosophy of science, vol 13. Elsevier, Amsterdam

Ariely D (2009) The end of rational economics. Harvard Bus Rev 87:78–84

Boulding KE (1961) Contemporary economic research. In: Ray DP (ed) Trends in social science. Philosophical Library, New York, pp 9–26

Brzeziński M, Gorynia M, Hockuba Z (2008) Ekonomia a inne nauki społeczne na początku XXI w Między imperializmem a kooperacją. Ekonomista 2:201–232

Buczek SB (2005) Efektywność informacyjna rynków akcji - teoria a rzeczywistość. Oficyna Wydawnicza SGH, Warszawa

Camerer CF, Loewenstein G (2004) Behavioural economics: past, present, future. In: Camerer CF, Loewenstein G, Rabin M (eds) Advances in behavioral economics. Princeton University Press, Princeton, NJ, pp 3–59

Cartwright E (2011) Behavioral economics. Abingdon, UK Routhledge

Cyert R, March J (1963) Behavioral theory of firm. Prentice-Hall, Englewood Cliffs, NJ

Czaja S (2011) Paradygmat ekonomii głównego nurtu i ekonomii zrównoważonego rozwoju. In: Poskrobko B (ed) Kanony ekonomii zrównoważonego rozwoju. Białystok, Wydawnictwo Wyższa Szkoła Ekonomiczna, pp 28–50

Czerwonka M, Gorlewski B (2008) Finanse behawioralne. Oficyna Wydawnicza SGH, Warszawa

Esther-Mirjam S (2004) Behavioral economics: how psychology made its (limited) way back into economics. Hist Polit Econ 36(4):735–760

Frydman R, Goldberg MD (2013) Mechaniczne rynki a świat realny: wahania cen aktywów, ryzyko i rola państwa. Wydawnictwo Krytyki Politycznej, Warszawa

Gul F, Pesendorfer W (2008) The case for mindless economics. In: Caplin A, Schotter A (eds) The handbook of economic methodologies. Oxford University Press, Oxford, pp 3–39

Harrison GW (2008) Neuroeconomics: a critical reconsideration. Econ Philos 24:303–344

Heukelom F (2009) Kahneman and Tversky and the making of behavioral economics. Thela thesis, Amsterdam

Kahneman D, Tversky A (1979) Prospect theory: an analysis of decisions under risk. Econometrica 47(2):263–292

Kahneman D, Tversky A (1996) On the reality of cognitive illusions: a reply to Gigerenzer's critique. Psychol Rev 3:582–591

Kirkpatrick ChD, Dahlquist JR (2010) Technical analysis, the complete resource for market technicians. FT Press, USA

Kundera E (ed) (2004) Słownik historii myśli ekonomicznej. Oficyna Ekonomiczna, Kraków

Lambert CA (2006) The marketplace of perceptions. Harvard Mag 50–95

Mullainathan S, Thaler RH (2000) Behavioral economics. National Bureau of Economic Research, Cambridge

Polowczyk J (2009) Podstawy ekonomii behawioralnej. Przegląd Organizacji 12:3–7

Polowczyk J (2010) Elementy ekonomii behawioralnej w dziełach Adama Smitha. Ekonomista 4:493–522

Ratajczak M (2008) Dylematy współczesnej ekonomii. Zeszyty Naukowe PTE 6:69–84

Simon H (1955) A behavioral model of rational choice. Q J Econ 69:99–118

Simon H (1976) From substantive to procedural rationality. In: Latsis SJ (ed) Methods and appraisal in economics. Cambridge University Press, Cambridge, pp 129–148

Smith A (1989) Teoria uczuć moralnych. PWN, Warszawa

Smith VL (2013) Racjonalność w ekonomii. Oficyna Wolters Kluwer business, Warszawa

Solek A (2010) Ekonomia behawioralna a ekonomia neoklasyczna. Zeszyty Naukowe PTE 8:21–34

Sora M (2006) Ewolucja koncepcji człowieka gospodarującego – homo oeconomicus Na przykładzie prac Adama Smitha, Alfreda Marshalla i Gary'ego S Beckera. Kwartalnik Historii Myśli Ekonomicznej 2–3:103–119

Stankiewicz W (2000) Historia myśli ekonomicznej. Polskie Wydawnictwo Ekonomiczne, Warszawa

Stępień B, Szarzec K (2007) Ewolucja poglądów teorii ekonomii na temat koncepcji człowieka gospodarującego. Ekonomista 1:13–35

Stiglitz JE (2010) Freefall: America, free markets, and the sinking of the world economy. Norton, New York

Swacha-Lech M (2010) Homo oeconomicus a homo neuropsychologicus jako element dyskusji o nowym paradygmacie finansów. In: Frąckowiak W, Szambelańczyk J (eds) Ku nowemu paradygmatowi nauk o finansach, Zeszyty Naukowe Wydawnictwa Uniwersytetu Ekonomicznego w Poznaniu vol 144, pp 71–82

Tomer JF (2007) What is behavioral economics? J Socio Econ 36:463–479
Wach K (2010) Od człowieka racjonalnego do emocjonalnego. Zmiana paradygmatu nauk ekonomicznych. Horyzonty Wychowania 9(17):95–105
Waerneryd KE (2004) Psychologia i ekonomia. In: Tyszka T (ed) Psychologia ekonomiczna. Gdańskie Wydawnictwo Psychologiczne, Gdańsk, pp 7–34
Wilkinson N (2008) An introduction to behavioral economics. Palgrave Macmillan, New York
Zaleśkiewicz T (2011) Psychologia ekonomiczna. PWN, Warszawa
Zielonka P (2008) Behawioralne aspekty inwestowania na rynku papierów wartościowych. CeDeWu, Warszawa

Chapter 2
Behavioral Aspects of Cost Management

Teresa Kiziukiewicz and Elzbieta Jaworska

Abstract Economic results of a company mostly depend on proper cost management that determines its competitive position. The condition for an effective cost management is possession of information provided by cost accounting. The nature and scope of information regarding costs depend on the chosen model of cost accounting. Therefore, an economic entity should attempt to create such a cost accounting model that will ensure not only the fulfillment of duties resulting from the provisions of the Accounting Act, but also the provision of information necessary for decision-making. However, the shape of cost accounting model, information about costs and managing them are all influenced by human behavior. The aim of the chapter is to present the areas of influence of behavioral factors on effective cost management, especially on planning and controlling costs. Therefore, the following topics are presented in the chapter:

- Design of a cost accounting model supporting the decision-making process in the context of behavioral interactions.
- Impact of the selected model on management usefulness of information on costs —with respect to the behavior of people working in accounting.
- Choices in decision-making as part of cost management, especially in the field of cost planning (budgeting).

For the purpose of the chapter, the following methods are used: literature analysis, source analysis method, as well as inductive and deductive reasoning methods.

T. Kiziukiewicz
Department of Financial and Management Accounting, Faculty of Economics and Management, Institute of Accounting, University of Szczecin, Mickiewicza 64, 71–101 Szczecin, Poland
e-mail: tkiziukiewicz@wp.pl

E. Jaworska (✉)
Department of Economics and Accounting, Faculty of Economics, West Pomeranian University of Technology Szczecin, Zołnierska 47, 71–206 Szczecin, Poland
e-mail: elzbieta.jaworska2@gmail.com

K. Nermend and M. Łatuszyńska (eds.), *Problems, Methods and Tools in Experimental and Behavioral Economics*, Springer Proceedings in Business and Economics, https://doi.org/10.1007/978-3-319-99187-0_2

Keywords Behavioral accounting · Behavioral factors · Cost management Cost accounting · Cost planning and control · Decision-making

2.1 Introduction

Costs are of particular interest to the managers. Their decisions have a greater impact on the level of costs than on revenues, which are largely determined by external factors, especially the market situation, independent of the individual. On the other hand, costs are the result of decision-making choices relating not only to external factors, but above all to a number of internal factors. Therefore, costs are particularly sensitive to behavioral activities. On the one hand, it results from different ranges of cost management at particular levels of the organizational structure—from the chief executive officer to direct contractors (Dobija and Kucharczyk 2009). At each level, there are different tasks, the possibilities of their implementation and motivations in the field of cost formation. On the other hand, information about costs necessary for making decisions arises as a result of the information process, during which it can be manipulated by accountants to adjust costs to the level guaranteeing achievement of the expected financial result as a business objective (Piosik 2016). It should be emphasized that the preferences of managers as well as accounting activities may be bidirectional depending on the strategy adopted by the enterprise. It may be oriented toward maximizing the result or minimizing it due to tax reasons. It is also worth emphasizing that the information about costs prepared by accountants is determined by the cost accounting model employed in a given entity.

The aim of the chapter is to consider behavioral aspects of cost management, in particular, in the area of planning (budgeting), measurement (determination), recording, accounting, monitoring, control, reporting, and analysis. These activities are closely related to the provision of relevant information by the cost account, whose model can also be subject to behavioral effects both at the stage of its formation in a given unit, as well as during the implementation of the information process. The form of the cost model, as well as the information obtained, its use, and cost management are influenced by the behavior of both people preparing information about costs and managers from various levels of the organizational structure who use this information in the decision-making process. These three areas, i.e., the impact of behavioral attitudes on the cost accounting model, the quality of the formation of costs, and the way they are used in management, will be the subject of further considerations.

Bearing in mind the broad spectrum of cost management, it should be emphasized that the discussed issues, as already mentioned, are particularly susceptible to multidimensional behavioral and moral impacts. The shape of the cost accounting model, the obtained cost information, its use, and cost management are influenced by the behavior of both people preparing information on costs, as well as people from various levels of the organizational structure who use this information in the decision-making process.

For the purposes of the chapter, there will be used methods of analysis of the literature in the field of cost accounting, management, psychology, and sociology, as well as methods for analyzing sources and inductive and deductive reasoning.

2.2 Costs as a Subject of Management

Running a business is inseparably connected with incurring costs, the size of which significantly affects the company's financial result. To ensure its optimization, it is necessary to identify the factors affecting the formation of costs. From this perspective, it is important to effectively operate and effectively use the resources of a given enterprise, in particular, fixed assets, raw materials, other materials, energy, and workforce.

Cost management can be defined as a set of techniques and methods for the implementation of basic management functions (planning, organizing, motivating, and controlling) to control the costs of the company's operations in terms of their optimal level and structure, as well as the organization of activities aimed at achieving the business objective through appropriate motivation of employees and control and analytical activities. This kind of management is characterized by constant striving to improve and optimize business processes and products (Nita 2008).

Reflecting the involvement of a number of tangible and intangible factors in the enterprises operations, costs constitute a measure and, at the same time, a carrier of economic information necessary to make decisions. This information is the basis of management processes in both the short and long term. The ultimate goal is to focus on optimizing the use of resources in the most profitable areas of economic activity and increasing the efficiency of their use (Nowak 2015; after VanDerbeck 2013). Cost management also includes undertaking activities related to the systematic monitoring and control of costs toward a justified reduction of cost levels and optimization of their structure in order to achieve customer satisfaction (Horngren et al. 2003; Bhimani et al. 2007), which translates directly into revenues and financial results of operations. Cost management can also be defined as a combination of all activities and tools in order to influence costs to achieve the company's goals (Charifzadeh and Taschner 2017).

The literature distinguishes two approaches to cost management: operational and strategic (Nowak 2015). The first approach is subordinated to the current tasks performed in connection with the pursuit of the assumed objectives, e.g., by improving the efficiency of resource use, reducing energy consumption, increasing the productivity of employees, minimizing deficiencies. In current cost management (making short-term decisions), it is advisable to determine the significant costs. However, their designation may cause behavioral problems, such as: controversies regarding significant positions, free interpretation of certain quantities that generates abuses, especially when important factors and decisions are influenced by important factors, but of nonmeasurable, quantitative nature, resulting from the experience of accountants or managers, their intuition, or following their own preferences. They may concern, for example, safety, supervision, control, acceptable risk. Since they are not quantitatively or qualitatively measured, they will not be reported in the cost statements and reports, even though they have in fact influenced decisions that result in a certain level of costs. These factors may be used, despite the objections of other people, to force or abandon specific actions as so-called difficult to measure arguments (Dobija and Kucharczyk 2009). This may give rise to ethical problems and lack of transparency in the decision-making process and lead to loss of control over costs.

Strategic cost management is oriented toward long-term goals, e.g., broadening the potential of an economic entity, increasing its value, and ensuring the continuity of its existence (continuation of operations). The undertaken strategic decisions refer to the intentions and commitment of resources in the future.

Among the main goals of cost management, there can be mentioned (Zyznarska-Dworczak 2012), for example:

- learning the causes and mechanisms of cost creation,
- achieving and maintaining the assumed level of costs,
- identifying cost optimization possibilities, including their reduction as a result of the elimination of ineffective and unnecessary actions,
- increasing the company's productivity,
- improving the efficiency of using its resources.

Therefore, it can be concluded that cost management concerns the objective cost formation in line with the current company policy and its strategy in relation to the future. It requires, taking into consideration, the specific features of a given economic unit and its market position, as well as the multidirectional impact of behavioral factors.

2.3 Areas and Tools of Cost Management and Behavioral (Factors) Impacts

The information about costs for the purpose of their management may apply to various areas, presented in Fig. 2.1.

The management of the areas listed in Fig. 2.1 is supported by a cost account, which provides information necessary to create decision accounts for decision-making, development of cost assumptions, and monitoring of the implementation of costs. This allows to specify the improvement possibilities, as well as to prepare reports on the progress of the implemented methods of cost optimization in order to implement the adopted strategy. It also favors the development of the control system implemented in this area of improvements (Hansen et al. 2009).

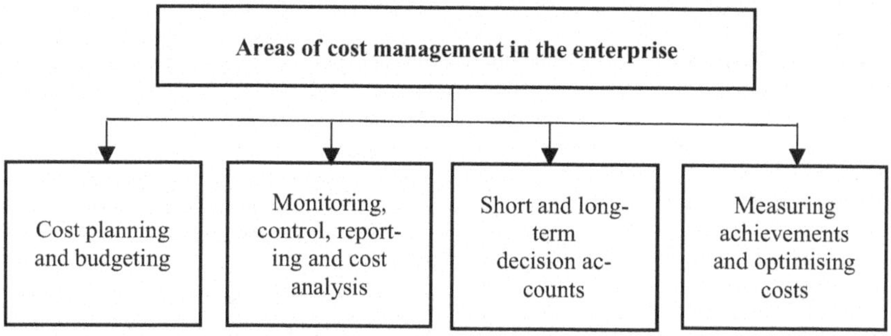

Fig. 2.1 Areas of cost management in the enterprise

Therefore, cost management tools and decision accounts, in which the selection criterion is cost, can be included in the cost management tools used in a given economic unit. The condition for effective cost management is to have information, which—as already pointed out—is a cost account. Its scope includes the measuring the consumption of economic process factors, determining the related costs, their settlement, and calculation, i.e., determining the unit cost of a product or service. The nature of the cost model depends on the nature, scope (detail), and quality (reliability, accuracy, keeping deadlines) of cost information. Therefore, each unit should treat the construction (development) of the cost accounting model as a fundamental area of cost management, which will ensure not only the fulfillment of obligations under current regulations, but which will also create the decision-making basics. In the first case, the cost accounting model is subordinated to the reporting tasks imposed by the Accounting Act and providing the basis for assessing the impact of costs on the profitability of operations, and in the second, the manageability of the cost accounting model is taken into account, with enrichment most often combined with (supplementing) reporting full cost accounting for a suitable management variant of cost accounting, in particular, partial cost account, future cost account, including budgeting, activity-based costing, target costing, life cycle costing. The selected variety should meet the information needs of the managers due to the specificity and conditions of running a business by a given economic unit. Premises for the selection of specific varieties are presented in Table 2.1.

In connection with the various features and objectives of individual cost accounting variations, one should strive to create an individual integrated cost accounting model for a given unit, providing information on costs that meet reporting needs and meeting the expectations of cost managers (planning, monitoring, analysis, making adjustments) through the prism of the unit's viability and its continuity (of existence).

Table 2.1 Management kinds of cost accounting

Kind of cost accounting	Usefulness in management
Variable (partial) cost accounting	Breakdown of costs by response to a change in production volume (variable and fixed costs) Determining the break-even point Short-term decision accounts (financial result, pricing policy, use of production capacity, assessment of responsibility centers, distribution channels, cutting additional orders)
Activity costs (processes) accounting	Selection of the basis for precise settlement of indirect costs for products. Linking cost-generating activities with manufactured products
Future costs accounting Budgeting costs	Cost planning (benchmarks: planned costs, standards, norms, budgets) Assessment of the implementation of the planned cost assumptions—disclosure of deviations and analysis of their causes, places of origin, consequences, responsible persons, reaction method
Target cost accounting	Cost optimization at the product design stage Management of the product's profitability within its life cycle
Quality cost accounting	Linking costs to places of their origin (analysis) Control of quality costs, prevention of deficiencies
Account for the cost of the life cycle of the product	Maximizing profitability of products Managing the costs of individual phases of the product's life cycle
Risk cost accounting	Risk hedging program—creating provisions for risk Risk projections versus the financial result

Source Own study based on Kiziukiewicz (2003)

2.4 The Use of Selected Psychological Theories in Managing Enterprise Costs

By implementing a specific business strategy, the company uses its resources to achieve the set goals. From the perspective of the cost management process, it is important to be aware of their alignment for effective implementation of the company's strategy. As already emphasized, management in this area is based on information from the calculation of costs generated and processed by man. For this reason, the information provided will not always be rational. Studies presented in the literature (e.g., Kotchetova and Salterio 2004) indicate that all, accountants, controllers, and managers who use information provided by the cost accounting, use identical mental shortcuts, make the same mistakes, and are subject to similar biases as other people who carry out specific actions, judgments, and choices, and who make decisions. Therefore, it is important to pay attention to behavioral and moral issues in broadly understood cost management.

The starting point of the cost management process is proper planning of activities and related costs and revenues. These processes are influenced by the behavior of not only the creators, but also by contractors of plans and cost budgets. Behavioral aspects are associated, for example, with the quality of information contained in plans or budgets of costs, the involvement in the process of their creation, and decisions made based on them during the implementation of cost assumptions. Furthermore, they are often guided by various motivations, as well different approaches to measuring costs and evaluating the achieved results compared to plans (budgets). This may be due to the lack of acceptance or belief in the accuracy of assumptions adopted during their development. As a result, they can be perceived as too easy or too difficult, or even unrealistic, which is reflected in the behavior of employees. Theories of cognitive, motivational, and social psychology may be helpful in their understanding and interpretation (Brinberg et al. 2007; Basel and Dalia Via 2014).

The importance of selected psychological theories for cost management by planning (budgeting) in the perspective of research presented in the literature on the subject is presented in Table 2.2.

Table 2.2 The meaning of selected psychological theories for managing costs by budgeting in the perspective of research presented in the literature on the subject

Behavioral aspects	Budgeting research
Theories of cognitive psychology	
Anchoring heuristics	Creators of the cost budgets may undergo the heuristics of "anchoring," especially in the case of incremental budgets. Cognitive limitations may result from relying on information about previous budgets, e.g., from the previous year. Such output values (anchors) may be conducive to duplicating errors from other periods
Overconfidence	Budgets may tend to overestimate profits (Moore and Healyth 2008; Kahneman and Lovallo 1993; Cesarini et al. 2006)
Optimism bias	When creating a budget, the most optimistic variant is usually assumed, which may cause underestimation of costs (Kahneman 2011; Montier 2002)
Approach to risk: framing effect, prospect theory	Decisions on budgets can be made on the basis of various reference points (profit/loss, positive/negative). This may affect the scale of the cost budget gap due to the assumption of too high or too low risk, which translates into costs, the level of expected costs and deviations from them (Brown et al. 2017; Harwood et al. 1991)

(continued)

Table 2.2 (continued)

Behavioral aspects	Budgeting research
Aspirations as a reference point for risk perception	If the assumptions for the budget are lower than the employee's aspirations, they may consider that the implementation of the budget assumptions will be easy, and they will make more risky decisions during the implementation of the budget. If, however, they consider the budget targets as too difficult to implement, they may approach risk with great reluctance, assuming that they are unable to reach the budgeted volumes (Sprinkle et al. 2008)
Theories of psychology of motivation	
Theory of expectations	This theory assumes that a person has a tendency to take action if he assesses that he will receive an award in line with his expectations. Different values are assigned to possible effects of actions (Schultz and Schultz 2011). Budgeters who make choices about their behavior, as well as other people, will take into account the subjective probability whether the specific effort to meet budget goals and whether the implementation of the budget will result in receiving rewards
Theory of aspirations	This theory assumes that the desire to achieve success and avoid the feeling of failure motivates a person to take a specific action. Therefore, the attractiveness and difficulty level of a given task affect the level of an individual's aspirations (Brinberg et al. 2007) Efficient implementation of the objectives included in the budgets therefore requires linking the company's aspirations with the level of employees' aspirations (Brinberg et al. 2007). Budgetary assumptions lower than the employees' aspirations may have a demotivating effect on the budget implementation, while too high budget assumptions may discourage action, because they will appear to the employees be unobtainable under the existing conditions
Theory of social justice (Libby)	The feeling of injustice may also have an impact on the motivation to implement the budget, especially if the budget is not related to real needs and conditions, but will depend on the influence and contacts of the manager of the given responsibility center (Libby 1999). Subsequent research (Libby 2001) indicated that individual employee performance is lower if they do not accept the budgeting process and perceive the resulting budget as unfair
Theory of goal setting (E. Locke)	According to this theory, the employee is motivated to perform specific tasks if their behavior leads to the achievement of set goals, including those resulting from budgets, provided that they accept and recognize them as achievable (Walker and Johnson 1999)
Theories of social psychology	
Theory of attribution	In this theory, attention is paid to the tendency to present positive results of the budget implementation as a result of the employee's or supervisor's own merits, while negative

(continued)

Table 2.2 (continued)

Behavioral aspects	Budgeting research
	results are considered as effects of external factors independent of a given person At the same time, when information about specific behavior is incomplete, supervisors and employees may have different opinions about the consequences of a given behavior (Shields et al. 1981)

Source Own study based on the given literature

The choice of cost information and the way in which it is presented is significantly influenced by the cognitive abilities of people participating in the cost management process. These possibilities include their ability to learn and the speed of information processing for a particular situation (Kiziukiewicz and Jaworska 2017b; Jaworska 2015) and can be determined by the abbreviations that simplify the thinking and the decision-making process, which sometimes results in committing various cognitive errors (Kahneman and Tversky 1996; Kiziukiewicz and Jaworska 2017a), because behavioral factors affect the understanding of phenomena, the attitude to them, and thus the behavior of people.

In the case of people responsible for developing budgets, the following behavioral issues are important:

- succumbing to errors and cognitive tendencies that affect the quality of information contained in budgets,
- one's own budgeting priorities that may affect the data,
- opportunism, i.e., presenting budget assumptions and assessing its implementation against the actual state and own conviction, but in a manner adapted to the expectations of other people, in particular, supervisors, budget creator and further environment, which may result from competition with other centers of responsibility, striving for approval and prizes.

Among the behavioral factors affecting the behavior of budget contractors there are, for example:

- aversion to imposed directives, especially when they do not coincide with the goals or aspirations of those who implement them,
- failure to accept restrictions imposed by the budget, e.g., cost limits,
- negative approach to budgets as a basis for assessing the work efficiency of those responsible for costs and results, especially in the case of individual competition or responsibility centers for costs.

This may result in the employees' lack of involvement in the implementation of budgets and in the search for their circumvention. This means that the employees, in order to ensure the achievement of the standards included in the budgets, may consciously (intentionally) underestimate their efficiency (productivity) (Young 1985). In their own interest, they can also lower costs or inflate revenues, or underestimate their results (Kren 1993). This phenomenon is referred to as a budget gap or slack. The research on presented behaviors included in the literature concerns both factors affecting the existence of the gap, such as the employee's own interest, contradiction between the goals of employees and their superiors (Chow et al. 1991; Fisher et al. 2002; Anthony and Govindarajan 2004), as well as formal and informal control mechanisms. According to Chong and Ferdiansah (2004), the level of budget gap and its scope is influenced by the level of trust in the superior. The higher this level, the smaller the budget gap affected by the employees. Greater trust in the supervisor may be connected with the reduction of the asymmetry of information, and it may lead to cooperation and redirecting the employees' efforts not toward personal preferences, but toward the company's goals. The issues of creating and reducing the budget gap from the perspective of confidence in the superior and sense of justice in a given unit were also examined by Özer and Yilmaz (2011), while Gilabert-Carreras et al. (2014) studied trust in the superior and the influence of cash incentives on the behavior of employees.

The purpose of cost planning and budgeting is to create a basis for assessing the implementation of cost assumptions. Cost control, in particular, the relationship between planned and actual costs, direct and indirect costs, and in the case of applying partial cost costs between variable and fixed costs, is one of the most important aspects of cost management. The analysis based on the results of the audit shows the relationship between individual cost groups, allowing for the assessment of the correctness of their management and for the indication of the desired actions in the event of worsening results, especially when the costs are high and the relations between them are inadequate, which may cause problems with the continuation of activity. However, limiting certain groups of costs, for example, indirect or fixed—due to inappropriate reading of the influence of behavioral factors—may be the cause of inadequate actions, for example, deciding to outsource work due to subjective reasons (Dobija and Kucharczyk 2009), due to which some costs may decrease, but at the price of the dependence of the unit on external entities, which may, over time, increase prices, fail to meet the quality requirements, or set deadlines. Therefore, in the long run, costs can increase significantly, and the unit will have limited control over them. As a consequence, the unit's existence may be threatened. It should also be remembered that the transition to outsourcing may mean not using the production potential, which may be wasteful.

Another important aspect of cost management is the reporting of cost information and making decisions on that basis, which should lead to proper allocation of resources and improvement of company results due to lower costs and thus higher profits. In this regard, the use of mental shortcuts by decision-making users of cost information may, based on the same information, lead to different conclusions depending on the way the information is presented. The form of the presentation, i.e., the form and layout of the information presented, may affect the quality of judgments and decision-making choices (Kotchetova and Salterno 2004). Experimental research on the profitability of a company is influenced by the relationship between the form of presenting information on costs and the knowledge of managers about the cost accounting conducted by Cardinaels (2008). He pointed out that decision-makers with a low level of knowledge on activity-based costing (ABC) achieved better results (lower costs and higher profits) if they used the graphical form of presenting cost information. It was worse, however, when they used information on costs presented in a tabular form. The opposite was true for people with a high level of such knowledge. This may mean that—having this behavioral factor in mind—enterprises should adapt the forms of the presentation of information about costs to the level of knowledge about the cost accounting of the users of reports used in cost management. With reference to the profit and loss account, the above-mentioned exemplary activities related to financial management (Ronen and Yaari 2010 after Piosik 2016) may occur, aimed at overestimating or underestimating profit or financial loss under the influence of behavioral factors from the environment or individual preferences.

2.5 Conclusions

Cost management involves planning and budgeting, monitoring, reporting cost information, analysis, and decision-making, as well as continuous measurement and improvement of the company's performance. Continuous improvement means looking for opportunities to improve the efficiency and effectiveness of the business unit, including achieving it by optimizing costs in both the short and long term.

The conducted research shows the necessity of a multifaceted approach to cost management. It is not enough to limit it to the decision-making process, because the condition for its effectiveness is to have information about costs that are the result of the information process implemented as part of the cost calculation. This means that its model should be adapted to the specifics of the business unit's activity, its organization and decision-making needs, taking into account the time horizon they relate to. In addition, cost management should be assessed in relation to revenues and the financial result.

Bearing in mind the broad spectrum of this process, it should be emphasized that the issues discussed in this chapter are particularly susceptible to multidirectional behavioral interactions. The shape of the cost accounting model, the information obtained, its use in cost management are all influenced by specific preferences, knowledge, aspirations, and expectations of both people information about costs and managers from various levels of the organizational structure who use this information in the decision-making process.

Due to the importance of behavioral aspects in cost accounting and cost management, the chapter identifies the impact of behavioral implications on the model of cost accounting, the impact of the persons developing cost information on their reliability, credibility, presentation, and persons using information on costs in decision-making processes. In pursuit of the management's expectations regarding costs perceived through the financial result, as well as their own intangible benefits (recognition) and material benefits (prize bonuses, promotion), accountants may manipulate the choice of measurement methods, price, cost accounting, and settlement of costs, especially with the use of estimates, inadequate allocation of costs to the period, creation of artificial reserves, or their concealment. In the case of decision-makers, actions may be taken to overestimate or underestimate the profit or financial loss due to behavioral factors stemming from the environment or resulting from the individual preferences of the interested parties.

What is important here is the systematics of behavioral factors (cognitive, emotional, previous experiences, mental image phenomenon, and others) affecting the cost information, and using them in decision-making processes with the indication of factors which, on the one hand, limit the decisive usefulness of accounting information, on the other hand, cause its inadequate and incomplete use in cost management. In order to understand the mechanism of presented behaviors, it is necessary to know the psychological theories presented in the chapter as a condition for taking actions that strengthen positive behaviors and counteract negative ones. This is an important reason for effective cost management and growth of the company's financial result.

References

Anthony RN, Govindarajan V (2004) Management control systems. McGraw-Hill, Boston

Basel JS, Dalia Via N (2014) Behavioral aspects and decision-making research in accounting: history, recent developments, and some future directions, (3 Apr 2014). Available at SSRN: https://ssrn.com/abstract=2244363 or http://dx.doi.org/10.2139/ssrn.2244363. Accessed 25 Jan 2018

Bhimani A, Horngren ChT, Foster G, Datar SM (2007) Management and cost accounting. Prentice-Hall, London

Brinberg JG, Joan L, Shields MD (2007) Psychology theory in management accounting research. In: Chapman CS, Hopwood AG, Shields MD (eds) Handbook of management accounting research vol 1, pp 113–135

Brown JL, Fisher JG, Peffer SA, Sprinkle GB (2017) The effect of budget framing and budget-setting process on managerial reporting. J Manage Acc Res 29(1):31–44

Cardinaels E (2008) The interplay between cost accounting knowledge and presentation formats in cost-based decision-making. Acc Org Soc 33(6):582–602

Cesarini D, Sandewall O, Johannesson M (2006) Confidence interval estimation tasks and the economics of overconfidence. J Econ Behav Org 61:453–470

Charifzadeh M, Taschner A (2017) Management accounting and control: tools and concepts in a Central European context. Wiley-VCH Verlag GmbH, Germany

Chong VK, Ferdiansah I (2011) The effect of trust-in-superior and truthfulness on budgetary slack: an experimental investigation. Adv Manage Acc 19:55–73

Chow C, Cooper J, Haddad K (1991) The effects of pay schemes and ratchets on budgetary slack and performance: a multiperiod experiment. Acc Org Soc 16(1):47–60

Dobija D, Kucharczyk M (2009) Rachunkowość zarządcza. Teoria. Praktyka. Aspekty behawioralne. Wydawnictwa Akademickie i Profesjonalne, Warszawa

Fisher JG, Frederickson JR, Peffer SA (2002) The effect of information asymmetry on negotiated budgets: an empirical investigation. Acc Org Soc 27:27–43

Gilabert-Carreras M, Naranjo-Gil D, Gago S (2014) Trust in superiors and dysfunctional behaviors: an experimental study on budgetary slack. J Positive Manage 5(1):54–66

Hansen DR, Moven MM, Guan L (2009) Cost management. In: Accounting and control, 6th edn. South-Western, Cengane Learning Inc

Harwood GB, Pate JL, Schneider A (1991) Budgeting decisions as a function of framing: an application of prospect theory's reflection effect. Manage Acc Res 2(3):161–170

Horngren C, Dater S, Foster G (2003) Cost accounting: a managerial emphasis, 11th edn. Prentice Hall

Jaworska E (2015) Poznawcze aspekty formułowania sądów i podejmowania decyzji w rachunkowości behawioralnej – wybrane zagadnienia. Prace Naukowe Uniwersytetu Ekonomicznego we Wrocławiu 389:130–138. https://doi.org/10.15611/pn.2015.389.12

Kahneman D (2011) Thinking, fast and slow. Farrar, Straus and Giroux, New York

Kahneman D, Lovallo D (1993) Timid choices and bold forecasts: a cognitive perspective on risk taking. Manage Sci 39:17–31

Kahneman D, Tversky A (1996) On the reality of cognitive illusions. Psychol Rev 103(3):582–591

Kiziukiewicz T (2003) Rachunkowość w systemie zarządzania. In: Kiziukiewicz T (ed) Zarządcze aspekty rachunkowości. PWE, Warszawa, pp 28–36

Kiziukiewicz T, Jaworska E (2017a) The impact of behavioral factors on the decisive usefulness of accounting information. In: Nermend K, Łatuszyńska M (eds) Neuroeconomic and behavioral aspects of decision making. Springer Proceedings in Business and Economics. Springer, Cham 2017, pp 201–213. https://doi.org/10.1007/978-3-319-62938-4_13

Kiziukiewicz T, Jaworska E (2017b) Obszary oddziaływań behawioralnych na rachunkowość finansową i zarządczą. Finanse, Rynki Finansowe, Ubezpieczenia 4/2017 (88) Part 1 Szczecin, pp 105–118. https://doi.org/10.18276/frfu.2017.88/1-10

Kotchetova N, Salterio S (2004) Judgment and decision-making accounting research: a quest to improve the production, certification, and use of accounting information. In: Koehler DJ, Harvey N (eds) Blackwell handbook of judgment and decision making. Blackwell Publishing, Oxford, UK

Kren L (1993) Control system effects on budget slack. Adv Manage Acc 2:109–118

Libby T (1999) The influence of voice and explanation on performance in a participative budgeting setting. Acc Org Soc 24(2):125–137

Libby T (2001) Referent cognitions and budgetary fairness: a research note. J Manage Account Res 13:91–105

Montier J (2002) Behavioral finance: insights into irrational minds and markets. Wiley, West Sussex

Moore D, Healy P (2008) The trouble with overconfidence. Psychol Rev 115:502–517

Nita B (2008) Rachunkowość w zarządzaniu strategicznym przedsiębiorstwem. Oficyna Volters Kluver Business, Kraków

Nowak E (2015) Rachunek kosztów a zarządzanie kosztami. Rozważania o relacjach. Studia Ekonomiczne, Zeszyty Naukowe Uniwersytetu Ekonomicznego w Katowicach 245:162–172

Özer G, Yilmaz E (2011) Effects of procedural justice perception, budgetary control effectiveness and ethical work climate on propensity to create budgetary slack. BERJ (Bus Econ Res J) 2:1–18

Piosik A (2016) Kształtowanie wyniku finansowego przez podmioty sprawozdawcze w Polsce: diagnoza dobrej i złej praktyki w rachunkowości. Wydawnictwo Uniwersytetu Ekonomicznego, Katowice

Ronen J, Yaari V (2010) Earnings management. In: Emerging insights in theory, practice and research. Springer, New York

Schultz DP, Schultz SE (2011) Psychology and the challenges of contemporary work. PWN, Warszawa (in Polish)

Shields MD, Birnberg JG, Frieze IH (1981) Attributions, cognitive processes and control systems. Acc Org Soc 6:69–93

Sprinkle G, Williamson M, Upton D (2008) The effort and risk-taking effects of budget-based contracts. Acc Org Soc 33(4–5):436–452

VanDerbeck EJ (2013) Principles of cost accounting. South-Western Cengage Learning, Mason

Walker KB, Johnson EN (1999) The effects of a budget-based incentive compensation scheme on the budgeting behavior of managers and subordinates. J Manage Acc Res 11:1–28
Young SM (1985) Participative budgeting: the effects of risk aversion and asymmetric information on budgetary slack. J Acc Res 23:829–842
Zyznarska-Dworczak B (2012) Jak zrządzać kosztami w przedsiębiorstwie?. Difin, Warszawa (in Polish)

Chapter 3
The Financial Management of Households—Behavioral Economics Perspective

Katarzyna Włodarczyk

Abstract This chapter is the theoretical discussion based on the literature on the subject. The elements of behavioral economics and behavioral finances are key tools that help to identify and explain motivating processes that occur when household members take financial decisions. As far as economic determinants are concerned, income generated by a household is undoubtedly the most important factor in determining consumer behavior. Income, along with savings and debt level, defines the final amount of money spent on consumption. The aim is to present characteristic patterns in the financial management of modern households in light of changes in these patterns that are attributed to the development of economic psychology and behavioral economics.

Keywords Households · Finances · Behavioral economics

3.1 Introduction

The market behavior of households on the one hand stems from preferences expressed by household members as to the selection of goods and services and on the other hand is equated with financial capability of household. Therefore, in order to satisfy their needs, household members not only have to undertake purchasing activities, but also take actions that will enable them to generate income and manage their finances efficiently. The aim of this chapter is to present characteristic patterns in the financial management of modern households in light of changes in these patterns that are attributed to the development of economic psychology and behavioral economics. This chapter presents theoretical discussion based on the literature on the subject.

K. Włodarczyk (✉)
University of Szczecin, Mickiewicza Str. 64-66, 71-101 Szczecin, Poland
e-mail: k.w-s@wp.pl

K. Nermend and M. Łatuszyńska (eds.), *Problems, Methods and Tools in Experimental and Behavioral Economics*, Springer Proceedings in Business and Economics, https://doi.org/10.1007/978-3-319-99187-0_3

3.2 Selected Issues Relating to Household Decisions—A Classical Approach

Household functions thank different actions and activities undertaken by household members to meet their individual and collective needs (Hodoly 1971; Kieżel 2010). These needs can be satisfied by using a combination of specific elements, namely money, means of consumption, time, effort, and abilities. The market behaviors of households means all decisions taken by household members, i.e. all actions, activities and steps taken once an individual (individuals) has realized and identified his/her (their) needs owing to which he/she has become a consumer (consumers). After all, market behavior involves the utilization of goods and services and takes account of conditions essential for satisfying consumer needs (Szczepański 1981; Antonides and van Raaij 2003; Solomon 2006; Murray 2008).

The market behavior of households may involve the following sequence of events: a household member identifies a specific need, he/she places this need in a hierarchy, he/she collects information about the available objects of consumption, he/she makes a market selection from the available means of consumption, and finally, he/she uses the objects of consumption that he/she has selected (East et al. 2014).

The comprehensive nature of research on the market behavior of households as well as an interdisciplinary approach to this issue contributes to the fact that it is a subject of an ongoing discussion. Household buying behavior is explored as part of such scientific disciplines as economics, sociology, and psychology. For instance, psychology investigates motive underlying consumer buying behavior, the influence of consumer personality on decisions he/she makes, consumer's ability to learn as well as consumer's perception. Sociology, on the other hand, deals with the identification of social characteristics determining specific human behavior. Last but not least, economics highlights the importance of such factors determining household behavior as income, prices, supply, or marketing tools. Other scientific disciplines that address the market behavior of consumers and households are as follows: history, anthropology of culture, clinical psychology, social psychology, and experimental psychology (Solomon 2006; Zalega 2012).

Factors determining the market behavior of households have been a subject of numerous studies for some time now. The analysis of individual decisions indicates that factors shaping household buying behavior may have different characters. Market behavior is not always determined by economic factors such as income, supply, and prices, but is often affected by psychological and social factors, i.e., relating to the membership of a social group or a class or an occupational group, as well as factors relating to the place of residence or cultural factors (Falkowski and Tyszka 2002; Swamm 2002; Bywalec 2010; Stasiuk and Maison 2017).

Research on factors determining change in consumer behavior and household behavior has made attempts to provide a classification and typology of these factors. However, in the literature on the subject, different authors offer different classifications of determinants under consideration. Although these classifications vary considerably, there is one element common to most of them, namely they make a clear distinction between economic and non-economic factors (Kieżel 2010; Włodarczyk 2013).

Recent studies on factors determining the market behavior of consumers and households have not introduced a rigid division into economic and non-economic factors. Income, prices, credit, savings, and supply to some extent govern consumer behavior and may be considered as factors that stimulate their purchasing activity. As for the typology of consumption determinants, they are generally divided into internal (individual) and external (social) factors (Schiffman and Kanuk 1987; Kassarijan and Robertson 1968; Hawkins et al. 1989; Engel et al. 1995; Schewe and Smith 1980; Kieżel 2010; Schiffman and Wisenblit 2015). The external factors determining consumption include culture, value system, demography, social status, reference group, and household size. By contrast, internal determinants include information acquisition, learning, memorizing, motives, personality, emotions, lifestyle, and attitudes (Hawkins et al. 1989). Another approach to organizing and classifying factors determining consumption proposes a division into the following three categories: individual differences, environmental influences, and psychological process. Individual differences are reasons behind purchasing activity, knowledge, attitudes, motivation, personality, value system, and lifestyle. On the other hand, environmental influences include the impact of culture, social class, family, and opinion leaders. Finally, psychological process refers to the role of information collected by consumers in making buying decisions, consumers' ability to learn, as well as a change in consumer attitudes and behavior (Engel et al. 1995; Falkowski and Tyszka 2002; Schiffman and Wisenblit 2015; Stasiuk and Maison 2017).

Research on consumer buying behavior may refer to individual consumers and households of which these consumers are members. On a microeconomic scale, studies on consumer behavior address directly the subjects of consumption, i.e., consumers. Such a perspective enables researchers to present factors that have a direct effect on the behavior of individual consumers and consequently to observe their behavior both on the market and in a household. Research on consumer buying behavior on a microscale addresses the following issues: consumer characteristics, consumer preferences, consumer opinions and attitudes, consumer behavior, motives underlying consumer behavior, or consumer intentions (Antonides and van Raaij 2003; Zaleśkiewicz 2015; Zimbardo and Gerrig 2017; Wójcik 2017).

Studies on consumer behavior are based on paradigms, i.e., sets of believes held by researchers about what is being analyzed and how it is being analyzed. Nowadays, a sort of "rivalry" can be observed between a prevailing positivist (modernist) paradigm and a new postmodern (interpretive). The latter paradigm questions the former paradigm. As for the assumptions underlying the positivist paradigm, emphasis is placed on explaining any phenomenon using one's mind. Hence, there is one objective truth to be discovered by science. From this perspective, the world is rational and organized. Postmodern analysis rejects the positivist assumptions since the modern world is characterized by social and cultural diversity and hence cannot be organized. Postmodern research assumes that every human being develops his/her own believes (different from believes held by other people) based on his/her cultural experience (Solomon 2006). Consumers, who are at the same time household members, take actions because they are inspired by external incentives, and the main task of researcher is to identify certain regularities and thus foresee certain situations and behavior. Knowledge acquired in this way can be used at any given moment and in any market or sociohistorical situation. In addition, researchers are experts on their subjects and theorists, and therefore, they apply their knowledge to interpret what has been discovered in the course of research, namely judgements, opinions, and attitudes. The postmodern approach enables respondents to describe their behavior and enables researchers not to impose theoretical patterns of thought upon respondents. The postmodern research focuses on socially construed reality which is not a sum of objective rules and regulations. A consumer is an active individual who freely exercises his/her will. Research conducted in such fashion provides the description of consumer actions and activities based on the interpretation made by consumers themselves (Falkowski and Tyszka 2002; Sagan 2004).

3.3 Household Behavior in Light of Income

As far as economic determinants are concerned, income generated by a household is undoubtedly the most important factor in determining consumer behavior. Income, along with savings and debt level, defines the final amount of money spent on consumption. Income is of major importance to the analysis of household consumption for the following reasons (Bywalec 2010):

- Income influences consumer behavior prior to price;
- Income can be treated as a key, measurable and quantitative factor in determining demand and consumption;
- Income allows to analyze demand in many groups of consumers that have different characteristics;
- Income allows to indirectly account for changes in other economic and non-economic factors determining the structure of consumption.

Household behavior may be determined by any change in household income as well as in the structure of this income. In the literature on the subject, such a correlation is discussed, among others, by Friedman and Tobin. Friedman divided total consumer income into two components, namely permanent and transitory. Consumption depends only on the former, i.e., the permanent component of income. On the contrary, the latter, i.e., the transitory component of income, has a marginal effect on consumption since this component is usually put aside in the form of savings (Friedman 1957). Quite a different view is presented by Tobin who is inclined to believe that any extra increase in income is not saved but most likely spent on durables and necessities (Stankiewicz 2000). Both views may be the case with societies, and therefore, it is difficult to decide which one is correct. It can be stated without a doubt that increase in regular income triggers a significant change in the structure of consumer expenditure and lifestyle, whereas increase in additional income causes a short-term change.

Needless to say, households should attempt to adjust to continually changing socioeconomic situation on which their financial situation depends. In order to do so, household members take a number of actions, namely (Bywalec 2017):

- Take up extra jobs and engage in different forms of activity in the labor market;
- Raise credit or loan;
- Request financial assistance from institutions, family, or acquaintances;
- Use household savings;
- Change their consumption patterns and reduce consumption level.

As it has already been stated, household income together with savings and debt level determines the final amount of money spent on consumption. All these factors define the purchasing power of household and hence consumer demand. Household savings can be defined as a difference between income and current consumption. Savings, or so-called past income, are treated as financial resources that have been taken from net disposable income and have not been spent. These resources enable a household to buy durables. In order to make a purchase, substantial amount of money is paid from the savings account. Needless to say, the wider the range of goods purchased, the lower the level of past income. Credit, or so-called reverse of savings, raised by a household is money granted by financial institutions (mainly banks) or other natural persons and legal persons. Credit is giving the possibility to households of purchase goods before their otherwise low income allows them to do so. As a general rule, a greater part of credit is spent on durables such as cars or domestic appliances.

Numerous economic hypotheses confirm that credit and savings to a great extent shape the structure of household expenditure. One of such hypotheses, developed by Modigliani and Ando, is referred to as the life cycle hypothesis (LCH) (Ando and Modigliani 1963; Zalega 2012). According to LCH, people attempt to foresee their income over their entire lifetime. Human life can be divided into three stages during which people generate income the level of which changes over time. The first stage refers to young people and is characterized by low income and high expenditure. During this period, people raise credit but do not save any money. The second stage involves increase in income which enables people to repay their loans and build up some savings. This stage is the case with middle-aged people who have already achieved certain social and professional standing, as well as financial stability. The third stage is the case with elderly people who have retired and live on their savings (Modigliani 1988). Another hypothesis suggesting that credit and savings have a significant effect on consumption is referred to as the permanent income hypothesis (Schab 2004; Zalega 2012; Friedman 1957). It was developed by Friedman who proved that consumption levels depend on total income generated by households. If people believe that their income is exceptionally high over a given period of time, they increase their consumption only slightly in order not to feel a striking difference. They save up the remaining amount of this extra money for the time when their income is lower, and it might be difficult to maintain the usual consumption level. In the market economy, a hypothesis developed by Keynes can partially be proven. According to him, extreme tendency to save money increases along with income growth, while extreme tendency to consume is subject to reduction. Empirical research suggests that such a regularity is observed only from a certain income level (Kieżel 1999; Galbraith 1992).

3.4 The Financial Management of Modern Households

If household members want to fulfill their goals, and most of all if they want to satisfy their needs, they should take actions that will guarantee an optimum use of their finances as well as financial capability. Bywalec (2017) refers to such actions as *financial management*. According to him, the financial management of household should be understood as: "(…) all actions taken by household members in order to earn money and spend it in accordance with the household's goals."

The financial management of household is treated as a process and consists of the following sub-processes (Bywalec 2017; Bodie and Merton 2003; Lindqvist 1981; Warneryd 1983; Van Raaij and van Wijck 1984):

(1) Risk management, i.e., actions aimed at reducing uncertainty, consists of the following successive stages: identification of possible sources of risk, determination of possible consequences following from risk factors, selection and implementation of the method for risk management, evaluation of the method for reducing uncertainty;
(2) Wealth management, i.e., purchase of physical assets, exploitation, and liquidation or modernization of assets;
(3) Capital management, i.e., evaluation of investments and intangible assets, determination of the amount and structure of equity capital, determination of liquidity and the period of conversion of assets into cash;
(4) Budget management, i.e., forecasting household income, planning household expenditure, and generating money surplus over a given period of time;
(5) Savings management, i.e., evaluation of present and future financial situation of household, identification of market terms under which savings are built up as well as selection of the form (forms) of savings;
(6) Debt management, i.e., evaluation of current and future financial situation of household, identification of market terms under which debt is incurred as well as selection of the form (forms) of debt.

It should be emphasized that a household may take only some of the aforementioned actions or take completely different steps. The configuration and order in which these actions are taken depend solely on household needs and preferences (Iwanicz-Drozdowska 2011; Dąbrowska et al. 2015).

Therefore, the financial management of household should be treated as a series of actions taken by household members to earn money (e.g., by taking up a decent job or starting a business) and maintain a decent standard of living so that household members could satisfy their needs and preferences (e.g., by purchasing goods and services that they consider as attractive). Furthermore, financial management involves activities that are the most favorable and satisfying to household members. Financial management should entail actions that are taken deliberately by household members in order to use their assets as efficiently as possible and avoid falling into unnecessary debt (or accumulating the already incurred one) (Antonides and van Raaij 2003; Bywalec 2017; Zaleśkiewicz 2015; Falkowski and Tyszka 2002).

Research on household behavior is largely based on psychological factors that determine decisions taken by individual consumers (Cooper et al. 2007). Psychological factors also play a profound role in financial management. In this context, motives behind taking specific actions are of major importance. As far as building up savings is concerned, households can be inspired by the following motives: buying plans, providing for oneself or one's children in the future, protecting oneself and one's family against unexpected events, as well as managing the financial surplus by making profitable investments. The role of motives is also highlighted in the context of debt incurred by a household. On the one hand, borrowing money is generally accepted and enables households to maintain a decent standard of living at a given moment or purchase some extra goods. On the other hand, debt indicates that household members have poor ability to control their finances and poses a risk of uncontrolled and unnecessary buying decisions. Furthermore, repayment schedule is often interpreted incorrectly which may foster a neutral or positive attitude toward incurring debt and therefore lure a household into a debt trap. Consequently, a financial problem may become a mental issue (Zaleśkiewicz 2015; Bielawska-Batorowicz 2012).

As for the ongoing discussion on the financial management of households, the observation of actual market behavior enables researchers to challenge a number of economic assumptions completely or at least partly. One of such assumptions entails that individuals make only rational choices. However, an insight into the market behavior of households questions this assumption. To be more specific, decisions made by household members about buying specific goods and services are often impulsive, whereas decisions taken by household members on the financial markets are often based on so-called misconception. Similar conclusion may be drawn from the assumption that all individuals strive to maximize their profit. Research on consumer behavior proves the above statement but only to a limited extent (Goszczyńska and Górnik-Durose 2010). Another economic assumption entails that all individuals rely solely on their own opinion while making a decision. This assumption can also be questioned since in the age of global consumption, most consumers are inspired by other consumers and public opinion when making the final choice (Włodarczyk 2013).

Since this chapter discusses the financial management of modern households, attention should also be paid to behavioral finance hypothesis. One of the issues addressed as part of behavioral finance is the rationality of decisions made by investors. Studies and analyses of the market behavior of households suggest that financial decisions taken by household members are often irrational as well as impulsive and related to habit. Individual decisions about the financial management of household make up a decision-making process that consists of pre-decision-making actions, the actual decision, and post-decision-making actions. The first stage involves preparation for making a decision as well as collecting and analyzing information. During the third stage, the consequences of the decision made by a household are evaluated. Needless to say, household members may take wrong decisions. Errors that may lead to decisions that will have a number of negative financial consequences to a household are presented below.

Errors in foreseeing a situation on the financial market—a household perspective (Zaleśkiewicz 2015):

- Excessive self-confidence—Overestimation of one's competence and knowledge as well as strong belief that one's decisions are always right. It may be a consequence of previous experience shared by household members (in this case also decision makers). Forecasts often prove to be incorrect, and hence, household members make wrong decisions, which has a negative effect on household finances
- Unrealistic optimism—A belief shared by household members that their household will always be successful, whereas failure is to be expected by other households, a belief in an extremely positive outcome. Unrealistic optimism distorts the real picture and inspires household members to make decisions that are not always good in terms of financial management
- Illusion of control—A belief that household members can control all actions taken with reference to their households. A belief shared by household members that they can affect these actions significantly. Thanks to the illusion of control household members become more optimistic, self-confident, and willing to take risky decisions
- Anchoring—Foreseeing the financial situation of household based on past experiences, decisions, opinions, judgments. Such an approach may distort every newly collected piece of information and hence may have a negative effect on household finances.

As for the key notions used as part of behavioral economics, it is worth exemplifying how they can be used in reference to a household, namely

(1) When household members keep their accounts, they use only some items of information. In other words, they highlight some pieces of information and they completely ignore other pieces of information. Such an approach is known as "using mental shortcuts" (heuristic thinking) (Nęcka et al. 2008);
(2) Household members base their decisions on one specific perspective (e.g., they assume that they will manage to avoid loss or that they will make profit

constantly). Such an approach is known as "framing" (Kahneman and Tversky 1979; Tversky and Kahneman 1992; Camerer 2000);

(3) When household members take financial decisions, they often employ so-called mental accounting, i.e., a process during which people categorize different types of income and expenditure on so-called mental account and try not to change their assumptions (Thaler 1980, 1985, 1999; Kahneman and Tversky 2000).

Therefore, the elements of behavioral economics and behavioral finances are key tools that help to identify and explain motivating processes that occur when household members take financial decisions. However, in order to get a full picture of decision-making process taking place in a household, it is worth employing both the classical economics approach and the behavioral economics approach.

3.5 Conclusion

Household is a social unit that, together with other social units, plays an important role in the market. The identification of household behavior may help to explain a number of processes occurring on the market. While making an insight into the functioning of household, and particularly into specific elements of this functioning such as financial management, it should be highlighted that these elements are strongly correlated with one another and at the same time closely correlated with external environment. The functioning of household is subject to analysis in such disciplines as economics, sociology, and psychology. It is also in the center of attention of such disciplines as economic psychology and behavioral economics. These disciplines address issues relating to the financial management of household since the behavioral approach enables researchers to capture and explore actual human behavior by taking account not only of the existing theories, but also of actual human tendencies. Therefore, growing importance is placed on the role that personality traits, value system, motives, and emotions occupy in making financial decisions. Based on the elements of the financial management of households presented in this chapter, it seems important to develop a set of uniform indicators and measures that would enable researchers to make valid comparisons and draw conclusions. As a matter of fact, it seems even more important to develop research methodology, systematize the existing knowledge and then conduct a comprehensive questionnaire survey using theoretical foundations laid in the course of previous studies and analyses.

References

Ando A, Modigliani F (1963) The life-cycle hypothesis of saving: aggregate implication and tests. Am Econ Rev 53(March):55–84
Antonides G, van Raaij WF (2003) Zachowania konsumenta. Podręcznik akademicki (Consumer behavior. A european perspective). PWN, Warszawa
Bielawska-Batorowicz E (ed) (2012) Wprowadzenie do psychologii dla ekonomistów (Introduction to psychology for economists). PWE, Warszawa
Bodie Z, Merton RC (2003) Finanse (Finances). PWE, Warszawa
Bywalec C (2010) Konsumpcja a rozwój gospodarczy i społeczny (Consumption and socio-economic development). C.H. Beck, Warszawa
Bywalec C (2017) Gospodarstwo domowe. Ekonomika. Finanse. Konsumpcja (Household. Economics. Finances. Consumption). Wydawnictwo Uniwersytetu Ekonomicznego w Krakowie, Kraków
Camerer CF (2000) Prospect theory in the wild. In: Kahneman D, Tversky A (eds) Choices, values and frames. Russell Sage Foundation, New York
Cooper JO, Heron TE, Heward WL (2007) Applied behaviour analysis. Prentice-Hall, Upper Saddle River, NJ
Dąbrowska A, Bylok F, Janoś-Kresło M, Kiełczewski D, Ozimek I (2015) Kompetencje konsumentów. Innowacyjne zachowania, zrównoważona konsumpcja (Competences of consumers. Innovative behavior, sustainable consumption). PWE, Warszawa
East R, Wright M, Vanhuele M (2014) Zachowania konsumentów (Consumer behaviour). Oficyna a Wolters Kluwer business, Warszawa
Engel JF, Blackwell RD, Miniard PW (1995) Consumer behavior, 8th edn. The Dryden Press, Harcourt Brace College Publishers
Falkowski A, Tyszka T (2002) Psychologia zachowań konsumenckich (Psychology of consumer behavior). GWP, Gdańsk
Friedman M (1957) A theory of consumption function. Princeton University Press, Princeton, NJ
Galbraith JK (1992) Ekonomia w perspektywie. Krytyka historyczna (Economics in perspective. A critical history). PWE, Warszawa
Goszczyńska M, Górnik-Durose M (eds) (2010) Psychologiczne uwarunkowania zachowań ekonomicznych. Przedsiębiorczość – Pieniądze – Konsumpcja (Psychological determinants of economic behavior. Entrepreneurship - Money – Consumption). Difin, Warszawa
Hawkins DJ, Best RJ, Coney KA (1989) Consumer behavior: implications for marketing strategy, 4th edn. Homewood Il, Boston
Hodoly A (1971) Gospodarstwo domowe i jego rola społeczno- ekonomiczna (Household and its socio-economic role). KiW, Warszawa
Iwanicz–Drozdowska M (ed) (2011) Edukacja i świadomość finansowa. Doświadczenia i perspektywy (Education and financial awareness. Experience and perspectives). Oficyna Wydawnicza SGH, Warszawa
Kahneman D, Tversky A (1979) Prospect theory: an analysis of decision under risk. Econometrica 47:263–291
Kahneman D, Tversky A (2000) Choice, values and fames. Russell Sage Foundation, Cambridge University Press, New York
Kassarijan H, Robertson T (1968) Perspectives in consumer behavior. Scott, Foresman and Co., Glenview
Kieżel E (ed) (1999) Rynkowe zachowania konsumentów (Market behavior of consumers). Wydawnictwo Akademii Ekonomicznej w Katowicach, Katowice
Kieżel E (ed) (2010) Konsument i jego zachowania na rynku europejskim (The consumer and his behavior on the European market). PWE, Warszawa
Lindqvist A (1981) A note on the determinants of households saving behaviour. J Econ Psychol 1:39–57

Modigliani F (1988) The role of intergenerational transfers and life-cycles saving in the assumption of wealth. J Econ Perspect 2:15–40
Murray HA (2008) Explorations in personality. Oxford University Press
Nęcka E, Orzechowski J, Szymura B (2008) Psychologia poznawcza (Cognitive psychology). PWE, Warszawa
Sagan A (2004) Badania marketingowe. Podstawowe kierunki(Marketing research. Basic directions). Wydawnictwo Akademii Ekonomicznej w Krakowie, Kraków
Schab I (2004) Dochód i konsumpcja (Income and consumption). In: Panek T, Szulc A (eds) Statystyka społeczna. Wybrane zagadnienia (Social statistics. Selected Issues). Wydawnictwo SGH, Warszawa
Schewe Ch, Smith R (1980) Marketing, concepts and applications. McGraw–Hill Book Co., New York
Schiffman LG, Kanuk LL (1987) Consumer behavior, 3rd edn. Prentice Hall, New Yersey, Englewood Cliffs
Schiffman LG, Wisenblit J (2015) Consumer behavior. Pearson, Essex
Solomon MR (2006) Zachowania i zwyczaje konsumentów (Consumer Behavior). Helion, Gliwice
Stankiewicz W (2000) Historia myśli ekonomicznej (History of economic thought). PWE, Warszawa
Stasiuk K, Maison D (2017) Psychologia konsumenta (Psychology of consumer). PWN, Warszawa
Swamm GM (2002) Innovation in consumption and economic growth. In: Michie J, Smith JG (eds) Globalization, growth and governance: towards innovative economy. Oxford University Press, New York
Szczepański J (1981) Konsumpcja a rozwój człowieka. Wstęp do antropologicznej teorii konsumpcji (Consumption and human development. Introduction to the anthropological theory of consumption). PWE, Warszawa
Thaler RH (1980) Toward a positive theory of consumer choice. J Econ Behav Organ 1:39–60
Thaler RH (1985) Mental accounting and consumer choice. Mark Sci 4:199–214
Thaler RH (1999) Menontal accounting matters choice. J Behav Decis Mak 12:183–206
Tversky A, Kahneman D (1992) Advances in prospect theory: cumulative representation of uncertainty. J Risk Uncertainty 5:297–323
Van Raaij WF, van Wijsc H (1984) Saving and borrowing behaviour. Bank-en Effectenbedrijf 33:280–285
Warneryd KE (1983) The saving behavior of households. Katholieke Hoge-School, Tilburg
Włodarczyk K (2013) Rynkowe zachowania polskich konsumentów w dobie globalizacji konsumpcji (Market behaviors of Polish consumers in the age of globalization of consumption). Wydawnictwo Adam Marszałek, Toruń
Wójcik P (2017) Psychografia konsumentów (Consumers psychographics). Wydawnictwo Słowa i Myśli, Lublin
Zalega T (2012) Konsumpcja. Determinanty. Teorie. Modele (Consumption. Determinants. Theories. Models). PWE, Warszawa
Zaleśkiewicz T (2015) Psychologia ekonomiczna (Economic psychology). PWN, Warszawa
Zimbardo PG, Gerrig RJ (2017) Psychologia i życie (Psychology and life). PWN, Warszawa

Chapter 4
Propensity to Risk and the Prospect Theory

Mariusz Doszyń

Abstract The main aim of the chapter is a discussion of the prospect theory in context of propensity to risk. In prospect theory and, generally, in behavioural economics, there are many methodological attitudes. Propensity theory gives possibility to standardise them, and this is the general motivation of the chapter. Presented methods of analysing propensity could help operationalise the prospect theory and other behavioural economics concepts. In the first part, general definition of propensity, as well as methods of measuring propensities is shortly discussed. In the next part of the chapter, propensity to risk is analysed in context of the prospect theory. Frequency measures of propensity to risk are used to specify a value function in the prospect theory. The first measure is based on nominal scale. This method might be useful when we have two outputs (safe and risky one), such as in the first version of the prospect theory (Kahneman and Tversky in Econometrica 47:2, 1979). Also, method of measuring propensity to risk that is based on game against nature is proposed. This method might be used in case of cumulative prospect theory, where we have more than two outputs.

Keywords Propensity · Propensity theory · Propensity measures
Propensity to risk · Prospect theory

JEL D01 · D81 · D91 · C18

M. Doszyń (✉)
Econometrics and Statistics, Institute Faculty of Economics and Management,
University of Szczecin, Mickiewicza 64, 71-101 Szczecin, Poland
e-mail: mariusz.doszyn@usz.edu.pl

K. Nermend and M. Łatuszyńska (eds.), *Problems, Methods and Tools in Experimental and Behavioral Economics*, Springer Proceedings in Business and Economics, https://doi.org/10.1007/978-3-319-99187-0_4

4.1 Introduction

Nowadays, there is a growing number of researches, mostly in behavioural economics, in which impact of psychological factors is emphasised. In behavioural economics, it is stated that people make many systematic errors in judgements and use certain heuristics while making decisions (*heuristics and biases paradigm*). People also make mistakes while evaluating past and future utility, which is contradictory with the assumption about utility maximisation. With respect to social behaviours, not only selfishness, but also rule of reciprocity seems to be important (Wilkinson 2008; Rabin 1996).

In context of these studies the question arises, how to measure intensity of psychological features and their impact on economic events? It is connected with more general problem: how to apply the very interesting findings of behavioural economics to real phenomena analysis? In the following monographs (Hozer and Doszyń 2004; Doszyń 2008, 2013) conception of propensity was proposed. Generally, in these monographs problems connected with measuring propensities are discussed. Also, analysis of human propensities' impact on economic occurrences and a proposal of econometric tools enabling identification of this impact are presented. Problems connected with measuring propensities are also considered in Doszyń and Majewski (2016) and Doszyń (2017).

In this chapter, measures of propensity to risk will be used in context of the prospect theory. With respect to these measures, value function will be specified. The hypothesis will be verified if proposed measures of propensity to risk are consistent with conclusions that stem from the prospect theory.

4.2 Measures of Propensities

In the philosophy of science, there are many varieties of propensity theories which generally could be divided into two groups: (1) theories in which propensity is understood as a result of all conditions that generate events (K. R. Popper), (2) theories in which propensity is an internal characteristic of an object (C. Peirce). These concepts are described in Popper (1959, 1990) and Gillies (2000). Classification of propensity theories is presented in Doszyń (2013, 2017). In the prospect theory, propensity to risk is understood as a tendency that depends both on external circumstances and psychological traits. In this theory, such factors as prospects, level of gains and losses, probability of events are influencing behaviours. Therefore, in this chapter propensity to risk is understood as a tendency dependent both on internal and external incentives.

How to define a propensity? Propensity might be defined as a "slope of posture" towards something (or somebody) that makes probability of certain event higher (Hozer and Doszyń 2004). Generally, propensity could be measured by means of frequency and trigonometric methods (Hozer and Doszyń 2004). In the frequency method, level of propensity is a:

$$s = \frac{m}{n} \tag{4.1}$$

where

s The frequency measure of propensity,
m Number of cases in which propensity appears,
n Number of all possible cases.

Therefore, in the frequency measure, propensity (***s***) is calculated as a share of cases in which propensity appears (***m***) in all possible cases (***n***). Propensity might be also presented in degrees, by means of trigonometric measure, where propensity is defined as a specified angle (Hozer and Doszyń 2004) (Fig. 4.1).

In the trigonometric method, propensity is measured as an angle γ. Tangent of this angle could be obtained as:

$$tg\gamma = \frac{1-s}{s} \tag{4.2}$$

where

s Frequency measure of propensity.

The higher the propensity, the higher the "slope" (and the lower angle γ). The trigonometric method could be useful while presenting the strength of propensity in a graphical way.

Fig. 4.1 Trigonometric interpretation of propensity. *Source* Individual study

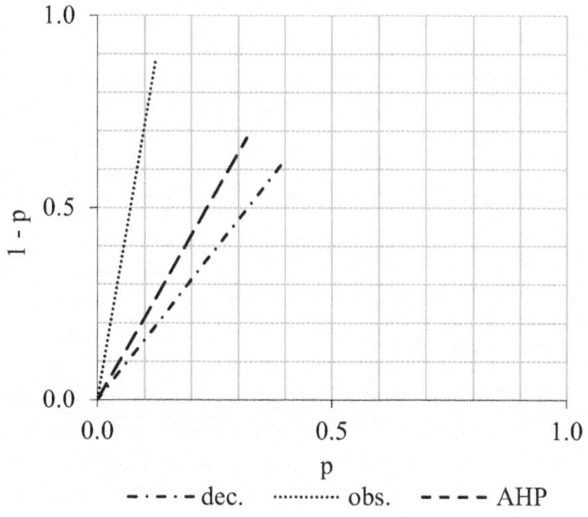

The frequency measure (4.1) could be used to estimate propensity to risk if information about propensity is presented on nominal scale. In that case, n is a number of people and m is a number of people who make risky choices. Such measure describes propensity to risk of a given collectivity, but this measure might be also used for individuals. Then, m stands for risky decisions of a given person and n is a number of all possible cases, when risky decisions could be made.

Therefore, the frequency measure (4.1) could be used to calculate propensity to risk if we have two outcomes: risky one and safe (safer) one. That kind of decision problems was analysed by D. Kahneman and A. Tversky in their famous article about the prospect theory (Kahneman and Tversky 1979).

If there are many outcomes, propensity to risk could be estimated by means of measure constructed on the basis of the game against nature (Doszyń 2008). Decision problems with many outcomes were analysed by D. Kahneman and A. Tversky in the cumulative prospect theory (Tversky and Kahneman 1992).

Output matrix in the game against nature should be constructed in such a way that strategies are ordered with respect to propensity to risk (Table 4.1). To each strategy, different levels of propensity to risk are assigned. According to Hurwicz criterion, strategy A is an optimum for propensity s_A, strategy B is an optimum for propensity s_B, etc.

Let us assume that Hurwicz criterion is used to make a choice (d_i is maximised):

$$d_i = s_i k_i + (1 - s_i) l_i,$$

where s_i is a given propensity to risk and k_i, l_i are outputs for analysed strategy $(k_i > l_i)$.

With respect to Hurwicz criterion, output matrix could be constructed in such way that strategy A is an optimum for propensity to risk s_A, strategy B is an optimum for propensity to risk s_B and so on:

$$\begin{aligned} d_A &= s_A k_A + (1 - s_A) l_A \rightarrow max \\ d_B &= s_B k_B + (1 - s_B) l_B \rightarrow max \\ &\ldots \\ d_Z &= s_Z k_Z + (1 - s_Z) l_Z \rightarrow max \end{aligned}$$

The higher propensity to risk, the higher dispersion of the results in a given strategy. Output matrix should be specified exactly in this way. If we know that n_A

Table 4.1 Game against nature with strategies characterised by different level of risk

Strategy	Case L	Case K
A	l_A	k_A
B	l_B	k_B
…	…	…
Z	l_Z	k_Z

Source Own work

is a number of people who choose strategy A, n_B is a number of people who choose strategy B, etc., propensity to risk (s_r) for n people might be estimated as a weighted average:

$$s_r = \frac{s_A n_A + s_B n_B + \cdots + s_Z n_Z}{n} \tag{4.3}$$

4.3 Prospect Theory and Propensity to Risk

The first version of the prospect theory was described in the famous article *Prospect Theory: An Analysis of Decision Under Risk*, published in 1979 by D. Kahneman and A. Tversky in *Econometrica*. It is now accepted that the model proposed in this article has, however, some limitations. Primarily, it can be only applied to gambles with two nonzero outcomes. In 1992 D. Kahneman and A. Tversky published a new version of the model, which is called cumulative prospect theory. There is a lot of literature on these topics. A brief description is presented for example in Barberis (2013). Nowadays cumulative prospect theory is usually implemented.

This theory is based on the following findings (Kahneman and Tversky 1992):

- Framing effects. According to the rational theory of choice, equivalent formulations of the same choice problem should result in the same preference order. However, there are a lot of proofs that variations in the framing options lead to systematically different preferences.
- Nonlinear preferences. It is known that utility of a risky prospect is not a linear function of outcome probabilities. For instance, the difference between such probabilities as 0.99 and 1.00 has much greater impact on preferences than the difference between 0.10 and 0.11.
- Source dependence. In betting on uncertain events, not only the degree of uncertainty but also its source is important. A lot of recent evidence shows that people usually prefer a bet on an event in the area of their competence, also when the probability is more vague than in other options.
- Risk seeking. In economic analysis of decision under uncertainty, the risk aversion is generally assumed. However, there are two classes of decision problems where risk-seeking behaviours are usually observed. The first class contains choices when people prefer a small probability of winning a large prize over the expected value of such prospect. In the second are these decisions when people must choose between a sure loss and a larger loss with moderate probability.
- Loss aversion. According to this assumption, people are more sensitive to losses than to gains of the same magnitude.

In the cumulative prospect theory gambles with many outcomes are considered:

$$(x_{-m}, p_{-m}; x_{-m+1}, p_{-m+1}; \ldots, x_0, p_0; \ldots, x_{n-1}, p_{n-1}; x_n, p_n)$$

where x_{-m} is a gain occurring with probability p_{-m}, x_{-m+1} is a gain with probability p_{-m+1} and so on Barberis (2013). Outcomes are in increasing order and $x_0 = 0$. Under expected utility theory, every individual makes decision on the basis of the utility levels weighted by objective probabilities of events:

$$\sum_{i=-m}^{n} p_i U(W + x_i)$$

where W is a state of wealth and U is a concave utility function.

In case of cumulative prospect theory, each decision is based on values of changes (with respect to reference point) weighted by the so-called decision weights

$$\sum_{i=-m}^{n} \pi_i v(x_i)$$

where v is a value function, and π_i are decision weights (Kahneman and Tversky 1992; Barberis 2013). State of wealth (*W*) is omitted. Therefore, in the cumulative prospect theory not state of wealth is important, but changes of wealth (gains, losses) with comparison to settled reference point.

Usually, four elements of prospect theory are emphasised (Barberis 2013):

(a) Reference dependence,
(b) Loss aversion,
(c) Diminishing sensitivity,
(d) Probability weighting.

As it was mentioned, the prospect theory states that people derive utility not from absolute levels of wealth but from gains and losses, with relation to the reference point. This is why value function $v(x_i)$ (with changes) and not utility function $U(W + x_i)$ (with wealth state) is considered. General explanation for this assumption, known as reference dependence, was proposed by D. Kahneman and A. Tversky. After many experiments, they noted that our perception works in such way, that we are rather more sensitive to changes of attributes than to absolute magnitudes.

Another very important feature is that the value function captures loss aversion, so people are much more sensitive to losses than to gains of the same level. Loss aversion makes the value function much steeper in the region of losses (Figs. 4.2 and 4.3). The value function is also concave in the region of gains and convex in the region of losses. This is known as a diminishing sensitivity and it implies that, for example, a change of gain (or loss) from \$100 to \$200 has a higher utility impact than change of gain (or loss) from \$1000 to \$1100. The concavity in case of gains

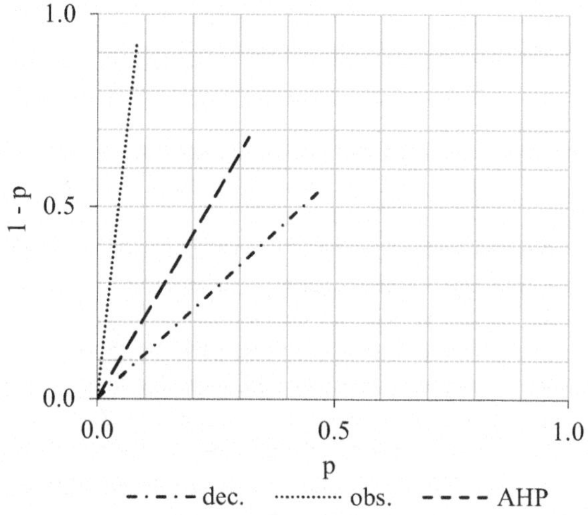

Fig. 4.2 The weighting function. *Source* Own calculations

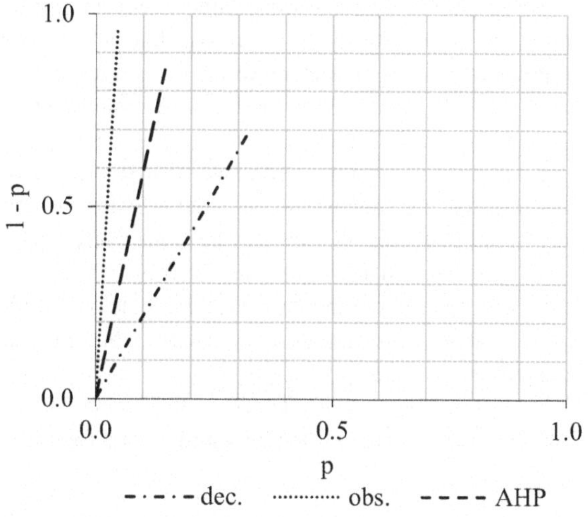

Fig. 4.3 Distribution of respondents according to sex and age. *Source* Own calculations

makes that people are risk averse over moderate probability of gains. In losses regions, people tend to be more risk seeking (over moderate probability).

The last feature of the prospect theory is that people don't weight outcomes by using objective probabilities p_i, but rather by decision weights π_i. The decision weights are obtained by means of a weighting function, where objective probability is taken as an argument. The weighting function is presented in Fig. 4.2. It was proposed by A. Tversky and D. Kahneman (Kahneman and Tversky 1992). They estimated the following model:

$$w(p) = \frac{p^{\delta}}{\left(p^{\delta} + (1-p)^{\delta}\right)^{1/\delta}} \tag{4.4}$$

where p is an objective probability and the δ was estimated from experimental data ($\delta = 0.65$).[1] The dotted line refers to $\delta = 1$, in which case we have linear probability weighting. The function (4.4) has many interesting features. At first, it is compatible empirical data (Kahneman and Tversky 1992). It has only one parameter and encompasses both concave and convex regions. The condition that: $w(0.5) = 0.5$ is also not necessary.

The general conclusion is that the weighting function overestimates low probabilities and underestimates high probabilities. People usually have tendency to overweight unlikely extreme outcomes. D. Kahneman and A. Tversky found that it is consistent with the fact that people like both lotteries and insurance. In case of lotteries, value of winning $1000 with probability 0.001 is higher than sure gain of $1. But at the same time, people prefer to pay $1 than to lose $1000 with probability equal to 0.001.

When people evaluate uncertainty, two natural boundaries are considered: certainty and impossibility. It is known that an increase of 0.05 in the probability of winning has stronger impact when it changes the probability from 0.95 to 1.0 or from 0 to 0.05. When the probability of winning changes from 0.40 to 0.45 or from 0.7 to 0.75, the influence is much weaker. The diminishing sensitivity is a reason why weighting function is concave near 0 and convex near 1. It is however worth noticing that the function is not well—behaving near the endpoints. If we have a very small probability, they can be both overestimated and neglected.

It is also worth noticing that the transformed probabilities π_i do not represent erroneous beliefs, but they are exactly decision weights. So someone who is offered a 0.01 chance of winning knows exactly what it means to have a 0.01 probability of occurrence.

D. Kahneman and A. Tversky also proposed a specific value function, with different form in region of gains and losses (Kahneman and Tversky 1992):

$$v(x) = \begin{cases} x^{\alpha} & if\, x \geq 0 \\ -\lambda(-x)^{\alpha} & if\, x < 0 \end{cases} \tag{4.5}$$

The author's estimates are $\alpha = 0.88$ and $\lambda = 2.25$. One of the parameters (λ) expresses loss aversion in the losses region.

In case of the value function, the following problem arises: does the propensity to risk affect its parameters? We could assume that presented estimate of parameter

[1] At first, D. Kahneman and A. Tversky estimated the weighting function separately for gains and for losses, but differences were very small, so one function is usually considered.

α is not constant and could be different in other groups of people. So how this parameter could be specified? In this chapter, an attempt is made to treat one of the parameters (α) as a propensity to risk, calculated by means of proposed measures of propensity to risk.

4.4 Empirical Example

The main aim of the undertaken research was to use proposed measures of propensity to risk (frequency measure (4.1) and measure based on game against nature (4.3)) to specify the value function (4.5) proposed by D. Kahneman and A. Tversky. Mainly, students took part in the survey. 48 respondents were asked to fulfil the questionnaire. Most of the participants were women (75%). Majority of respondents were 21–22 years old. Most of the men were at least 23 years old. Structure of the respondents according to sex and age is presented in the Fig. 4.3.

In the first part, the frequency measure of propensity (4.1) was applied. In this measure propensity to risk is measured on the nominal scale. In these decision problems, we have only two outputs. That kind of problems was analysed by D. Kahneman and A. Tversky in the first version of the prospect theory. Intensity of propensity to risk is a share of respondents who make risky choices. The respondents had to answer the following question (problem S1):

You can get for sure 950 PLN or take part in a lottery where you can win 1000 PLN with probability of 90% and 500 PLN with probability of 10%. Will you take part in the lottery?

Expected value of the lottery is the same as a sure gain. It was assumed that people who choose lottery have strong propensity to risk. Although they could win 1000 PLN with high probability equal to 90%, but they could also have only 500 PLN, but with probability 10%.

In the next part, propensity to risk was measured by means of measure (4.3), where there are many outputs presented in the form of game against nature. That kind of measures could be used in context of cumulative prospect theory. The respondents had to decide, which strategy to choose in the following problem (problem S2):

You participate in a lottery in which two results may appear: K or L (Table 4.2). For example, if you choose strategy A you might win 2000 PLN, if you choose strategy B you might win 1800 or 2800 PLN, if you choose strategy C you might win 1600 or 3200 PLN, and so on.

Which option you choose, if you do not know whether K or L will appear?

The above output matrix was constructed in such a way that strategy A is an optimum for propensity to risk $s = 0$, strategy B is an optimum for propensity to risk $s = 0.25$, strategy C is an optimum for propensity to risk $s = 0.5$, strategy D is

Table 4.2 Lottery results depending on the selected option (payment in PLN)

	K	L
A	2000	2000
B	1800	2800
C	1600	3200
D	1200	3400
E	400	3600

Source Own work

Table 4.3 Hurwicz criterion (d_i) for different values of propensity to risk for output matrix presented in Table 4.2

Strategy/ propensity	0	0.25	0.50	0.75	1
A	**2000**	2000	2000	2000	2000
B	1800	**2050**	2300	2550	2800
C	1600	2000	**2400**	2800	3200
D	1200	1750	2300	**2850**	3400
E	400	1200	2000	2800	**3600**

Source Own work
Bolded values are highest, for given strategy

Table 4.4 Propensity to risk measures (4.1) and (4.3) calculated for the two problems: S1 and S2

Problem	S1	S2
Men	0.333	0.521
Women	0.361	0.299
Total	0.354	0.354

Source Own calculations

an optimum for propensity to risk $s = 0.75$ and strategy E is an optimum for propensity to risk $s = 1$.

To build that kind of output matrix Hurwicz criterion was applied: $d_i = s_i k_i + (1 - s_i)l_i$. Values of Hurwicz criterion (d_i) for different values of propensity to risk are presented in Table 4.3.

If someone is risk averse ($s = 0$), the best is strategy A. For people with high propensity to risk ($s = 0.75$), the best is strategy D, etc. If we know how many respondents choose each strategy, we could calculate propensity to risk on the basis of the formula (4.3).

Propensities to risk obtained for problems S1 and S2 are presented in Table 4.4. What seems to be very interesting, propensity to risk calculated for all respondents by means of the two measures is the same and equal to 0.354. The general conclusion is that propensity to risk among all respondents is rather low. Propensities to risk, also according to sex, are presented in Figs. 4.4, 4.5 and 4.6. Also, trigonometric measure of propensity (4.2) was applied. According to this measure, the higher propensity, the higher slope and smaller angle γ.

According to sex, in the first problem (S1), in which propensity is measured on nominal scale (4.1), propensity is a little higher for women. In the second problem

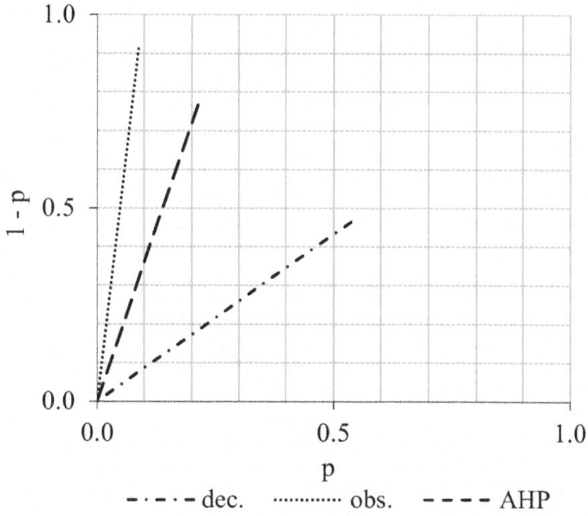

Fig. 4.4 Trigonometric measure of propensity to risk for all respondents ($\gamma = 63.3°$). *Source* Own calculations

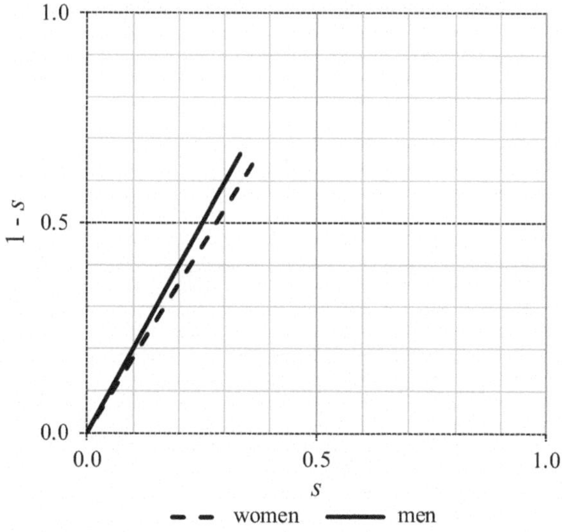

Fig. 4.5 Trigonometric measure of propensity to risk of men ($\gamma = 63.4°$) and women ($\gamma = 60.5°$)—problem S1. *Source* Own calculations

(S2), where propensity is calculated on the basis of output matrix with many strategies, propensity is much higher in case of men. These differences are probably due to fact, that only 12 men took part in the research and it is hard to make a valid conclusion. Despite this drawback, obtained results were used to specify the value function proposed in cumulative prospect theory to show how propensity to risk could affect choices under risk and uncertainty. In problem S1, probabilities are known, so decisions under risk are considered. In problem S2 there is uncertainty, because respondents didn't know probabilities.

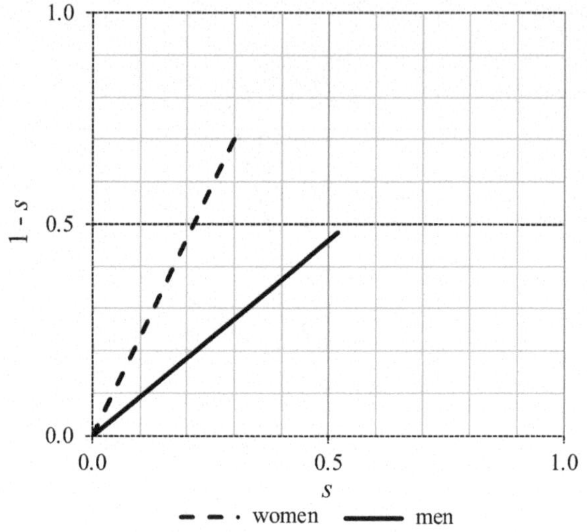

Fig. 4.6 Trigonometric measure of propensity to risk of men ($\gamma = 42.6°$) and women ($\gamma = 66.9°$)—problem S2. *Source* Own calculations

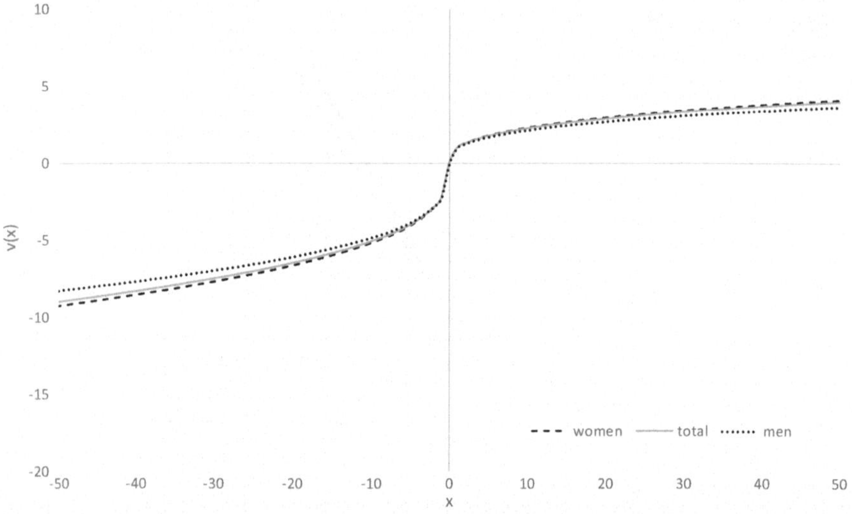

Fig. 4.7 Value functions for propensities to risk in problem S1. *Source* Own calculations

Figures 4.7 and 4.8 present value functions (4.5), whereas a parameter α respective measure of propensity to risk was applied. In analysed problems, only gains were analysed, but value functions were presented also for losses.

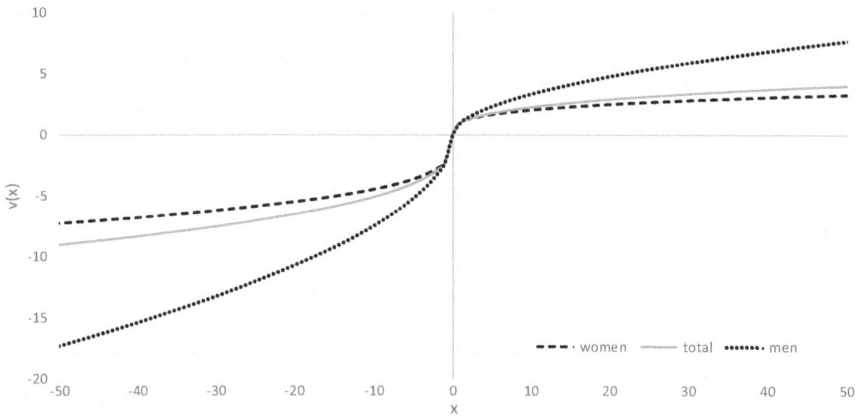

Fig. 4.8 Value functions for propensities to risk in problem S2. *Source* Own calculations

On the whole, the value functions suggest low propensity to risk. On Fig. 4.7, differences between functions are very small, because propensities to risk were almost the same for men and women. Much higher were the differences in propensities in problem S2, where there were many outputs. These differences are visible especially in case of propensity to risk of men. The value function constructed for men is generally much steeper but, as it was mentioned before, number of men was too small to make valid conclusions.

4.5 Conclusions

Many researchers state that it is hard to implement very interesting findings of behavioural economics. In this chapter, conception of propensity was proposed that could be useful in behavioural economics. Definition of propensity and propensity measures were discussed, mainly in context of propensity to risk. Two versions of the prospect theory were also considered, the first version (Kahneman and Tversky 1979) and the cumulative prospect theory (Kahneman and Tversky 1992).

The main aim of the chapter was to propose a new possibility of specification of the value function in the prospect theory, where the measures of propensity to risk are used as parameters. Two measures of propensity to risk were introduced. The first measure (4.1) is a share of risky choices in all considered cases. This measure is useful if we have two outputs with known probabilities (decisions are made under risk), as in the first version of the prospect theory. The information about propensity to risk is exhibited on the nominal scale.

The second measure of propensity is based on the game against nature (4.3) with unknown probabilities (decisions are made under uncertainty). Output matrix is constructed with respect to Hurwicz criterion. It enables identification of the intensity of the propensity to risk. This measure might be useful in situations, where we have many outputs, such as in the cumulative prospect theory. Presented ideas should be verified in further research to confirm that proposed specification of the value function is consisted with real decisions made under risk and uncertainty.

References

Barberis NC (2013) Thirty years of prospect theory in economics: a review and assessment. J Econ Perspect 27

Doszyń M (2008) Statystyczno – ekonometryczna analiza skłonności ludzkich [Statistical and econometric analysis of human propensities]. WNUS, Szczecin

Doszyń M (2013) Skłonności w ekonomii. Ujęcie ilościowe [Propensities in economics. The quantitative approach]. WNUS, Szczecin

Doszyń M (2017) Measuring economic propensities. In: Łatuszyńska M, Kesra N (eds) Neuroeconomic and behavioral aspects of decision making, Springer proceedings in business and economics, pp 77–90

Doszyń M, Majewski S (2016) Is there enough psychology in behavioural economics? Personality types and human propensities. In: Łatuszyńska M, Kesra N (eds) Selected issues in experimental economics, Springer proceedings in business and economics, pp 271–284

Gillies D (2000) Varieties of propensity. Br J Philoso Sci 51

Hozer J, Doszyń M (2004) Ekonometria skłonności [Econometrics of propensities]. PWE, Warszawa

Kahneman D, Tversky A (1979) Prospect theory: an analysis of decision under risk. Econometrica 47:2

Popper KR (1959) The propensity interpretation of probability. Br J Philos Sci 10

Popper KR (1990) A world of propensities. Thoemmes, Bristol

Rabin M (1996) Psychology and economics. Department of Economics, University of California —Berkeley

Tversky A, Kahneman D (1992) Advances in prospect theory: cumulative representation of uncertainty. J Risk Uncertainty 5

Wilkinson N (2008) An introduction to behavioural economics. Palgrave Macmillan

Chapter 5
Some Theoretical Aspect of Equilibrium in Behavioral Economics

H. Kowgier

Abstract Behavioral economics is closely related to the theoretical aspects that result from it. An especially important aspect is the problem of equilibrium. Experience shows that stock market investors often behave irrationally. Nevertheless, it was noted that in the long term, their activity is related to the equilibrium surface, which is a rotary cone. The chapter shows how using the method of least squares you can get a spiral line of the vector $[q_i, p_i, t_i]$ (p_i—means the price of the *i*th good, q_i—means the amount of the *i*th good, t_i—time characterizing a certain economic process) using a hyperbolic spiral which in space creates a equilibrium surface that is a cone. Having a general solution, we can experiment by adopting certain values that are coordinates of the vector, $[q_i, p_i, t_i]$, obtaining different cones of economic equilibrium. An important tool used in behavioral economics is game theory. The stock market can be treated as a game without the possibility of concluding a coalition. The chapter shows how to find the stock exchange state number, knowing the stock exchange information matrix and vice versa, how to find the state form of the stock exchange, knowing the stock market state number. In addition, the matrix boundary for the stock market is given, which is also the equilibrium matrix for the ideal economy. According to E. Noether's theorem, certain principles of conservation are associated with every symmetry. There is no equilibrium without symmetry. The third part of the work presents the problem of symmetry of economic quantities using the Shubnikov method. In addition, this chapter discusses the symmetry groups of some of the equilibrium surfaces encountered in economics.

Keywords Method of least squares · Equilibrium surfaces · Symmetry of economic quantities · Stock market · E. Noether's theorem · Hyperbolic spiral The W. Shubnikov method

H. Kowgier (✉)
Faculty of Economics and Management, Institute of Econometrics and Statistics, University of Szczecin, Mickiewicza 64, 71-101 Szczecin, Poland
e-mail: kowhenry@interia.eu

K. Nermend and M. Łatuszyńska (eds.), *Problems, Methods and Tools in Experimental and Behavioral Economics*, Springer Proceedings in Business and Economics, https://doi.org/10.1007/978-3-319-99187-0_5

5.1 Introduction

Economics as a social science is closely related to human activity. The tendencies and preferences of investors determine many things in economics. Interesting investors' behavior on the stock exchanges has been observed for many years. Although there are quite objective analyzes of how to invest in securities on the stock market, they are not always fully applied.

In view of the many factors affecting effective investments, investors are often based on their own intuition. This is manifested by the fact that in many situations instead of a cold analysis, "herd instinct" prevails the so-called sheep rush. To minimize the risk of investment, a statistical investor places his capital on the stock exchange in such securities as most investors. A psychological principle works here —it is safer in the group. The hypothesis concerning the centrifuging vectors in economics which move on centrifuging-spiral trajectories creating precessive cones of equilibrium or other precessive rotating surfaces of the second degree has been empirically verified on the example of a time series covering daily stock exchange data from a period of over one hundred years (Juzwiszyn 2007). The observed regularity is interesting because the herding instinct on the stock market also leads to a kind of equilibrium. The aim of the chapter is to present three theoretical aspects related to the problem of equilibrium in behavioral economics. The first one concerns how one can simulate the motion of the vector $[q_i, p_i, t_i]$ characterizing a certain economic process on the surface of equilibrium which is a cone with the use of a hyperbolic spiral. The second aspect concerns the stock exchange as an example's of a game conducted by investors without the possibility of concluding a coalition and how to find individual states of the stock exchange and a border matrix that characterizes the state of the ideal economy. The third aspect concerns the problems of symmetry of economic quantities and the resulting conclusions, as well as the issues of the equilibrium surface (their gradation) encountered in behavioral economics. The methods of mathematical analysis and linear algebra were used to perform the relevant research.

5.2 Determination of the Equilateral Cone Using a Hyperbolic Spiral

The essence of economics is the whirling movement. He is associated with a desire to equilibrium. The Earth came whirling circles full precession cone. The cone is the second-degree algebraic surface that the helix curve generates (Fig. 5.1). The cone has an equation:

$$\frac{x^2}{a^2} + \frac{y^2}{b^2} - \frac{z^2}{c^2} = 0 \tag{5.1}$$

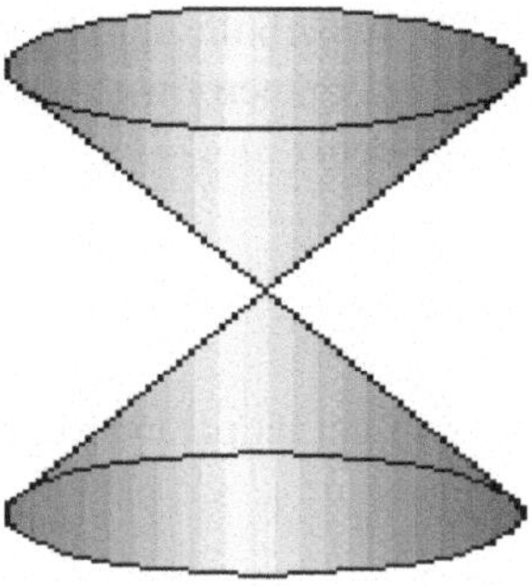

Fig. 5.1 Cone as the surface of equilibrium. *Source* Own studies

The cone can be treated as an asymptotic surface for a double-coat hyperboloid which has the equation (Fichtenholz 1985):

$$\frac{x^2}{a^2} + \frac{y^2}{b^2} - \frac{z^2}{c^2} = -1 \tag{5.2}$$

It is located inside the cone. Similarly, one-coat hyperboloid an the equation:

$$\frac{x^2}{a^2} + \frac{y^2}{b^2} - \frac{z^2}{c^2} = 1 \tag{5.3}$$

is the outer sheath of the cone.

On the surface of the cone, there are states of instantaneous equilibrium, which are unstable. In any neighborhood of the point on the cone, there are states from other classes. The states inside the cone form an open set and are stable (Smoluk 2007). Similarly, states outside the cone create an open set and are stable. The size of the gaping of this cone speaks of stability. The larger the gaping angle of the cone, the less stable the economy is. A smaller gaping angle means that the economy is more stable. Because the dynamic process of shaping prices and quantity of goods runs continuously, new vortex trajectories are created. There may also be a reverse process associated with the development of vortices. Achieved equilibrium in behavioral economics is relatively short, because it may be associated with some economic stagnation, which is not desirable. All cybernetic systems occurring in nature react to changing conditions in such a way that the whirling movement is constantly around a certain ideal state. The equation of hyperbolic spiral in polar coordinates has the form:

(Bronsztejn et al. 2001):

$$\rho = \frac{a}{\varphi} \tag{5.4}$$

where $a > 0,\ -\infty < \varphi < 0,\ 0 < \varphi < \infty$.

The hyperbolic spiral consists of two branches, one of which is the image of the other in symmetry with respect to the vertical axis. If the hyperbolic spiral is wound on the cone:

$$\frac{x^2}{r^2} + \frac{y^2}{r^2} = \frac{z^2}{l^2}, \tag{5.5}$$

we will get its parametric representation:

$$S_{hip} = [\frac{a}{\varphi}\cos\varphi, \frac{a}{\varphi}\sin\varphi, \frac{a}{\varphi}\frac{l}{r}]. \tag{5.6}$$

We consider the vector $[q_i, p_i, t_i]$ where p_i—means the price of the *i*th good, q_i—means the amount of the *i*th good, t_i—time characterizing a certain economic process. Let the vectors with given coordinates be subjected to market processes. Considering the motion of such vectors in the three-dimensional Cartesian system, we obtain the vortex trajectories characteristic of these vectors. The increase or decrease in the prices of given goods affects the quantity of goods appearing on the market and vice versa. By presenting studied the economic processes on the plane, we obtain flat zigzag graphs where one of the coordinates of the vector is time. The adjustment of the price level and the quantities of the equilibrium of the considered economic goods can be presented by means of the so-called of spiderweb model. This model was independently proposed by three economists J. Tymimen, R. Ricci, T. Hanau. The hyperbolic spiral can be approximated with vectors $[q_i, p_i, t_i]$ using the least squares method:

$$\begin{aligned} W &= \sum_{i=1}^{n}\left([\frac{a}{\varphi_i}\cos\varphi_i, \frac{a}{\varphi_i}\sin\varphi_i, \frac{a}{\varphi_i}\frac{l}{r}] - [q_i, p_i, t_i]\right)^2 \\ &= \sum_{i=1}^{n}\left([\frac{a}{\varphi_i}\cos\varphi_i - q_i, \frac{a}{\varphi_i}\sin\varphi_i - p_i, \frac{a}{\varphi_i}\frac{l}{r} - t_i]\right)^2 \end{aligned}$$

$$\begin{aligned} \frac{\partial W}{\partial a} &= 2\sum_{i=1}^{n}\left([\frac{a}{\varphi_i}\cos\varphi_i - q_i, \frac{a}{\varphi_i}\sin\varphi_i - p_i, \frac{a}{\varphi_i}\frac{l}{r} - t_i][\frac{\cos\varphi_i}{\varphi_i}, \frac{\sin\varphi_i}{\varphi_i}, \frac{l}{r\varphi_i}]\right) \\ &= 2\sum_{i=1}^{n}\left(\frac{a\cos^2\varphi_i}{\varphi_i^2} - q_i\frac{\cos\varphi_i}{\varphi_i} + a\frac{\sin^2\varphi_i}{\varphi_i^2} - p_i\frac{\sin\varphi_i}{\varphi_i} + \frac{al^2}{\varphi_i^2 r^2} - t_i\frac{l}{\varphi_i r}\right) = 0. \end{aligned}$$

Therefore, we receive:

$$\sum_{i=1}^{n}\left(\frac{a}{\varphi_i^2}(1 + \frac{l^2}{r^2}) - \frac{1}{\varphi_i}(q_i\cos\varphi_i + p_i\sin\varphi_i + \frac{l}{r}t_i)\right) = 0$$

from here

$$a\sum_{i=1}^{n}\frac{r^2+l^2}{r^2\varphi_i^2}-\sum_{i=1}^{n}\frac{1}{\varphi_i}\left(q_i\cos\varphi_i+p_i\sin\varphi_i+\frac{l}{r}t_i\right)=0$$

and

$$a=\frac{\sum_{i=1}^{n}\left(\frac{1}{\varphi_i}(q_i\cos\varphi_i+p\ \sin\varphi_i+\frac{l}{r}t_i)\right)}{\frac{r^2+l^2}{r^2}\sum_{i=1}^{n}\left(\frac{1}{\varphi_i^2}\right)}=\frac{\sum_{i=1}^{n}\left(\varphi_i^{-1}(q_i\cos\varphi_i+p_i\sin\varphi_i+lr^{-1}t_i)\right)}{(r^2+l^2)r^{-2}\sum_{i=1}^{n}\varphi_i^{-2}}. \tag{5.7}$$

By analogy, we get:

$$\begin{aligned}\frac{\partial W}{\partial r}&=2\sum_{i=1}^{n}\left([\frac{a}{\varphi_i}\cos\varphi_i-q_i,\frac{a}{\varphi_i}\sin\varphi_i-p_i,\frac{a}{\varphi_i}\frac{l}{r}-t_i][0,0,\frac{-al}{r^2\varphi_i}]\right)\\&=2\sum_{i=1}^{n}\left(\left(\frac{al}{r\varphi_i}-t_i\right)\left(\frac{-al}{\varphi_i r^2}\right)\right)\\&=2\sum_{i=1}^{n}\left(\frac{alt_i}{r^2\varphi_i}-\frac{a^2l^2}{r^3\varphi_i^2}\right)=0,\end{aligned}$$

and therefore, we receive:

$$\frac{al}{r}\sum_{i=1}^{n}\frac{1}{\varphi_i^2}=\sum_{i=1}^{n}\frac{t_i}{\varphi_i}$$

and

$$r=\frac{al\sum_{i=1}^{n}\varphi_i^{-2}}{\sum_{i=1}^{n}t_i\varphi_i^{-1}}. \tag{5.8}$$

We note that from (5.8), we receive:

$$r^{-1}=\frac{\sum_{i=1}^{n}\varphi_i^{-1}t_i}{al\sum_{i=1}^{n}\varphi_i^{-2}},\quad r^{-2}=\frac{\sum_{i=1}^{n}\varphi_i^{-1}t_i}{a^2l^2\left(\sum_{i=1}^{n}\varphi_i^{-2}\right)^2}.$$

Substituting expressions for r^{-1} and r^{-2} to (5.7), we get:

$$a=\frac{\sum_{i=1}^{n}\left(\varphi_i^{-1}(q_i\cos\varphi_i+p_i\sin\varphi_i+lr^{-1}t_i)\right)}{(1+\frac{l^2}{r^2})\sum_{i=1}^{n}\varphi_i^{-2}}=\frac{\sum_{i=1}^{n}\left(\varphi_i^{-1}\left(p_i\sin\varphi_i+q_i\cos\varphi_i+l\frac{\sum_{i=1}^{n}\varphi_i^{-1}t_i}{al\sum_{i=1}^{n}\varphi_i^{-2}}t_i\right)\right)}{\left(1+l^2\frac{\sum_{i=1}^{n}\varphi_i^{-1}t_i}{a^2l^2\left(\sum_{i=1}^{n}\varphi_i^{-2}\right)^2}\right)\sum_{i=1}^{n}\varphi_i^{-2}}$$

$$=\frac{\sum_{i=1}^{n}\varphi_i^{-1}(p_i\sin\varphi_i+q_i\cos\varphi_i)+\frac{\left(\sum_{i=1}^{n}\varphi_i^{-1}t_i\right)^2}{a\sum_{i=1}^{n}\varphi_i^{-2}}}{\sum_{i=1}^{n}\varphi_i^{-2}+\frac{\sum_{i=1}^{n}\varphi_i^{-1}t_i}{a^2\sum_{i=1}^{n}\varphi_i^{-2}}}$$

$$\Leftrightarrow a\sum_{i=1}^{n}\varphi_i^{-2}+\frac{1}{a}\frac{\sum_{i=1}^{n}\varphi_i^{-1}t_i}{\sum_{i=1}^{n}\varphi_i^{-2}}-\frac{1}{a}\frac{\left(\sum_{i=1}^{n}\varphi_i^{-1}t_i\right)^2}{\sum_{i=1}^{n}\varphi_i^{-2}}-\sum_{i=1}^{n}\varphi_i^{-1}(p_i\sin\varphi_i+q_i\cos\varphi_i)=0$$

$$\Leftrightarrow a^2\sum_{i=1}^{n}\varphi_i^{-2}-a\sum_{i=1}^{n}\varphi_i^{-1}(p_i\sin\varphi_i+q_i\cos\varphi_i)+\frac{\sum_{i=1}^{n}\varphi_i^{-1}t_i-\left(\sum_{i=1}^{n}\varphi_i^{-1}t_i\right)^2}{\sum_{i=1}^{n}\varphi_i^{-2}}=0.$$

The obtained equation is square.

$$\Delta=\left(\sum_{i=1}^{n}\varphi_i^{-1}(p_i\sin\varphi_i+q_i\cos\varphi_i)\right)^2-4\left(\sum_{i=1}^{n}\varphi_i^{-1}t_i-\left(\sum_{i=1}^{n}\varphi_i^{-1}t_i\right)^2\right)>0$$

Therefore, we receive:

$$a_{1/2}=\frac{\sum_{i=1}^{n}\varphi_i^{-1}(p_i\sin\varphi_i+q_i\cos\varphi_i)\pm\sqrt{\left[\sum_{i=1}^{n}\varphi_i^{-1}(p_i\sin\varphi_i+q_i\cos\varphi_i)\right]^2-4\left[\sum_{i=1}^{n}\varphi_i^{-1}t_i-\left(\sum_{i=1}^{n}\varphi_i^{-1}t_i\right)^2\right]}}{2\sum_{i=1}^{n}\varphi_i^{-2}} \quad (5.9)$$

$$r_{1/2}=l\frac{\sum_{i=1}^{n}\varphi_i^{-2}}{\sum_{i=1}^{n}\varphi_i^{-1}t_i}\frac{\sum_{i=1}^{n}\varphi_i^{-1}(p_i\sin\varphi_i+q_i\cos\varphi_i)\pm\sqrt{\left[\sum_{i=1}^{n}\varphi_i^{-1}(p_i\sin\varphi_i+q_i\cos\varphi_i)\right]^2-4\left[\sum_{i=1}^{n}\varphi_i^{-1}t_i-\left(\sum_{i=1}^{n}\varphi_i^{-1}t_i\right)^2\right]}}{2\sum_{i=1}^{n}\varphi_i^{-2}}. \quad (5.10)$$

At certain values $p_i, q_i, t_i, \varphi_i, l$, we receive $a > 0$ and $r > 0$ and we can write the equation of the hyperbolic spiral. Having a general solution, we can experiment by adopting certain values that are coordinates of the vector, $[q_i, p_i, t_i]$, obtaining different cones of economic equilibrium. The hyperbolic spiral explains the essence of the market game.

$$\lim_{\varphi \to 0} y = \lim_{\varphi \to 0} \frac{a}{\varphi} \sin \varphi = a, \quad \lim_{\varphi \to 0} x = \lim_{\varphi \to 0} \frac{a}{\varphi} \cos \varphi = \infty$$

i.e., financial spiral strives for asymptote $y = a$ when $\varphi \to 0$. Similarly, $\lim_{\varphi \to \infty} y = \lim_{\varphi \to \infty} \frac{a}{\varphi} \sin \varphi = 0$, $\lim_{\varphi \to \infty} x = \lim_{\varphi \to \infty} \frac{a}{\varphi} \cos \varphi = 0$. The hyperbolic spiral in this case approaches the equilibrium point (0, 0).

5.3 Stock Exchange States, the Boundary Matrix of Equilibrium for the Ideal Economy

The area of interest of game theory is problems related to decisions in systems with many players, each of whom has their own preferences, defining the mode of operation within the set rules on which his payment depends. An example of a multiplayer game is the stock exchange. It is a game without the possibility of creating a coalition. Let on the stock exchange there are n companies of comparable size offering their securities, e.g., shares. In addition, let the daily change in the share price be such that either the share price drops or grows by a unit. The condition of the stock exchange describes a vector from the real space R^n. This vector informs whether the quotations of each company are decreasing, fixed, or growing. It can be assumed that the state of the stock exchange has components belonging to the set $\{-1, 0, 1\}$, which symbolize the quotations of companies. Because we have n companies, so all possible states we have as much as we can create variations of n elements with repetitions from the three element sets, i.e., 3^n. Each state can occur with a certain probability, although some states are very unlikely, for example, that all companies will simultaneously receive a discount or increase in the rate. With n companies, the stock exchange state matrix $A_{n \times 3^n}$ will have n rows and 3^n columns. For example, for n = 1 we get $A_{1 \times 3^1} = [-1, 0, 1]$. For n = 2, we receive:

$$A_{2 \times 3^2} = \begin{bmatrix} -1 & -1 & -1 & 0 & 0 & 0 & 1 & 1 & 1 \\ -1 & 0 & 1 & -1 & 0 & 1 & -1 & 0 & 1 \end{bmatrix} = \begin{bmatrix} -1-1-1 & 000 & 111 \\ A_{1 \times 3^1} & A_{1 \times 3^1} & A_{1 \times 3^1} \end{bmatrix}. \tag{5.11}$$

Inductively for a matrix with $n + 1$ rows and 3^{n+1} columns, we have:

$$A_{(n+1)\times 3^{n+1}} = \begin{bmatrix} -1,-1,\ldots,-1 & 0,0,\ldots,0 & 1,1,\ldots,1 \\ A_{n\times 3^n} & A_{n\times 3^n} & A_{n\times 3^n} \end{bmatrix}, \quad (5.12)$$

where in the top row of the matrix there are 3^n times -1, 3^n times 0, and 3^n times 1 which after adding gives 3^{n+1} columns. Each investor on the stock market maximizes his payment with a fixed distribution of stock levels $(p_1, p_2, \ldots, p_{3^n})$, where $\sum_{l=1}^{3^n} p_l = 1$ and $p_l \geq 0$. Let us mark the exchange information matrix by A. The columns of this matrix are stock exchange states.

To find the state number, should be found the appropriate column number in the matrix A.

Each state of the stock exchange is given by the vector $[g_1, g_2, \ldots, g_n]$ where $g_j \in \{-1, 0, 1\}$ for $j = 1, 2, 3, \ldots, n$, because we have n companies. To find the number of state of stock exchange in the A matrix, use formula:

$k = 1 + (g_n + 1) \cdot 3^0 + (g_{n-1} + 1) \cdot 3^1 + \ldots + (g_1 + 1) \cdot 3^{n-1}$ where $k \in \{1, 2, , \ldots, 3^n\}$.

For example, when $[g_1, g_2, \ldots, g_n] = [1, 1, \ldots, 1]$, we receive:

$$k = 1 + 2 + 2 \cdot 3^1 + 2 \cdot 3^2 + \ldots + 2 \cdot 3^{n-1} = 3 + 2 \cdot \frac{3 \cdot (1 - 3^{n-1})}{1 - 3} = 3^n$$

When $[g_1, g_2, \ldots, g_n] = [-1, -1, \ldots, -1]$, we get $k = 1$. For $[g_1, g_2, \ldots, g_n] = [-1, -1, \ldots, -1, 0]$, we have $k = 2$,

etc. Let us assume that $\delta_0 = g_n + 1$, $\delta_1 = g_{n-1} + 1, \ldots, \delta_{n-1} = g_1 + 1$ then we have:

$$k = 1 + \delta_{n-1} \cdot 3^{n-1} + \delta_{n-2} \cdot 3^{n-2} + \ldots + \delta_0 \cdot 3^0$$

where $\delta_i \in \{0, 1, 2\}$, $i = 0, 1, \ldots, n-1$ because $g_j \in \{-1, 0, 1\}$ for $j = 1, 2, 3, \ldots, n$.

Knowing the column number (state) can also find the state form. It results from the relationship:

$$k - 1 = \delta_{n-1} \cdot 3^{n-1} + \delta_{n-2} \cdot 3^{n-2} + \ldots + \delta_0 \cdot 3^0$$

and equality:

$$g_1 = \delta_{n-1} - 1,\ g_2 = \delta_{n-2} - 1,\ \ldots,\ g_n = \delta_0 - 1.$$

Thus, kth state of the stock exchange is a vector $[\delta_{n-1} - 1, \delta_{n-2} - 1, \ldots, \delta_0 - 1]$.

With the family of states of companies of stock exchange which denote a decline, constancy, growth, the transition matrix is bound

$$\hat{A} = \begin{bmatrix} \frac{1}{3} & \frac{2}{3} & 0 \\ \frac{1}{6} & \frac{2}{3} & \frac{1}{6} \\ 0 & \frac{2}{3} & \frac{1}{3} \end{bmatrix}. \tag{5.13}$$

From the first row of matrix $\hat{A}$, it appears that out of all companies recording declines, 1/3 of them will remain in a state of decline, 2/3 will go to a stable state, and none of them will grow.

By analogy, we interpret the second and third rows of the matrix $\hat{A}$. From matrix $\hat{A}$, it follows that the probability of transition to the permanent state in each case is 2/3.

Practice shows that there is an approximate matrix equation:

$$\hat{A} \approx \frac{1}{n} \sum_{i=1}^{n} \hat{A}_i. \tag{5.14}$$

where $\hat{A}$ is the transition matrix for the ith company.

In addition, it happens (Gelfand 1975):

$$\lim_{n \to \infty} \begin{bmatrix} \frac{1}{3} & \frac{2}{3} & 0 \\ \frac{1}{6} & \frac{2}{3} & \frac{1}{6} \\ 0 & \frac{2}{3} & \frac{1}{3} \end{bmatrix}^n = \begin{bmatrix} \frac{1}{6} & \frac{2}{3} & \frac{1}{6} \\ \frac{1}{6} & \frac{2}{3} & \frac{1}{6} \\ \frac{1}{6} & \frac{2}{3} & \frac{1}{6} \end{bmatrix} = \tilde{A} \tag{5.15}$$

where $\tilde{A}$ is a boundary matrix and $\tilde{A}^n = \tilde{A}$. In the model economy, which can be treated as a state of equilibrium, 1/6 of the companies record declines, 2/3 maintain stable standards, and 1/6 have increased. Transitions on the stock exchange, related to −1, 0, 1 numbers, create peculiar whirls. The main core of the stock exchange is companies that stick to a stable standard.

5.4 Symmetry of Economic Quantities, Surfaces of Equilibrium

Because many economic quantities are described by means of vectors, scalars, and tensors, point symmetry can be attributed not only to economic values, but also to the mathematical quantities used to describe them. We owe this innovative approach to matters of symmetry of mathematical quantities to the Soviet mathematician and physicist W. Shubnikov, who introduced this concept in the 1950s.

The extension of the idea of symmetry to mathematical quantities describing economic quantities transfers the consideration of economic phenomena to the plane of strict laws and mathematical rules. Below, after a short introduction, we define the concept of symmetry group: vector, scalar, tensor.

The ordered pair $< G, \circ >$ we call the Abelian group if the "∘" operation satisfies the conditions: "∘" is combined operation, "∘" is an alternate operation, "∘" operation does not lead out of the set G, each element of the G set has the inverse element, and in the set G, there is a neutral element of operation "∘".

The ordered pair $< H, \circ >$ we call the subgroup of the group $< G, \circ >$ if H is contained in G and H is the group due to the "∘" operation. The group's row is the number of its elements. When a group has a finite number of elements, we call it finite. Otherwise, the group is called infinite. Conversion that converts each vector $[a_1, a_2, a_3]$ into a vector $[-a_1, -a_2, -a_3]$ and that is alternating with any rotation in space we call an inversion and denotes I.

$$(I \circ g)([a_1, a_2, a_3]) = (g \circ I)([a_1, a_2, a_3]) \tag{5.16}$$

g—any rotation in space.

The set W with the operation of assembling transformations, which includes rotations and inversion–rotation assemblies, we call a full orthogonal group and denotes $< W, \circ >$.

Each subgroup of the group $< W, \circ >$ we call point group and denote $< P, \circ >$.

The element of symmetry of a given point group is a group consisting of powers of one symmetry operation.

Straight C we call the axis of the point group if the rotation around C is in this group.

The multiplicity of a given axis of symmetry is called the natural number n: $n = \frac{2\pi}{\alpha}$ where α it is the smallest angle of rotation about this axis, so that it introduces a given geometrical figure into an indistinguishable from the original one. Axes of symmetry with multiples $n = 3, 4, 5, \ldots n, \ldots, \infty$ can be treated as a result of the coexistence of three, four, and five to the infinity of the number of symmetry planes containing a given axis and intersecting along it.

According to the W. Shubnikov method, instead of considering symmetry (symmetry groups) of economic quantities, it is possible to consider the symmetry of mathematical quantities that these economic quantities describe.

We say that a vector treated as an ordered three of numbers has one or another element of symmetry, if as a result of acting on this vector by the appropriate symmetry operation, each of its coordinates takes a numerical value the same as before the operation of symmetry transformation. For research in three-dimensional space, we use clockwise and counterclockwise systems. To transform an old XYZ system into a new $X'Y'Z'$ with a fixed start, just enter the using matrix of the direction cosines:

$$A = \begin{bmatrix} a_{11} & a_{12} & a_{13} \\ a_{21} & a_{22} & a_{23} \\ a_{31} & a_{32} & a_{33} \end{bmatrix} \tag{5.17}$$

where $a_{ij}(i,j = 1,2,3)$—cosine of the angle between the old and the new coordinate axes, i—the number of the old axis; j—the number of the new axis. The sum of squares of cosines standing in one row or column of matrix A is equal to 1. The sums of the products of elements of different rows or columns are equal to 0. It can be shown that the coordinates of the vector $\boldsymbol{p} = [p_1, p_2, p_3]$ in the new $X'Y'Z'$ coordinates system they are given by the formula (Nedoma 1984):

$$p'_i = \sum_{j=1}^{3} a_{ji} p_j \tag{5.18}$$

where p_j (j = 1, 2, 3)—coordinates in the old XYZ layout.

Conversely—the old coordinates of the vector $\boldsymbol{p}$ are expressed by the new coordinates as follows (Nedoma 1984):

$$p_i = \sum_{j=1}^{3} a_{ij} p'_j \tag{5.19}$$

Equations (5.18) and (5.19) are true in clockwise and left-handed coordinate systems. They are also true when we move from one system to another about opposite torsion.

If the coordinates of the second-order tensor (b_{ij}) are subject to the transformation laws (Nedoma 1984):

$$b_{ij} = \pm a_{il} a_{jm} b'_{lm} \tag{5.20}$$

$$b'_{ij} = \pm a_{li} a_{mj} b_{lm}, \; (l, m = 1, 2, 3; i, j = 1, 2, 3) \tag{5.21}$$

we call it axial. The plus sign occurs when the old and the new system have the same twist and minus when the systems have the opposite steer. Similarly, if the coordinates of the second-order tensor (b_{ij}) are subject to the transformation laws (Nedoma 1984):

$$b_{ij} = a_{il} a_{jm} b'_{lm} \tag{5.22}$$

$$b'_{lm} = a_{il} a_{jm} b_{ij} \; (l, m = 1, 2, 3; i, j = 1, 2, 3) \tag{5.23}$$

we call it polar.

Equations (5.22) and (5.23) are true irrespective of the twist of the coordinate system.

We say that a second-order tensor treated as ordered nine numbers has a specific symmetry element, if as a result of acting on this tensor by a corresponding symmetry operation, each of its coordinates takes the same numerical value as before the symmetry operation.

It can be shown that the polar tensor can be represented as the sum of the symmetrical and anti-symmetric tensor:

$$(b_{ij}) = (b_{ij})_{sym} + (b_{ij})_{antys}$$

where

$$\begin{bmatrix} b_{11} & b_{12} & b_{13} \\ b_{12} & b_{22} & b_{23} \\ b_{13} & b_{23} & b_{33} \end{bmatrix} = (b_{ij})_{sym} \begin{bmatrix} 0 & b_{12} & b_{13} \\ -b_{12} & 0 & b_{23} \\ -b_{13} & -b_{23} & 0 \end{bmatrix} = (b_{ij})_{antys}.$$

Using the formulas of transformation (5.22) and (5.23), we can show that symmetrical tensors can be assigned to points groups of symmetry: $<vvv, \circ>$, $<C_{\infty vv}, \circ>$, $<C_{\infty\infty v}, \circ>$.

In geometric interpretation, $<vvv, \circ>$ represents a fixed ellipsoid, $<C_{\infty vv}, \circ>$—represents a rotary ellipsoid (second-degree rotary surface), and $<C_{\infty\infty v}, \circ>$—a fixed sphere.

It can be shown by means of formulas (5.22) and (5.23) that the anti-symmetric tensor has a boundary group of symmetry $<C_{\infty h}, \circ>$.

The group image $<C_{\infty h}, \circ>$ is a rotating cylinder. This is the second-degree rotary surface.

Analogously, it can be demonstrated by means of formulas (5.20) and (5.21) that the axial tensor of the second order of the form:

$$\begin{bmatrix} b_{11} & b_{12} & 0 \\ -b_{12} & b_{11} & 0 \\ 0 & 0 & b_{33} \end{bmatrix} \tag{5.24}$$

has a point group of symmetry of form $<C_{\infty}, \circ>$.

The geometric image of the $<C_{\infty v}, \circ>$ group is a immobile cone, while the $<C_{\infty}, \circ>$ groups—the rotary cone.

Vector $[l, c, s] \in R^3_+ \cup \{0, 0, 0\}$ where l—work, c—capital, s—organization is closely related to the state of behavioral economics at a given moment in time. The condition of the behavioral economy can be represented by vector $[l, c, s]$.

Vector $[l, c, s]$ treated as an ordered three numbers has a point group of symmetry $<C_{\infty v}, \circ>$.

To see this consider at the beginning of the vector $[0, 0, s]$ where $l = 0, c = 0, s > 0$. *LCS* system rotation around the axis of S to any angle can be specified by using matrix of the direction cosines.

$$\begin{bmatrix} a_{11} & -a_{21} & 0 \\ a_{21} & a_{11} & 0 \\ 0 & 0 & 1 \end{bmatrix}.$$

Then using the formula (5.18) we get:

$$\begin{aligned} l' &= a_{11} \cdot l + a_{21} \cdot c + a_{31} \cdot s = a_{11} \cdot 0 + a_{21} \cdot 0 + 0 \cdot s = 0, \\ c' &= a_{12} \cdot l + a_{22} \cdot c + a_{32} \cdot s = -a_{21} \cdot 0 + a_{11} \cdot 0 + 0 \cdot s = 0, \\ s' &= a_{13} \cdot l + a_{23} \cdot c + a_{33} \cdot s = 0 \cdot 0 + 0 \cdot 0 + 1 \cdot s = s. \end{aligned}$$

So, we have $[0, 0, s] = [0, 0, s']$. Because we considered rotation around the *S*-axis by any angle and the numerical values of the vector coordinates have not changed, the *S*-axis is the axis of symmetry of the vector with a multiplicity equal to ∞.

By analogically considering the *LCS* reflection in the planes containing the *S*-axis, we obtain directional cosine matrix of the following form:

$$\begin{bmatrix} a_{11} & a_{12} & 0 \\ a_{21} & a_{22} & 0 \\ 0 & 0 & 1 \end{bmatrix}.$$

Substituting the appropriate words of the obtained matrix to the formula (5.18), we have for the vector $[0, 0, s]$:

$$l' = 0, c' = 0, s' = s.$$

Thus, the infinitely many planes containing the *S*-axis are planes of symmetry for the vector $[0, 0, s]$. In particular, the vector $[0, 0, s]$ does not have a *LOC* symmetry plane perpendicular to the *S*-axis, because in this case the cosine matrix has the form:

$$\begin{bmatrix} 1 & 0 & 0 \\ 0 & 1 & 0 \\ 0 & 0 & -1 \end{bmatrix}$$

which, taking into account formula (5.18) gives $l' = 0$, $c' = 0$, $s' = -s$ thus, the vector $[0, 0, s]$ does not retain its coordinates. In summary, we note that although we were taking a vector $[l, c, s]$ in a special position (directed along the *S*-axis), our considerations were of a general character, because the properties of the vector do not depend on the choice of the coordinate system. If the origin of the vector $[l, c, s]$ is at the beginning of the *LCS* coordinate system and at the same time we rotate the said system around an axis coincident with the vector $[l, c, s]$ direction, then the vector components will change their orientation in space, but their values will remain unchanged. Thus, the vector $[l, c, s]$ actually has a symmetry group

$<C_{\infty v}, \circ>$. For the same reason, the vector $[p, q, t]$ often used in economics, where p—means the price of a given commodity, q—the quantity of a given commodity, t—time, also has a symmetry group $<C_{\infty v}, \circ>$. It follows from the above that all economic values expressed by means of a (polar) vector with three coordinates have the so-called boundary group of symmetry $<C_{\infty v}, \circ>$. By the way—interesting information on the use of vector calculus in economics can be found in the monograph (Nermend 2009).

The size of the budget of investors participating in the market game is of great importance in issues related to behavioral economics.

Let us now analyze the scalar product of vectors: $\mathbf{p} = [x_1, x_2, x_3]$—the price of goods, $\mathbf{x} = [x_1, x_2, x_3]$—the quantity of goods, i.e. size, in the context of the point group of symmetry which describes it, assuming that we are considering the market of three goods. Using the transformation formula (5.18) in relation to the considered vectors, we obtain:

$$
\begin{aligned}
a' = p'_1x'_1 + p'_2x'_2 + p'_3x'_3 &= (a_{11}p_1 + a_{21}p_2 + a_{31}p_3)(a_{11}x_1 + a_{21}x_2 + a_{31}x_3) \\
&\quad + (a_{12}p_1 + a_{22}p_2 + a_{32}p_3)(a_{12}x_1 + a_{22}x_2 + a_{32}x_3) \\
&\quad + (a_{13}p_1 + a_{23}p_2 + a_{33}p_3)(a_{13}x_1 + a_{23}x_2 + a_{33}x_3) \\
&= p_1x_1(a_{11}^2 + a_{12}^2 + a_{13}^2) + p_2x_2(a_{21}^2 + a_{22}^2 + a_{23}^2) \\
&\quad + p_3x_3(a_{31}^2 + a_{32}^2 + a_{33}^2) + p_1x_2(a_{11}a_{21} + a_{12}a_{22} + a_{13}a_{23}) \\
&\quad + p_2x_1(a_{11}a_{21} + a_{12}a_{22} + a_{13}a_{23}) + p_1x_3(a_{11}a_{31} + a_{12}a_{32} + a_{13}a_{33}) \\
&\quad + p_3x_1(a_{11}a_{31} + a_{12}a_{32} + a_{13}a_{33}) + p_3x_2(a_{31}a_{21} + a_{32}a_{22} + a_{33}a_{23}) \\
&\quad + p_2x_3(a_{21}a_{31} + a_{23}a_{33} + a_{22}a_{32}) = p_1x_1 + p_2x_2 + p_3x_3 = a,
\end{aligned}
$$

because the sum of the squares of words standing in one row or column of the directional cosine matrix is equal to one, while the sums of the products of the elements of different rows or columns are equal to zero. In addition, the scalar value a does not depend on the transition from a given XYZ system to a new one $X'Y'Z'$ with any twist. It is easy to check that in the case of a scalar a, the Z-axis is an axis with a multiplicity equal to infinity. Taking into account the directional cosine matrix concerning rotation by any angle around the Z-axis, we have:

$$
\begin{aligned}
a' = p'_1x'_1 + p'_2x'_2 + p'_3x'_3 &= (a_{11}p_1 + a_{21}p_2)(a_{11}x_1 + a_{21}x_2) \\
&\quad + (a_{11}p_2 - a_{21}p_1)(a_{11}x_2 - a_{21}x_1)p_3x_3 = p_1x_1(a_{11}^2 + a_{21}^2) \\
&\quad + p_2x_2(a_{21}^2 + a_{11}^2) + p_3x_3 = p_1x_1 + p_2x_2 + p_3x_3 = a.
\end{aligned}
$$

Since the scalar a is a non-directional value, it can be equally well assumed that the axis with infinite multiplicity has any other direction. Similarly, using the general relationship shown in this example, we get that along each axis of symmetry of the scalar a intersects the infinite many planes of symmetry of this scalar, and the plane perpendicular to each axis is the plane of symmetry. To sum up, we have obtained that the scalar product $<\boldsymbol{p},\boldsymbol{x}>$ has a point symmetry group that can be symbolically written $<C_{\infty\infty v}, \circ>$. The geometric image of the group $<C_{\infty\infty v}, \circ>$ is a fixed sphere. There are infinitely many symmetry axes of infinite multiplicity passing through the center of this sphere. In addition, each axis is a common part of infinitely many symmetry planes containing it, and additionally, perpendicular to each axis, there is a separate symmetry plane containing the center of the sphere. The scalar product $<\boldsymbol{p},\boldsymbol{x}>$ can be treated as the investor's budget. All other economic quantities that are expressed in a similar way as the budget have a symmetry group of a fixed sphere. In economic considerations, there is often a correlation matrix:

$$\begin{bmatrix} \rho_{11} & \rho_{12} & \rho_{13} \\ \rho_{21} & \rho_{22} & \rho_{23} \\ \rho_{31} & \rho_{32} & \rho_{33} \end{bmatrix}.$$

Because it is a symmetric matrix, it can be treated like a symmetrical polar tensor. This tensor has a symmetry group $<vvv, \circ>$.

If $\rho_{ij} = 0$ for $i \neq j$ and $\rho_{ij} = 1$ for $i = j$, this correlation matrix treated as a symmetric second order tensor has a symmetry group $<C_{\infty\infty v}, \circ>$.

Above, only some examples of the application of the W. Shubnikov method concerning the symmetry of economic quantities described with the help of vectors, scalars, and second-degree tensors are shown. A certain principle of conservation is connected with each symmetry (Smoluk 2007). This is the famous E. Noether's theorem. The E. Noether theorem is also given in the works of D. Hilbert and F. Klein. In a simplified wording, E. Noether's statement says that if the system's properties do not change with certain transformations of variables, it is related to a specific principle of conservation. According to E. Noether's thesis, the principle of conservation also applies to economic quantities. The principles of conservations also revealed the existence of hidden invariances, called symmetries.

Let $A = <C_{\infty\infty v}, \circ>$, $B = <C_{\infty\infty}, \circ>$, $C = <C_{\infty vv}, \circ>$, $D = <C_{\infty 2}, \circ>$, $E = <C_{\infty v}, \circ>$, $F = <C_{\infty h}, \circ>$, $G = <C_{\infty}, \circ>$.

In geometric interpretation:

$B = <C_{\infty\infty}, \circ>$—represents a sphere with rays rotating in the same direction,
$D = <C_{\infty 2}, \circ>$—represents a cylinder rotating in two directions, which is also twisted.

The subordination of point groups is shown below.

Figure 5.2 shows that the border point group $G = <C_{\infty}, \circ>$ is a subgroup of all border groups, i.e., the most important equilibrium surface appearing in economics has a border group of symmetry, which is a subgroup of all border groups of symmetry.

From the above, it also follows that if we consider various types of equilibrium in the economy expressed by point border groups, the point border group of the rotating cone is the smallest point group and the equilibrium expressed by the pre-cone is the most basic equilibrium.

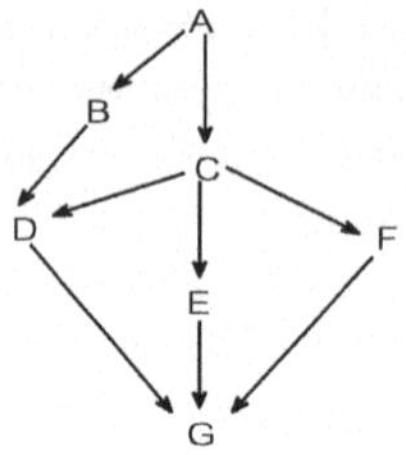

Fig. 5.2 Subordination of border point groups. *Source* Own studies

5.5 Conclusions

To sum up, all the goals set at the beginning of the chapter have been realized.

Equilibrium is the basic concept of behavioral economics and science. Nothing can exist without it. The equilibrium surfaces in behavioral economics can be described by means of point groups of symmetry. We can assign symmetry groups to the economic quantities and the equilibrium surface in behavioral economics. Often, this causes the transfer of our considerations to purely mathematical ground. Using the Shubnikov method, we obtain that economic quantities have specific symmetry groups. An interesting problem to be solved, which was omitted in the chapter, is the aspect interaction with each other of groups of symmetry of economic quantities. Interesting economic conclusions may result from this.

By virtue of E. Noether's theorem, these quantities are subject to the principle of conservation. Equilibrium surfaces are often rotating surfaces of the second degree. They can be described using so-called boundary groups of symmetry. A special surface of equilibrium is the rotary cone. The border group of symmetry the rotary cone is a subgroup of other boundary groups of symmetry the second-degree rotary surfaces. These surfaces, just like a cone, can also be surfaces of equilibrium. Using the hyperbolic spiral, we can describe in a space the whirling motion of vectors $[q_i, p_i, t_i]$ forming an equilibrium surface, which is a cone. The stock market as an example of a multiplayer game without the possibility of concluding a coalition has an interesting property. The boundary matrix of the equilibrium associated with it illustrates the state of the ideal economy.

References

Fichtenholz GM (1985) Differential and integral calculus. PWN, Warszawa
Gelfand IM (1975) Wykłady z algebry liniowej. PWN, Warszawa
Juzwiszyn J (2007) Form of vortex in nature and economics. Math Econ 4(11):95–124
Nedoma J (1984) Grupy punktowe elementy symetrii. Wydawnictwo AGH, Kraków
Nermend K (2009) Vector calculus in regional development analysis: comparative regional analysis using the example of Poland. Physica-Verlag, Berlin
Smoluk A (2007) Mathematics, economics and probability. Math Econ 4(11):5–36

Part II
Methods and Tools of Contemporary Economics

Chapter 6
Intuitive Methods Versus Analytical Methods in Real Estate Valuation: Preferences of Polish Real Estate Appraisers

Iwona Foryś and Radosław Gaca

Abstract Market analysis is one of the basic and essential stages in the process of estimating the market value of real property. In this context, both the legal provisions in force in Poland and the methodological guidelines contained in the valuation standards leave appraisers with considerable flexibility in the use of specific methods. The research referred to only that part of the market analysis which focuses on a dependency study and ultimately aimed at determining materiality and subsequently the magnitude of the impact of market characteristics on the differentiation of transaction prices. The chapter analyzes the methods used by Polish real estate appraisers and the context of using the conclusions resulting from the analyses. The study provided the response on the appraisers' preference for valuation approaches and methods. On the basis of the conclusions of the study, a critical assessment of the causes influencing the range of applied analytical tools identified was also carried out. In summary, on the basis of the collected results, recommendations regarding possible changes to legal regulations and professional norms relating to the studied area of professional activity were presented.

Keywords Intuitive methods · Real estate valuation · Real estate market analysis
Market value

6.1 Introduction

The analysis of the data constituting the basis for deducting the value of real estate is one of the basic elements of the valuation process and falls within the obligatory activity, which is the analysis and characteristics of the market (Isakson 1998).

I. Foryś (✉)
WNEiZ, Uniwersytet Szczeciński, Szczecin, Poland
e-mail: forys@wneiz.pl

R. Gaca
Kancelaria Rzeczoznawcy Majątkowego R.Gaca, Bydgoszcz, Poland

K. Nermend and M. Łatuszyńska (eds.), *Problems, Methods and Tools in Experimental and Behavioral Economics*, Springer Proceedings in Business and Economics, https://doi.org/10.1007/978-3-319-99187-0_6

Both the market analysis itself and its component, i.e., the analysis of relations between prices and characteristics of real estate, have not yet been specifically codified (Foryś and Gaca 2016). To date, both practical and scientific studies covering market analysis issues have basically only referred to specific methods and techniques that can be used (Dell 2004, 2013; Emerson 2008; Fanning 2014; Fleming and Nellis 1994; Foryś 2009). However, there is no analysis in the literature referring to the current scope of the use of the analytical methods described in the literature and applied in practice (Gaca 2016). This chapter is an attempt to complement this area of knowledge by presenting and analyzing the experience of real estate appraisers, both in relation to the methods of analysis and the valuation methods used in the comparative approach.

Under the property valuation system in force in Poland, regulations of a legal and substantive nature are distinguished. Currently, within the framework of the latter group, apart from scientific and professional literature, there is also a set of valuation standards prepared and edited by the Polish Federation of Valuers' Associations under the name of the General National Valuation Rules. Both the provisions of law and methodological guidance in the valuation standards leave appraisers with considerable discretion in the use of market analysis methods.

The basic document that provides some guidance on the scope and detail of the analysis is now Interpretative Note (IN)—applying a comparative approach to property valuation. In this document (IN), which is one of the elements of the General National Valuation Rules in point 3.5. It was pointed out that the purpose of market analysis is to establish the characteristics (attributes) of real estate properties, hereinafter referred to as market characteristics. A real estate appraiser should assess the magnitude of the impact of market characteristics on the differentiation of transaction prices which may constitute market characteristics weights. The following section provides only general guidance on the principles for assessing the impact of market characteristics on the differentiation of transaction prices which include:

(a) the results of analysis of data on prices and market characteristics of similar real estate being traded on the market for the purpose of real estate market valuation;
(b) analogy with similar local markets in terms of type and area;
(c) examination and/or observation of preferences of potential purchasers of real estate;
(d) other reliable means.

Of course, market analysis is not only the analysis of relationships between prices and the factors influencing them. Market analysis is also a study of macroeconomic as well as microeconomic conditions constituting a broad market environment in relation to the object of valuation, which is a specific real property. The market analysis must also include an extremely important activity consisting in separating a collection of similar real estate which will ultimately form the basis for further deducting the market value of the property being valued.

In light of the above, the investigation generally referred to only that part of the market analysis which focuses on a dependency study and ultimately aimed at determining materiality and subsequently the magnitude of the impact of market characteristics on the differentiation of transaction prices. As it results from the analysis of objections raised by recipients to the content of appraisal studies, this element is currently one of the basic critical elements influencing the evaluation of the reliability of the work of appraisers. This is also evidenced by the conclusions of the Professional Responsibility Committee at the Ministry of Infrastructure as well as arbitration committees at local appraisers' associations.

6.2 Literature Review

The main problem in the real estate market is its low information efficiency. Therefore, decisions of many market participants are irrational and are the result of intuitive actions, imitation, and not decisions supported by a collection and analysis of reliable information (Thaler 2016). As Skinner (1978) stated, all human activity was a result of their genetic conditions and the influence of the environment in which they operated, in particular the social and physical environment. Ingrained views, the lack of openness to further professional development experiences, are a frequent reason for rejecting new solutions and methods. In addition, disseminating views about the absence of the need for change justifies part of the professional environment and discourages the use of innovative techniques and tools.

It is no longer disputed in developed real estate markets that it is necessary to use advanced statistics for the analysis of large data collections, market analysis, and mass valuation (Kane et al. 2004; Wolverton 2014). The use of advanced statistical methods for the valuation of a single property is problematic, and this still requires an in-depth market analysis in the estimation process (Kummerow 2002; Betts and Ely 2008). Therefore, in the educational process of real estate appraisers, more and more emphasis is placed on increasing competence of appraisers in the use of statistics and statistical analyses in valuation, and more and more people are convinced that the use of advanced statistical tools and models is appropriate (Pasymowski 2006).

The development of modern technologies and software of computational tools, with increasingly easy access to large databases, induces a change in the way of thinking about the problem of appraisal, in particular through traditional methods of data selection (Dell 2017). It requires appraisers to change their approach to the valuation process, from collecting and evaluating the quality of data and their ability to select them using statistical tools relevant to the analysis of large databases, the so-called *Big Data Analysis Interoperability Framework* (2015) techniques. This is particularly important both in the process of establishing a collection of similar properties and the ability to generalize the results obtained.

In the past, the challenge for appraisers was a lack of good data and the need to represent them with deliberately selected samples. Now the challenge is the opposite: how to properly sort, examine, and draw conclusions from large collections of available data? The new situation requires a change of thinking about data collection and analysis for valuation purposes which are the basis of a properly conducted analytical process.

Hence, as Dell (2017) observes, proper use of quantitative analyses and econometric modeling is necessary for a new paradigm of market analyses for property valuation purposes. Big Data analysis and data mining allow the "new paradigm of real estate value modeling" to evolve. Historically, the valuation theory has been developed in the context of few transaction data. The new concept continues on the path from the world of rare data to a world of large data resources. It forces real estate appraisers to a new vision of the traditional valuation process.

Psychological, demographic, social, and cultural factors are a barrier to a new perception of the role of real estate appraiser. Recalling once again the behavioral concept of man in psychology, one can refer to conscious and forced stimuli (Majewski 2012). The first is the result of human disabilities in the interpretation of perceived phenomena (so-called anchorage effect) or from the system memory (e.g., cognitive load). Forced stimuli are triggered by subconsciousness (pulse action). These include stress, panic, and herd effects. In the demographic context, there is a tendency or aversion to take up new challenges related to the gender or age of individuals. In the issues discussed, age or work experience can play an important role in a new perception of reality. Social factors are environmental elements, shaping social, ethical, and opinion-forming attitudes, which in a closed professional environment may become decisive for shaping new attitudes toward the aforementioned professional challenges.

6.3 Scope of Data and Organization of the Study

In order to diagnose both the scope of applied methods of analysis and applied valuation methods, a survey was conducted on the group of real estate appraisers, participants in the National Discussion List. Therefore, the survey carried out referred to a targeted rather than a random sample, which has to be taken into account in the sample of generalizations of the results obtained.

The survey carried out with the use of an online form asked questions relating to the type of methods used to determine the effect of the characteristics on price differentiation, the range of methods used in the comparative approach, the number of collections of similar real estate properties used as the basis for the analysis, and the collection constituting the basis for determining the effect of the characteristics on price differentiation when using mathematical methods.

The survey was carried out in July and August 2016 and repeated in January and February 2018, with 105 and 109 responses, respectively. As at February 1, 2018, a total of 7086 persons are registered in the Central Register of Real Estate Valuers maintained by the Minister of Infrastructure, and no persons who are deceased or not practicing the profession are deleted from the register. Hence, the sample in both cases represents 1.5% of the total population of this occupational group, which meets basic expectations in terms of number.

Due to the type of research tool used, no non-response questionnaires were found and only for some questions the number of responses was incomplete. The maximum difference in this case was three responses. In the case of a question relating to the methods of analysis used and comparative approach methods, respondents were given the opportunity to make multiple choices. In the other cases, the questions were closed-ended with one answer possible. However, in the context of the questionnaire question relating to the collection being the basis for determining the influence of characteristics on price differentiation, mathematical methods were used and an open question was adopted, leaving open the possibility for the respondent's own answer. The survey was supplemented with personal information concerning the number of years of practicing the profession of a real estate appraiser.

6.4 Test Results

As evidenced by the results of an examination of the methods used in market analysis, and more precisely the impact of characteristics on price differentiation, the intuitive approach continues to play a dominant role in this respect. In a study conducted in 2016, its use as at least one of the methods was declared by as many as 46.70% of respondents, while in a study conducted in 2018 it was still 40.37%. Along with work experience, there is a growing tendency to use other than intuitive approaches to determine the impact of characteristics on price differentiation (correlation coefficient 0.93 in 2016 and 0.88 in 2018) and to analyze an increasing number of data collections for this purpose (correlation coefficient 0.85) according to the 2018 surveys, while there is no clear correlation in 2016 (correlation coefficient 0.22).

Among the methods of analysis, a significant share is also held by methods of analyzing the preferences of purchasers the application of which in 2016 was declared by 40.0%. However, the percentage of respondents using such methods decreased significantly in the 2018 study, in which 18.35% of respondents indicated the use of this method. Under the indicated methods, respondents were asked to indicate all methods used. It should be noted that the concept of examining the preferences of purchasers does not usually mean a professional survey of real estate purchasers, but intuitive decisions based on, at most, poll opinions among real estate agents.

The number of respondents declaring to use the classical *ceteris paribus* method was also significantly reduced. According to the 2016 survey, 25.71% of the respondents declared its use in 2018 to fall to 16.51% in 2018. The result obtained is very interesting in comparison with the experience of the authors gathered during numerous meetings with appraisers, where the percentage of people declaring using this method was 1–2%. Perhaps, in non-anonymous responses given at training courses on statistical methods, the respondents did not dare to admit poor activity in the area of advanced methods of analysis, or it was the fact that those methods were favored encouraged them to participate in such training.

In the case of mathematical methods, the use of a simple correlation account (Pearson's linear correction) was declared by 34.29% in 2016 and only 21.10% in 2018. On the other hand, the number of people declaring to use nonparametric correlation supported by the method of adjusting prices to the "ceteris paribus" state increased from only 1.90% in 2016 to 6.42 in 2018. Relatively high proportion of appraisers declared the use of regression models. As for 2016, there were 47.62% declarations made in this respect. The percentage rose slightly to 50.46% in 2018 (Table 6.1).

In the case of a comparative approach, the basic method is still the method of comparing real estate properties in pairs, utilization of which declared 72.1% of the surveyed in 2016, but only 66.06% in 2018.

An important place in valuation practice is also occupied by the method of adjusting the average price which according to the data presented in 2016 was used by 54.8% of respondents, while in the next survey 54.13%. The smallest number of appraisers, amounting to only 7.62% in 2016 and 8.26% in 2018, declared the use of the market statistical analysis method which requires a more advanced technique of using statistical software. In reference to the methods used, the share of particular age groups is very interesting (Table 6.2).

According to the data from both studies, respondents with more than 16 years of experience were the dominant group. The situation was similar also in the case of persons declaring that the method of adjusting the average price was applied. However, this was not the case for respondents declaring the application of the method of statistical analysis of the reexamination market carried out in 2018. While in the first study the dominant group consisted of valuers with more than 16 years of experience, in the second study as many as half of the valuers were practitioners with less than three years of experience.

Another area of the study referred to the number of collections that were the basis for the deduction. In this case, the respondents could choose between close-ended answers, specifying number ranges. Within the scope of possible options, five collections of various real estate properties number were listed (Table 6.3).

Table 6.1 Methods used to determine the impact of characteristics on price differentiation (%)

Method	2016	2018	Change 2016/2018
Intuitive method	46.67	40.37	−6.30
Analysis of customer preferences (surveys)	40.00	18.35	−21.65
Ceteris paribus method (classic)	25.71	16.51	−9.20
Linear correlation (Pearson's)	34.29	21.10	−13.18
Rank correlation (Spearman's)	1.90	6.42	4.52
Multiple regression	47.62	50.46	2.84
Other (neural networks, etc.)	4.76	2.75	−2.01

Table 6.2 Methods used to determine the impact of characteristics on price differentiation (%)

Method	2016	2018	Change 2016/2018
Method of comparing real estate properties in pairs	71.43	66.06	−5.37
Method of adjusting the average price	54.29	54.13	−0.16
Method of statistical market analysis	7.62	8.26	0.64

Table 6.3 Number of collections of similar real property constituting the basis for analyses

Number intervals	2016		2018		Change 2016/2018
	Number of responses	Interest %	Number of responses	Interest %	
From 3 to 5	8	7.62	1	0.92	−6.70
From 6 to 10	14	13.33	6	5.50	−7.83
From 11 to 20	31	29.52	22	20.18	−9.34
From 21 to 30	20	19.05	29	26.61	7.56
More than 30	32	30.48	50	45.87	15.40

Table 6.4 Collection underlying the determination of the effect of characteristics on price differentiation

Collection definition	2016		2018		Change 2016/2018
	Number of responses	Interest %	Number of responses	Interest %	
Collection of similar real property constituting the basis for valuation	42	40.78	55	53.40	12.62
Collection of similar real property larger than the basis for valuation	49	47.57	45	43.69	−3.88
Collection(s) of different real property	12	11.65	6	5.83	−5.83

The survey results indicate a clear decrease in the share of small and very small collections. At this point, it should only be recalled that it is practically impossible to make any conclusion about the influence of real estate volatility on price volatility on the basis of collections with numbers below $n = 6$ (Czaja and Parzych 2007).

Another issue covered by the survey was the verification of respondents' knowledge of the principles of statistical reasoning. In this context, the survey participants were asked a question relating to the identity of the collection which is the basis for determining the influence of characteristics on price differentiation in relation to the collection constituting the direct basis of valuation, i.e., a collection of similar real property (Table 6.4).

The results clearly indicate an increase in the number of respondents who use collections of similar real property as a basis for estimating which are the direct basis for valuation. However, the percentage of respondents using data from wider collections is still quite high. A detailed analysis of the responses in 2016 shows that among those declaring such a basis for concluding 41.86% were people declaring the method of comparing real property in pairs as the basic method. In such a case, it is possible to adopt for the assessment of the impact of characteristics on prices a collection of real property larger than the collection of real property accepted for comparison, provided that both the gap and impact of the characteristics resulting from the collection constituting the basis for determining the variability (Gaca 2016) are observed.

6.5 Conclusions

The results obtained allow for preliminary conclusions concerning the inclination of real estate appraisers to methods other than intuitive ones in everyday professional practice. However, they cannot be generalized to the entire population because of the failure to meet the requirements of a representative survey, although some assumptions can be made because of the way in which the survey was conducted (voluntary survey on an Internet forum, accessible only to real estate appraisers).

The results of the survey clearly indicate that the intuitive approach is still the dominant way of recognizing the influence of particular characteristics on prices and, consequently, the value of real estate among respondents. This circumstance may result from the appraisers' belief that it is not possible to use mathematical tools for real estate market analysis. Unfortunately, this state of affairs is very negative. While it cannot be excluded that in many cases of simple valuations, experienced appraisers are able to correctly recognize the influence of particular factors and characteristics on price volatility, the manner of their determination is not subject to any verification as a whole. This situation forces the appraiser to indicate his own experience and professional authority as the only source of findings. Unfortunately, this has seriously reduced public confidence.

The profession of real estate appraiser, which plays an extremely important role in a market economy, is a profession with all the prerogatives of the profession of public confidence. Those involved in this type of professions are expected not only to be ethical, but above all to have reliable answers, to use legible and verifiable methods of conclusion-finding. In this context, an improvement in the state of affairs should be seen in the popularization of mathematical methods, in particular statistical methods and econometric models in property valuation.

The existing scientific achievements in this field certainly constitute an excellent basis for the development of the educational sphere. Increased awareness of recipients of valuations and relative ease in gaining knowledge in the field of new techniques of drawing conclusions will lead, in the absence of development of the described methods, to further deterioration of the image of the profession. This state of affairs may, unfortunately, have a decisive impact on the acceleration of the implementation of automated models, making full use of the latest developments in statistics and econometrics, including data mining.

It should be emphasized that the survey is of a pilot nature; therefore, in subsequent stages, both the substantive scope of the survey and the respondent base will be extended, in the direction of representative surveys, allowing for far-reaching generalizations concerning the aversion of appraisers to use specialized analytical tools in the process of real estate valuation.

References

Betts RM, Ely SJ (2008) Basic real estate appraisal: principles and procedures, 7th edn. Thomson South-Western (printed the USA), Mason

Big Data Interoperability Framework. In: Definitions, National Institute of Standards and Technology, vol 1. NIST, Washington, DC, US Department of Commerce, 16 Sept 2015, p 8

Czaja J, Parzych P (2007) Szacowanie rynkowej wartości nieruchomości w aspekcie międzynarodowych standardów wyceny. Wydawca Stowarzyszenie Naukowe im St. Staszica. Kraków 2007

Dell G (2004) The myth and the reality; the problem and the solution. In: Valuation insights & perspectives, vol 9/3. Chicago, IL

Dell G (2013) Common statistical errors and mistakes: valuation and reliability. Apprais J (Fall 2013)

Dell G (2017) Regression, critical thinking, and the valuation problem today. Apprais J (Summer 2017):217–230. www.appraisalinstitute.org

Emerson DM (2008) Subdivision market analysis and absorption forecasting. Apprais J (Fall 2008)

Fanning SF (2014) Market analysis for real estate. Concepts and applications in valuation and highest and best use, 2nd edn. Appraisal Institute, Chicago, IL

Fleming MC, Nellis JG (1994) The measurement of UK house prices: a review and appraisal of the principal sources. J Hous Financ 24

Foryś I (2009) The Cox proportional hazards model in the analysis of property transactions. Folia Oecon Stetinensia 8(1):71–81

Foryś I, Gaca R (2016) Theoretical and practical aspects of qualitative variable descriptions of residential property valuation multiple regression models. In: Proceedings, Foundation of the Cracow University of Economics, Cracow, 978-83-65173-48-5 (HTML), pp 36–44

Gaca R (2016) Terminy i zagadnienia statystyczne i ekonometryczne w wycenie nieruchomości. Biul Stowarzyszenia Rzeczoznawców Majątkowych Województwa Wielkopolskiego 45:31–35

Isakson H (1998) The review of real estate appraisals using multiple regression analysis. J Real Estate Res 15(2)

Kane MS, Linne MR, Johnson JA (2004) Practical applications in appraisal valuation modeling. Statistical methods for real estate practitioners. Appraisal Institute, Chicago, IL

Kummerow MA (2002) Statistical definition of value. Apprais J (October 2002)

Majewski S (2012) Wpływ czynników behawioralnych na rynkowa wycenę akcji. Ujęcie ilościowe. Szczecin, Wydawnictwo Naukowe Uniwerystetu Szczecińskiego

Pasymowski E (2006) Econometric Solutions for real estate valuation automated valuation models—friend or foe? MAI Published in the TriState REALTORS Commercial Alliance Newsletter Spring 27

Skinner BF (1978) Poza wolnością i godnością. PIW, Warszawa

Thaler RH (2016) Misbehaving: the making of behavioral economics. W.W. Norton, New York, London

Wolverton ML (2014) Comments on "common statistical errors and mistakes: valuation and reliability". Letters to the Editor. Apprais J (Spring 2014):176

Chapter 7
Methodology for Choosing the Location for In-Game Advertising Billboards

Kesra Nermend and Jarosław Duda

Abstract Recently, the market for in-game advertising is growing very dynamically. In 2015, profits out of this business were above 2.75 mio USD, and it is expected to be doubled by 2020. The proper location of the in-game commercial (billboard) is significantly important for the promotion of a given product (service). The paper presents the use of eye tracker and GSR to register behaviors and perception of the in-game advert placed in the computer game simulating car driving.

Keywords Advertisement · Computer games · Location choice
Cognitive neuroscience

7.1 Introduction

Advertisement is the form of communication with the consumers of given products or services. It aims to inform, persuade consumers to purchase goods (commercial advertising), or to change behavior (social issue advertising). The term advertisement originates from the Latin word *reclamare*, which means loud exhortation, calling out or evoking (Thyssen 2011). This word and alike (*reklamo and reclamatum*) have their genesis in the middle ages, when merchants in the streets encouraged people to buy their products. With such a behavior, they aimed at drawing the attention of prospective buyers at their offer. Over the time, first signboards focusing on display of own trademarks appeared. This referred both to manufacturers (e.g., a shoe was the sign of a shoemaker and a barrel of an innkeeper) and merchants selling goods manufactured by others (Nowacki 2005).

K. Nermend (✉)
Universty of Szczecin, Szczecin, Poland
e-mail: kesra.nermend@usz.edu.pl

J. Duda
Maritime University of Szczecin, Szczecin, Poland
e-mail: j.duda@am.szczecin.pl

K. Nermend and M. Łatuszyńska (eds.), *Problems, Methods and Tools in Experimental and Behavioral Economics*, Springer Proceedings in Business and Economics, https://doi.org/10.1007/978-3-319-99187-0_7

In Anglo-Saxon countries, a commercial is defined by the word "advertising" originating from an advert which means "reverse". Thus, advertising is the activity of attracting one's attention and targeting it at a specific product (Silayoi and Speece 2004). For example, it is estimated that while shopping in a mall, consumers have few seconds (3–5 s) to notice a product and based on collected information to decide whether to buy it or not (Gajzler 2010). It refers to various aspects of business activity. Hence, the problem of location of any objects is very important and still valid. These applies to both the location of distribution centers, warehouses (Brandeau and Chiu 1989), emergency services (Neebe 1988), places for investments (Gajzler 2010), wind energy (Wątróbski et al. 2015, 2016; Ziemba et al. 2017), industrial buildings (Grau and Caldas 2009), and advertising billboards. The problem of location of such banners is the major dilemma appearing during election campaigns or the promotion of a product. The example of using in-game advertising for election campaign was placed in the computer game "Need for Speed" available at Xbox 360 Live billboards for Barack Obama, a candidate for the President of the USA (2008). Obama used the similar solution before the second term of office.

Advertisements are placed on different objects, like building facades, fences, billboards. Choice of the appropriate location depends on various aspects among which one of the most important is the customer's profile (gender, age, financial condition, level of education). It is not always an efficient choice, not always the advertising message is well visible for every customer (pedestrian, car drivers, bicycle riders). Wrong decision in the form of an advert or location of an advertising medium may result in success or failure of the whole business project. One may say that it is strategic for the advertiser.

Firms and specialists in marketing try to use every possible method to have an effective impact on the customer's decision. For that they use various media, like radio, television, press (newspapers, magazines, etc.), or Internet (including social media). Different promotion materials are produced, like banners, posters, leaflets, the advert appears on cloths, competitions and events are organized (Yang et al. 2006; Martí-Parreño et al. 2013). More and more advertisement is located in computer games, both these run on desktop and mobile devices as well as different consoles. The popularity of social media makes that sponsors more and more willingly try to use this medium. Facebook may be an example (Terlutter and Capella 2013), where more and more interesting games are shared, like CityVille (88.8 mio players), FarmVille (47.9 mio), Texas HoldEm Poker (35.8 mio), Mafia Wars (16.8 mio), or FrontierVille (15.9 mio) (data according to socialbakers.com). In addition to games in which the main purpose is entertainment, there are also those that promote good habits, behavior, such as the promotion of good nutrition among children (Pempek and Calvert 2009). The value of the global market in this area is growing rapidly. According to "The Statistics Portal" (statista.com) in 2009, the global value of advertisements market for computer games amounts to USD mio, and projected value in 2020 will be already 5.05 billion USD.

One of the possibilities to use computer games for promotion of products is to place advertising billboards in these games, like in the real world (billboards along the roads). Due to the nature of such type of advert, which is fast moving by a car, the content of a billboard or its location is very important. A similar situation also occurs when users of computer games quickly change their place, e.g., combat games, simulators (Łatuszyńska 2012, 2016; Łatuszyńska and Borawska 2015). Hence, the choice of the location of a banner in computer games becomes an important task for both game developers and people or institutions responsible for promotion (advertising industry). The aim of the article is to study the possibility of using modern techniques of cognitive neuroscience (eye tracker and GSR) to collect information for the development of principles, rules, and criteria for choosing the location for in-game advertising billboards.

7.2 Research Experiment

For the purposes of the research experiment, a computer game was developed, which was designed according to general principles, that is, it had to be funny, entertaining, and educational (Backlund and Hendrix 2013). Research has shown that unlike more conventional media formats, games are more eye-catching, increase engagement, encourage learning and to change behavior (Bellotti et al. 2013). The developed game was a car driving simulator, and its aim was to drive through the whole route in the shortest possible time. The experiment participant started the game from the parking lot in a small residential area. The place from which the player started the game (driving a car) was marked with a white square in Fig. 7.1. He followed the designated route (along barriers), which was marked by road traffic signs (no entry, one-way road, etc.). In the game, the same rules (road traffic regulations) as in the real world applied. Within the residential area, nine small advertising billboards were placed along the route (marked with white dots in the Figure). The advertisements were allocated in accordance with the general

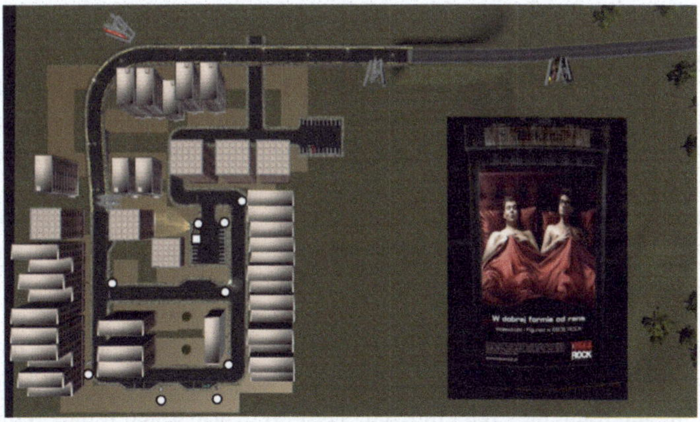

Fig. 7.1 The starting point of the game, the layout of small advertising billboards, and their example

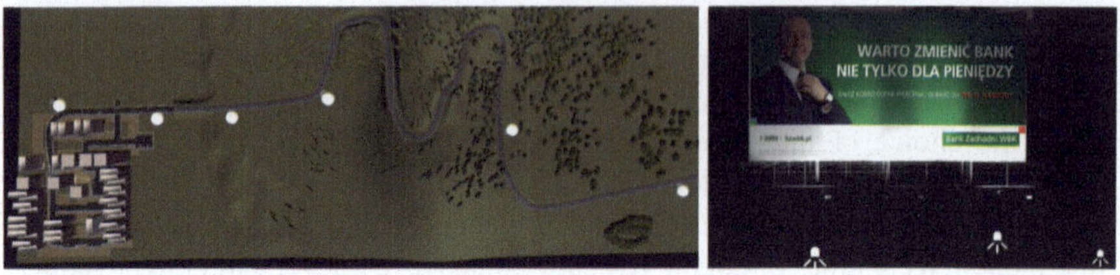

Fig. 7.2 The layout of large advertising billboards and their example

principles of promotion, following the similar solutions used in the real residential area and in the city streets. Due to the fact that the ride took place at night, the billboards were illuminated from the inside. Thanks to that the content presented on the billboards was noticeable and visible from a relevant distance while driving.

The participant of the experiment, leaving the city passed through the viaduct, still had to overcome the mountain (driving serpentine), where on its other side the game ended. Six large advertising billboards were also placed along the route. The locations are shown in Fig. 7.2. (marked with white dots). The sizes of these billboards are similar to the sizes of billboards placed along the routes outside the residential area in the real world. Each such advertisement was highlighted with three directional lightings, like it is in reality. Thus, they were clearly visible, and the content of the message was clear to a customer.

A total of 26 people in good health condition, aged 18–39, participated in the experiment. Consent for being tested was obtained from each subject person. The experiment was carried out following the principles specified in the Helsinki Declaration of 1975, amended in 2000. During the entire experiment, a skin-galvanic reaction, eye tracking, and keyboard pressing time were recorded as well as all events taking place during the game. At the beginning of the test, the eye tracker was calibrated. For this purpose, the participants of the experiment were asked to focus their eyes on specific points on the screen (Piwowarski 2017; Nermend and Piwowarski 2018). In addition, before the start of the game, the subjects were asked to calm down, at the same time watching the black screen of the monitor. In order to excite the participant in the experiment, after 1 min of silence and watching this black screen, a picture of a spider was displayed to shock (Fig. 7.3). This operation enabled to determine the delay of the GSR reaction. After this situation, the game began.

After the experiment was completed, the participants were surveyed (using a questionnaire). Personal data and data confirming some of the participants' experiences were collected, for example, gender, year of birth, right-/left-handedness, whether a subject has a car, driving license, for how many years he/she is having a driving license, or does he/she like games simulating driving, and if so, for how many years he/she has been playing this type of game. In addition, data about visibility of billboards were collected. Surveyed people were asked what billboards located along the route they remembered. They were also asked if they remembered any graphic elements and texts displayed on billboards. Next, the participants of experiment were asked if they saw specific advertisements on the billboards.

Fig. 7.3 The picture of a spider before the start of the game

Fig. 7.4 The view on the in-game small billboard and its zoom in

In total, they were asked about 15 advertising billboards nine of which were placed in the game (six big-sized and three small-sized). Six small-sized billboards which appeared in the game were not included in the survey. In the last part of survey, the participants saw 15 billboards which were included in the questionnaire. They were asked if the subjects had seen these ads in the game and whether they had already seen these ads somewhere else.

During the tests, many people reported problems with the readability of small advertising billboards. This was due to two reasons. The first one was the high speed of the player's car. A small-sized billboard is clearly visible when a car is very close. So the player has only a few seconds to notice the billboard and possibly read the content. From a distance, such a billboard is hardly visible, and its texture is blurred by the game engine. The second reason was the billboard lighting. In the night game, the car has lights on, which causes additional lighting of an advertisement, and thus reduces its readability. It is illustrated in Fig. 7.4.

The survey shows that advertisements on small billboards were mainly remembered by those who collided with them. The collision causes the player's car to stop in front of a billboard so that he/she has time to see the ad and possibly read its contents. Figure 7.5 shows the player's collision with a billboard. It occurred

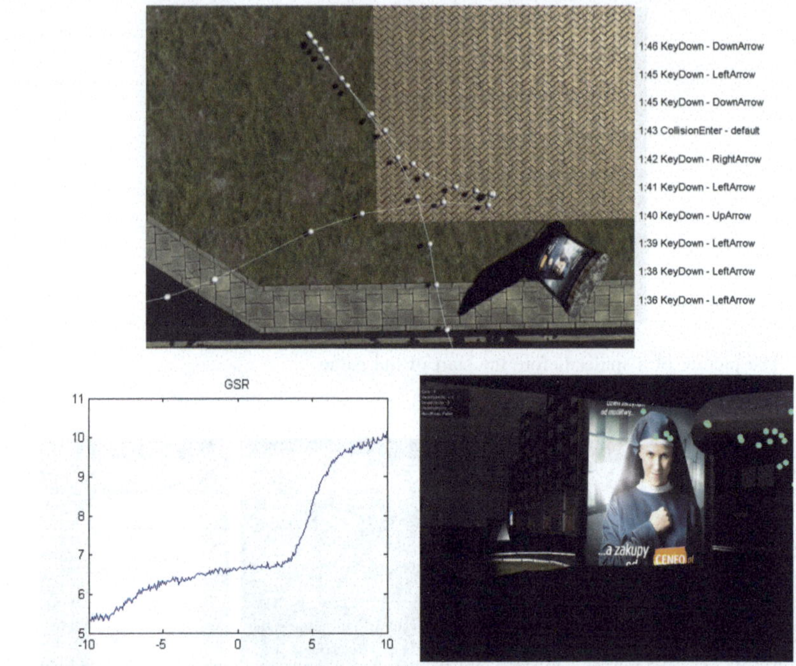

Fig. 7.5 Collision of the player's car with a small billboard

after 1 min and 43 s from the game start. As the picture shows, the player after the collision for 2 s stood in front of the billboard, and then for the next 4 s, he was moving backward. So it took enough time for the ad to be noticed. It shows that small-sized billboards should be placed so that they are obstacles for which a car can crash. For example, it may be at dangerous bents.

The Coca-Cola billboard was the most noticeable one from the large size billboards (Fig. 7.6). It was most probably due to its specific color and popularity.

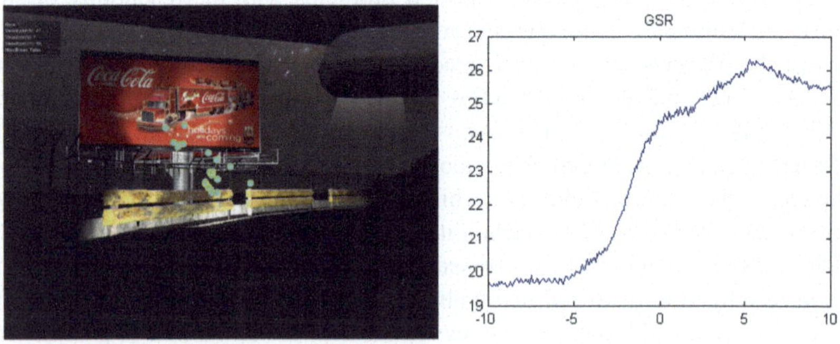

Fig. 7.6 Coca-Cola billboard

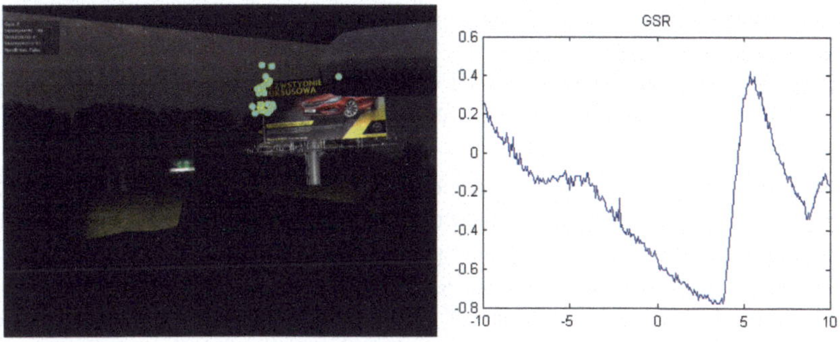

Fig. 7.7 Billboard along the straight road

All surveyed declared that they had seen this ad much earlier, and many people indicated that they remembered the red color of the ad.

Large billboards were remembered when they were put along straight sections of the route, on which the player had no problems to control a car. The problem to control appeared mainly when driving in the mountain serpentines or in bents. With a straight road, players are generally not focused only on what is in front of the car, but also pay attention to what is along the road. Figure 7.7 shows billboard on the straight road. The GSR graph shows that the player's emotions are falling, because there were no difficult obstacles at a longer distance (which was straight). Emotions increased after passing the billboard. Then while driving, the player was not only focusing on the road. You can see by the place where he looked at that he managed to read the advertising slogan on the billboard.

However, driving along a straight section of the road cannot last too long, because it would be less attractive and not very interesting for a player. The more the track in a game is complicated and more emotional, the more the player is involved in a game. In this way, the game gains on attractiveness and becomes more popular. As the result, in such types of games, the product promotion will reach the larger number of customers. Pilot studies have shown that the originally designed track is not very diverse, and in the night conditions, billboards are hardly visible. As a result, the track has been modified in such a way that hills and long straight sections have been added. In addition, lighting similar to that used for real advertising banners were added. This improved significantly visibility and noticeably.

Despite the fact that the pilot version of the game has been amended, studies carried out using the GSR and eye tracker still indicated the poor visibility of some of the ads. However, by increasing the number of advertisements, some of the billboards should be moved to other places and their surroundings (houses, trees, etc.) should be changed. It would be necessary to repeat the tests for the new layout of billboards. If the location were still not very satisfying, it would be necessary to move the billboards again and repeat the tests. As you can see, it is an iterative process that ends after achieving a satisfying effect. Therefore, a computer game that is a good medium of advertising message must be subjected to multiple tests before it reaches the target client.

Acquiring data on the behavior of game participants using cognitive neuroscience techniques and tools such as Web tracker or eye tracker can be used to develop rules and criteria for choosing the location of advertising billboards. The created rules can be used in the construction of e.g., multicriteria models or artificial intelligence. Results obtained in this way may be helpful for software companies developing computer games in choosing appropriate places for sponsors.

The use of cognitive neuroscience techniques (EEG, GSR, HR, EMG, etc.) in the study of the behavior of users of computer games (the degree of emotion, memory, interest, involvement, or brain activity level) can also be used to improve the quality of the game itself (design tips). Finally, the inclusion of recommendations for amendments by programmers may result in a better reception of the game by potential users, which may translate into the increase in its popularity. The procedure of choosing the location of advertising billboards should consist of the following stages: determining the final customer, developing a computer game scenario, designing the game, iterative testing of the game using cognitive neuroscience techniques (examining the participant's involvement in the game), and making iterative amendments. Data collection by means of cognitive neuroscience techniques is aimed at precise determination of location variants, ranking, and optimization of selected locations.

7.3 Conclusions

The methodology of selecting the location of advertising billboards based on gaining data on the behavior of game participants using cognitive neuroscience (GSR) and tools such as Web tracker and eye tracker presented in the article allows to study the degree of emotion, commitment, and visibility of products on billboards. These studies allow for the development of rules and appropriate criteria for the assessment of decision-making variants related to the placement of advertising billboards in computer games. Then employment of multicriteria and optimization methods allows for ranking the set of received variants, determining the location of advertising billboards. As a result, in a computer game, one can predict places suitable for billboards location but also locations in which they should not be placed. In practical terms, the suggested location selection procedure can be used by companies from the computer games industry as a tool for making decisions in the game design process and using them as a medium for advertising.

References

Backlund P, Hendrix M (2013) Educational games—Are they worth the effort? A literature survey of the effectiveness of serious games. In: 2013 5th international conference on games and virtual worlds for serious applications (VS-GAMES), pp 1–8

Bellotti F, Kapralos B, Lee K, Moreno-Ger P, Berta R (2013) Assessment in and of serious games: an overview. Adv in Hum-Comp Int 1(1–1):1. https://doi.org/10.1155/2013/136864

Brandeau ML, Chiu SS (1989) An overview of representative problems in location research. Manage Sci 35:645–674. https://doi.org/10.1287/mnsc.35.6.645

Gajzler M (2010) Text and data mining techniques in aspect of knowledge acquisition for decision support system in construction industry. Technol Econ Dev Econ 16:219–232

Grau D, Caldas C (2009) Methodology for automating the identification and localization of construction components on industrial projects. J Comput Civil Eng 23(1):3–13

Łatuszyńska M (2012) Computer simulation methods in economics and management. Actual Probl Econ 131:170–179

Łatuszyńska M (2016) Experiment versus simulation in economics. In: Silva P, Guerreiro A, Quaresma R (eds) Academic conferences and publishing international limited, reading, UK. The University of Evora, Portugal, pp 117–123

Łatuszyńska M, Borawska A (2015) Economic experiments in virtual world. Transformations Bus Econ 14:495–506

Martí-Parreño J, Aldás-Manzano J, Currás-Pérez R, Sánchez-García I (2013) Factors contributing brand attitude in advergames: entertainment and irritation. J Brand Manag 20:374–388. https://doi.org/10.1057/bm.2012.22

Neebe AW (1988) A procedure for locating emergency-service facilities for all possible response distances. J Oper Res Soc 39:743–748. https://doi.org/10.1057/jors.1988.129

Nermend K, Piwowarski M (2018) Cognitive neuroscience techniques in supporting decision making and the analysis of social campaign. Erbil, Iraq, pp 1–12

Nowacki R (2005) Reklama. DIFIN, Warszawa

Pempek T, Calvert S (2009) Tipping the balance: use of advergames to promote consumption of nutritious foods and beverages by low-income African American children. Arch Pediatr Adolesc Med 163:633–637

Piwowarski M (2017) Cognitive neuroscience techniques in examining the effectiveness of social advertisements. In: Nermend K, Łatuszyńska M (eds) Neuroeconomic and behavioral aspects of decision making. Springer International Publishing, pp 341–352

Silayoi P, Speece M (2004) Packaging and purchase decisions: an exploratory study on the impact of involvement level and time pressure. Br Food J 106:607–628

Terlutter R, Capella ML (2013) The gamification of advertising: analysis and research directions of in-game advertising, advergames, and advertising in social network games. J Advertising 42:95–112. https://doi.org/10.1080/00913367.2013.774610

Thyssen O (2011) Aesthetic communication. Palgrave Macmillan, New York

Wątróbski J, Ziemba P, Jankowski J, Zioło M (2016) Green energy for a green city—a multi-perspective model approach. Sustainability 8. https://doi.org/10.3390/su8080702

Wątróbski J, Ziemba P, Wolski W (2015) Methodological aspects of decision support system for the location of renewable energy sources, pp 1451–1459

Yang M, Roskos-ewoldsen DR, Dinu L, Arpan LM (2006) The effectiveness of "In-game" advertising: comparing college students' explicit and implicit memory for brand names. J Advertising, 143–152

Ziemba P, Wątróbski J, Zioło M, Karczmarczyk A (2017) Using the PROSA method in offshore wind farm location problems. Energies 10:1755

Chapter 8
Neuromarketing Tools in Studies on Models of Social Issue Advertising Impact on Recipients

Mateusz Piwowarski

Abstract Multi-step models of advertising impact on the recipient (e.g., AIDA) are often used to design social issue advertising. The effectiveness of achieving desired objectives of some steps can be analyzed applying modern cognitive neuroscience techniques (EEG, GSR, HR). They enable to read and analyze the pulses generated by the brain, myocardium, or skin surface while watching advertisements. Thus, there is the opportunity to monitor emotions, level of interests, or level of memorization of the subsequent advert sequences.

Keywords Advertisement · Social advertisement · Model of advertising impact AIDA · Cognitive neuroscience · EEG · GSR · HR

8.1 Introduction

At present time, an advertisement accompanies a human everywhere. Every day an average person watches or listens to even hundreds of ads. They are placed in mass media (TV, radio, Internet, press), but they are also visible in other places (streets, buses, mailboxes, stadiums, etc.) Typically, these are commercials, but we also meet other ad categories, such as social issue and political adverts (not discussed in this chapter). Social campaigns as well as commercial campaigns are based on similar principles and techniques in spite of the fact that their goals are different. The aim of commercial advertising refers usually to advertising products or services whose sale will bring measurable benefits and profits. On the other hand, the aim of the social campaign refers to providing, widening of social knowledge, engaging in social affairs, or sensitizing to certain issues (Barry 2016). The rules determining the effectiveness of social issue advertising are comparable to the rules of

M. Piwowarski (✉)
Department of Computational Methods in Experimental Economics, Faculty of Economics and Management, Institute of IT in Management, University of Szczecin, Mickiewicza 64, 71-101 Szczecin, Poland
e-mail: mateusz.piwowarski@usz.edu.pl

K. Nermend and M. Łatuszyńska (eds.), *Problems, Methods and Tools in Experimental and Behavioral Economics*, Springer Proceedings in Business and Economics, https://doi.org/10.1007/978-3-319-99187-0_8

commercials' assessment. They are based on the functioning of a human, an opportunity to influence his behavior. They refer to regularities involving human cognitive processes, emotions, or motivations. Advertising is effective when the recipient notices and then remembers contents being the intent of the message (company logo, product name, name of a candidate in election, desired social behavior, etc.). If the result is different, it means that an ad is pointless. Thus advertising, including social issue ads, must attract the recipient's attention. To recognize the role of attention in advertising, differences between conscious and automate processes should be understood. Studies in this field have been conducted for years, but the complexity of a brain is still a great mystery (Gail 1995; Bock 1986; Gilbert et al. 1993; Tversky and Kahneman 1973; Jankowski et al. 2016a, b). In order to reach recipients and achieve goals planned by creators of the advertisement, various techniques of influencing human sub-consciousness awareness and control are implemented. They include, among others, influencing the memory, emotions, sub-consciousness. Additionally, various techniques of the sociological advertising and social engineering techniques are implemented (Barry 2016; Gobe 2010). As noticed by Ohme (2001) showing negative effects in social issue advertising, talking about what can be lost is more effective. It is in line with the Kahneman and Tversky concept (1979) assuming that for people, the negative value of the loss is greater than the positive value of profit. Therefore, the social issue ads often include data about improper habits or behaviors. However, one should remember that showing negative behavior as typical might be risky. Conducted studies prove that common negative behavior might be an excuse (even if wrong) (Cialdini et al. 2006). Vast majority of social issue advertising is based on emotions and these are usually messages associated with fear or compassion. Fear is usually used in social issue campaigns, which focus on care of own or one's family welfare (to quit smoking, to drive safely, etc.). While compassion is where one should help others (giving blood, helping the hungry people, etc.) (Rogers and Prentice-Dunn 1997).

Cognitive psychology theories state that human being has an active participation in information receipt, including this conveyed through advertising. Based on this assumption, human communication models have been developed. In the context of advertising, models of advertising impact on the recipient have been elaborated. They describe the mechanism of advertising as well as processes of processing and utilizing information by recipients.

They differ by number, type, and sequence of particular steps occurrence. The most popular models of advertising impact are linear models, while less common are multi-track models (more extensive). Linear models of effects hierarchy include three-element sequence: think-feel-do models, which may be configured variously. Each of them assumes that an advert may bring on one of the three reactions (Fennis 2015):

- Cognitive—related to the level of knowledge of the purchaser which is the result of information carried by an advert message that reached his/her mind. The

names of the indicators: advertising awareness, advertising recall, advertising recognition, brand awareness, brand salience.
- Emotional—related to shaping customer's attitude toward a product and company being influenced by an advert. The names of the indicators: brand attitude, user image, brand preference.
- Behavioral—associated with inducing the customer to act according to the sender of an advert message expectations. The names of the indicators: intentions of buying a brand, use of the brand.

Models of advertising impact on the recipient present also hierarchy of advertising effects in various combinations of such elements as comprehension, emotions, and behavior. It is related to the existence of different communication objectives, such as providing information to the recipient's mind, pushing for action, change of habits or beliefs. Thus, this is to trigger a cognitive, emotional, or behavioral reaction. The best-known models of the advert impact (including various stages) are:

- SLB stages: Stay, Look, Buy;
- AIDA stages: Attention, Interest, Desire, Action (Priyanka 2013);
- AIDAS, AIDAL, AIDAR, AIDAE, AIDCAS stages: Attention, Interest, Desire, Conviction, Action, Satisfaction (Barry and Howard 1990);
- DAGMAR stages: Unawareness, Awareness, Comprehension, Conviction, Action (Yorke 2015; Colley 1961);
- DIPADA stages: Definition, Identification, Proof, Acceptance, Desire, Action (Furnham 2008);
- Lavidge'a-Steinera stages: Awareness, Knowledge, Liking, Preference Conviction, Purchase (Lavidge and Steiner 1961);
- Ray's model (Ray 1973):
  - Scheme 1, stages: Awareness, Comprehension, Conviction, Action;
  - Scheme 2, stages: Action, Conviction, Awareness, Comprehension;
  - Scheme 3, stages: Awareness, Comprehension, Action, Conviction;
- FCB: Foote, Cone, Belding (Vaughn 1980);
- ELM: Elaboration Likelihood Model (Cacioppo and Petty 1986);
- Reed's and Ewing's model (Reed and Ewing 2004).
- More detailed information on assumptions of models of advertising impact is in the works of A. Kozłowska (e.g., Kozłowska 2014).

While designing an advert particular steps of adopted model should be included. Thus, the advertisement should (e.g., in accordance with the AIDA model) attract the recipient's attention, arise interest in the product, focus on the benefits and create the desire to own and eventually buy. You should remember that objectives put for social issue advertising are different than those for other commercial adverts. Therefore, the selection of models to influence a recipient must take into account the nature of planned advertising activities. In the case of social campaigns, models including, for example, the stages of purchasing products will not be applicable. It should be noted that there is no single universal model that would be able to determine the basic conditions for choosing a particular manner of affecting the consumer's decisions. The impact of advertising on the recipient depends on a number of different factors, such as the type of a product, the nature of a target group, or the value of the decision for a consumer (Glowa 2002). However, the effectiveness of achieving the intended goals at some steps can be well analyzed by applying modern research techniques, such as the cognitive neuroscience techniques. It is possible to examine what emotions are caused by particular scenes of advertising, what elements of advertising the recipients were paying particular attention to, or what was remembered (Borawska 2016; Piwowarski 2017; Nermend and Piwowarski 2018). This type of research apparatus has been developed and used for many years in various scientific centers, including the author's environment (Borawski and Nermend 2016; Borawski 2017; Łatuszyńska and Borawska 2015; Nermend 2017). Conducting such studies requires the application of appropriate research techniques and methods allowing for the reading and analyzing impulses generated by the brain, heart muscles, skin surface, etc. The aim of this chapter is to present the opportunity to verify the effectiveness of selected steps of the models of the social advertising impact on the recipient by applying the cognitive neuroscience techniques (EEG, GSR, HR). Research refers to the AIDA model, but may apply to similar steps in other models of advertising impact.

8.2 Materials and Methods

The research experiment was carried out using the selected social issue advertising. The purpose of the ad was to make drivers aware of the need to observe traffic rules and to provide information about the role of the automatic traffic supervision system in improving safety. The slogan used in the campaign "SLOW DOWN! Do not be a ram … on the road" refers to more and more common negative social evaluation of irresponsible driving style. The advertising spot lasting 30 s has been analyzed.

The AIDA model was applied to analyze the impact of advertising on the recipient. Three out of four steps of these models have been analyzed, namely Attention, Interest, and Desire. The last stage (Action) was omitted due to the inability to verify the actions taken by the recipients after watching the commercial spot. Table 8.1 presents the characteristics of the steps of the AIDA model.

This model can be also used to evaluate an advertisement by viewers. The advertisement's viewers may use a questionnaire to evaluate fulfilling or not fulfilling this model's (Attention, Interest, Desire, Action) conditions (elements). Assessment of advertising as, e.g., AID means that the first three conditions were met, while advertising did not cause the expected action (Action). This type of tests is not the subject of this publication, although they have been carried out.

The experiment was conducted in 2017–2018 for a group of 30 persons (16 men and 14 women) of different ages, from 18 to 50 years old.

Table 8.1 AIDA model (Priyanka 2013)

Stages	Description	Area of influence
Attention	To attract the viewer's attention, appearing positively in the recipients' mind, offering the benefits of watching the rest of the advertisement. Used techniques: – using images, colors, backgrounds, themes, layouts, etc., – using famous personalities, animals, and children, etc., – using powerful words, scenes or using them creatively or in an unexpected way, – music, jingles, etc., – asking provocative questions	Cognitive stage
Interest	Arising recipient's interest through elaborated content of the message. Viewers must have interest in the advertisement (its part) even after they give their attention for a short span of time. If the message is something that they can relate to, they will be interested and listen to what you have to say	Affective stage
Desire	To induce certain needs (desire), action in relation to the message presented in the advertising. Desire is associated with emotions, which should be stimulated. Recipient should be convinced that presented proposal will also work in his case, solve his problems	Affective stage
Action	The next task is to make people aware of their emotions or desire so that they immediately act on it. When people are persuaded that, for example, a product, service, or behavior can solve their problems, they will perform appropriate actions. Examples of activities: – purchase of a product or service, – e-book download, – newsletter subscription, – like a profile on Facebook, – change of behavior, e.g., driving according to traffic law regulations	Behavior stage

Such measurements included the examination of the brain activity by means of electroencephalography (EEG), the measurements of galvanic skin response (GSR), and heart rate (HR). Electroencephalography (EEG) constitutes one of the neuroimaging techniques. With the use of the electroencephalograph, the recording of the bioelectrical activity of the brain (neurons) is read. An important part of this examination refers to electrodes placed on the head of the examined person and registering the electrical potential in a given place (Bear et al. 2006). For the needs of the examination, electrodes have been installed on the scalp in compliance with the guidelines of the 10–20 system. In the area of the frontal part of the frontal lobe, only 7 electrodes were taken into consideration (Fp1, Fp2, F7, F3, Fz, F4, and F2). The measurements of the galvanic skin reaction (GSR) were conducted by means of the galvanometer measuring the skin conductivity changing depending on the general simulation of the sympathetic nervous system. The activation of the autonomic nervous system is related to the physiological stimulation, and thus, changes in electrical resistance of the skin may mean experiencing emotions or a spontaneous reaction to the stimulus (Boucsein et al. 2012; Dawson et al. 2007).

The measurements of the heart rate (HR) are registered for the purpose of establishing the frequency of heart beats per minute (Dulleck et al. 2014). The measurement was taken at the wrist of the left hand, but it may also be taken on the chest.

To check the impact of advertising on recipients, based on the obtained test results (EEG, GSR, HR), indices of memorization, interest, and emotions were determined.

Memorization index (MI) is established in compliance with the formula:

$$MI = \frac{1}{N_Q} \sum_{i \in Q} x_{\theta_i}^2(t) = Average\,Power_{\theta_{left\,frontal}}, \quad (1)$$

where x_{θ_i} represents the ith EEG channel in the theta band that has been recorded from the left frontal lobe, Q is the set of left channels, and N_Q represents its cardinality.

The increase of the MI value is related to enhanced memorization (Werkle-Bergner et al. 2006; Summerfield 2005; Vecchiato et al. 2014).

Approach-withdrawal (AW) index—is calculated on the basis of the formula:

$$\begin{aligned} AW &= \frac{1}{N_P} \sum_{i \in P} x_{\alpha_i}^2(t) - \frac{1}{N_Q} \sum_{i \in Q} y_{\alpha_i}^2(t) \\ &= Average\,Power_{\alpha_{right\,frontal}} - Average\,Power_{\alpha_{left\,frontal}}, \end{aligned} \quad (2)$$

where x_{α_i} and y_{α_i} represent the ith EEG channel in the alpha band that has been recorded from the right and left frontal lobes, respectively, P and Q are the sets of right channels and left channels, and N_P and N_Q represent their cardinality.

The value of the AW index is related to the increase in interest, its drop together with the decrease in interest. The AW signal measured has been transformed and averaged in such a manner so as to obtain the averaged course (Davidson 2004; Vecchiato et al. 2014).

Emotional index (EI) is established according to the dependency:

$$EI = 1 - \frac{\beta}{\pi}, \quad (3)$$

where

$$\beta = \begin{cases} \frac{3}{2}\pi + \pi - \vartheta & if\ GSR_Z \geq 0,\ HR_Z \leq 0, \\ \frac{\pi}{2} - \vartheta & otherwise. \end{cases} \quad (4)$$

GSR_Z, HR_Z represent the Z-score variables of GSR and HR, respectively; ϑ—arctan $g(GSR_Z, HR_Z)$. The angle β is defined in order to obtain the EI varying between [−1, 1].

According to (2) and (3), negative $HR_Z < 0$ and positive $HR_Z > 0$ values of the *EI* are related to negative and positive emotions (Astolfi et al. 2008; Mauss and Robinson 2009; Vecchiato et al. 2014).

8.3 Results and Discussion

EEG, GSR, and HR signals record allowed to determine neurometric indices of memorization (MI), interest (AW), and emotions (EI) level. The volatility of the values of these indices against adopted time segments allows assessing the perception of the advertisement. Figures 8.1, 8.2, and 8.3 present the average values of the memorization index (MI), the approach-withdrawal (AW), and the emotional index (EI) for all participants in the experiment. The borders also outline approximate areas consistent with the steps of the AIDA model (for 30 s of advertising).

While analyzing the obtained values of the AW index, it should be noted that apart from one fragment, the advertisement does not generate much interest. Only between 11th and 14th second, there is a clear increase in the value of the AW index. At its peak, this value was 0.6515. Then, only the final scenes of the ad (the 23rd–26th s) and about the 29th second assumed positive values (weak interest). Referring the obtained values of the AW index to the scenes of an advertising spot (Fig. 8.4), you can see which shots caused increase of interest (frames marked in red). These are scenes in which the driver (the father driving accompanied by his son) is speeding (breaking traffic regulations) and approaches the traffic lights on which the red lights up. The culminating moment is in about the 13th second of the spot, in other words a situation in which the speeding car approaches the pedestrian crossing. The participants watched this piece of advertising with interest—will he be able to stop or he will run on the red light.

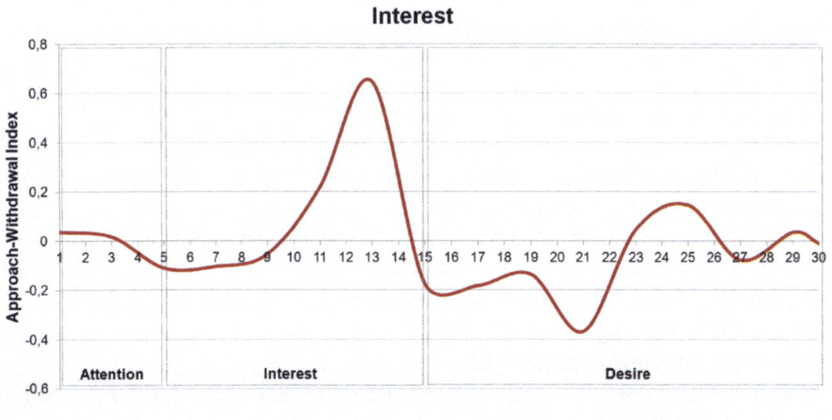

Fig. 8.1 Averaged values of the approach-withdrawal index (AW) for all the participants of the experiment

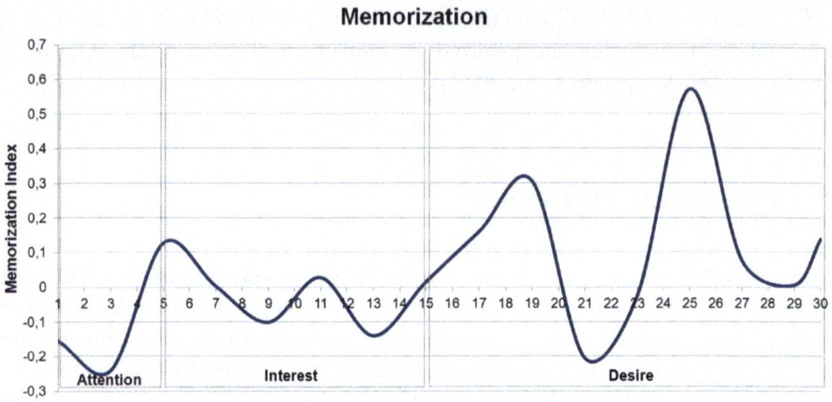

Fig. 8.2 Averaged values of the memorization index (MI) for all the participants of the experiment

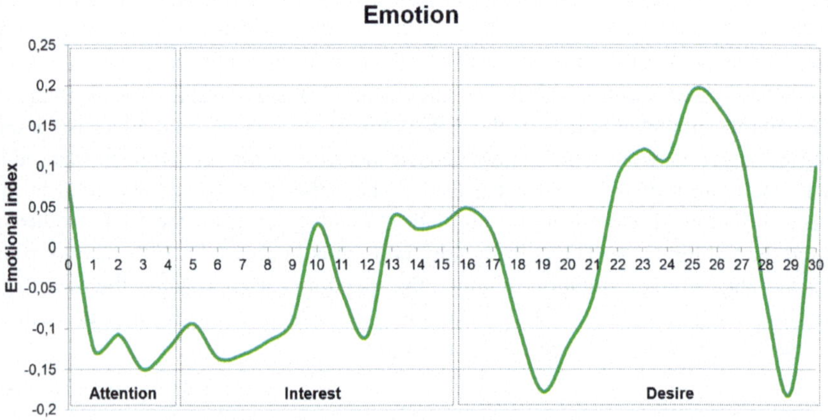

Fig. 8.3 Averaged emotional index (EI) for all the participants of the experiment

MI index values indicate the level of memorization (Formula 1). Figure 8.2 shows that there was one such moment in the advertisement (the 24th–26th s), which particularly stuck in the viewers' memory (value 0.5718). This is the situation, when the child can hear the crash of the 'road pirate's crashed car, and then the shots of the crashed car are shown. A few seconds earlier (the 18th–19th s), this value has also increased, but to the lower level (0.3075). These frames are distinguished in Fig. 8.4 in blue. This scene concerns overtaking the car by the car at the pedestrian crossing. Slight increase is also visible around the 5th–6th s of the spot, but only up to the level of just 0.1273.

Results of emotion tests (EI) presented in Fig. 8.3 show level of emotions excited by advertising in its subsequent parts. The end of the movie turned out to be particularly emotional (the 23rd–28th s). The value of the EI index reached the

Fig. 8.4 Film frames (seconds) of the analyzed advertisement. *Source* https://www.youtube.com/watch?v=UNJcIKuTCJo

value above 0.1 (max. 0.1935). These are the scenes with the accident of the speeding car (crash, boy's worried face, view of the crashed car, and the beginning of the slogan of the ad) and are marked in Fig. 8.4 in red. In the earlier parts of the movie, you can also notice momentary increases in emotions (about the 1st second, the 11th second, the 11th–18th s), but at a much lower level.

Analyzing this advertisement in terms of the assumptions of the linear model of advertising impact on the AIDA recipient, one can state that it was not properly designed. This mainly refers to the first step, namely Attention. Details of this analysis are included in Table 8.2.

What is particularly striking is the low impact of the first part of the advertisement (Attention) on the recipients. None of the analyzed indices confirms special attention to the message, it does not excite emotions, and it is not memorized. Only after 10 s, the level of interest is growing rapidly, and in about the 14th second already decreasing. It can be concluded that the expected effect (though short-lived) was achieved in this element (Interest). However, taking into account the first 10 s of advertising, it should be noted that the recipients cannot wait for this second step and simply switch the channel, go away from the receiver or turn it off. The third element of the AIDA (Desire) model is related to the induction of certain needs, in this case behavior, which is related to the excitation of emotions. The analysis of the EI index results shows that this effect has been achieved (especially in the 23rd–28th s). The AW, MI, and EI indices can be analyzed separately, but also together—the "Key Frame" index (Vecchiato et al. 2013). The distribution of MI and EI index values (from about 1/3 of the movie's length) is very similar. This allows to carefully assuming that where emotions appear, the spot scenes are better remembered. The last element of the AIDA (Action) model for these tests is not verifiable. The action that should be taken under the impact of this advertisement is related to safer driving, compliance with traffic rules.

Table 8.2 Elements of AIDA models in the analyzed advertising

AIDA steps	Assumption	Effect in advertising	Notes
Attention	The first seconds of the spot should catch viewer's attention to the ad. It is often assumed that for 30 s an advertising spot is a time segment of around the first 5 s	The expected effect has not been achieved	Change the story. Replace the scene with the running man in the hood by more dynamic and interesting ones
Interest	The next advertising seconds (10th–15th s) should arouse the viewer's interest. If the message is well-chosen, the recipients will watch the rest of the ad with interest	The assumed effect was achieved. High level of interest has been achieved, although it was short-lived	The effect of interest could have appeared few seconds earlier
Desire	Next, that is from about the 15th second an increase in emotions should appear so as to induce a desire to change behavior	The effect was achieved. There is also a visible decline in emotion	One should consider why between the 18th–22nd s there was such a drop in emotions
Action	Typically, the last seconds of the ad should stimulate the recipient to any action. In case of this advertising, such actions were not planned	Not measurable with this experiment	After watching advertising, carrying out a test, e.g., in a form of interview

8.4 Conclusions

The aim of this chapter was to present a methodical apparatus (techniques of cognitive neuroscience) to study the effectiveness of selected steps of the models of the social issue advertising impact of social advertising on the recipient. The study was based on the AIDA model. The results of the analyzed advertisement showed that it is possible to assess with great accuracy whether the advertisement was properly designed (in relation to the adopted model). Analyzing various indices (in this case AW, MI, EI) determined on the basis of EEG, GSR, HR research, appropriate corrections can be made at the stage of advertising implementation. Referring directly to the analyzed advertisement, it should be stated that its beginning (the first 10 s) did not fulfill its task (it did not attract attention, did not arise interest). Thus, this part should be redesigned.

The conducted research concerned the AIDA model, but the applied research techniques can be used to verify some of the steps of other models of the advertising impact. It is possible to analyze whether the designed advertisements arouse the assumed recipients' reactions in accordance with the methodology of given models.

Acknowledgements The project was financed with the National Science Centre funds allocated according to the decision DEC-2016/21/B/HS4/03036.

References

Astolfi L, De Vico Fallani F, Cincotti F, Mattia D, Bianchi L, Marciani MG, Salinari S, Colosimo A, Tocci A, Soranzo R, Babiloni F (2008) Neural basis for brain responses to TV commercials: a high-resolution EEG study. IEEE Trans Neural Syst Rehabil Eng 16(6): 522–531

Barry P (2016) The advertising concept book: think now, design later. Thames & Hudson, New York

Barry TE, Howard DJ (1990) A review and critique of the hierarchy of effects in advertising. Int J Advertising 9(2):121–135

Bear MF, Connors BW, Paradiso MA (2006) Neuroscience: exploring the brain. Lippincott, Philadelphia

Bock M (1986) The influence of emotional meaning on the recall of words processed for form or self-reference. Psychol Res 48:107–112. https://doi.org/10.1007/BF00309324

Borawska A (2016) Neuroscience techniques in economic experiments. In: Nermend K, Łatuszyńska M (eds) Selected issues in experimental economics. Proceedings of the 2015 computational methods in experimental economics (CMEE) conference, springer proceedings in business and economics, Springer International Publishing, pp 125–133

Borawski M, Nemrend K (2016) Methods of data collection in experimental economic games. In: Silva P, Guerreiro A, Quaresma R (eds) Proceedings of the 10th European conference on information systems management, academic conferences and publishing international limited, Evora, Portugal, pp 12–19

Borawski M (2017) Convolutional representation in brain simulation to store and analyze information about the surrounding environment for the needs of decision making. In: Nermend K, Łatuszyńska M (eds) Neuroeconomic and behavioral aspects of decision making, proceedings of the 2016 computational methods in experimental economics (CMEE) conference, Springer International Publishing, pp 91–105

Boucsein W, Fowles DC, Grimnes S, Ben-Shakhar G, Roth WT, Dawson ME, Filion DL (2012) Publication recommendations for electrodermal measurements. Psychophysiology 49(8):1017–1034

Cacioppo J, Petty R (1986) Communication and persuasion: central and peripheral router to attitude change. Springer-Verlag, New York

Cialdini RB, Demaine LJ, Sagarin BJ, Barrett DW, Rhoads K, Winter P (2006) Activating and aligning social norms for persuasive impact. Psychology Press Ltd Social Influence 1:3–15. https://doi.org/10.1080/15534510500181459

Colley R (1961) Defining advertising goals for measured advertising results. Association of National Advertisers, New York

Davidson RJ (2004) What does the prefrontal cortex "do" in affect: perspectives on frontal EEG asymmetry research. Biol Psychol 67(1–2):219–233

Dawson ME, Schell AM, Filion DL (2007) The electrodermal system. In: Cacioppo JT, Tassinary LG, Berntson G (eds) Handbook of psychophysiology, Cambridge University Press, Cambridge

Dulleck U, Schaffner M, Torgler B (2014) Heartbeat and economic decisions: observing mental stress among proposers and responders in the ultimatum bargaining game. PLoS ONE 9(9)

Fennis BM, Stroebe W (2015) The psychology of advertising. Psychology Press, New York

Furnham A (2008) How advertising works. In: Head & heart management, Palgrave Macmillan, London

Gail T (1995) Classical conditioning of unattended stimuli. Psychol Mark 12:79–87. https://doi.org/10.1002/mar.4220120106

Gilbert DT, Tafarodi RW, Malone P (1993) You can't not believe everything you read. J Pers Soc Psychol 65:221–233. https://doi.org/10.1037/0022-3514.65.2.221

Glowa T (2002) White paper: advertising process models. http://www.academia.edu/5302471/Advertising_Process_Models_White_Paper_White_Paper_Advertising_Process_Models. Accessed 21 Feb 2018

Gobe M (2010) Emotional branding: the new paradigm for connecting brands to people. Allworth Press, New York

Jankowski J, Kolomvatsos K, Kazienko P, Wątróbski J (2016a) Fuzzy modeling of user behaviors and virtual goods purchases in social networking platforms. J Univ Comput Sci 22(3):416–437

Jankowski J, Ziemba P, Wątróbski J, Kazienko P (2016b) Towards the tradeoff between online marketing resources exploitation and the user experience with the use of eye tracking. Asian conference on intelligent information and database systems. Springer, Berlin Heidelberg, pp 330–343

Kahneman D, Tversky A (1979) Prospect theory: an analysis of decision under risk. Econometrica XLVII:263–291

Kozłowska A (2014) The model of advertising impact: a review of existing assumptions. Zeszyty Naukowe Uniwersytetu Szczecińskiego, Problemy Zarządzania, Finansów i Marketingu 36:279–294

Lavidge R, Steiner G (1961) A model for predictive measurements of advertising effectiveness. J Mark 25(6):59–62. https://doi.org/10.2307/1248516

Łatuszyńska M, Borawska A (2015) Economic experiments in virtual world. Transformations Bus Econ 14(36C):495–506

Mauss IB, Robinson MD (2009) Measures of emotion: a review. Cogn Emot 23(2):209–237

Nermend K (2017) The implementation of cognitive neuroscience techniques for fatigue evaluation in participants of the decision-making process. In: Nermend K, Łatuszyńska M (eds) Neuroeconomic and behavioral aspects of decision making, proceedings of the 2016 computational methods in experimental economics (CMEE) conference, Springer International Publishing

Nermend K, Piwowarski M (2018) Cognitive neuroscience techniques in supporting decision making and the analysis of social campaign. In: Proceedings book international conference on accounting, business, economics and politics (ICABEP-2018), Erbil, Iraq, pp 1–12. https://doi.org/10.23918/icabep2018p1

Ohme RK (2001) Social influence in media: culture and antismoking advertising. In: Wosińska W, Cialdini RB, Barrett DW, Reykowski J (eds) The practice of social influence in multiple cultures. Erlbaum, Mahwah, pp 309–324

Piwowarski M (2017) Cognitive neuroscience techniques in examining the effectiveness of social advertisements. In: Nermend K, Łatuszyńska M (eds) Neuroeconomic and behavioral aspects of decision making, proceedings of the 2016 computational methods in experimental economics (CMEE) conference, Springer International Publishing, pp 341–352

Priyanka R (2013) AIDA marketing communication model: stimulating a purchase decision in the minds of the consumers through a linear progression of steps. Int J Multi Res Soc Manag 1:37–44

Ray ML (1973) A decision sequence analysis of development in marketing communication. J Mark 1

Reed PR, Ewing M (2004) How advertising works: alternative situational and attitudinal explanations. Mark Theory 4(1/2)

Rogers RW, Prentice-Dunn S (1997) Protection motivation theory. Phys Rev Lett 1

Summerfield C, Mangels JA (2005) Coherent theta-band EEG activity predicts item-context binding during encoding. NeuroImage 24(3):692–703

Tversky A, Kahneman D (1973) Availability: a heuristic for judging frequency and probability. Cogn Psychol 5(2):207–232. https://doi.org/10.1016/0010-0285(73)90033-9

Vaughn R (1980) How advertising works. a planning model. J Advertising Res 5

Vecchiato G, Cherubino P, Trettel A, Babiloni F (2013) Neuroelectrical brain imaging tools for the study of the efficacy of TV advertising stimuli and their application to neuromarketing. Springer, Berlin, Heidelberg, pp 89–112

Vecchiato G, Maglione AG, Cherubino P, Wasikowska B, Wawrzyniak A, Latuszynska A, Latuszynska M, Nermend K, Graziani I, Leucci MR, Trettel A, Babiloni F (2014) Neu-rophysiological tools to investigate consumer's gender differences during the observation of TV commercials. Hindawi Publishing Corporation Computational and Mathematical Methods in Medicine 2014, article ID 912981

Werkle-Bergner M, Muller V, Li S, Lindenberger U (2006) Cortical EEG correlates of successful memory encoding: implications for lifespan comparisons. Neurosci Biobehav Rev 30(6): 839–854

Yorke D (2015) DAGMAR Model. In: Cooper CL, Lee N, Farrell AM (eds) Wiley Encyclopedia of Management. https://doi.org/10.1002/9781118785317.weom090406

Chapter 9
Impact of Negative Emotions on Social Campaigns Effectiveness—Measuring Dilemmas

Anna Borawska and Dominika Maison

Abstract In the case of social campaigns, the often-used method of increasing their impact is appealing to the negative emotions of recipients. This is quite a controversial approach, because the results of some studies indicate that when the emotions are too negative (this is particularly true in case of fear), the effect may be counterproductive and lead to the emergence of defensive mechanisms in the audience. It is important, therefore, to evoke emotions of adequate intensity. Thanks to the use of cognitive neuroscience tools (electroencephalography, measurement of galvanic skin response and heart rate), the researchers can check reactions to different media messages (varying in intensity of negative emotions) which go beyond declaration of recipient and ascertain which ones are the most effective in terms of increasing awareness of the problem and the involvement of the recipient. These additional methods of measuring the effectiveness (apart from questionnaires) offer new possibilities in conducting social campaigns research. The chapter presents a scenario of the experiment aimed to check whether the relationship between the intensity of negative emotions in the media message of the social campaign and its effectiveness is consistent with the curvilinear model proposed in the literature. The study is prepared for a campaign concerning road safety.

Keywords Social campaigns · Negative emotions · Experiment
Cognitive neuroscience measures

A. Borawska (✉)
Faculty of Economics and Management, University of Szczecin,
Mickiewicza 64, 71-101 Szczecin, Poland
e-mail: anna.borawska@usz.edu.pl

D. Maison
Faculty of Psychology, University of Warsaw,
Stawki 5/7, 00-183, Warsaw, Poland
e-mail: dominika.maison@psych.uw.edu.pl

K. Nermend and M. Łatuszyńska (eds.), *Problems, Methods and Tools in Experimental and Behavioral Economics*, Springer Proceedings in Business and Economics, https://doi.org/10.1007/978-3-319-99187-0_9

9.1 Introduction

Social campaigns are an important tool for promoting positive change in social attitudes (in ecology, health prevention, tolerance promotion, etc.). Improving their effectiveness may therefore have a very tangible effect on many aspects of life—both for individuals and for whole societies. Social campaign, also known as public awareness campaign, is defined as "a comprehensive effort that includes multiple components (messaging, media relations, government affairs, budget, etc.) to help reach a specific goal" (Bouder 2013). Usually, a campaign attempts to raise awareness about a key issue and induce a desired positive behavioral change (Coffman 2002). Among the most widespread activities that are undertaken within the framework of social campaigns, one can mention: communication campaigns, press publications, brochures, events and happenings, and sometimes more direct educational actions. They also include promotion through different types of media—television, radio, Internet, and print. The advertising is not usually the main component of a well-prepared social campaign, but it plays an important role in terms of its public perception and draws the attention of a wide audience to the problem.

Thanks to the occurrence of the campaign in the media, it can reach the larger number of potential customers and initiate a number of positive changes. However, media messages of this kind could fulfill their task only if they are prepared in the right way. Due to the cost of their emissions, before they can be shared with the audience, they should be evaluated in terms of accomplishing the expectations. Therefore, it is needed to assess the effectiveness of such media messages. It is usually assumed that an effective message is one that captures the attention of the target audience, is easy to understand and remember, and does not require any further explanation (Raab and Rocha 2011).

Generally, evaluation can be categorized into four basic types. These are formative, process, outcome, and impact evaluation (Coffman 2002). The first type is performed before the campaign is launched; the other three are used to assess the outcomes of the campaign during and after its release. Media messages used for campaigns are mostly assessed during the formative evaluation. This approach helps to sense what messages work best and how they should be framed and identifies the factors that can facilitate or impede the campaign (Valente 2001; Maison 2005). During this phase, messages are designed and pretested on representatives of campaign's target audience.

The most commonly used methods in this scope are methods based on questionnaires (e.g., Gibson et al. 2014) and focus groups (e.g., Freimuth et al. 2001). It is increasingly recognized, however, that the results obtained with the use of such methods are not quite reliable, because the study subjects are not always able to evaluate media messages in accordance with their true feelings (Zaltman 2003). Moreover, research of this type relies on measures that are proximal, such as perceptions of message effectiveness (Noar et al. 2010). Although it is assumed that perceived effectiveness is causally antecedent to actual effectiveness

(Dillard et al. 2007), it would be advisable to find the way of assessing actual effectiveness more directly and not only based on respondents' declarations. One of the approaches that aim to solve the problem of direct measures based mostly on conscious information processing is the application of the tools of cognitive neuroscience into advertising pretesting methods (Plassmann et al. 2007; Ohme et al. 2009; Craig et al. 2012; Plassmann et al. 2012). Methods of this kind offer access to information that cannot be obtained as a result of the survey or declarations in focus groups. They also give a better understanding of the mechanisms underpinning the formation of consumer attitudes and behavior that lead to the emergence of a new field of science described as consumer neuroscience. Under this name, scientists utilize neurophysiological signals to gain deeper insight into a consumer brain (Agarwal and Dutta 2015; Lin et al. 2018).

Considering the specific nature of social campaigns, different from campaigns aimed at inducing the consumer to purchase a particular product or service, the assessment methodology with the use of cognitive neuroscience tools used in commercial marketing cannot be directly applied to media messages in social campaigns. They require not only the message memorization, but also understanding the importance of behavior being promoted. According to the theory (supported by Kahnemann 2011) about the existence in the human mind of two "modes" of thinking—rapid, intuitive and slow, logical—during examining the effectiveness of media messages the activation of this second mode is more relevant in the context of advertising research. Taking into account the current state of knowledge, a recognition of this kind of activation is possible with the use of the techniques of cognitive neuroscience. Such research should also allow to acquire new knowledge on the relationship between forms of advertising and mental processes activation. This problem is often omitted in researches of commercial advertising messages due to its low priority in this respect. An important element of the research is also an indication of the strength and the kind of impact that emotions and visual/sound impressions have on the perception of advertising message. In the case of social campaigns, an awareness and an understanding of the media are also very important, because they increase the impact of the campaign. Some pioneering research in this scope was already done (e.g., Zelinková et al. 2014; Falk et al. 2015; Piwowarski 2017), but still methods and procedures used to discover unconscious opinions of recipients and the actual effectiveness of media messages need to be done.

The use of cognitive neuroscience techniques for evaluating media messages in social campaigns requires properly designed research. It can go beyond testing single messages for different kinds of media. In broader sense, using these methods, effectiveness of certain elements used in messages and their general emotional appeal can be assessed. To test their effectiveness, one can use the indicators obtained on the basis of registration of psychophysiological signals (index of emotions, memory and approach–withdrawal, facial muscle tension, galvanic skin response, heart rate) and data obtained with the help of questionnaires (opinion on the presented stimuli, their reasonableness and effectiveness, declaration on changing the driving style in the future under the influence of the stimuli seen by the participant during the experiment).

The aim of this chapter is to present a scenario of the experiment that applies cognitive neuroscience techniques aimed to check whether the relationship between the intensity of negative emotions in the media message of the social campaign and its effectiveness is consistent with the curvilinear model proposed in the literature.

9.2 Research on the Use of Negative Emotions in Social Campaigns

In the case of social campaigns, the often-used method of increasing their impact is appealing to the negative emotions of recipients. Among the main reasons for that one can mention (Witte and Allen 2000; Grancea 2012; McGraw et al. 2015):

- "Drawing attention" of the recipient,
- Increasing the engagement of the recipient in advertising,
- Shocking the recipient to mobilize him to take specific actions,
- Causing anxiety, feelings of guilt or worry to change attitudes,
- Inspiring behavior aimed to solve the problem,
- Appealing to fear motivates changes in attitude, intent, and behavior,
- Inducing more intensive information processing in the recipients' mind,
- Increasing reliability—negative messages are perceived as more reliable and informative.

Appealing to negative emotions is quite a controversial approach because the results of some studies indicate that when the emotions are too negative (this is particularly true in case of fear), the effect may be counterproductive and lead to the emergence of defensive mechanisms in the audience (Witte and Allen 2000). It is important, therefore, to refer to this kind of emotion in the correct proportions (Brennan and Binney 2010). Thanks to the use of cognitive neuroscience tools (electroencephalography, measurement of galvanic skin response and heart rate), the researchers can present media messages that cause negative emotions of varying intensity and check which ones are the most effective in terms of increasing awareness of the problem and the involvement of the recipient. Exemplary research in this field has been already carried out. They are listed in Table 9.1.

These studies did not focus on examining the effectiveness of the level of negative emotions intensity; only on the determination of whether appealing to such emotions is generally effective or ineffective in advertisements accompanying various types of social campaigns.

Table 9.1 Research on the use of negative emotions in social campaigns

Research	Campaign	Emotions used	Stimuli	Cognitive neuroscience technique	No. of subjects
Boshoff and Teorien (2017)	Health warnings (photographs on cigarette packs)	Fear	Pictures and texts	Eye tracking, galvanic skin response	90
Hamelin et al. (2017)	Safe driving	Generally negative	Video clips	GfK-EMO Scan (software for recognizing facial expressions)	60
Wang et al. (2015)	Health warnings (photographs and information on cigarette packs)	Depression, sadness, guilt, disgust, discouragement, anxiety,	Pictures and texts	Electroencephalography	25
Suckfüll and Reuter (2013)	Safe driving	Fear, shock, anxiety	Video clips	Heart rate, galvanic skin response	118
Missaglia et al. (2014)	Raising awareness about female circumcision	Sadness, anger	Video clips	Galvanic skin response, electromyography	40
Ordoñana et al. (2009)	Promotion of tetanus vaccines	Fear, threat	Pictures with audio	Heart rate, galvanic skin response	92

Source own elaboration

9.3 Experimental Research—Assumptions and Design

The aim of the proposed study is to check whether the relationship between the intensity of negative emotions in the media message of the social campaign and its effectiveness is consistent with the curvilinear model proposed in the literature (Janis 1967; Krisher et al. 1973; Hale and Dillard 1995); that is, whether exceeding a certain degree of negative emotions in the media message of a social campaign may reduce the effectiveness of this message, due to the occurrence of so-called defense mechanisms. The theoretical shape of the model that is examined is shown in Fig. 9.1.

The study also aims to develop and present a procedure for testing and evaluating advertisements within social campaigns in terms of their effectiveness depending on the intensity of negative emotions in the message. As research methods questionnaires to obtain self-report measurements and cognitive neuroscience techniques to check unconscious and automatic reaction to advertising are used.

In the experiment, the following research questions have been posed:

– Will the exceeding a certain level of intensity of negative emotions reduce the effectiveness of the media message in the social campaign?

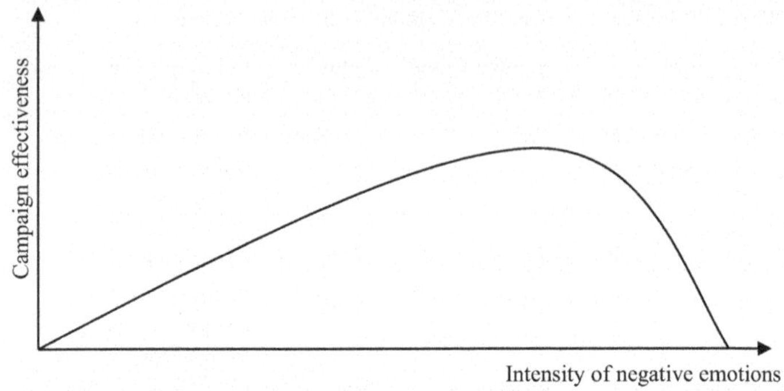

Fig. 9.1 Curvilinear model of dependence between intensity of negative emotions and effectiveness of social campaign. *Source* based on (Hale and Dillard 1995)

- What level of intensity of negative emotions in the media message of the social campaign is the most appropriate from the point of view of their effectiveness?
- Does the effectiveness of negative emotions in media messages is dependent on the style of driving?

For these questions, research hypotheses were formulated:

***H1**: Increasing the intensity of negative emotions in advertising increases its effectiveness only to a certain level. When advertising carries too negative emotional charge, its effectiveness decreases.*
***H2**: During the presentation of social advertising with high intensity of negative emotions, defense mechanisms have the greatest chance of revealing themselves in people who have an irresponsible driving style than in people who drive safely.*
***H3**: The measurement of psychophysiological responses of participants using the cognitive neuroscience techniques will allow for registering unconscious and automatic reaction to advertising.*

The experiment has two stages. In the first step (pretest of research materials), three versions of the message with varying emotional intensity were prepared. The goal of this stage of the study was the validation of three advertising variants in terms of their difference in intensity of negative emotions evoked. For this purpose, the respondents, with the help of a questionnaire, evaluated pictures shown in Fig. 9.2.

From the list of basic emotions proposed by Ekman (1992), three negative emotions relevant to the researched object (social advertising campaign)—fear, disgust, sadness—were chosen. With its help, the subjects could evaluate the emotions felt after viewing picture stimulus types of situations in the virtual world on a scale from 1 to 7 (from minimal to maximum level of sensations). Each of the basic negative emotions was assessed independently. In order to determine the type and level of emotions evoked by prepared research materials, the three versions of advertising were tested by independent group of respondents (between subject

Fig. 9.2 Stimuli used in the experiment: **a** low intensity of negative emotions, **b** medium intensity of negative emotions, and **c** high intensity of negative emotions. *Source* own elaboration

experimental design) and evaluated on the same scale using the same questions. The study was conducted online by 160 people (86 female and 74 male). For the analysis, a one-way analysis of variance (ANOVA) and t tests were performed that allowed to determine whether the differences of averaged intensity of emotion felt between groups are significant. The results of the pretest were used to determine whether the graphic materials for the experiment have been prepared in a proper manner and whether the intensity of negative emotions is appropriately graded. When the obtained results would not confirm the hypothesis that the stimuli shown to the respondents differ in the intensity of the negative emotions induced, it would be necessary to introduce changes regarding the stimuli and to repeat the pretest.

In the final step, focus is put on achieving the main goal of the experiment and on verifying its hypotheses presented earlier. The participants for this stage of study will be people who have previously completed the survey on the driving style (Reason et al. 1990; Aberg and Rimmo 1998). All respondents are going to be divided into two groups. In one group, there will be people who have obtained a questionnaire result indicating a tendency to irresponsible driving, while in the second one those that are characterized by a responsible driving style. Assignment to groups is done on the basis of the total score obtained in the questionnaire. People with the highest results were classified as careless drivers and those with the lowest as cautious ones. In this phase of experiment, each participant will be exposed to one of the three versions of social advertising showing car accident in more or less drastic way (evaluated in the pretest of material). During the exposition, psychophysiological and self-report measurements of every person will be collected. This part of research is still in progress. The rest of the chapter is focused on detailed results of the pretest stage.

9.4 Results of the Pretest

The pretest part of the experiment allowed to check how recipients assess the level of negative emotions shown on three versions of stimulus (social ads with different level of negative emotions). The questionnaire was filled by 160 persons. Table 9.2

Table 9.2 Distribution of participants in the pretest by gender and stimulus variant

Intensity of negative emotions	Male	Female	Total
Low	21	34	55
Medium	33	26	59
High	20	26	46
Total	74	86	160

Source own elaboration

Table 9.3 One-way ANOVA and t tests results—significance of mean assessments differences for three negative emotions and three variants of stimulus

	Intensity of emotion			F	p	Simple effects
	Low	Medium	High			(paired samples t tests)
Fear	$M_{FL} = 3.31$	$M_{FM} = 3.24$	$M_{FH} = 4.33$	5.8	0.004	M_{FL} and M_{FM}: $t = 0.21$; $p = 0.833$ M_{FL} and M_{FH}: $t = -2.96$; $p = 0.004$ M_{FM} and M_{FH}: $t = -3.15$; $p = 0.002$
Disgust	$M_{DL} = 1.55$	$M_{DM} = 2.42$	$M_{DH} = 4.57$	63.59	0.000	M_{DL} and M_{DM}: $t = -3.98$; $p < 0.001$ M_{DL} and M_{DH}: $t = -11.15$; $p < 0.001$ M_{DM} and M_{DH}: $t = -6.7$; $p < 0.001$
Sadness	$M_{SL} = 3.78$	$M_{SM} = 3.8$	$M_{SH} = 4.59$	2.49	0.086	M_{SL} and M_{SM}: $t = -0.04$; $p = 0.969$ M_{SL} and M_{SH}: $t = -1.95$; $p = 0.055$ M_{SM} and M_{SH}: $t = -1.92$; $p = 0.058$

Source own elaboration

shows how many participants evaluate each variant and what was their distribution in relation to gender and stimulus variant.

The focus of the analysis was put on three negative emotions: fear, sadness, and disgust. For all obtained results, descriptive statistics, student's t tests, and one-way ANOVA calculations were performed. These statistical methods were used to determine whether the emotional assessments of each stimulus variant differ significantly in their means. The analysis was performed for each emotion separately. An alpha level of 0.05 for all statistical tests was used.

The results of ANOVA and t tests showing the significance of the differences in mean assessments are presented in Table 9.3.

The data presented in Table 9.3 showed that in case of three tested versions of advertising there are differences in the intensity of evoked negative emotions. However, analysis of variance was significant only in case of fear and disgust, but in case of sadness, the results were only approaching significance. The simple effects showed that in case of fear and sadness, the biggest (and significant) difference was between ads with low and high and medium and high intensity of emotions, while between low and medium version of ad the difference in experienced emotions was not significant. In case of disgust, for a change, there was difference in the level of felt emotions between all three versions of ad. The lack of significant results between two versions of ads (low vs. medium) in case of fear and sadness led to the hypothesis that maybe ads with varying intensity of negative emotions are perceived differently by women and men. To check this assumption, the same tests as previously were conducted, but this time for female and male participants separately. The results of these analyses are shown in Tables 9.4 and 9.5.

Results of the tests performed for each gender separately allowed to confirm the difference in assessment for the disgust (ANOVA results for women: $F = 54.96$, $p < 0.001$; for men: $F = 18.69$, $p < 0.001$). They have also revealed additional information. Medium variant of stimulus is perceived differently than the low one, although at first, for all participants the difference was not so obvious. Men and women have various opinions in that matter and that was the premise to control the number of male and female participants in the second part of the experiment (with the use of cognitive neuroscience techniques). Moreover, it is necessary to control the number of responsible and irresponsible drivers among men and women to check whether these two variables are dependent or not.

The average assessments of stimuli for all three emotions are shown graphically on the charts in Fig. 9.3.

Table 9.4 One-way ANOVA and t tests results—significance of mean assessments differences for three negative emotions and three variants of stimulus (female participants)

	Intensity of emotion			F	p	Simple effects
	Low	Medium	High			(paired samples t tests)
Fear	$M_{FL} = 4$	$M_{FM} = 3.54$	$M_{FH} = 4.88$	3.67	0.030	M_{FL} and M_{FM}: $t = 0.95$; $p = 0.348$ M_{FL} and M_{FH}: $t = -1.92$; $p = 0.061$ M_{FM} and M_{FH}: $t = -2.58$; $p = 0.013$
Disgust	$M_{DL} = 1.76$	$M_{DM} = 2.42$	$M_{DH} = 5.08$	54.96	0.000	M_{DL} and M_{DM}: $t = -2.22$; $p = 0.032$ M_{DL} and M_{DH}: $t = -9.64$; $p < 0.001$ M_{DM} and M_{DH}: $t = -6.5$; $p < 0.001$
Sadness	$M_{SL} = 4.32$	$M_{SM} = 4.08$	$M_{SH} = 5.62$	4.85	0.010	M_{SL} and M_{SM}: $t = 0.48$; $p = 0.633$ M_{SL} and M_{SH}: $t = -2.60$; $p = 0.012$ M_{SM} and M_{SH}: $t = -2.89$; $p = 0.006$

Source own elaboration

Table 9.5 One-way ANOVA and t tests results—significance of mean assessments differences for three negative emotions and three variants of stimulus (male participants)

	Intensity of emotion			F	p	Simple effects
	Low	Medium	High			(paired samples t tests)
Fear	$M_{FL} = 2.19$	$M_{FM} = 3$	$M_{FH} = 3.6$	4.82	0.011	M_{FL} and M_{FM}: $t = -2.06$; $p = 0.045$ M_{FL} and M_{FH}: $t = -3.9$; $p < 0.001$ M_{FM} and M_{FH}: $t = -1.48$; $p = 0.146$
Disgust	$M_{DL} = 1.19$	$M_{DM} = 2.42$	$M_{DH} = 3.9$	18.69	0.000	M_{DL} and M_{DM}: $t = -4.09$; $p < 0.001$ M_{DL} and M_{DH}: $t = -7.14$; $p <= 0.001$ M_{DM} and M_{DH}: $t = -3.15$; $p = 0.003$
Sadness	$M_{SL} = 3.78$	$M_{SM} = 3.8$	$M_{SH} = 4.59$	0.82	0.443	M_{SL} and M_{SM}: $t = -1.3$; $p = 0.12$ M_{SL} and M_{SH}: $t = -0.64$; $p = 0.525$ M_{SM} and M_{SH}: $t = 0.615$; $p = 0.542$

Source own elaboration

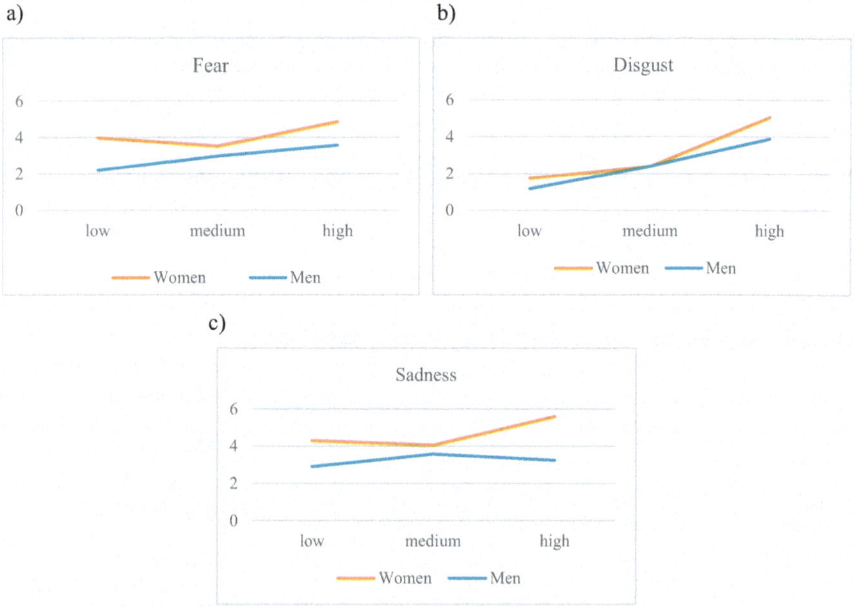

Fig. 9.3 Average assessment of stimuli for women and men: **a** fear, **b** disgust, and **c** sadness. *Source* own elaboration

The observed differences in the stimulus variants' reception allowed for the conclusion that on the basis of pretest results, graphical materials prepared for the experiment fulfill the condition of representing three various levels of negative emotions intensity. Based on this, they were used in the second part of the experiment.

9.5 Conclusion

Measuring the effectiveness of media messages in social campaigns is a complex issue. Application of cognitive neuroscience techniques along with the questionnaires can improve the accuracy of such measurements. However, in order to obtain good results, the experiment that aims to achieve this goal has to be prepared very carefully. The study presented in this chapter conceptualizes the procedure that needs to be followed in the research design. The pretest study allowed for choosing appropriate stimuli that will be used in the second part of the experiment, what was shown in the analyses results presented in the previous section. In order to measure the effectiveness of the presented message, this step of the research will be based on different effectiveness indicators that will be calculated from the questionnaire and psychophysiological data. These indicators will include:

- Emotional reaction (emotion index calculated using data obtained from galvanic skin response and heart rate measurement).
- Index of memorization and of approach–avoidance determined on the basis of registered brain activity.
- Fixation and heat maps registered with the eye tracker.
- Self-report measurement (e.g., a declaration on changing the driving style, maintaining greater caution on the road).

Recordings of psychophysiological signals and questionnaire responses for the second phase of the experiment have been already completed at the Cognitive Neuroscience Laboratory at the Faculty of Economics and Management (University of Szczecin). Analysis of the obtained data is currently in progress. Comparison of the results obtained on the basis of psychophysiological measurements and on the basis of a questionnaire (self-report—measurement) will be the basis for verifying or possibly rejecting the main research hypotheses. Verification of these hypotheses will help to formulate guidelines for the appropriate use of negative emotions in social advertising.

Acknowledgements The project was financed with the National Science Centre funds allocated according to the decision DEC-2016/21/B/HS4/03036.

References

Aberg L, Rimmo PA (1998) Dimensions of aberrant driver behaviour. Ergonomics 41(1):39–56

Agarwal S, Dutta T (2015) Neuromarketing and consumer neuroscience: current understanding and the way forward. Decision 42(4):457–462

Bouder S (2013) Critical components for public awareness campaigns. Advocacy Unleashed. https://advocacyunleashed.kontribune.com/articles/1371. Accessed 25 March 2018

Boshoff C, Toerien L (2017) Subconscious responses to fear-appeal health warnings: an exploratory study of cigarette packaging. S Afr J Econ Manag Sci 20(1). https://doi.org/10.4102/sajems.v20i1.163

Brennan L, Binney W (2010) Fear, guilt, and shame appeals in social marketing. J Bus Res 63(2):140–146

Coffman J (2002) Public communication campaign evaluation: an environmental scan of challenges, criticisms, practice, and opportunities. Harvard Family Research Project, Cambridge

Craig AW, Loureiro YK, Wood S et al (2012) Suspicious minds: exploring neural processes during exposure to deceptive advertising. J Mark Res 49(3):361–372

Dillard JP, Shen L, Vail RG (2007) Does perceived message effectiveness cause persuasion or vice versa? 17 consistent answers. Human Commun Res 33(4):467–488

Ekman P (1992) An argument for basic emotions. Cogn Emot 6:169–200

Falk EB, O'Donnell MB, Tompson S et al (2015) Functional brain imaging predicts public health campaign success. Soc Cogn Affect Neurosci 11(2):204–214

Freimuth V, Cole G, Kirby S (2001) Issues in evaluating mass media-based health communication campaigns. In: Rootman I, Goodstadt M, Hyndman B et al (eds) Evaluation in health promotion: principles and perspectives. World Health Organization, Regional Office for Europe

Gibson LA, Parvanta SA, Jeong M et al (2014) Evaluation of a mass media campaign promoting using help to quit smoking. Am J Prev Med 46(5):487–495

Grancea I (2012) When images hurt: a closer look at the role of negatively-valenced images in advertising. Argumentum: J Semin Discursive Logic, Argumentation Theory Rhetoric 10:153–164

Hale JL, Dillard JP (1995) Fear appeals in health promotion campaigns. Too much, too little, or just right. In: Maibach E, Parrott RL (eds). Design health messages. Approaches from communication theory and public health practice. Sage

Hamelin N, El Moujahid O, Thaichon P (2017) Emotion and advertising effectiveness: a novel facial expression analysis approach. J Retail Consum Serv 36:103–111

Janis IL (1967) Effects of fear arousal on attitude change: recent developments in theory and experimental research. In: Berkovitz L (ed) Advances in experimental social psychology. Academic Press, New York

Kahneman D (2011) Thinking, fast and slow. Macmillan

Krisher HP, Darley SA, Darley JM (1973) Fear-provoking recommendations, intentions to take preventive actions, and actual preventive actions. J Pers Soc Psychol 26:301–308

Lin MH, Cross SNN, Jones WJ et al (2018) Applying EEG in consumer neuroscience. Eur J Mark 52(1/2):66–91

Maison D (2005) Pre-test research—how to foresee effectiveness of future advertisement basing on research. In: Nowak AZ, Glinka B, Hensel P (eds) Business administration in Central Europe: challenges, problems and opportunities. Wydawnictwo Naukowe Wydziału Zarządzania UW, Warsaw

McGraw AP, Schiro JL, Fernbach PM (2015) Not a problem: a downside of humorous appeals. J Mark Behav 1(2):187–208

Missaglia A, Mauri M, Oppo A, Russo V (2014) The impact on emotions on recall: an empirical study on social ads. In: Proceedings of measuring behavior 2014, Wageningen, The Netherlands 27–29 August 2014, pp 1–6

Noar SM, Palmgreen P, Zimmerman RS et al (2010) Assessing the relationship between perceived message sensation value and perceived message effectiveness: analysis of PSAs from an effective campaign. Commun Stud 61(1):21–45

Ohme R, Reykowska D, Wiener D et al (2009) Analysis of neurophysiological reactions to advertising stimuli by means of EEG and galvanic skin response measures. J Neurosci Psychol Econ 2(1):21

Ordoñana JR, González-Javier F, Espín-López et al (2009) Self-report and psychophysiological responses to fear appeals. Hum Commun Res 35:195–220

Piwowarski M (2017) Cognitive neuroscience techniques in examining the effectiveness of social advertisements. In: Nermend K, Latuszynska M (eds) Neuroeconomic and behavioral aspects of decision making. Springer International Publishing, Cham, Switzerland

Plassmann H, Ambler T, Braeutigam S et al (2007) What can advertisers learn from neuroscience? Int J Advertising 26(2):151–175

Plassmann H, Ramsøy TZ, Milosavljevic M (2012) Branding the brain: a critical review and outlook. J Consum Psychol 22(1):18–36

Raab M, Rocha J (2011) Campaigns to end violence against women and girls. http://www.endvawnow.org/uploads/modules/pdf/1342724232.pdf. Accessed 25 March 2018

Reason J, Manstead A, Stradling S et al (1990) Errors and violations on the roads: a real distinction? Ergonomics 33:1315–1332

Suckfüll M, Reuter M (2013) Emotions elicited by a road safety campaign. Int J Commun Health 2:64–69

Valente T (2001) Evaluating communications campaigns. In: Rice RE, Atkin CK (eds) Public communication campaigns. Sage, Thousand Oaks, CA

Wang A, Romer D, Elman I et al (2015) Emotional graphic cigarette warning labels reduce the electrophysiological brain response to smoking cues. Addict Biol 20(2):368–378

Witte K, Allen M (2000) A meta-analysis of fear appeals: Implications for effective public health campaigns. Health Educ Behav 27(5):591–615

Zaltman G (2003) How customers think: essential insight into the mind of the market. Harvard Business School Press, Cambridge

Zelinková J, Shaw DJ, Mareček R et al (2014) An evaluation of traffic-awareness campaign videos: empathy induction is associated with brain function within superior temporal sulcus. Behav Brain Funct 2014:10–27

Chapter 10
Use of Computer Game as an Element of Social Campaign Focusing Attention on Reliability of Information in the Internet

Mariusz Borawski

Abstract The chapter presents an example of analysis of the game created for the purpose of social campaign, taking into consideration its playability and impact of the message included in the game. Methods of cognitive neuroscience were used for the analysis. The recording included what the player was looking at, the GSR signal and EEG, on the basis of which the Memorization Index was calculated. It allowed to specify, which parts of the game were boring, as well as what parts of the message in the game might have been remembered by the player.

Keywords Cognitive neuroscience methods · Social campaigns
Games

10.1 Introduction

Game is a form of entertainment, which might easily be connected with science. Through games that imitate behaviors of adults, children learn proper behaviors, specific activities, etc. It is typical not only for people but also for many species of animals. That might be the reason why the computer games in which children, as well as adults play specific roles, become heroes, and sometimes solve riddles, are very popular. In 1952, A. S. Douglas came to realize that computers might become media for playing games and created the game Noughts and Crosses for EDSAC computer. It was one of the first computer games (Jorgensen 2009).

Nowadays, the computer games market achieved the status of the industry. As shown by the GAMR (Desjardins 2017) research, currently there are 2 billion players throughout the world, half of it in Asia. Average age of the player is 38 years. In Poland, the situation is slightly different, according to Ipsos (2014),

M. Borawski (✉)
West Pomeranian University of Technology Szczecin,
Żołnierska 49, 71-210 Szczecin, Poland
e-mail: mborawski@usz.edu.pl

K. Nermend and M. Łatuszyńska (eds.), *Problems, Methods and Tools in Experimental and Behavioral Economics*, Springer Proceedings in Business and Economics, https://doi.org/10.1007/978-3-319-99187-0_10

research. Ninety-five percent of Polish players is below 30, and the biggest percentage (35%) are aged between 16 and 19.71% of all players are pupils or students.

Large number of players in the world causes that the games are often used in commercials. In 2015, gains only from the commercials in the games amounted 2.75 billion dollars. It is foreseen that the gains will increase to 5.05 trillion dollars in 2020 (Statista 2017). There are two tendencies to use games in the commercials:

- IGA (In-game advertising) means use of the game as a medium of advertisement;
- Advergaming (advertising + gaming) is the advertisement games created specially for advertising specific product or service.

There are various ways to use game as a means of advertisement. The easiest is placing advertising billboards. In the 3D games, the advertising billboards are placed according to the same principles as in the real world. An example might be the advertising campaign of President Barack Obama from 2008, which used 18 games, including Need for Speed: Carbon in 2008. In the game, the player drives a car and advertisements of the presidential candidate are presented to him on big billboards allocated along the road (Yenigun 2012). The products might be placed in the games, as items used by the characters in the games. A good example might be placement of the phone Sony Xperia Z5 in the Uncharted 4 game. The character that one becomes in the game has possibility to take selfies using this phone and there is no possibility to change it to another type of phone. The type of the phone is not specified directly, but its size, color, logo, etc., indicate that it is Sony Xperia Z5 (Peckham 2015). Other interesting way of the product placement is the game Alan Wake (Microsoft Game Studios and Remedy Entertainment 2010). In this game, the main character Alan Wake uses a torch, in which periodically the batteries have to be replaced. The batteries are marked with the Energizer logo.

Advergaming are the games created on order, and their aim is to advertise specific goods, services, etc. In 2006, Burger King launched the game Sneak King created by Blitz Games. The game was sold with the meal in special price 3.99 USD. In total, there were created three games, which were not well accepted by the critics but generated great income. They are assigned significant input to the company's sale's growth. The main character of the game was a king toy of Burger King, and his task was to deliver burgers to hungry people (Hyman 2007). Other example of the game created on order was America's Army: Proving Grounds (U.S. Army 2017). It is the game created on order of the American army, whose aim was promoting army and encouraging young people to join it.

According to The Motion Monkey (2017), the main advantages of using advergaming are:

- combining advertisement and entertainment;
- interactivity—the recipient of the advertising message is a participant rather than a passive viewer;
- creating positive associations;

– long lifetime of the computer game (in comparison to a standard advertisement);
– enables presenting story of the company or product.

These are the reasons why advergaming is more and more often used in the advertising campaigns, including social campaigns. The advantages of using games in social campaigns: possibility to implement educational elements, good game scenario allows compensating for a low budget; non-commercial campaigns may use free libraries, model databases, etc.

An example of a game created for social campaign is Food Force. It was published by United Nations World Food Programme (WFP) in 2006. The players participate in missions related to campaigns against hunger. In this way, they learn about problems related to hunger and activities of WFP (United Nations World Food Programme 2017).

The games might be addressed to children in order to develop specific behaviors. As an example, there are games available on the Nourish Interactive Web site, which promotes healthy diet. In the section for children, there are available games aiming at raising awareness as to how important is healthy diet and developing healthy habits. Good example of such type of game is Kevin's Build-a-Meal Game (Nourish Interactive 2017). During the game, a child has to compose properly balanced meals for an entire day. Meals have to include specific amounts of products of four types. The selection is evaluated by the game on the basis of information gathered from the child at the beginning, which includes their sex and age. It gives the opportunity to teach the child how much of which group of products they should eat in order for the meals to be balanced.

In the Internet, there can be found games of educational and ecological nature, e.g., Waste Segregation, which is available on the Zyraffa (Zyraffa 2017) Web site. The game teaches children how to throw waste into properly market waste bins. The child needs to recognize type of waste and select proper waste bin.

The increasing popularity of the games as the means of advertisement causes the researchers to try to find out to what extent the information included in the game have the impact on the players. The main ways of gathering information are questionnaires, interviews, and observations. The example of research on impact of advertisements is the research "Can advergames boost children's healthier eating habits?" presented in this work. A comparison between healthy and non-healthy food (Dias and Agante 2011). The research focused on impact of advergames on children's healthy diet. Children (231) were divided into two groups. One was playing the game promoting healthy diet, and the second was playing a standard game. Impact of the game was examined by means of the questionnaire. No impact related to increasing children's knowledge on healthy diet was demonstrated due to the fact that they already had such knowledge. On the other hand, it turned out that children have tendency to choose what was advertised in the game.

The work "Marketing Fruit and Vegetable Intake with Interactive Games on the Internet" (Buller et al. 2009) describes researches related to three Internet games developed for the Web site Centers for Disease Control and Prevention, which subject were fruit and vegetables. The games promoted eating fruit and vegetables.

Internet users were invited to the researches, and data were collected by means of self-descriptive measures. The research showed that the games did not increase consumption of fruit and vegetables but increased the conviction on profits related to consumption of fruit and vegetables in large quantities.

The work "A Hierarchy-of-Effects Approach to Designing a Social Marketing Game" (Russell-Bennett et al. 2016) presents researches which specified impact of the online game related to physiological effects of water drinking on our body. The game was played by the students of high schools, out of which 223 took part in the online questionnaire. Results of the research indicated that the elements of the game related to enjoyment (feel), knowledge (learn), and challenge (do) significantly influenced attitude of the students. Similar research was conducted in the work "Electronic games: can they create value for the moderate drinking brand?" (Mulcahy et al. 2015). One hundred and seven male teenagers were surveyed in order to verify relation between experiential value a consumer-based brand equity dimensions. The game "Don't Turn a Night Out into a Nightmare", developed on request of was the Australian Federal Government within the scope of the marketing campaign against excessive alcohol drinking, was used for the research.

The work "Educational video game for juvenile diabetes: results of a controlled trial" (Brown et al. 1997) focuses on examining impact of the game teaching diabetics rules of proper diet and taking medicines. Fifty-nine persons suffering from diabetes of the age between 8 and 16 were examined, out of which 31 played the game, while the remaining 28 played other entertainment games. Sick persons were interviewed, and their parents filled in the questionnaires. The research indicted that the group playing the educational game showed increased awareness related to observance of the diet and taking medicines. Moreover, number of urgent medical appointments for this group was smaller than for the control group.

In the study "Tipping the balance: Use of advergames to promote consumption of nutritious foods and beverages by low-income African American children" (Pempek and Calvert 2009) observation was used as a method of data collection. An online advergame was used for the research in order to verify its influence on the selection of snacks by poor Afro-American children. Thirty children from public schools were assigned to three groups. The first group played the games promoting healthy snacks, the second group played the games promoting less healthy snacks, and the third group was the control group. The researchers were observing what types of snacks were selected by children from various groups. The research proved that the games influenced the choice of snacks and children playing the games promoting healthy snacks chose them more often.

The study "How does serious m-game technology encourage low-income households to perform socially-responsible behaviors?" (Yam et al. 2017) examined impact of the game on mobile devices Reduce Your Juice and energy-saving behavior. The group interviews were conducted in six households in Brisbane Australia. The study indicated that the experiences gained through the game were transferred to the daily life and resulted in energy-saving behavior.

Success of the social campaign, which uses the game, mainly depends on its playability and strength of its message. These are the key factors, although not always taken into consideration when planning the campaign. The good example might be the Waste Segregation, which has only one stage and one level of difficulty. That causes the game to be monotonous and its players might easily get bored. Playability of the game and its influence might be measured using the cognitive neuroscience methods. That enables verification of the game's "construction" at the final stage of its development and implementation of necessary changes. The chapter presents the computer game focusing on reliability of information in the Internet and research on the game's playability, as well as impact of its message.

10.2 Computer Games Used for Purposes of Social Campaign, Focusing Attention on Reliability of Information in the Internet

Introduction of the game engines onto the market significantly simplified the development process. Development of the game is possible engaging one programmer, and in case of easier projects even an amateur-programmer. Currently, there are two leading commercial game engines: Unity (Unity Technologies 2017) and Unreal engine (EpicGames 2017). In both cases, costs of engine application can be avoided. In case of Unity, the engine is available for free, if the gross income and the company's capital are lower than 100 thousand dollars. Unreal engine requires license fees, if the gross income from the sales of product per calendar quarter exceeds 3000 dollars. There are also available game engines with the open-source license. An example might be Godot (Godot Engine 2017). In the presented game, there were used the engines of the Unity game as well as free models and textures delivered by the Internet societies related to Unity. In the game, there were used: Mega Fantasy Props Pack (http://u3d.as/NBP), MCS Male: Wood Elf Scout (http://u3d.as/kLn) RPG inventory icons (http://u3d.as/oCk), character systems MCS Male (http://u3d.as/jxH), i UMA 2—Unity Multipurpose Avatar (http://u3d.as/fDS), Make Your Fantasy Game—Lite (http://u3d.as/4w2), graphics presenting a studded bed (http://niemodlinzamek.pl/wp-content/uploads/2015/08/rys1.jpg).

The developed game is connected with social campaign aiming at making people aware of low reliability of the Internet treated as a source of information. The game's plot takes place in non-specified past in a small village nearby a castle. The Internet is presented as Jan Pokątny-Internet (John Illicit-Internet). He is the source of numerous bad events, which happened in the village. During the game, the player learns various stories related to his activities. The game begins at the sea shore. The players see the world with the eyes of the character controlled by them. The first thing the player sees is a poster (Fig. 10.1).

The poster placed in the game is a part of the story related to John Illicit-Internet. The player gets to know the story by talking to the village inhabitants. It warns against buying medicines of unknown origins. Prince's daughter decided to take

Fig. 10.1 Poster warning traders trading medicines of unknown origin (content of the poster: The Prince's Inn Special offer! Free accommodation for traders of the unknown origin medicines)

part in the Miss of the Castle Boroughs competition. She believed she was a bit overweight, and when John Illicit-Internet showed up, she got convinced to purchase the slimming medicine. Due to the medicine effect, she fell into a coma. It turned out that other candidates to the competition also took this medicine and died. The Prince got furious and forbid his subordinates to use any medicines. The story transfers into the game real events related to the death of people who took slimming medicines. The example can be DNP FAT Burner product, which became known due to the death of a 22-year-old woman in Warsaw. The product is still available on the Internet (Fig. 10.2a). There are also less harmful products for sale. The example might be pills with tapeworms larvae for carrying tapeworm diet (Fig. 10.2b).

The game has additional functions enabling synchronization with recording devices, which record what the player is looking at (eye-tracker), skin galvanic

a) b)

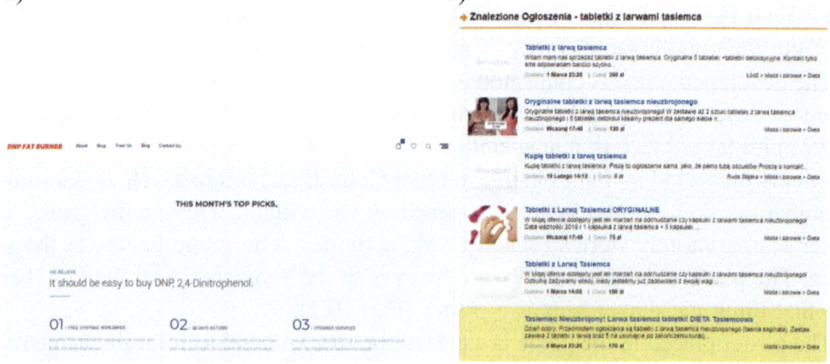

Fig. 10.2 Sales advertisements: **a** fat burner (DNP Fat Burner n.d.); **b** pills with tapeworms larvae (Oglaszamy24 n.d.)

	A	B	C	D	E	F	G	H	I	J	K	L	M
2289	ChangeRotate	2017	9	25	12	12	27	846		moduleDe(	Player	0	
2290	ChangeRotate	2017	9	25	12	12	27	875		moduleDe(	Player	-0,18276	
2291	ChangeRotate	2017	9	25	12	12	28	351		moduleDe(	Player	0	
2292	StartSpeakYN	2017	9	25	12	12	28	380	save	speakPlay	Player		
2293	StopSpeakYN	2017	9	25	12	12	31	196	save	speakPlay	Player	true	
2294	StartSpeak	2017	9	25	12	12	31	196	save	speak	Shoemaker		
2295	Speak	2017	9	25	12	12	31	197	save	speak	Shoemake	FirstConversation1	
2296	Speak	2017	9	25	12	12	48	665	save	speak	Shoemake	FirstConversation2	
2297	Speak	2017	9	25	12	13	32	710	save	speak	Shoemake	FirstConversation3	
2298	StopSpeak	2017	9	25	12	13	36	13		speak	Shoemaker		
2299	ChangeMove	2017	9	25	12	13	36	13		moduleDe(	Player	0	
2300	ChangeMove	2017	9	25	12	13	37	446		moduleDe(	Player	-0,64999	
2301	ChangeRotate	2017	9	25	12	13	37	845		moduleDe(	Player	0,18664	
2302	ChangeMove	2017	9	25	12	13	38	25		moduleDe(	Player	0	
2303	ChangeMove	2017	9	25	12	13	39	554		moduleDe(	Player	0,972008	
2304	ChangeRotate	2017	9	25	12	13	39	693		moduleDe(	Player	0	
2305	StartSpeakYN	2017	9	25	12	13	40	18	save	speakPlay	Player		

commands

Fig. 10.3 Messages recorded during reading the story of Dratewka by the player

response, and the EEG signal. That required designing the game on the basis of the messages transferring mechanism. Individual modules of the game transfer to each other commands and information, through messages. Each message includes name, generating time, recipient, and sender, as well as additional parameters related to nature of the message itself. All messages pass through central messages manager. The manager transmits messages from the sender to the receiver, simultaneously recording them on the disc. The manager can stop accepting messages from the senders and read them from the file, which enables replaying course of the game. Additional advantage of recording the messages is possibility to specify the time used by the player for specific parts of the game and synchronization, e.g., with the eye-tracker. Messages facilitate specification of the time used by the player for specific activities during the game. Figure 10.3 presents example of the events recorded at the moment when the player was reading story of Szewczyk Dratewka (Dratewka Shoemaker). The story is composed of three pages of the text. The first page was read by the player for 17.468 s, the second part took him 44.045 s, and the third one 3.303 s which, more or less, reflects content of the text on the pages. The time anomalies might indicate that the player did not read the text. The stories, independently told by the characters, include clues how to end the game. It encourages players to read the text.

10.3 Examining Playability and the Campaign Message Reception

The game can be divided into ten stages:

(a) Talks with characters. The player talks with the game characters in order to learn about the aim of the game and find first clue enabling its execution. The aim of the game is finding brother of the person living by the seaside. The missing person's name is Wiesław. The innkeeper asks the player to regain the

mixture guarded by the rabbits. In return, he offers items belonging to missing Wiesław.
(b) A fight with the rabbits. The player has to defeat rabbits (shoot them using sling), in order to get a mixture requested by the innkeeper.
(c) Second talk with the innkeeper. In return for the mixture, the innkeeper offers a key and asks guests for help (sympathy during the talk) in searching Wiesław.
(d) Conversation with the innkeeper's guests. One of the guests gives the player a clue to talk with Miss of the Castle Boroughs.
(e) Conversation with Miss of the Castle Boroughs. Miss of the Castle Boroughs tells that in one of the houses of the castle, Wiesław has left a chest.
(f) An attempt to enter the castle. Requires distracting guards (guards cannot be killed).
(g) Searching the castle. Aims at finding Wiesław's chest. Clues found in the chest lead the player to the cemetery.
(h) Creating magic weapon. Elimination of skeletons requires creation of a magic weapon by combining available items.
(i) A fight with the skeletons. Upon elimination, the skeletons are reborn. Complete elimination of the skeletons requires blocking doors to the coffin from which they come out.
(j) Finding the mixture and passing it to the Miss of the Castle Boroughs.

The game was initially tested on three players. The tests aimed at catching mistakes, specifying how much players are involved in the game and how visible is the message of the game. The tests included observation of the players, tracking messages recorded by the game, recording GSR, EEG, and points which the players looked at (by use of the eye-tracker function).

Observation of the players indicated difficulty in executing phase 1. The players themselves had difficulties finding out that the doors should be blocked. The problem was solved by implementing clues from the innkeeper, who gives hints upon each instance of the player's elimination. In this case, he is informing about the necessity to block the doors. Further difficulty was finding the item to block the doors, even though it was near the doors. Still, the biggest difficulty was the action of blocking the doors. The blocking mechanism, even though seemed logical, was not coherent with application of the item, and the players could not block the doors. Lack of coherence resulted from the fact, that it required pressing the button of object dropping instead of the button of the object use. It was necessary to change the doors blocking mechanism.

The cognitive neuroscience methods could be used to examine the players' reaction. Those methods enable, among others, examining the emotional status of the players and the moments remembered by the players. The emotional status can be recognized by measuring the galvanic skin response (GSR). Figure 10.4 presents recorded skin and galvanic reaction of the player throughout the entire game. Subsequent stages executed by the player were marked with letters a, b, etc. As you

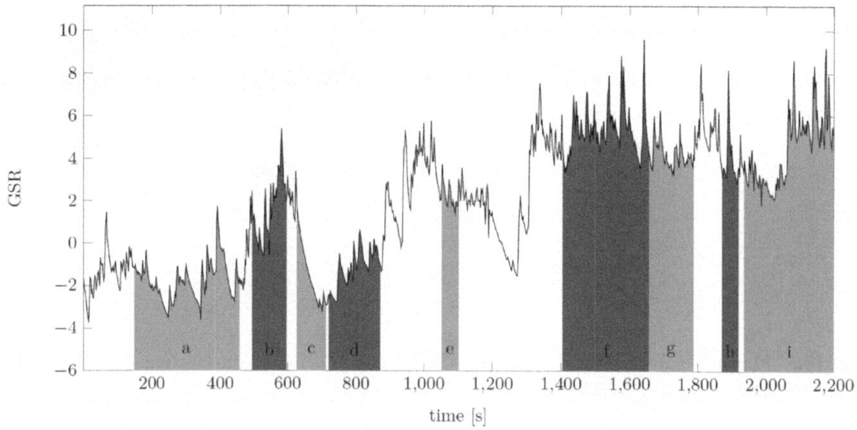

Fig. 10.4 Galvanic skin response (GSR) of the player during the entire game

can see, the player does not always execute all stages of the game. He/she takes some time to sightsee the terrain, get to know its topography and placement of the character.

GSR represents the emotional status of the player, which may indicate their involvement in the game. Gradual decrease of the GSR means boredom of the player. It often happens when the examined person remains passive, e.g. Watches the movie. In such case, the GSR gradually decreases, with a few increases when the person gets sad or amused. During the game, it is possible to see on the chart that the graph increases, which might mean that the person got involved in the game. There are parts of the graph which are slowly decreasing. These can be related to the elements of the game in which the examined person reads statements of other characters. The most uniform and longest decrease of the graph is visible on the stage c. It is the conversation with the innkeeper. The graph shows that none of the elements of the conversation influenced emotions of the player. Nothing made him sad or amused. Such statement can be perceived by the player as boring. That means, either the statement should be shortened or a humorous element should be introduced.

The Memorization Index can be used for checking what the player has remembered (Giovanni Vecchiato et al. 2014):

$$\mathrm{MI} = \frac{1}{N_Q} \sum_{i \in Q} x_{\theta_i}^2(t) = \text{Average Power}_{\theta_{\text{left,frontal}}} \tag{10.1}$$

where $x_{\theta_i}(t)$ represents i-channel in the band θ at the moment of time t recorded for left frontal lobe, N_Q represents number of all channels of the left front lobe.

Figure 10.5 presents graphs of the GSR and MI for advertisement of the Prince's Inn. The dot marks place of the player's eye-spot at a given moment. The eye-spot was identified by the eye-tracker. On the graphs, the zero time reflects the moment

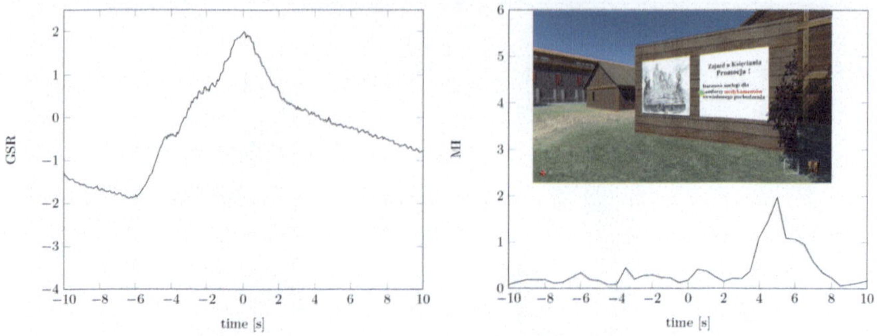

Fig. 10.5 Player's galvanic skin reaction (GSR) and MI index during viewing the Inn's advertisement

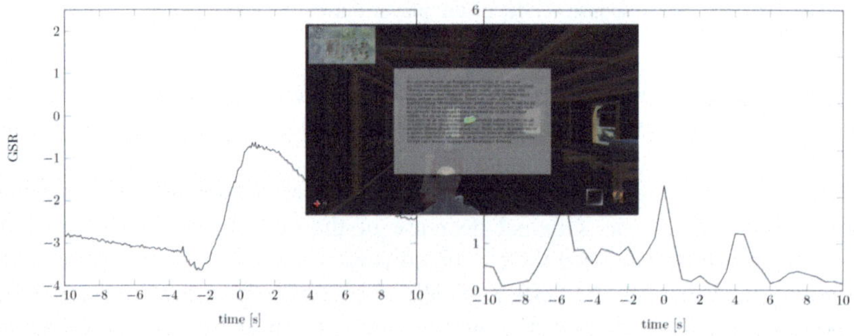

Fig. 10.6 Player's galvanic skin reaction (GSR) and the MI index when reading the end of the story about Dratewka the Shoemaker

at which the player was looking on the indicated place. GSR reached maximum when the player reached the word traders (free services for traders of the medicines of unknown origin). The increase of the GSR means that the player's emotions were influenced during reading of the text, probably due to humorous mood of the text in combination with a picture placed next to the text, showing the studded bed. The MI index reached maximum when the reader reached the word medicines. That might be caused by the fact that the word was highlighted with red color, which made the word look important.

Figure 10.6 presents response of the player to the part of the story of the Dratewka Shoemaker: So there came the John Illicit-Internet. And they said that the sulfur was obsolete, that it was good in the grandfather's times, but now the alchemists from across the sea prepared a mixture for all types of pests: cockroaches, flies, rats, snakes, wolves, crocodiles, dragons, and other riff-raff. You give it to the dragon, and it immediately falls onto its back, swings its legs, and drops dead. No blood, everything clean, and in order.

I have bought the mixture, soaked the lamb and slipped it to the dragon. I told him it was a starter, the main dish would follow, he should wait, not burning the village. The dragon ate the lamb, fell onto its back, and swung its legs. But he wouldn't stop swinging.

We were waiting till evening. Suddenly, the dragon turned and run to the river, he kept drinking and drinking, and suddenly attacked as from its back. I have never seen such diarrhea. The village was covered with brown substance. The smell was so horrible that I have almost fainted. The peasants wanted to kill me; I have hardly managed to escape. Well, burnt village can be re-built but after such incident, they had to leave their houses.

Since that time, everyone calls me Dratewka the Diarrheamaker.

The GRS graph for the story about Dratewka the Shoemaker slowly decreases up to the moment when the dragon starts drinking and gets diarrhea. This part significantly influenced emotions of the players. The MI index reached the highest value at the sentence. Suddenly, the dragon turned…. It is the part of the story related to the dragon's diarrhea (Fig. 10.6). Slightly increased values were recorded also for sentence: The village was covered with brown substance. That also indicates this fragment of the story focused the players' attention and was partly remembered by him. The MI index indicates also that the player remembered the sentence about developing a miraculous mixture against all types of pests by the alchemist. Taking into consideration the GRS value and MI index recorded during reading the text by the player, the first part of the text should be shortened, because it did not evoke any emotions. It is worth, however, to leave sentence about mixture developed by the alchemists, because this fragment was most probably remembered.

Figure 10.7 presents player's reaction at the end of the story about the Castle Boroughs Competition. The whole story did not evoke any emotions of the player. Throughout the whole story, the GRS graph was decreasing. At the end of the story, there was notified high MI index value, which was connected with information that Grypselda was the only candidate of the competition. Due to lack of emotions of the player, the story should be shortened or changed.

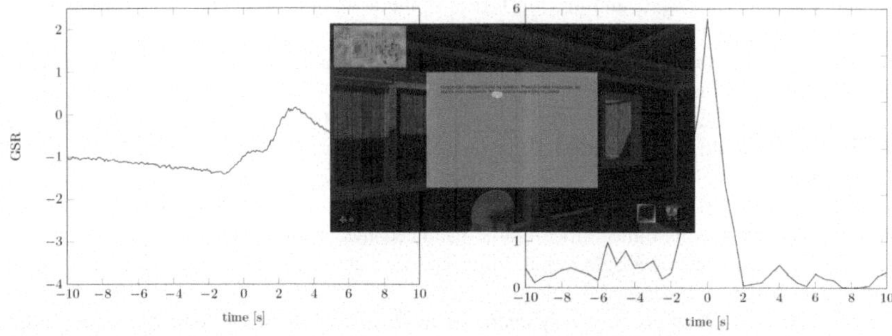

Fig. 10.7 Player's galvanic skin reaction (GSR) and the MI index when reading the end of the story about the Miss Castle Boroughs competition

10.4 Conclusions

Computer games became very popular and due to this fact are more often used in the advertisement campaigns. They are very useful in social campaigns because they enable implementation of the educational elements. The efficiency of the game depends on its playability and to what extend the players will get the message of the game.

The chapter includes the example of analysis related to the game's playability and strength of the message on the Internet unreliability. The analysis was conducted with use of the cognitive neuroscience methods. It allowed to specify, which parts of the game might be boring to the player, as well as what might have been remembered by the player. That allows for implementing improvements to the game prior to its launching.

Acknowledgements The project was financed with the National Science Centre funds allocated according to the decision DEC-2016/21/B/HS4/03036.

References

Brown SJ, Lieberman DA, Gemeny BA et al (1997) Educational video game for juvenile diabetes: results of a controlled trial. Med Inform (Lond) 22:77–89. https://doi.org/10.3109/14639239709089835

Buller MK, Kane IL, Dunn AL et al (2009) Marketing fruit and vegetable intake with interactive games on the internet. Soc Mark Q 15:136–154. https://doi.org/10.1080/15245000903038316

Desjardins J (2017) The history and evolution of the video games market. http://www.visualcapitalist.com/history-video-games-market/. Accessed 10 Dec 2017

Dias M, Agante L (2011) Can advergames boost children's healthier eating habits? A comparison between healthy and non-healthy food. J Consum Behav 10:152–160. https://doi.org/10.1002/cb.359

DNP Fat Burner (n.d.) DNP fat buner. http://dnpfatburner.com/. Accessed 3 July 2018

EpicGames (2017) Unreal engine. https://www.unrealengine.com. Accessed 10 Dec 2017

Godot Engine (2017) Godot. https://godotengine.org/. Accessed 10 Dec 2017

Hyman P (2007) Burger King has it their way with advergame sales. Hollywood Report

Ipsos (2014) #jestemgraczem. Ipsos, Polska

Jorgensen AH (2009) Context and driving forces in the development of the early computer game Nimbi. IEEE Ann Hist Comput 31:44–53

Microsoft Game Studios, Remedy Entertainment (2010) Alan Wake. http://www.alanwake.com. Accessed 12 Dec 2017

Mulcahy R, Russell-Bennett R, Rundle-Thiele S (2015) Electronic games: can they create value for the moderate drinking brand? J Soc Mark 5:258–278. https://doi.org/10.1108/JSOCM-06-2014-0043

Nourish Interactive (2017) Kevin's build-a-meal Game. http://www.nourishinteractive.com/kids/healthy-games/6-kevins-build-a-meal-game-balanced-meals. Accessed 6 Dec 2017

Oglaszamy24 (n.d.) Darmowe ogłoszenia. http://www.oglaszamy24.pl/szukaj/ogloszenia/tabletki-z-larwami-tasiemca. Accessed 3 Jul 2018

Peckham J (2015) Well of course every character in Uncharted 4 uses a Sony Xperia Z5. https://www.techradar.com/news/phone-and-communications/mobile-phones/well-of-course-every-character-in-uncharted-4-uses-a-sony-xperia-z5-1310986. Accessed 11 Dec 2017

Pempek TA, Calvert SL (2009) Tipping the balance: Use of advergames to promote consumption of nutritious foods and beverages by low-income african american children. Arch Pediatr Adolesc Med 163:633–637. https://doi.org/10.1001/archpediatrics.2009.71

Russell-Bennett R, Leo C, Rundle-Thiele S, Drennan J (2016) A hierarchy-of-effects approach to designing a social marketing game. J Nonprofit Public Sect Mark 28:105–128. https://doi.org/10.1080/10495142.2014.988081

Statista (2017) Video games advertising spending worldwide from 2010 to 2020 (in billion U.S. dollars). https://www.statista.com/statistics/238140/global-video-games-advertising-revenue/. Accessed 5 Dec 2017

The Motion Monkey (2017) UK advergame design & development. https://www.themotionmonkey.co.uk/advergames/. Accessed 6 Dec 2017

United Nations World Food Programme (2017) Food force. https://web.archive.org/web/20050605073447/http://www.food-force.com. Accessed 12 Jun 2017

Unity Technologies (2017) Unity. https://unity3d.com/. Accessed 10 Dec 2017

U.S. Army (2017) America's army. https://www.americasarmy.com/. Accessed 12 Jun 2017

Vecchiato G, Maglione AG, Cherubino P et al (2014) Neurophysiological tools to investigate consumer's gender differences during the observation of TV commercials, computational and mathematical methods in medicine. Comput Math Methods Med, 1–12

Yam A, Russell-Bennett R, Foth M, Mulcahy R (2017) How does serious m-game technology encourage low-income households to perform socially-responsible behaviors? Psychol Mark 34:394–409. https://doi.org/10.1002/mar.20996

Yenigun S (2012) Presidential campaigns rock the gamer vote. https://www.npr.org/2012/10/01/162103528/presidential-campaigns-rock-the-gamer-vote. Accessed 10 Dec 2017

Zyraffa (2017) Segregowanie śmieci. http://www.zyraffa.pl/ekologia/kat/Gry/smieci. Accessed 6 Dec 2017

Chapter 11
Application of the Survival Trees for Estimation of the Propensity to Accepting a Job and Resignation from the Labour Office Mediation by the Long-Term Unemployed People

Beata Bieszk-Stolorz and Krzysztof Dmytrów

Abstract The obstacles in finding a job by the long-term unemployed people are their behaviours resulting from cognitive and emotional mistakes. Long-term unemployment results in depreciation of the human capital and discouragement to further job searching. In order to lead the effective social policy, identification of threatened group is essential. The goal of the research was estimation of the influence of gender, age and education on the probability of exit from the long-term registered unemployment and resignation from the labour office mediation. Due to the fact that there were censored observations, survival analysis methods were used. Survival trees were built by means of the Kaplan–Meier estimators, and the statistics of the log-rank test were used as splitting criteria. They are the example of methods of recursive binary partitioning, which aim in creation of homogeneous subsets with respect to the analysed response variables. In the analysis, the conditional inference trees were used.

Keywords Survival trees · Kaplan–Meier estimator · Log-rank test
Registered long-term unemployment

B. Bieszk-Stolorz · K. Dmytrów (✉)
University of Szczecin, Institute of Econometrics and Statistics,
ul. Mickiewicza 64, 71-101 Szczecin, Poland
e-mail: krzysztof.dmytrow@usz.edu.pl

B. Bieszk-Stolorz
e-mail: beatus@wneiz.pl

K. Nermend and M. Łatuszyńska (eds.), *Problems, Methods and Tools in Experimental and Behavioral Economics*, Springer Proceedings in Business and Economics, https://doi.org/10.1007/978-3-319-99187-0_11

11.1 Introduction

Behavioural economics describes and explains the people's economic behaviours. People do not always make decisions with accordance to the *homo oeconomicus* model. Behavioural economics comprises behavioural anomalies, or the events that are hard to explain by the mainstream economics. It even completely denies the standard model (Just 2014). People constantly learn, communicate, consult and influence on mutual assessments, including the risk perception. All this together makes that individual behaviours gain social significance, which has influence on the macroeconomic occurrences. Works of the behavioural economists are mostly the extension and complement of the neo-Keynesian theories. Empirical researches confirm the existence of human behaviours that are partly contradictory to standard economic assumptions. Humans can make systematic mistakes, become discouraged, postpone their actions and have non-standard preferences and opinions (DellaVigna 2009). If we consider the labour market, behavioural economics most often deals with two problems: the existence of voluntary unemployment and relations between inflation and unemployment.

The obstacles in finding job by the unemployed are their personal behaviours resulting from cognitive and emotional mistakes. Job searching is most often the unpleasant and cost-generating activity with profits that are postponed. Many unemployed people regularly delay job searching and agree to be unemployed (Warr and Jackson 1987). The state economic policy connected with the excess protection of the unemployed people can also influence the extension of unemployment duration. Researches confirm that receiving the unemployment benefit influence the extension of the unemployment duration (Bieszk-Stolorz and Markowicz 2015). Consequently, the number of the long-term unemployed people increases as well as the risk of depreciation of the human capital.

We can observe steady improvement of the situation on the Polish labour market, confirmed by decrease of the unemployment rate. Processes occurring on the Polish labour market are similar to these on the Slovak and Hungarian markets (Hadaś-Dyduch et al. 2016). Social policy of the state influences the situation on the labour market. This policy is realised—among the other things—by the labour offices. The activisation activities that are focused on the particularly threatened by the unemployment people have positive impact on this situation.

Labour market analyses generally focus on the persons that leave the unemployment by finding a job. However, on the basis of rich data collected by the labour offices, we can also analyse other reasons of de-registration, such as: retirement, receiving pension, going abroad for period longer than 30 days, change of residence, death, granting pre-retirement allowance. There are two main causes of de-registrations: finding a job and removal from the register. Removal happens when the unemployed person refuses to accept proposed employment or is absent in the labour office in due time. In years 2008–2016, the share of removal in total de-registrations decreased from approximately 32% in 2008 to 19.6% in 2016 (Fig. 11.1). The removal is often followed by punishment the unemployed person,

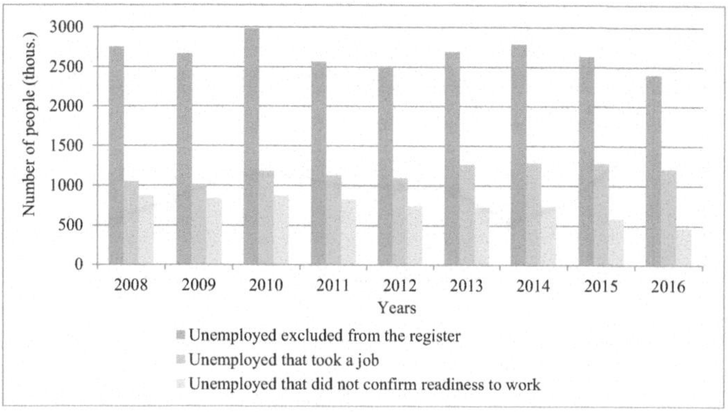

Fig. 11.1 Number of de-registrations from labour offices in Poland in years 2008–2016 (in thousands) [own study on the basis of the: Yearbook of Labour Statistics 2010, 2012, 2015, 2016 (2011, 2013, 2016, 2017)]

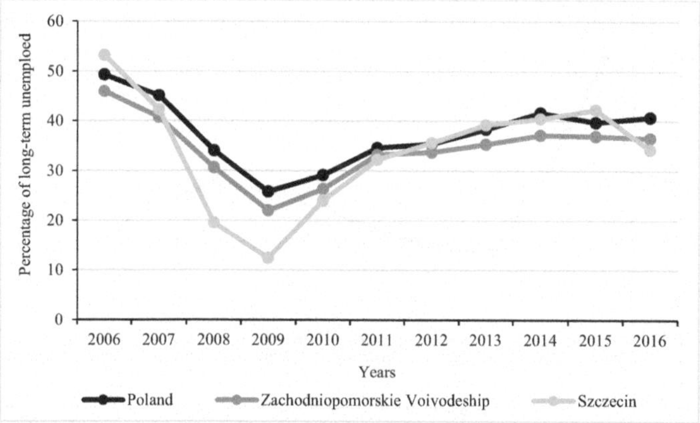

Fig. 11.2 Percentage of the long-term unemployed persons in total registered unemployed persons in years 2006–2016 (own study)

which is the difficulty of reclaiming the status of the unemployed, hence the right to the health insurance and benefit. Among the removed persons, there are also the long-term unemployed people. The long-term unemployment happens if person remains in the register for at least 12 months during two last years. The share of the long-term unemployed persons in total number of registered unemployed persons in Poland in the period from the year 2006 to the beginning of the crisis in 2009 decreased (minimum in 2009 was 25.8%), after which it rose to about 40% in years 2014–2016 (Fig. 11.2). The registered unemployment rate in years 2006–2008 decreased from 14.8 to 9.5%. Afterwards, it increased to 13.4% in 2013, while in the subsequent years it decreased to 8.2% (Fig. 11.3). In the analysed period,

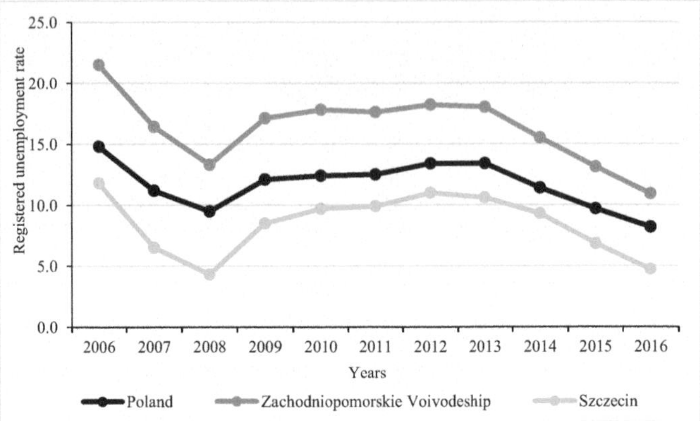

Fig. 11.3 Registered unemployment rate in Poland, Zachodniopomorskie Voivodeship and Szczecin in years 2006–2016 (own study)

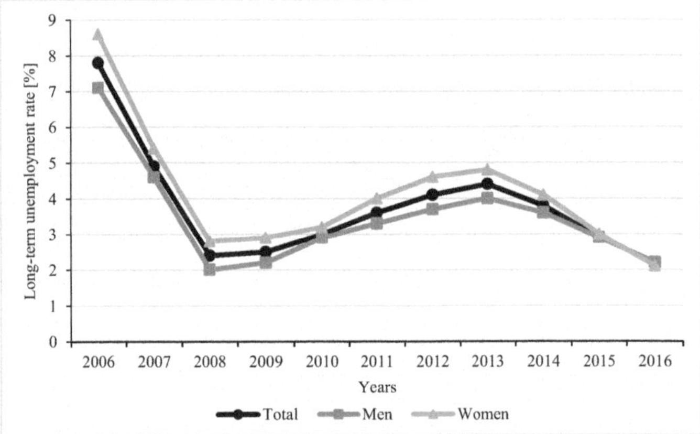

Fig. 11.4 Long-term unemployment rate in Poland in years 2006–2016 according to BAEL (own study on the basis of http://bdm.stat.gov.pl/)

the registered unemployment rate in the Zachodniopomorskie Voivodeship was higher than in Poland and in Szczecin—it was lower. The directions of changes were the same. Similar directions of changes were observed for the long-term unemployment rate (Fig. 11.4). However, the decrease in years 2006–2008 was much stronger (from 7.8 to 2.4%) than for the general registered unemployment rate. It is characteristic that this rate was higher for women than for men (with the exception of the year 2016).

The goal of the research was estimation of the influence of gender, age and education on the probability of exit from the long-term registered unemployment and resignation from the labour office mediation. The analysis carried out is important in order to implement effective labour market policies. It enables to indicate the groups of long-term unemployed people, to whom the additional supporting programmes should be addressed. Selected methods of survival analysis will be applied in the research.

11.2 Data Used in the Research

In the analysis, the individual data about the long-term unemployed persons de-registered from the Poviat Labour Office in Szczecin (Poland) in the year 2015 were used. They contain information about gender, age, education, time of registration and the cause of de-registration. In 2015 in Szczecin, 25,881 unemployed persons were de-registered. Among them, the data referring to 5266 long-term unemployed persons were extracted (about 20% of all unemployed).

The event that terminated each observation was the moment of de-registration from the labour office list. The unemployment duration was the time since the registration until de-registration and was denoted by T. Among many others, the two main reasons of de-registration were considered—finding a job and removal. Together they consisted almost 82% of all terminating events (37 and 45%, respectively). The size of each group is presented in Table 11.1. The job-finding (Job) consists of three main subgroups: finding a job or another form of employment, taking up a government subsidised form of employment and entrepreneurial activity. The removal from register category includes the unemployed individual's

Table 11.1 Structure of analysed long-term unemployed people (own study)

Group	Total	Job	Removal
Total	5266	1960	2371
Gender			
Women (K or 1)	2730	1108	1100
Men (M or 0)	2536	852	1271
Age			
18–24 (W_1)	270	102	140
25–34 (W_2)	1264	569	535
35–44 (W_3)	1293	508	634
45–54 (W_4)	1022	367	511
55–59 (W_5)	791	288	341
60–64 (W_6)	626	126	210
Education			
At most lower secondary (S_1)	1420	375	806
Basic vocational (S_2)	1384	457	691
General secondary (S_3)	575	238	242
Vocational secondary (S_4)	998	408	379
Higher (S_5)	889	482	253

reluctance to cooperate with the labour office and have been removed from the register through their own fault or on their own request. The remaining causes of de-registration are less numerous and, as previous research showed, each of them had a marginal effect on the probability of de-registration (Bieszk-Stolorz 2017a).

11.3 Research Methodology

The first fields, in which the survival analysis methods were applied, were the medicine, demography and reliability theory. Nowadays, it is more and more often used in analysis of the social and economic occurrences, e.g. in the labour market analysis. Such approach helps to analyse the economic activity of the population (Landmesser 2013) or duration of unemployment (Bieszk-Stolorz 2017b; Bieszk-Stolorz and Markowicz 2012). The duration at given state (duration of the company activity, duration of unemployment, duration of debt payment) is the random variable T. The basis for such analysis is the survival function, defined as follows (Kleinbaum and Klein 2005):

$$S(t) = P(t > T) = 1 - F(t) \tag{11.1}$$

where

T the event duration,
$F(t)$ the cumulative distribution function of the random variable T.

The most widely used estimator of the survival function is the Kaplan–Meier estimator (Kaplan and Meier 1958):

$$\hat{S}(t) = \prod\nolimits_{j:t_j \leq t} \left(1 - \frac{d_j}{n_j}\right) \tag{11.2}$$

where

d_j the number of events at the moment t_j,
n_j the number of individuals at risk by the moment t_j.

The survival function $S(t)$ determines the probability that specific event will not occur at least by the time t. For certain events, it is more convenient to analyse the cumulative distribution function $F(t)$, which is the probability that the event will occur at most by the time t. In case of definition of the event as de-registration from the labour office, the survival function estimator is the probability that the long-term unemployed person remains in the register, while the estimator of the cumulative distribution function is the probability of de-registration. On the basis of the survival function, quartiles of survival time can be estimated. They are determined in the point, where the survival function takes the values of 0.25, 0.5 and 0.75 (Aalen et al. 2008).

Analysed population of long-term unemployed people, de-registered in 2015 can be divided into various groups on the basis of analysed variables. For each group, the survival function can be estimated and the hypothesis about the significant differences between these function for each group can be verified. Due to the fact that the duration times are unknown, the rank-based, nonparametric tests are used. Their main drawback is that they are effective only for large samples, while their effectiveness in case of small samples is not well recognised. The most commonly used test for comparison of two survival curves is the log-rank test (Klein and Moeschberger 2003; Moore 2016). It verifies the hypothesis that the survival curves for two groups are the same. Assuming that the null hypothesis is true, the test statistics is chi-square distributed with one degree of freedom. This test has the highest power, when the difference between the hazard functions for single subgroups is constant in time (Landmesser 2013). Because of the limitations resulting from assumptions of other tests and initial analysis with use of the function $\ln(-\ln S(t))$, the validity of application of the log-rank test in the study was confirmed.

If we want to distinguish homogeneous groups from the analysed population with respect to the shape of survival curves, the survival trees become a very useful tool. They are constructed on the basis of the idea of binary partitioning and belong to the group of conditional inference trees. Their advantage over other methods results from the fact that they require less assumptions and they are applicable to various data structures (Al-Nachawati et al. 2010; Bou-Hamad et al. 2009; Zhou and McArdle 2015; LeBlanc and Crowley 1993). There are two opposite aspects of constructing any tree—partitioning the data and pruning the tree (Cappelli and Zhang 2007). The idea that stands behind partitioning is selection of homogeneous groups with respect to the level of analysed covariates. It is done on the basis of splitting criterion, which can be based on the impurity measure or on the value of the log-rank test statistics. Partitioning occurs until the stopping criterion is reached. Splitting is necessary in order to obtain the homogeneous groups of units; however, it very often happens (especially for large samples) that the tree becomes very large, with too many final nodes and, as a consequence, overfitted and illegible. The partitioning stops when the stopping criterion is achieved, i.e. when the empirical significance level of the log-rank test statistics exceeds assumed value (if the log-rank test is used for data partitioning). Especially for large samples, this approach is not always effective (and leads to too large tree). In order to stop partitioning before the stopping criterion is achieved, several approaches can be used. One of them is defining the minimum group size, for which the partitioning may occur. Other, similar to this approach is defining the minimum group size in the final node. Eventually, we can define the maximum tree depth (Mudunuru 2016).

Presented in the chapter, survival trees were constructed by using the `ctree` function in the `partykit` package in R language. Every observed long-term unemployed person was described by the following triplet: $\{y_i, \delta_i, \mathbf{x}_i\}$, where y_i was the duration of registration, δ_i indicated whether the observation is censored or not (1—uncensored, 0—censored) and the $\mathbf{x}_i$ vector contained three covariates: gender, age and education. The duration of registration was the numerical continuous variable, censoring was the dichotomic variable. The covariates were the categorical variables. In the `ctree_control` function, two default parameters were changed: the `mincriterion` was set at 0.99 in order to set the significance level at 0.01 and by means of the `maxdepth` parameter the tree was pruned at the third level.

11.4 Results of the Empirical Analysis

The analysis was conducted in two stages. The first one consisted in selection of homogeneous groups of long-term unemployed people with respect to the probability of exit from long-term unemployment to work. Figure 11.5 shows that in the first step, the long-term unemployed people were divided with respect to education—into persons with higher education and the remaining ones. In the next step, both education groups were divided with respect to age—the group of long-term unemployed people with at most secondary education was divided into two groups—persons up to 59 years old and the remaining ones. The first group was further divided again with respect to the education into the group with at most lower secondary and the one with vocational and secondary education. The second group (long-term unemployed persons at the age of 60 years and more with at most secondary education) was further divided with respect to gender. The second group obtained in the first step (long-term unemployed people with higher education) was further divided with respect to age—into the group of the long-term unemployed people at the age of 18–24, 25–34 and 45–54 years and the remaining ones. As a result, six final nodes (or six homogeneous groups of long-term unemployed people that were de-registered to work in the year 2015) were obtained. They are presented in Table 11.2. The lowest probability of exit from long-term unemployment to work was observed for long-term unemployed women at the age of 60 years and older with at most secondary education (node 8) and the highest—for the long-term

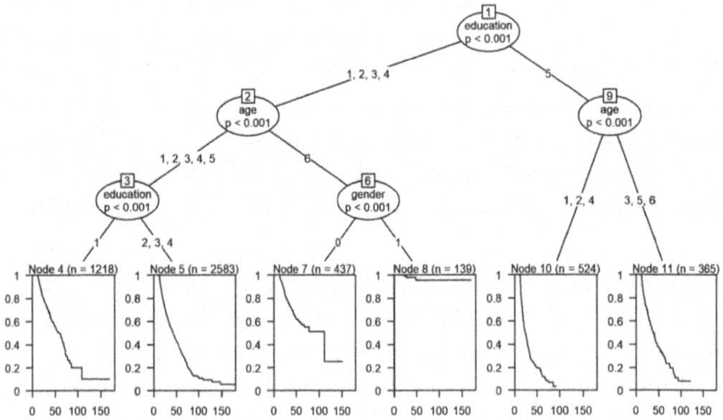

Fig. 11.5 Survival tree for de-registration to work (own study)

Table 11.2 Homogeneous groups of long-term-unemployed persons—de-registration to work (own study)

Specification	Number of the final node					
	4	5	7	8	10	11
Education	S_1	S_2–S_4	S_1–S_4	S_1–S_4	S_5	S_5
Age	W_1–W_5	W_1–W_5	W_6	W_6	W_1, W_2, W_4	W_3, W_5, W_6
Gender	K, M	K, M	M	K	K, M	K, M

Table 11.3 Quartiles of the time to finding a job (months) (own study)

Number of the final node	Lower quartile	Median	Upper quartile
4	30.09	58.66	80.08
5	22.68	42.14	72.41
7	33.37	79.11	–
8	–	–	–
10	15.84	23.74	40.46
11	20.25	37.17	65.31

unemployed people at the age of 18–24, 25–34 and 45–54 years with higher education (node 10). It is confirmed by the quartiles of the survival time presented in Table 11.3. All quartiles for the group in the node 8 were higher than 180 months. The lowest quartiles of the survival time (staying in the register) were observed for the group in the node 10—the median survival time for this group was less than 2 years. The exact courses of the Kaplan–Meier estimators for the long-term unemployed people de-registered to work are presented in Fig. 11.6. The distribution of time to de-registration to work was extremely positively skewed with the highest probability of leaving the register within first six months (starting from 12 months—Fig. 11.7).

In the second stage of the analysis, homogeneous groups of long-term unemployed people with respect to the probability of removal from the register were selected. As shown in Fig. 11.8, education was not the significant splitting criterion. In the first step, the long-term unemployed people that were removed from the register in the year 2015, were divided with respect to age—into persons at the age of at most 59 years and older. The first group was further divided with respect to gender. Males were further again divided with respect to age—into long-term unemployed males not older than 54 years and long-term unemployed males at the age group of 55–59 years. Females were also further divided with respect to age into long-term unemployed females not older than 24 years and long-term unemployed females at the age of 25–59 years. The group of oldest long-term unemployed people, obtained in the first step, was further divided with respect to gender. Eventually, six homogeneous groups of long-term unemployed people removed from the register in the year 2015 were selected. They are presented in Table 11.4.

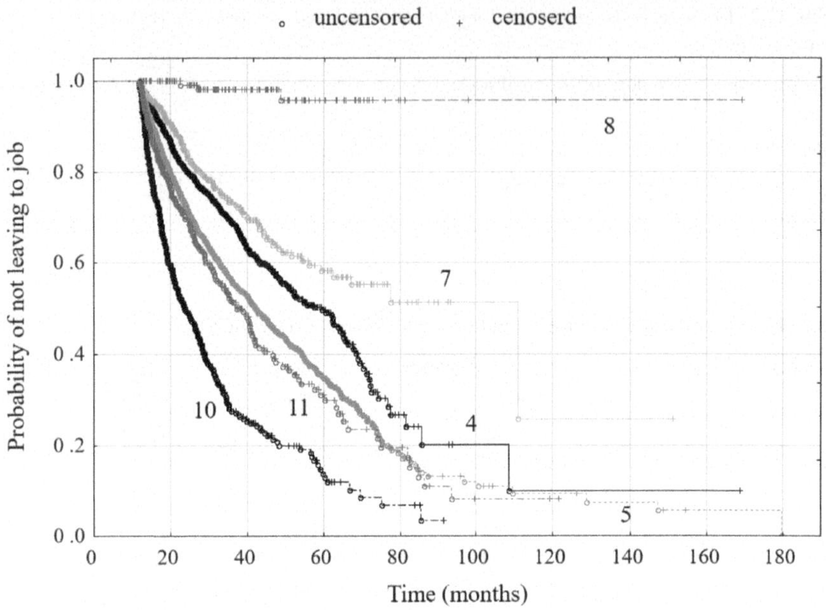

Fig. 11.6 The Kaplan–Meier estimators for not leaving to job (own study)

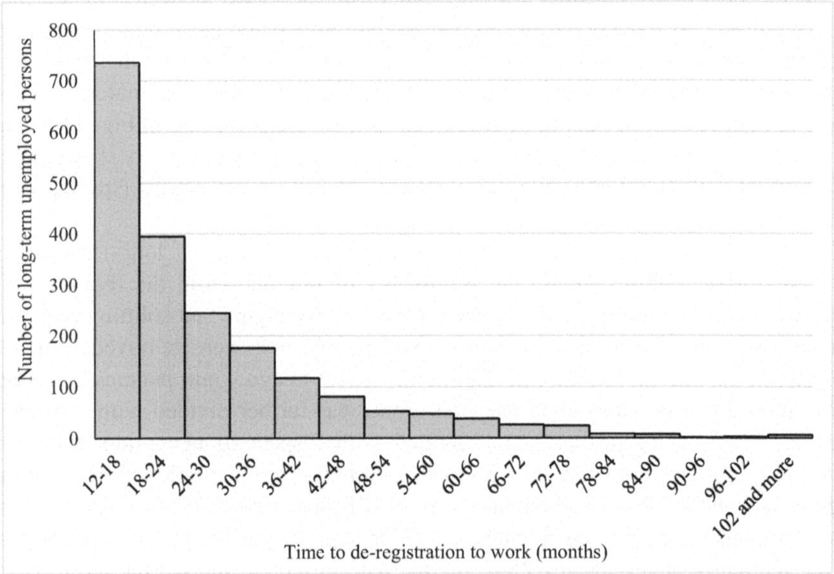

Fig. 11.7 Distribution of time to de-registration to work (own study)

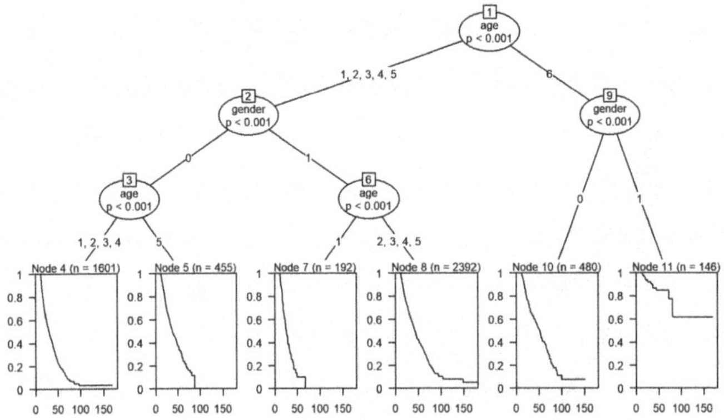

Fig. 11.8 Survival tree for removal from the register. *Source* Own study

Table 11.4 Homogeneous groups of long-term unemployed persons–removal from the register (own study)

Specification	Number of the final node					
	4	5	7	8	10	11
Age	W_1–W_4	W_5	W_1	W_2–W_5	W_6	W_6
Gender	*M*	*M*	*K*	*K*	*M*	*K*

Table 11.5 Quartiles of the time to removal from the register (months) (own study)

Number of the final node	Lower quartile	Median	Upper quartile
4	18.49	29.88	48.13
5	22.71	37.59	61.46
7	17.89	25.76	37.60
8	23.57	42.56	69.18
10	26.48	51.25	73.96
11	73.20	–	–

The lowest probability of removal from the register was observed for the oldest long-term unemployed women (node 11) and the highest—for the youngest long-term unemployed women (node 7). It is confirmed by the quartiles of duration time presented in Table 11.5. Only the lower quartile could have been estimated for the group in the node 11—it was over 73 months. On the other hand, the median time of staying in the register for the quickest removed group—the youngest long-term unemployed women—was just above 2 years and 1 month. The exact courses of the Kaplan–Meier estimators for the long-term unemployed people removed from the register are presented in Fig. 11.9. The distribution of time to

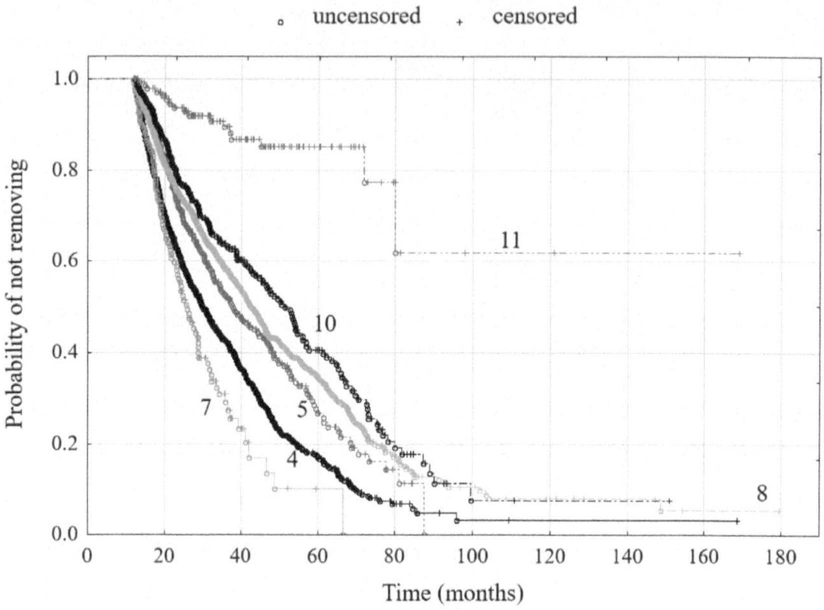

Fig. 11.9 The Kaplan–Meier estimators for not removing from the register (own study)

removal was extremely positively skewed with the highest probability of being removed from the register within first six months (starting from 12 months—Fig. 11.10).

11.5 Conclusions

In the chapter, the analysis of exit from the registered long-term unemployment was conducted by means of the survival trees. The two main causes of de-registration from the labour office were analysed: finding a job and removal from the register. The research allowed to distinguish homogeneous groups of long-term unemployed people de-registered in the year 2015 with respect to three covariates—gender, age and education. From the point of view of the labour market policy directed to particularly threatened groups, for de-registration to work the most threatened group is the group with the lowest probability of de-registration, while for removal, the most threatened group is the group with the highest probability of removal from the register. We also should bear in mind that the long-term unemployed people are themselves particularly threatened group on the labour market. However, special attention should be put on one group of long-term unemployed persons—women at

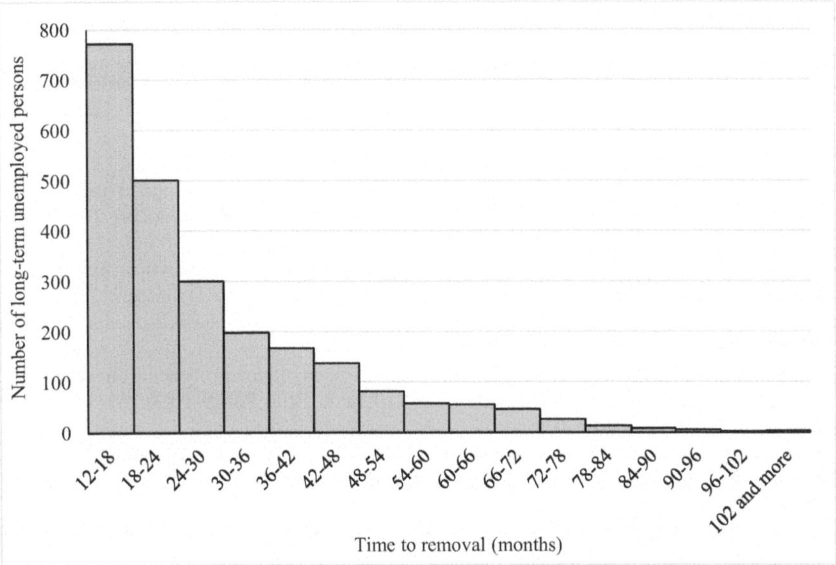

Fig. 11.10 Distribution of time to removal from the register (own study)

the age of 60 years and more. They are both de-registered to work and removed with the lowest probability. It is the result of the fact that it was the new group in the registers of labour offices. Its existence results from increase of the retirement age in Poland in the year 2013.[1] Low probability of leaving the register resulted from the fact that there were little job offers for this group. On the other hand, long-term unemployed persons that are removed from the register through their own fault or on their own request begun being tired of waiting for job offers. It could also have happened that these persons found jobs on their own (without the mediation of the labour office) and forgot to complete the formalities of de-registration or found jobs in the so-called grey economy. It is worth noting that in case of de-registration to work of long-term unemployed people all covariates (gender, age and education) were the significant splitting criteria, while for removal—only gender and age. Future area of research will include comparison of the results obtained in this chapter with the results obtained for non-long-term unemployed people, de-registered in the year 2015.

[1]In 2013, retirement age for women and men was raised from 60 to 67 years for women and from 65 to 67 years for men. Changes were supposed to take place gradually.

References

Aalen O, Borgan O, Gjessing H (2008) Survival and event history analysis. A process point of view. Springer, New York

Al-Nachawati H, Ismail M, Almohisen A (2010) Tree-structured analysis of survival data and its application using SAS software. J King Saud Univ (Science) 22:251–255

Bieszk-Stolorz B (2017a) Cumulative incidence function in studies on the duration of the unemployment exit process. Folia Oecon Stetin 17(1):138–150. https://doi.org/10.1515/foli-2017-0011

Bieszk-Stolorz B (2017b) The impact of gender on routes for registered unemployment exit in Poland. Equilibrium. Q J Econ Econ Policy 12(4):733–749. https://doi.org/10.24136/eq.v12i4.38

Bieszk-Stolorz B, Markowicz I (2012) Modele regresji Coxa w analizie bezrobocia. CeDeWu, Warszawa

Bieszk-Stolorz B, Markowicz I (2015) Influence of unemployment benefit on duration of registered unemployment spells. Equilibrium. Q J Econ Econ Policy 10(3):167–183. https://doi.org/10.12775/equil.2015.031

Bou-Hamad I, Larocque D, Ben-Ameur H, Mâsse LC, Vitaro F, Tremblay RE (2009) Discrete-time survival trees. Can J Statist Rev Can Statist 37(1):17–32. https://doi.org/10.1002/cjs.10007

Cappelli C, Zhang H (2007) Survival Trees. In: Vieu P (ed) Härdle W,·Mori Y. Statistical Methods for Biostatistics and Related Fields Springer-Verlag, Berlin, pp 167–179

DellaVigna S (2009) Psychology and economics. evidence from the field. J Econ Lit 47(2):315–372. https://doi.org/10.1257/jel.47.2.315

Hadaś-Dyduch M, Pietrzak MB, Balcerzak AP (2016) Wavelet analysis of unemployment rate in Visegrad Countries. In: Kliestik T (ed) 16th international scientific conference on globalization and its socio-economic consequences. University of Zilina, Zilina, pp 595–602

Just DR (2014) Introduction to behavioral economics. Noneconomic factors that shape economic decisions. Wiley, Hoboken

Kaplan EL, Meier P (1958) Non-parametric estimation from incomplete observations. J Am Stat Assoc 53:457–481

Klein JP, Moeschberger ML (2003) Survival analysis. Techniques for censored and truncated data. Springer, New York

Kleinbaum D, Klein M (2005) Survival analysis. A self-learning text. Springer, New York

Landmesser J (2013) Wykorzystanie metod analizy czasu trwania do badania aktywności ekonomicznej ludności w Polsce. Wydawnictwo SGGW, Warszawa

LeBlanc M, Crowley J (1993) Survival trees by goodness of split. J Am Statist Assoc 88 (422):457–467. https://doi.org/10.2307/2290325

Moore DF (2016) Applied survival analysis using R. Springer International Publishing. https://doi.org/10.1007/978-3-319-31245-3

Mudunuru VR (2016) Modeling and survival analysis of breast cancer: a statistical, artificial neural network, and decision tree approach. Graduate theses and dissertations. http://scholarcommons.usf.edu/etd/6120. Accessed 10 Dec 2017

Warr P, Jackson P (1987) Adapting to unemployed role: a longitudinal investigation. Soc Sci Med 25(11):1219–1224. https://doi.org/10.1016/0277-9536(87)90369-8

Yearbook of Labour Statistics 2010, 2012, 2015, 2016 (2011, 2013, 2016, 2017). Central Statistical Office, Warsaw

Zhou Y, McArdle JJ (2015) Rationale and applications of survival tree and survival ensemble methods. Psychometrika 80(3):811–833. https://doi.org/10.1007/s11336-014-9413-1

Chapter 12
Expressing Our Preferences with the Use of AHP: The Game Is not Worth the Candle?

Jacek Cypryjański and Aleksandra Grzesiuk

Abstract Multi-criteria decision-making methods are widely used for comparing alternatives when there are multiple objectives. There are many alternative methods differing in their ease of use, validity, results, and appropriateness to resource planning. This chapter describes the results of a laboratory study which investigates preference in decision-making under certainty with multiple conflicting objectives and continuous decision variables. Techniques for solving such problems are taken from the fields of decision analysis and optimization: direct rating technique (SMART-like) and AHP. The purpose of the experiment was to determine the ability of each method to correctly express the decision-maker's preferences. If multi-criteria methods always support the decision-making process and better reflect to existing pattern of preferences of decision-maker, choices made in the decision-making process, obtained through multi-criteria methods, should be closer than the overall assessment. The results obtained in the experiment indicate that this is not the case. Furthermore, the research shows that the AHP method does not better reflect preferences. The results obtained by the AHP method significantly differ from the results obtained by the direct rating and overall assessment method.

Keywords Multi-criteria analysis · Multi-criteria decision-making
AHP · SMART · Direct rating · Holistic assessment

J. Cypryjański
Department of Computer Methods in Experimental Economics,
Faculty of Economics and Management, Institute of IT in Management,
University of Szczecin, Mickiewicza 64, 71-101 Szczecin, Poland
e-mail: jacek.cypryjanski@wneiz.pl

A. Grzesiuk (✉)
Faculty of Economics, West Pomeranian University of Technology
in Szczecin, Żołnierska 47, 71-210 Szczecin, Poland
e-mail: aleksandra.grzesiuk@gmail.com

K. Nermend and M. Łatuszyńska (eds.), *Problems, Methods and Tools in Experimental and Behavioral Economics*, Springer Proceedings in Business and Economics, https://doi.org/10.1007/978-3-319-99187-0_12

12.1 Introduction

The decision-making process leading to many goals simultaneously is an object of interest for researchers at various levels. Decision analysis methods cover both the psychological problems that are associated with unaided managerial decision-making and the decision analysis methods designed to overcome them.

As for the psychological approach, it focuses mainly on intuitive decision-making. Simon (1982) indicates that the limitations of the human mind make the decision-makers strive only to choose a satisfactory, not optimal, solution which he called a bounded rationality. These approximate practical methods are often referred to as heuristics.

Research carried out by psychologists indicates that decision-makers have a ready set of strategies to adapt to each situation, choosing a strategy that they think is the best for a given decision (Goodwin and Wright 2009). However, when making decisions that lead to multiple objectives concurrently, there may be situations where it is impossible to achieve all of the objectives. Then the decision-maker usually does not seek a compromise between these goals, which may lead to the rejection of relatively attractive options due to the fact that the good result they achieve in terms of certain goals does not compensate for the poor result in other respects (Goodwin and Wright 2009). Thus, a decision-maker who deals with too much information simultaneously and when making a choice uses simplified strategies (heuristics), rejecting in the decision process selection options that could be optimal for him.

In the next analyzed approach to the decision-making process, the starting point is the possibility of using decision-making analysis to help decision-makers who pursue multiple objectives.

The main goal of the multi-criteria methods (MCDM) is to help the decision-maker to better understand the decision problem. This is to happen by dividing the decision process into smaller parts and focusing on each of them separately. This approach is to help make a better, more rational decision than if the decision problem was considered as a whole (as it happens in heuristic methods).

The above arguments are the starting point in the presented study. In this chapter, the authors accept the following assumptions. First of all, multi-criteria methods are designed to protect decision-makers from the subconscious use of heuristics. Secondly, the assumption was that, using multi-criteria methods, decision-makers are better able to reflect their existing pattern of preferences at a given moment.

Because the literature cites many types of MCDM, the authors formulate a broad research question that a comparison, which method is better, assuming that all methods support the decision-making process, is unjustified because we do not know whether the multi-criteria methods really support decision-makers at all. If multi-criteria methods always support the decision-making process and better reflect preferences of decision-maker (in relation to heuristic methods), choices obtained through multi-criteria methods should be closer than the overall assessment.

In the presented study (experiment), participants make a choice using three methods: AHP, direct rating technique (SMART-like), and a holistic method. A direct rating (SMART-like) plays a special role here. SMART and AHP are multi-criteria methods and are based on the same criteria. But simultaneously SMART is based on the same scale as the overall assessment method.

Therefore, a main hypothesis was formulated (H1): the difference between preferences expressed through multi-criteria methods should be smaller than the difference between preferences expressed in one of these methods and the overall assessment.

12.2 Literature Review

As mentioned above, the authors consider two cardinal multi-criteria methods: the analytic hierarchy process (Saaty 1980) and direct rating, simple direct rating technique (SMART-like approach) originated from Von Winterfeldt and Edwards (1986).

AHP is probably the most widely used multi-criteria method that has gained wide acceptance among academics and practitioners (Gass 2005). The SMART method, in turn, is valued for relative simplicity and clarity, which means that regardless of the decision-maker's preparation, it can be easily applied and understood (Goodwin and Wright 2009).

In the literature, we find many papers comparing different aspects of the use of AHP and SMART as multi-criteria methods, including the possibilities of their application in specific situations and the potential convergence of results obtained using different methods (Lipovetsky 2008; Morera and Budescu 1998; Montis et al. 2005; Pöyhnön and Hämäläinen 2001; Velasquez and Hester 2013).

Lootsma (1997) and Lootsma and Schuut (1997) confronted the decision-making results using the AHP method and the SMART method. In comparative study, Lootsma and Schuut (1997) revealed an encouraging degree of similarity between the end results of the multiplicative AHP, SMART, and ELECTRE.

Lootsma (1997) sought the compatibility of these choices and noted the clear discrepancies that he believes the result from the applied measurement scales in both methods. Lootsma concludes that the problem arises from how a human thinks and evaluates alternatives, depending on how they are presented.

The literature review shows that multi-criteria methods lead to better decisions than heuristic methods. There are also experiments conducted to assess the extent to which multi-criteria methods support decision-makers to help and which of them in this process show greater effectiveness.

However, as Ishizaka et al. (2011) state, there is no clear evidence that AHP provides its users with their "best" choice and not an arbitrary one. Perhaps managers want only to claim to use a scientific process for their decisions but would have taken the same decisions without AHP.

These doubts are fully justified because it is difficult to find studies that would compare the choices made in the multi-criteria process with the choices of decision-makers in real-life situations. Tyszka (1986) cites several examples of experimental research, the results of which were confronted with real decisions in real-life situations. In general, decisions made in real life coincided with earlier choices obtained as a result of a multi-criteria analysis. But Tyszka (1986) also indicates some facts and observations less decisive for the decision-making analysis. One of such facts is the small variation (flatness distribution) of weights for various attributes obtained in the analysis process.

Another interesting aspect is the mechanism of evaluation in multi-criteria methods, which is based on the formulation of criteria by decision-makers. Bond et al. (2008) examined the ability of decision-makers to generate self-relevant objectives for consequential decisions. The results of these studies are important because the multi-criteria methods are intended to lead to “better” decisions. However, these methods are based on the formulation of a set of criteria and their ranking by decision-makers. Bond, Carlson, and Keeney put two fundamental questions: (1) to what extent are decision-makers able to list their own objectives, and (2) how important are objectives that decision-makers omit, but later acknowledge as relevant? As a result of series of experiments, they argue that decision-makers may commonly undertake decisions without considering many personally relevant objectives. An implication of their findings is that decisions could be poorer as a consequence of the failure to adequately generate objectives.

Doubts about the ability to generate a list of criteria and their ranking are also formulated by Tyszka (1986). He presented several arguments that lead to fears that the final result of the analysis is slightly affected by the “true” preferences of the decision-maker and these preferences are somehow “flattened” by the formal requirements of decision-making analysis.

Another important element is the selection of the indicator enabling the comparison of assessments made with different methods between each other. The study used the “distance” method. From the definition adopted by the authors, distance is a way of evaluating the application of multi-criteria methods. In this way, there is a distance between the choice made by each of the multi-criteria methods and the overall assessment. In the presented experiment, the distance between AHP and SMART is the distance resulting from the use of different scales, while the distance between SMART and the overall method is the distance between the multi-criteria and the overall (the scales are the same).

“The distance” as a measurement criterion is not a new indicator. It has been used, among others by Ishizak et al. (2011), as an assessment of the distance between the choice made using the AHP method and the selection based on the overall assessment.

In the reported study, the study of the distance of the choices made using multi-criteria methods with each other in relation to one of the multi-criteria methods and the overall assessment was used. In this context, the measure used is unique.

12.3 Experimental Procedure

The experiment was conducted with the participation of 180 students of the Faculty of Economics and Management at the University of Szczecin.

According to the authors, the fact of using students as participants in the experiment does not affect its results. Druckman and Kam (2009) investigate the problem and according to their findings, student subjects do not intrinsically pose a problem for a study's external validity.

The participants' task was to evaluate three pens: yellow BIC, transparent Pentel, and automatic no name pen using three methods: AHP (for this method we will use the designation A), direct rating/SMART (for this method we will use the designation D), and holistic judgment (for this method we will use the designation H).

Participants of the experiment were randomly divided into 12 groups differing in the order of application of the methods and applied measuring scales in methods D and H.

Such an arrangement of the experiment was to eliminate the possible element of the participants' fatigue, which could potentially disrupt the response. Additionally, we want to check if the participants' preferences change during the experiment. And we formulate and verify another hypothesis (H2): during the experiment there was no change in preferences of decision-maker.

The sequential change of the order of the methods used by the participants (presented in Table 12.1) would allow to verify this hypothesis. If the change did not take place, then the average distance among participants between the first and second implemented method would be smaller than between the first and third methods.

During the experiment, participants gave answers to questions asked by the computer program. Participants were asked about criteria, weight, evaluation, etc., so that pen ratings could be calculated using each method. In the first stage, the participants were asked about the criteria they follow when choosing a pen. Each participant could define between two and five of their own criteria (see Scheme 12.2, designation Nc) which then appeared in the A and D grades. In the

Table 12.1 Structure of the experiment

Sequence	Scale for *D* and *H*		Total
	Absolute	Relative	
A–D–H	15	15	30
A–H–D	15	15	30
D–A–H	15	15	30
D–H–A	15	15	30
H–A–D	15	15	30
H–D–A	15	15	30
Total	90	90	180

Source Own research

second stage, the participants made an assessment using the first, second, and third methods. During the experiment, the participants were not informed about the results of the calculations.

At the end, participants received (as a gift) a pen that, according to their answers, best suited their preferences. Because the prize was not valuable, most of the participants proceeded to experiment with the word-of-mouth, to the extent to which the computer can determine their preferences on the basis of the answers they provide. Apart from the reward, the participants' involvement in the research was undoubtedly due to the fact that the co-organizers of the experiment were their fellow students who used some of the results of the experiment in their master's theses.[1]

In the experiment, ten-point scales (from 1 to 10) were used in methods D and H. In absolute scale, each variant was assigned any value from this range, while in the relative scale the worst case was automatically evaluated as 1, the best variant was 10, whereas the intermediate variant was automatically the participant individually assigned a value from 1 to 10.

For each participant of the experiment, three grades were calculated (each made by a different method), which were then normalized (the best pen—1, intermediate pen—$(x - x_{min})/(x_{max} - x_{min})$, worst pen—0).

Then the distances between these evaluations were calculated using Euclidean distance:

$$e(H,A) = \sqrt{(H_1 - A_1)^2 + (H_2 - A_2)^2 + (H_3 - A_3)^2}$$

$$e(H,D) = \sqrt{(H_1 - D_1)^2 + (H_2 - D_2)^2 + (H_3 - D_3)^2}$$

$$e(A,D) = \sqrt{(A_1 - D_1)^2 + (A_2 - D_2)^2 + (A_3 - D_3)^2}$$

where A_1 means the assessment of the first pen using the AHP and analogously in succession, using the accepted method designations.

12.4 Research Results

The results are presented on the basis of triangles, where the sides of the triangles correspond to the average Euclidean distances (see Schemes 12.1 and 12.2). Friedman's test was used to verify hypotheses (nonparametric test for many dependent tests).

[1]The authors express their thanks for the help in preparing and conducting the experiment to Mr. Piotr Rawski—prepared the application for research, Mr. Paweł Olędzki, Ms. Justyna Procukiewicz, Mr. Damian Wilmański.

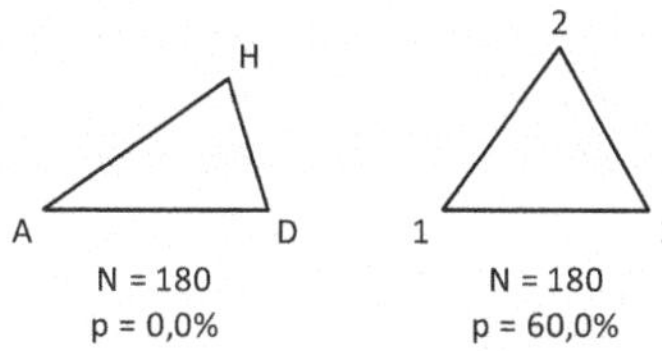

Scheme 12.1 Overall results. *Source* Own calculations based on the results of the experiment

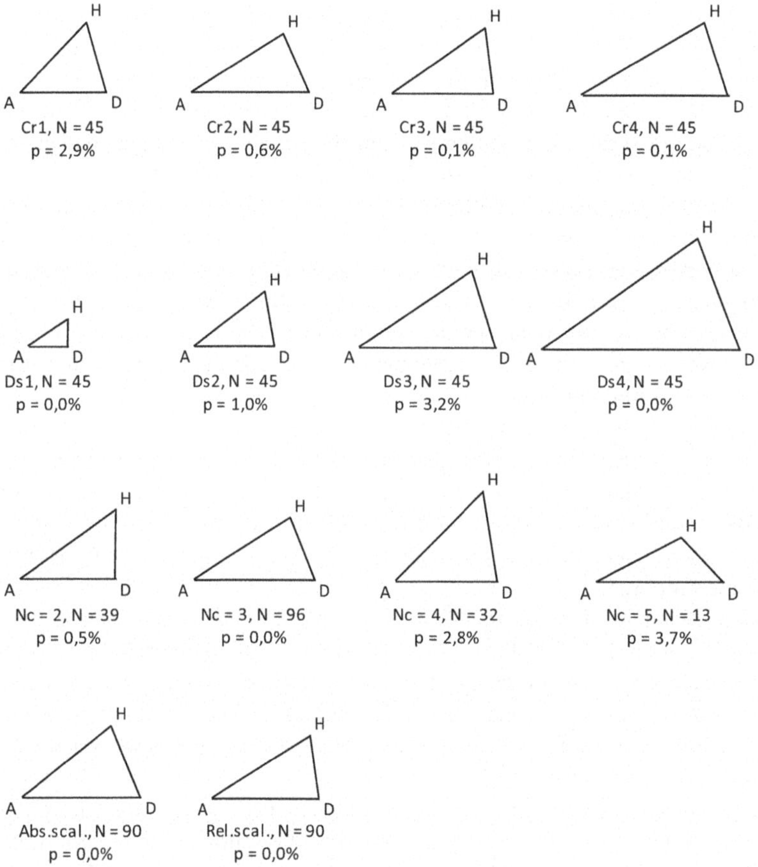

Scheme 12.2 Results presented in groups. Cr—Consistency ratio; Ds—Distance sum; Nc—the number of criteria defined by the experiment participants. *Source* Own calculations based on the results of the experiment

The presented research results negatively verify the proposed hypotheses (H1) that the difference between preferences expressed through multi-criteria methods should be smaller than the difference between preferences expressed in one of these methods and the overall assessment. The authors state that there is a statistically

Table 12.2 Distance calculation ($N = 180$)

	Average	Standard deviation
$e(H, D)$	0.433917	0.405899
$e(D, A)$	0.710106	0.462842
$e(H, A)$	0.723701	0.424168
Chi-square	41.98599	
p-value	0.0%	

Source Own calculations based on the results of the experiment

significant dependence that the evaluations performed by two different multi-criteria methods differ more than the multi-criteria and overall assessment if the same scale was used in both cases (the point of importance measurement method).

The obtained results show that it is not the results obtained by the holistic method that are significantly different from the results of MCDM, and the results obtained using the AHP method significantly differ from the others.

As we put the main hypothesis (H1): the difference between preferences expressed through multi-criteria methods should be smaller than the difference between preferences expressed in one of these methods and the overall assessment. Results presented in Scheme 12.1 do not support this hypothesis (see triangle with A, D, and H as the names of vertices and Table 12.2).

As presented in Table 12.1, participants evaluated alternatives using different methods set in different order.

Scheme 12.1 shows that the sequence of the methods in which the participants made the assessments did not affect the final results (see Scheme 12.1: triangle with numbers as the names of vertices). The distances between the first and second methods (regardless of which method for a given participant was the first and the second one) are comparable to the distances between the first and third. Hypothesis 2 was not supported.

The obtained result leads to the question whether the reason lies in the AHP method. The triangle 123 indicates that it was not a fatigue experiment or a change in the preferences of participants. It remains to check whether the reason is the organization of the experiment, especially the lack of interest of the participants.

To exclude issues related to the organization of the experiment, statistical tests for subgroups were carried out.

We have grouped the results of individual participants into four groups, according to the consistency of the answer. And the following three criteria for the division of the research sample into subgroups are distinguished—Cr factor, the sum of distances: Ds, number of criteria: Nc.

And so, in the Cr1 group were the most coherent answers, while in the Cr4 group—the least cohesive responses. As presented on Scheme 12.2, we calculate Cr for each participant and then divide into four groups.

Four subgroups were distinguished on the value of the factor: (Crl < 0.00; 0.14); (Cr2 < 0.14; 0.273); (Cr3 < 0.273; 0.49); (Cr4 < 0.49; 5.68). The use of this criterion was to verify the hypothesis (H3) that too large distance between AHP and

Table 12.3 Gamma correlation

	Gamma	p-value
$p(H)$ & e(Total)	−0.131852	0.031
$p(D)$ & e(Total)	0.056111	0.36
$p(A)$ & e(Total)	0.076296	0.213

Source Own calculations based on the results of the experiment

other methods corresponds to the fact that some participants in the AHP method provided inconsistent answers. Confirmation of this hypothesis would be a different shape of triangles, especially triangles Cr1 and Cr4.

In the same way, four subgroups were distinguished from on the value of the coefficient: (Ds1 < 0.18; 1.11); (Ds2 < 1.11; 1.70), (Ds3 < 1.70; 2.69); (Ds4 < 2.69; 3.92). The use of this criterion was to verify the hypothesis (H4) that the distance between the AHP and other methods is largely due to the fact that some participants were not involved and provided random answers. The confirmation of this hypothesis would be different shapes of triangles, especially triangles Ds1 and Ds4.

And finally, four subgroups were distinguished according to the number of criteria—participants who chose 2, 3, 4, and 5 criteria. In contrast to the two above-mentioned factors (Cr and Ds), these groups are not equal, as the choice of the number of criteria was left to the participants. The use of this criterion was to verify the hypothesis (H5) that the inaccuracies of the participants' responses/indications of participants, which increased with the number of criteria, were responsible for the large distance between AHP and other methods. The confirmation of this hypothesis would be different shapes of triangles, especially triangles Ds1 and Ds4.

As indicated in Scheme 12.2, hypotheses H3, H4, and H5 should be rejected because method A was distant in all triangles. In addition, Scheme 12.2 includes two triangles where the entire population is divided into relative and absolute scale (Abs.scal; Rel.scal). However, this division did not affect the results obtained.

The variable order of methods presented in Table 12.1 has also made it possible to check how the position of particular methods changes to the precision of the statements. We examined this by measuring gamma correlations between the place of the method and the sum of distances (see Table 12.3). It turned out that there is no correlation between the increase in AHP and direct rating. However, we found a negative correlation between the place of the total method and the sum of all distances. This may lead to the conclusion that together with the greater number of previously used MCDM, the decision-maker has a specific learning effect. The decision-maker deeply considered the decision (which was in a sense stimulated by the previously used MCDM) and better realizes its preferences, which is reflected in the overall assessment.

12.5 Conclusions

As presented above, the results negatively verify all the hypotheses: H1, H2, H3, H4, H5.

Therefore, the authors conclude that multi-criteria methods, in fact, do not allow to get rid of heuristics and make decisions better suited to our preferences. Particularly AHP is based on a pairwise comparison and people do not do it well. The experiment carried out by us suggests a lot of caution in the use of AHP. The results presented in the chapter are in contradiction with the results of research conducted by IIshizaka et al. (2011).

Following the discussion, the authors of the presented experiments claim that doubts about the use of MCDM come from the criteria generation problem. Is decision-maker able to define criteria in the selection process? It is possible that this is a problem—we can define two or three criteria. However, a larger number of criteria give decision-makers a clear problem, particularly when it is followed by the ranking procedure of these criteria. At this stage—the generation of criteria, and especially at the stage of assigning the ranks to these criteria, decision-makers can make mistakes resulting from the degree of difficulty of the task they faced. At the stage of generating criteria people, make mistakes and omit the criteria that are important to them, cannot verbalize their preferences well. As a result of these incorrectly assigned ranks or an incorrect set of criteria, the overall assessment is closer to the overall intuition of the decision-maker than the rational assessment, obtained by multi-criteria methods.

Suppose that the generic preferences of the decision-maker exist at the moment and they are interfered with by the heuristic. In such a situation, using the multi-criteria method should allow the decision-maker to eliminate heuristics by dividing the decision problem into smaller parts and introducing assessment criteria which means that two assessments made at the same time using different multi-criteria methods should give results closer to each other than the distance of each of these methods from the overall assessment (the overall assessment includes heuristics).

The discussion presented in the chapter suggests that such assumptions are incorrect. And thus, they ask the question whether multi-criteria methods, especially AHP, actually allow the decision-maker to better reflect preferences than overall assessment, including heuristics.

References

Bond SD, Carlson KA, Keeney R (2008) Generating objectives: can decision makers articulate what they want? Manage Sci 54(1):56–70

Druckman JN, Kam CD (2009) Students as experimental participants: a defense of the "narrow data base". https://ssrn.com/abstract=1498843

Gass S (2005) Model world: the great debate—MAUT versus AHP. Interfaces 35(4):308–312

Goodwin P, Wroght G (2009) Decision analysis for management judgement, 4th edn. Wiley, London

Ishizaka A, Balkenborg D, Kaplan T (2011) Does AHP help us make a choice? An experimental evaluation. J Oper Res Soc 62:1801–1812

Lipovetsky S (2008) Comparison among different patterns of priority vectors estimation methods. Int J Math Edu Sci Technol 39(3):301–311

Lootsma FA (1997) Multicriteria decision analysis in a decision tree. Eur J Oper Res 101:442–451

Lootsma FA, Schuut H (1997) The multiplicative AHP, SMART and ELECTRE in a common context. J Multi-Crit Decis Anal 6:185–196

Montis A, De Toro P, Droste-Franke B, Omann I, Stagl S (2005) Assessing the quality of different MCDA methods. In: Getzner M Spash CL Stagl S (eds) Alternatives for environmental valuation. Routledge Sigrid, pp 99–133

Morera OF, Budescu DV (1998) A psychometric analysis of the “divide and conquer” principle in multicriteria decision making. Organ Behav Hum Decis Process 75(3):187–206

Pöyhnön M, Hämäläinen RP (2001) On the convergence of multi attribute weighting methods. Eur J Oper Res 129:569–585

Saaty TL (1980) The analytic hierarchy process, planning, priority setting, resource allocation. McGraw-Hill, New York

Simon HA (1982) Models of bounded rationality. MIT Press, Cambridge

Tyszka T (1986) Analiza decyzyjna i psychologia decyzji. PWN Warszawa, pp 138–139

Velasquez M, Hester PT (2013) An analysis of multi-criteria decision making methods. Int J Oper Res 10(2):56–66

Von Winterfeldt D, Edwards W (1986) Decision analysis and behavioral research. Cambridge University Press, Cambridge

Chapter 13
Experimental Study of Consumer Behavior Using Agent-Based Simulation

Fatimah Furaiji and Małgorzata Łatuszyńska

Abstract The consumer is a key element in the marketing. Examining consumer behavior allows for a better understanding and forecasting factors influencing purchasing decisions, which in turn facilitates the formulation of effective marketing strategies. The aim of this study was to work out methodological basis for analyzing consumer behavior with application of agent-based simulation (ABS) as well as conducting simulation experiments using the elaborated methodology. The chapter presents ABS in the context of its applications in marketing research, proposes the methodology for consumer behavior analysis with the use of ABS, describes the concept of agent-based simulation model for investigating consumer behavior, and finally shows the results of simulation experiments executed for a case study. The case study focuses on the consumer behavior to buy electric appliances in Basra city and experiments relates to five exemplary marketing strategies. The results of the experiments confirm that the agent-based model can be a powerful tool for examining alternative marketing strategies rapidly, relatively cheaply, without requiring the actual commitment of resources.

Keywords Agent-based simulation · Consumer behavior · Simulation experiment

13.1 Introduction

The consumer is a key element in the marketing field. Examining consumer behavior allows for a better understanding and forecasting of factors connected with items purchased as well as motives and frequency of purchases. The process in

F. Furaiji
Faculty of Science, University of Basra, Karmt-Ali 1, 61004 Basra, Iraq
e-mail: fatmamoh1974@gmail.com

M. Łatuszyńska (✉)
Faculty of Economics and Management, University of Szczecin,
St. Mickiewicza 64, 71-101 Szczecin, Poland
e-mail: malgorzata.latuszynska@wneiz.pl

K. Nermend and M. Łatuszyńska (eds.), *Problems, Methods and Tools in Experimental and Behavioral Economics*, Springer Proceedings in Business and Economics, https://doi.org/10.1007/978-3-319-99187-0_13

which consumers make their purchase decisions has long been of great interest to researchers and practitioners. Current research in this field is trying to find answers to the following questions: How do consumers make purchase decisions? How can their behavior be checked under different conditions and scenarios? How can consequences of incorrect marketing plan decisions be eliminated? How can different marketing strategy alternatives be analyzed without any cost?

To find the answers to these questions, researchers apply many methods of modeling consumer behavior, including techniques based on econometrics, fuzzy logic, neural networks, decision trees, and genetic algorithms. These modeling techniques, while powerful, tend to be limited in the (1) number of factors that they can incorporate; (2) level of detail on each factor that they can accommodate; and (3) behavioral complexity that they can account for. Consequently, they may not be sufficient for holistically representing interdependent systems, such as those that commonly underlie the decisions of consumers (North et al. 2010). Hence, this study proposes applying agent-based simulation which is a relatively new approach in applications connected with investigating consumer behavior. It appeared as a perfect complement to other methods, because, thanks to the possibility of using business-driven rules in individuals descriptions, it allows defining holistic effects for system-level outcomes (North et al. 2010).

The aim of this study was to work out methodological basis for analyzing consumer behavior with application of agent-based simulation (ABS) as well as conducting simulation experiments using the elaborated methodology. The chapter presents ABS in the context of its applications in marketing research, proposes the methodology for consumer behavior analysis with the use of ABS, describes the concept of agent-based simulation model for investigating consumer behavior and finally shows the results of simulation experiments executed for a case study.

13.2 Agent-Based Simulation in Marketing Research

The origins of agent-based simulation come from complex adaptive systems, complexity science, and system science. As a form comprehensible for computers when it was first implemented, cellular automatons were created independently by S. Ulam and J. von Neumann in the 1940s. However, not until the beginning of the 1970s did it begin to take shape in the form which it is known today when J. Conway created the Game of Life (Gardner 1970). The current definition of an agent appeared in 1991 (Holland and Miller 1991). After this, the development of ABS accelerated and, during the last decade, has gained in popularity as a research method in many scientific fields (Latuszynska 2012).

In the agent-based simulation, the investigated system is modeled as a set of autonomous units, called agents. The decision-making processes are described at the micro-scale for each agent individually. Through the collective interaction between many agents and the environment in which they function, a macro-scale phenomenon emerges (Fig. 13.1) (Siebers and Aickelin 2008).

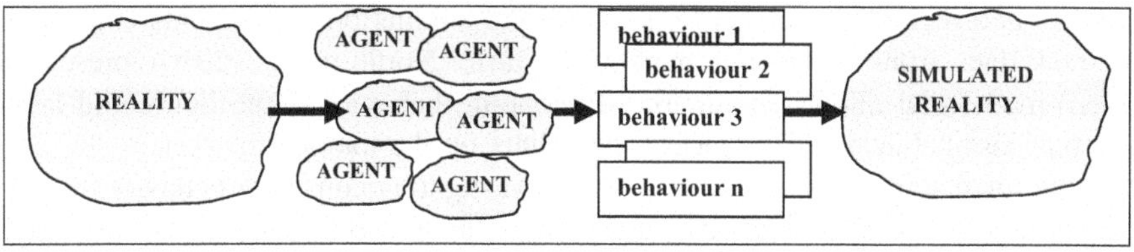

Fig. 13.1 Essence of an agent-based simulation. *Source* Based on Drogoul and Ferber (1994, p. 3)

There is no universal agreement in the literature on the precise definition of an agent beyond the essential property of autonomy. From a practical point of view, it is assumed that an agent has certain features (Macal and North 2014, p. 15): (1) is self-contained, modular, and uniquely identifiable individual; (2) is autonomous and self-directed, it can function independently in its environment and in contacts with other agents, at least in certain defined situations; (3) has a state that varies over time; (4) is social having dynamic interactions with other agents that influence its behavior. These assumptions particularly predestine agent-based simulation for applying in consumer behavior research, as it can show how out of many agents actions identifying individual and/or organizational consumers aggregated marketing phenomena arise.

During the last several years, scientific studies showing cases of agent-based simulation have been used in marketing research. These studies often concern consumer behavior in the context of innovation diffusion, such as in Watts (2002), Shaikh et al. (2006), Watts and Dodds (2007), Rahmandad and Sterman (2008), Goldenberg et al. (2009), and Delre et al. (2010). Another trend that applies ABS refers to research connected with the reception of products by the marketplace, as in Goldenberg et al. (2007, 2010). Many publications utilize agent-based approach in the analysis of companies positioning their influence on consumer behavior, including Buchta and Mazanec (2001), Wilkinson and Young (2002) and Tay and Lusch (2005, 2007), while others focus on the problem of moral behavior in relationship marketing, as in Hill and Watkins (2007, 2009), Watkins and Hill (2009), Midgley et al. (1997) and Marks et al. (2006).

Another important area that has applied agent-based simulation concerns shopping trends in specific markets. Many individual consumer choices are simulated to define how and why consumers choose a certain product or service. This type of approach is described by Collings et al. (2000), Brannon et al. (2000), Twomey and Cadman (2002), Wohltorf and Albayrak (2003), Robertson (2003), Kyrylov and Bonanni (2004), Schenk et al. (2007), Ulbinaite and Le Moullec (2010) and Kuhn et al. (2010).

Other studies presented more general deliberations on ABS approach in investigating consumer behavior, such as Janssen et al. (1999), Collings et al. (2000), Said et al. (2002), Janssen and Jager (2003), Jager (2006), Challet and Krause (2006), Rigopoulos et al. (2006) and Roozmand et al. (2011). These described agent-based models of consumer behavior based on marketing and behavior theories and then showed the results of several simulation experiments conducted by real data from a specific market. In turn, North et al. (2010) present a macro-model that allows simulation of shopping behavior at the household level and business behavior of producers and sellers on the national market.

Additional applications of ABS used in investigating consumer behavior include those on real supermarkets (Schwaiger and Stahmer 2003; Venables and Bilge 1998), consumer purchasing decision-making processes in the context of a decoy effect (Zhang and Zhang 2007) and those on advertising effectiveness (Cao 1999).

Despite a rich literature concerning agent-based simulation approaches in marketing applications along with a continual increase in its popularity, some researchers, e.g., Rand and Rust (2011) claim that the development of applications in this area is too slow. The reason is likely due to a lack of generally accepted standards for applying ABS in marketing research.

13.3 Methodology for Consumer Behavior Analysis Using ABS

Using agent-based simulation means obeying a certain defined modeling procedure (Fig. 13.2), which begins with formulating the problem and defining the aim for examining consumer behavior. In general, the goal of consumer research is the collection and compaction of information to support decision-making processes. This allows for an understanding of how consumers make purchase decisions, forecasting factors connected with the subject of purchase, determines the motives, and determines the frequency of purchase (Schiffman et al. 2008). Such research can significantly assist in the development of market strategies for a company.

The next step defines the simulation environment, especially the agents, space, and environment, and the system boundaries. An agent-based simulation model is a representation of a real-world system that incorporates time and the changes that occur over time (Helleboogh et al. 2007). First, a simulated environment can be divided into environmental entities represented by their own, distinct existence and characteristics of the real environment, which typically contains such entities as people, companies, branches, dealers, and projects. The entities are represented as agents who are connected with other agents who in some way influence their behavior. The interaction between entities occurs through existing social networks as well as information communicated by word-of-mouth.

The third step is responsible for defining the various methods and techniques for gathering and analyzing the data used to investigate the factors influencing consumers' purchase decision-making processes. For data gathering interviews, projective techniques, questionnaires, observations with check list, etc., can be used. The overview of the methods for gathering data from secondary and primary sources in marketing studies is included in Furaiji and Łatuszyńska (2012). In the study described in this chapter, authors used questionnaire method because

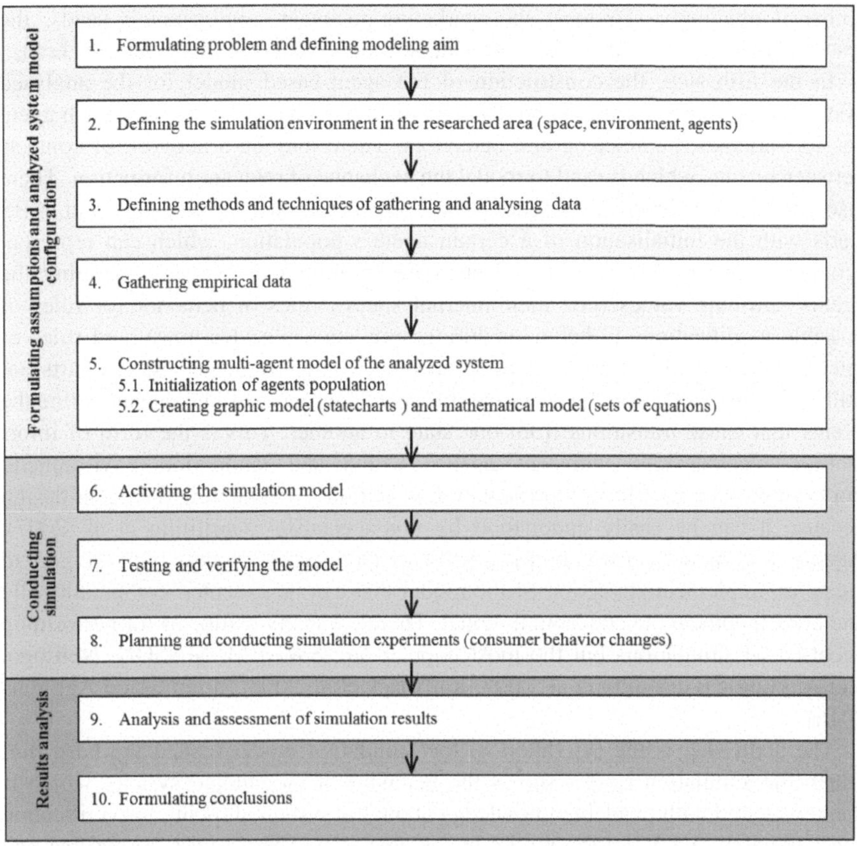

Fig. 13.2 Research procedure. *Source* Based on Wawrzyniak and Furaji (2013, p. 127)

it is the most common method of gathering data in marketing studies (Burns 1997; Crowther and Lancaster 2012; Lancaster 2007). Unfortunately, data obtained from questionnaires cannot provide information directly applicable to the agent creation process. Therefore, a statistical analysis of raw empirical data is performed to identify relations between variables and how precise the data appears. In addition to statistical analysis, artificial intelligence applications are used for creating a basis of consumer behavior rules for purchasing in the marketplace (Garifullin et al. 2007). In the current study, the rough set theory (Pawlak 2002) was used for searching the hidden, secret decision rules of consumers. More details on the rough set theory in marketing research are included for instance in Pawlak (2002) and Furaji et al. (2013).

Gathering empirical data occurs in the fourth step, which is the most arduous and expensive phase of the research project, so it deserves to be planned carefully. Researchers must determine the exact information needed and develop a plan to gather it efficiently. To meet the marketing manager's information needs, the research plan typically calls for gathering secondary data, primary data, or both.

In the fifth step, the construction of the agent-based model for the analysed system is developed basing on the data obtained from the previous step. Each agent has its variables, parameters, and behaviors. There may be a network of contacts between agents, which is used to model the exchange of relevant information. There also can be an environment affecting the agents and being affected by them. ABS starts with the initialisation of a certain agent's population, which can represent economic entities and other social phenomena. Initialization means defining the agents' attribute values (i.e., their internal states), rules of behavior (or rules of possible modifications to behavior during simulation, i.e., learning), and rules of interactive communication. For the conceptual design of agents, state charts are utilized in this work, which shows the different states an entity holds and define the events that cause transitions from one state to another. This is the form of information necessary to represent agents within the simulation environment. Furthermore, this graphical representation is helpful for validating the agent design because it can be easily understood by non-specialists (Garifullin et al. 2007). Agent-based model construction is a software engineering process with the goal to create an implemented version of the model that can be executed computationally and corresponds to the conceptual model. There are many platforms for performing agent-based simulations but the most popular are: SWARM, MASON, NetLogo, and AnyLogic (Garifullin et al. 2007; Railsback et al. 2006; Mourhir and Aklibous 2016).

The sixth step is the activation of the simulation model (called the base run) where the simulation results shows the behavior of the studied system, which is then compared with available knowledge about the system allowing for verification and validation (V&V) of the model in the next step. The model is re-verified and re-validated until it reflects the real system's behavior satisfactorily.

Verification and validation (step 7) is an essential part of the model development process. The difficulty for the V&V tasks is that there is no universal approach. O. Balci presents 75 validation, verification, and testing techniques that can be used in validating the models of manufacturing, engineering, and business processes. Detailed descriptions of these techniques are found in Balci (1997, 1998). For this research, Subject Matter Experts (SMEs) technique was used to validate the input and output of model because of the lack of real data connected with the investigation area.

The eighth step focuses on planning and conducting simulation experiments on consumer behavior changes. Experiments test the actual behavior of individuals under different conditions where individuals may be faced with choices under various circumstances, and the experimenter can observe how the consumers react. The experiments are conducted based on scenario planning techniques, which are used in the construction of different possible models for the future. Scenario planning in the field of consumer research is represented by marketing strategy tools used for improving decision-making against a background of possible future environments (Kosow and Gaßner 2008).

Analysis and assessment of simulation results occur in the ninth step where the base run results are compared with experimental run results. The simulation results are also analyzed and assessed using statistical methods. When the results of scenario are not able to provide information on the potential size of impacts in the real world, and where information about consumer beliefs and perceptions is required, another scenario is likely to be more useful.

The final step formulates conclusions resulting from the simulations and research, where the findings will be presented. This focuses on a detailed analysis by developing an experiment to study the effects of subjecting the simulation runs to different parameters representing different levels of the variables that were found to be most influential in the consumer behavior for the population studied. Researchers also will be exposed to the principal conclusions arising from the implementation of the methodology along with a conclusion with recommendations for future investigations.

13.4 The Structure of ABS Model

The structure of proposed ABS model of consumer behavior, as shown in Fig. 13.3, consists of components corresponding with defined by Macal and North (2014) basic elements of an agent-based model, i.e.,: (1) a set of agents and their attributes and behaviors; (2) a set of agent relationships and methods of interaction; (3) the agent's environment.

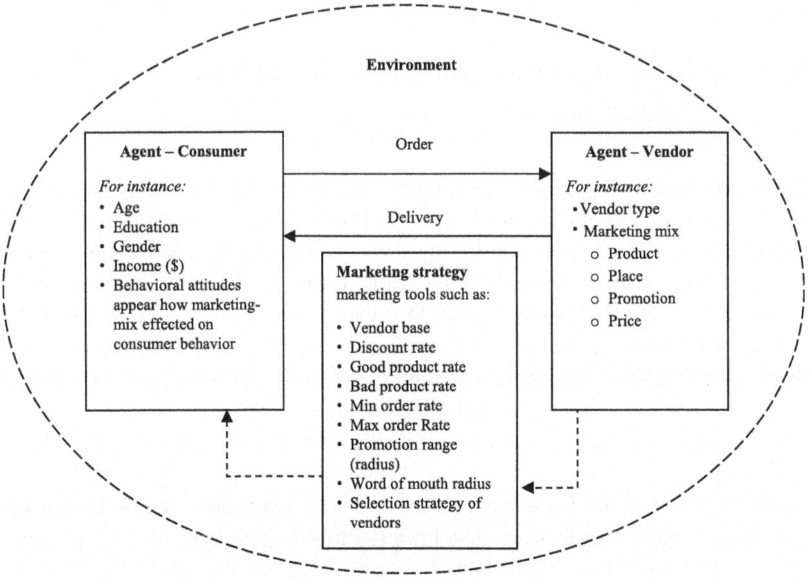

Fig. 13.3 Structure of the model of consumer behavior. *Source* Personal elaboration

13.4.1 A Set of Agents and Their Attributes and Behaviors

The proposed model of consumer behavior consists of agent objects, such as consumer and vendor. Each agent has a list of descriptive properties. The consumer agent has such properties as for instance: age, education, gender, income, and list of behavioral characteristics showing how marketing-mix affects consumer's behavior. Also, the vendor agent has properties, for example vendor type, product, place, promotion, price. Each agent has the probability of adopting a marketing strategy, such as advertising promotion, discounting promotion, and product quality, and even from word-of-mouth effects.

In this model, each agent has a set of neighboring agents. Agents numbering in the millions can be integrated into a model run on a computer, and each agent is designed with preliminary and untested rules of behavior, in order to test further scenarios and factors. Each individual agent is programmed to have individual characteristics and behaviors, which is the core intent of ABM. Behavior is diversified on the basis of the kind of agent (institutional versus individual) into what behaviors they can exhibit as conventional, vast, or bounded—as well as based on willingness to accept risk, and on the nature of the purchase.

State charts are used for the conceptual design of agents, show the different states of an entity, and define the events that cause a transition from one state to another based on rules. This is the information needed to represent agents later within the simulation environment. Furthermore, this form of graphical representation is also helpful for validating the agent design because it can be easily understood by non-specialists.

13.4.2 A Set of Agent Relationships and Methods of Interaction

Consumer behavior modeled in an agent-based method is formatted according to certain behavioral tendencies, guidelines, and interactions. Agents are informed by socioeconomic positions that are mirrored in reality and have individual character traits. In general, they follow two interfacing forms in the simulated market. The first form is between dissimilar consumer agents, which are based on social feedback (either positive or negative) from close relationship or through group gossip (Said et al. 2002). The second is when an agent interacts with other non-consumer agents, like vendors. Relevant activities include when they interact to discuss product quality, product cost, distribution areas, or commercial viewing.

The interaction process in agent-based model is formally defined following the recommendations of the Gaia methodology, the first complete methodology being proposed to guide the process of developing a multi-agent system from analysis to design (Wooldridge et al. 2000), and consists of the following:

- purpose (brief textual description of the nature of the interaction);
- initiator (the agent responsible for starting the interaction);
- responder (the agent with which the initiator interacts);
- inputs (information used by the agent initiator while enacting the interaction);
- outputs (information supplied by/to the protocol responder during the interaction);
- processing (brief textual description of any processing the protocol initiator performs during the interaction).

13.4.3 The Agent's Environment

ABM facilitates the representation of rich and dynamic environments. These environments can be as simple as two-dimensional abstract spaces or as realistic as a space derived from data contained in a geographic information system or a networked-based space derived with data from social network analysis. This allows ABM to capture the complexity of consumer adoption, from the influence of a convenience store location to a consumer's decision based on a peer network (Rand and Rust 2011). The consumer behavior model defines the environment as the market environment, in which many instances of consumer agents (each one having their behavior) are surfing the market environment to find a market to shop and meet their needs. Also, they may interact with each other to share information and exchange experiences about the purchasing process. The distribution of agents in the environment space is spread around randomly over a defined area. Each iteration of the simulation represents a unit of time, such as a day, week, month, or year.

The marketing research can be performed through several runs of the model and evaluate the results by changing the conditions of variables (relating to agents and the environment) to analyze the effects created by these variations in the results of the simulation.

13.5 Model for Case Study

The case study focuses on the consumer behavior to buy electric appliances in Basra city. Three methods were used to determine the elements of agent-based model: questionnaire, statistical analysis, and rough set theory. The model includes two types of agents: a consumer agent and a vendor agent. Figures 13.4 and 13.5 present a general structure of these types of agents developed with the use of AnyLogic software.

The consumer agent (Fig. 13.4) is a person who shops in an electric appliance market in Basra city and who is characterized by many parameters and variables,

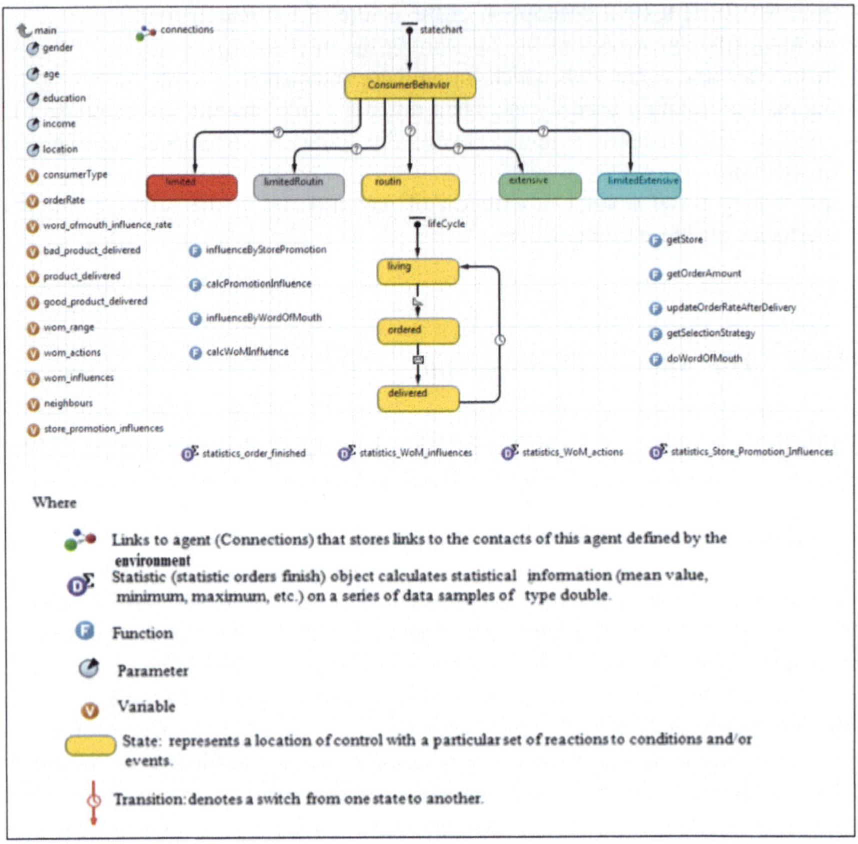

Fig. 13.4 Structure of the consumer agent. *Source* Personal elaboration

including demographics, behavioral attitudes, and influencing factors. The environment in which this agent acts is the electric appliance market where the agent is looking for information to decide on a purchase to satisfy a need. The consumer agent is modeled as animate, so it can act autonomously and interact with other agents. For the conceptual design of the agents, state charts are used, which show the different states in which an entity may be and define the events that cause a transition from one state to another. The structure of the consumer agent has two state charts. The first includes the consumer behavior types (with transition rules extracted by rough set theory), which are further divided into five kinds of behavior (limited, limited-routine, routine, extensive, and limited-extensive). Each consumer agent has an order rate for buying products per year, where the initial value depends on the behavior type. For example, the extensive consumer behavior may spend a long time collecting information before making a purchase decision compared with a consumer who has limited or routine behavior. The second state charts are life

Fig. 13.5 Structure of the vendor agent. *Source* Personal elaboration

cycles that represent the process of the consumer when they first enter the market until they receive an order and evaluate the product.

The vendor agent (Fig. 13.5) is a shop in the Basra market, which includes many features such as vendor type (warehouse, retail shop, and concept store), location, type of applied advertising (radio, billboard, and product placement), promotion (discount), and promotion range. This agent represents the external environmental influence on the consumer behavior. It is modeled as a source of the product and provides the two functions of promoting and delivering products.

In this environment, many instances of the consumer agent (each one having their own behavior) are looking for a vendor who will offer what they need from the environment. Two types of interactions take place in this environment. The first depends on consumer agents' communicating with each other when sharing information and exchanging experiences about the purchasing processes. The interaction between consumer agents occurs before making a final purchase decision. Each consumer agent observes their surroundings and looks for specific attributes from the other agents. This type of interaction may cause an agent to be influenced by others in its final decision. These attributes correspond to the variables representing word-of-mouth phenomena (WOM). In this case, each consumer agent takes into account these WOM values as a reference of the persuasive power from the surrounding agents. The second interaction appears when the vendor agent interacts with the consumer agent each time it is faced with the decision to purchase an electric appliance. This interaction occurs due to the consumer's influences by promotional factors from the vendors.

The simulation and experiments using the developed model run by following the case study over one year. For the model population, 100,000 consumers agents and 100 vendor agents were used, which represent the real population of consumers in one residential area of Basra city (1/20 population of Basra) and the real population of electric appliance vendors in Basra city.

For the verification and validation of the case study model, many experiments were run based on changes of parameters of agents, such as: the discount parameter value as a marketing strategy, the number of vendors in the city, the average promotion radius, the product quality, etc. The results of these experiments confirmed the correctness of the model and were accepted by subject matter experts.

13.6 Discussion of Experimental Results

Marketing managers make decisions on which marketing strategy to implement. The comparisons between the base simulation runs and the experimental scenarios can help guide the managers in making the best decision. The comparisons in this study were based on the four parameters of ordered products per month, the percentage of consumers satisfied with the delivered products, the percentage of consumers unsatisfied with the products delivered, and the percentage of people who did not buy products.

In this study, experiments were conducted on five exemplary marketing strategies:

- Strategy 1—increased percentage of vendors having discount promotion (from 20% in base run to 50% of all vendors).
- Strategy 2—increased number of vendors (from 100 to 110).
- Strategy 3—increased number of vendors and radiuses of advertising (number of vendors—from 100 to 110 and the average promotion radius—from 5 to 10 km).
- Strategy 4—decreased percentage of good-quality products in the entire volume (from 70 to 50%).
- Strategy 5—increased percentage of good-quality products in the entire volume (from 70 to 90%).

Table 13.1 Comparison between the base simulation and the results of the experiments

Index of strategies	Orders of products per month	Percentage of consumers satisfied with products delivered (%)	Percentage of consumers unsatisfied with products delivered (%)	Percentage of people who did not buy products (%)
Base run	13,474	71	19	10
Strategy 1	33,670	77	17	6
Strategy 2	16,123	72	18	10
Strategy 3	22,350	75	18	7
Strategy 4	9934	48	42	10
Strategy 5	31,905	87	7	6

Source Personal elaboration

Table 13.1 summarizes the value of the parameters for each strategy and the base simulation. The highest-ordered products per months are for strategy 1 (33,670 products) and the second highest for strategy 5 (31,905 products). At the same time, these two strategies (1 and 5) have the highest percentage of consumers satisfied with the products delivered of 77 and 87%, respectively. The lowest percentage of unsatisfied consumers was for strategy 5 (7%), so this suggests a very good value as consumers will likely attract other consumers to make similar purchase decisions. From the same table, both strategy 1 and strategy 5 have the same percentage of people who did not buy products (6%). On the other hand, the lowest value of ordered products per month was with strategy 2, which also has approximately the same values of the base simulation for satisfied consumers, unsatisfied consumers, and people who did not buy products. Based on Table 13.1, Strategy 1 and Strategy 5 can be recommended as the best strategies for the Basra market.

Figure 13.6 shows additional results of the experiment for Strategy 1 in the form of chart. The curve suggests that when the proportion of vendors offering discounted prices of the product increases from 20 to 50% of all vendors, then the number of orders for products (corresponding with the amount of deliveries) grows monthly (33,670 products) compared with the base run. The same figure includes a pie chart describing the average of products ordered based on the location of vendors. This illustrates that the most orders for products are placed with vendors in the residential area with the next percentage of the vendors located in the city center. These results suggest that most consumers prefer to buy products from the nearest vendor or in the city center.

This section describes only a few examples of experiments, but with the help of the presented agent-based model, we can conduct an unlimited number of simulation experiments that allow to verify different decision hypotheses relating to buying behavior, consumption patterns, and habits of different groups of consumers in the electric appliance marketplace, without interfering with the living organism of the system under investigation.

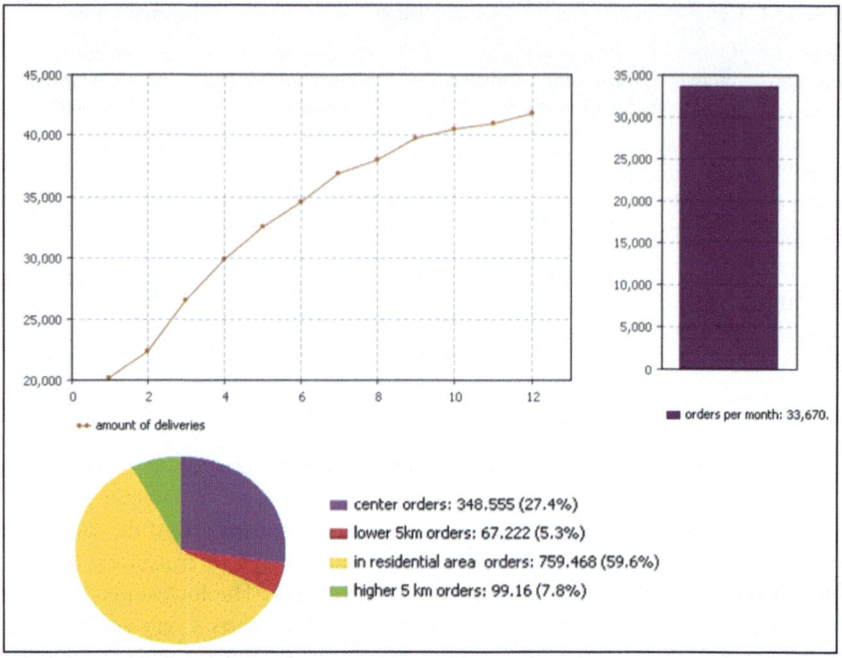

Fig. 13.6 Results of the experiment for Strategy 1. *Source* Personal elaboration

13.7 Conclusion

The considerations presented in the chapter allow formulating a general conclusion that agent-based simulation is a method that can be used successfully to study consumer behavior. An agent-based model allows conducting experiments taking into account the heterogeneous complexity both at the level of the individual consumer and the complex marketing environment. It also gives the possibility of modeling the interaction between different types of agents (consumers, vendors and other), which increases the credibility of the research results, because the modeled real world consists of individuals interacting with each other. Moreover, we can carry out an unlimited number of experiments in a short time using a computer (no harm to people and environment), which makes it possible to study the impact of many combinations of factors influencing consumer behavior and test many marketing strategies.

References

Balci O (1997) Verification validation and accreditation of simulation models. In: Proceedings of the 29th conference on Winter simulation, IEEE Computer Society, pp 135–141

Balci O (ed) (1998) Verification, validation and testing. In: Handbook of simulation, vol 10. John Wiley and Sons, New York

Brannon E, Ulrich P, Anderson L, Presley A, Thommesen S, Missam M (2000) Agent-based simulation of the consumer's apparel purchase decision. National Textile Centre Annual Report, November, Project I98-A09:1–10

Buchta C, Mazanec J (2001) SIMSEG/ACM. A simulation environment for artificial consumer markets. Working Papers SFB "Adaptive Information Systems and Modelling in Economics and Management Science", 79. SFB Adaptive Information Systems and Modelling in Economics and Management Science, WU Vienna University of Economics and Business, Vienna

Burns RB (1997) Introduction to research methods. Addison Wesley Longman

Cao J (1999) Evaluation of advertising effectiveness using agent-based modeling and simulation. Paper presented at the proceedings of 2nd UK workshop of SIG on multi-agent systems (UKMAS), Bristol, UK, Dec

Challet D, Krause A (2006) What questions to ask in order to validate an agent-based model. http://www.maths-in-industry.org/miis/107/1/Unilever-ABM-Report.pdf. Accessed on 10.8. 2017

Crowther D, Lancaster G (2012) Research methods. Routledge

Collings D, Reeder A, Adjali I, Crocker P, Lyons M (2000) Agent based customer modelling: individuals who learn from their environment. In: Proceedings of the 2000 congress on evolutionary computation, 2000, IEEE, pp 1492–1497

Delre SA, Jager W, Bijmolt TH, Janssen MA (2010) Will it spread or not? The effects of social influences and network topology on innovation diffusion. J Prod Innov Manag 27:267–282

Drogoul A, Ferber J (1994) Multi-agent simulation as a tool for modeling societies: application to social differentiation in ant colonies. In: Castelfranchi C, Werner E (eds) Artificial social systems. MAAMAW 1992. Lecture notes in computer science (Lecture notes in artificial intelligence), vol 830. Springer, Berlin, Heidelberg

Furaiji F, Łatuszyńska M (2012) Methods of gathering data for the study of consumer behavior. Stud Proc Pol Assoc Knowl Manag 58:77–88

Furaji F, Łatuszyńska M, Wawrzyniak A, Wąsikowska B (2013) Study on the influence of advertising attractiveness on the purchase decisions of women and men. J Int Stud 6:20–32

Gardner M (1970) The fantastic combinations of John Conways new solitaire games. Math Games 223(4):120–123

Garifullin M, Borshchev A, Popkov T (2007) Using AnyLogic and agent-based approach to model consumer market. In: Proceedings of the 6th EUROSIM congress on modelling and simulation, Ljubljana, Slovenia, 9–13 Sept 2007

Goldenberg J, Libai B, Moldovan S, Muller E (2007) The NPV of bad news. Int J Res Mark 24:186–200

Goldenberg J, Han S, Lehmann DR, Hong JW (2009) The role of hubs in the adoption process. J Mark 73:1–13

Goldenberg J, Libai B, Muller E (2010) The chilling effects of network externalities. Int J Res Mark 27:4–15

Helleboogh A, Vizzari G, Uhrmacher A, Michel F (2007) Modeling dynamic environments in multi-agent simulation. Auton Agent Multi-Agent Syst 14:87–116

Hill RP, Watkins A (2007) A simulation of moral behavior within marketing exchange relationships. J Acad Mark Sci 35:417–429

Hill RP, Watkins A (2009) The profit implications of altruistic versus egoistic orientations for business-to-business exchanges. Int J Res Mark 26:52–59

Holland JH, Miller JH (1991) Artificial adaptive agents in economic theory. Am Econ Rev 81(2): 365–370

Jager W (2006) Simulating consumer behaviour: a perspective. In: Faber A, Frenken K, Idenburg AM (eds) Environmental policy and modeling in evolutionary economics. Netherlands Environmental Assessment Agency, Groningen, Netherlands, pp 1–27

Janssen MA, Jager W (2003) Simulating market dynamics: interactions between consumer psychology and social networks. Artif Life 9:343–356

Janssen M, Vlek C, Jager W (1999) Consumats in a commons dilemma: testing the behavioral rules of simulated consumers. RUG-COV, Groningen

Kosow H, Gaßner R (2008) Methods of future and scenario analysis: overview, assessment, and selection criteria. Studies vol 39. DIE-Deutsches Institut für Entwicklungspolitik

Kuhn JR, Courtney JF, Morris B, Tatara ER (2010) Agent-based analysis and simulation of the consumer airline market share for Frontier Airlines. Knowl-Based Syst 23:875–882

Kyrylov V, Bonanni C (2004) Modeling decision making by telecommunications services providers in a strategy market game. Simul Ser 36:155

Lancaster G (2007) Research methods in management. Routledge

Latuszynska M (2012) Computer simulation methods in economics and management. Actual Probl Econ 131:170–179

Macal C, North M (2014) Tutorial on agent-based modeling and simulation. In: Taylor SJE (ed) Agent-based modeling and simulation. Palgrave Macmillan, pp 11–31

Marks R, Midgley D, Cooper L (2006) Co-evolving better strategies in oligopolistic price wars. In: Rennard JP (ed) Handbook of research on nature-inspired computing for economy and management. Idea Group, Hershey, pp 806–821

Midgley DF, Marks RE, Cooper LC (1997) Breeding competitive strategies. Manage Sci 43: 257–275

Mourhir A, Aklibous C (2016) Building a collaboration platform using agent-based modelling. School of Science and Engineering, Alkhawayn University, Marokko

North MJ, Macal CM, Aubin JS, Thimmapuram P, Bragen M, Hahn J, Karr J, Brigham N, Lacy ME, Hampton D (2010) Multiscale agent-based consumer market modeling. Complexity 15:37–47

Pawlak Z (2002) Rough sets and intelligent data analysis. Inf Sci 147:1–12

Rahmandad H, Sterman J (2008) Heterogeneity and network structure in the dynamics of diffusion: comparing agent-based and differential equation models. Manage Sci 54:998–1014

Railsback SF, Lytinen SL, Jackson SK (2006) Agent-based simulation platforms: review and development recommendations. Simulation 82:609–623

Rand W, Rust RT (2011) Agent-based modeling in marketing: guidelines for rigor. Int J Res Mark 28:181–193

Rigopoulos G, Patlitzianas KD, Karadimas NV (2006) Modeling consumer behavior towards payment system selection using multiagent based simulation. In: Proceedings of the IADIS virtual multi conference on computer science and information systems, 2006, pp 242–246

Robertson DA (2003) Agent-based models of a banking network as an example of a turbulent environment: the deliberate vs. emergent strategy debate revisited. Emergence 5:56–71

Roozmand O, Ghasem-Aghaee N, Hofstede GJ, Nematbakhsh MA, Baraani A, Verwaart T (2011) Agent-based modeling of consumer decision making process based on power distance and personality. Knowl-Based Syst 24:1075–1095

Said LB, Bouron T, Drogoul A (2002) Agent-based interaction analysis of consumer behavior. In: AAMAS '02 proceedings of the first international joint conference on autonomous agents and multiagent systems: part 1, Bologna, Italy, 15–19 July 2002, pp 184–190

Schenk TA, Löffler G, Rauh J (2007) Agent-based simulation of consumer behavior in grocery shopping on a regional level. J Bus Res 60:894–903

Schiffman LG, Hansen H, Kanuk LL (2008) Consumer behaviour. A European outlook. Pearson Education Limited

Schwaiger A, Stahmer B (2003) SimMarket: multiagent-based customer simulation and decision support for category management. In: Schillo M, Klusch M, Müller J, Tianfield H (eds) Multiagent system technologies. MATES 2003. Lecture notes in computer science, vol 2831. Springer, Berlin, Heidelberg, pp 74–84
Shaikh NI, Rangaswamy A, Balakrishnan A (2006) Modeling the diffusion of innovations using small-world networks. SSRN Electron J. https://doi.org/10.2139/ssrn.2032861
Siebers PO, Aickelin U (2008) Introduction to multi-agent simulation. In: Adam F, Humphreys P (eds) Encyclopedia of decision making and decision support technologies. Idea Group Publishing, Pennsylvania, pp 554–564
Tay NS, Lusch RF (2005) A preliminary test of Hunt's General Theory of Competition: using artificial adaptive agents to study complex and ill-defined environments. J Bus Res 58:1155–1168
Tay NS, Lusch RF (2007) Agent-based modeling of ambidextrous organizations: virtualizing competitive strategy. IEEE Intell Syst 22(5):50–57
Twomey P, Cadman R (2002) Agent-based modelling of customer behaviour in the telecoms and media markets. Information 4(1):56–63
Ulbinaite A, Le Moullec Y (2010) Towards an ABM-based framework for investigating consumer behaviour in the insurance industry. Economics 89:95–110
Venables M, Bilge U (1998) Complex adaptive modelling at J Sainsbury: the SimStore supermarket supply chain experiment. Business Process Resource Centre, Warwick University, Warwick
Watkins A, Hill RP (2009) A simulation of business-to-business decision making in a relationship marketing context. Ind Mark Manage 38:994–1005
Watts DJ (2002) A simple model of global cascades on random networks. Proc Natl Acad Sci USA 99(9):5766–5771
Watts DJ, Dodds PS (2007) Influentials, networks, and public opinion formation. J Consum Res 34:441–458
Wawrzyniak A, Furaji F (2013) The concept of simulation model to study consumer behavior. Zesz Nauk Uniw Szczecińskiego Stud Inform 32:121–136
Wilkinson I, Young L (2002) On cooperating: firms, relations and networks. J Bus Res 55: 123–132
Wohltorf J, Albayrak S (2003) An agent-based decision support system for the introduction of next generation mobile services. Dai-Labor at the Technische Universitat, Berlin
Wooldridge M, Jennings NR, Kinny D (2000) The Gaia methodology for agent-oriented analysis and design. Auton Agent Multi-Agent Syst 3:285–312
Zhang T, Zhang D (2007) Agent-based simulation of consumer purchase decision-making and the decoy effect. J Bus Res 60:912–922

Part III
Practical Issues—Case Studies

Chapter 14
The Relationship Between Doctors' Communication and Trust in Doctor: Some Behavioural Data

Iga Rudawska and Katarzyna Krot

Abstract Medical doctors' behaviour, including communication patterns, proves to be the most important set of variables affecting trust in the patient–doctor relationship. Therefore, the aim of the chapter is empirical verification of the relationship between doctor's communication and trust in doctors in the dimension of competence, benevolence and integrity. The research assumptions have been verified based on CATI, conducted on representative sample of Polish patients. The empirical findings support the hypothesis that there is a correlation between quality of communication and trust in all of the identified dimensions of patient–doctor relationship. The most prominent impact of the communication has been revealed in the dimension of benevolence.

Keywords Doctor–patient relationship · Communication · Trust

JEL I12

14.1 Introduction

As psychologists emphasize, in every medical practice—not just in the psychiatric one—the so-called non-intentional psychotherapy, i.e. the way in which a physician treats a patient (Tobiasz-Adamczyk et al. 1996, p. 15), plays a vital role. The dynamic development of medical technologies directs the focus of contemporary medicine chiefly on perfecting diagnostic and therapeutic methods and tools. What

I. Rudawska (✉)
Faculty of Economics and Management, Szczecin University,
Mickiewicza 64, 71-101 Szczecin, Poland
e-mail: igita@wneiz.pl

K. Krot
Bialystok University of Technology, Kleosin, ul. Ojca Tarasiuka 2,
16-001 Białystok, Poland
e-mail: katarzynakrot@gmail.com

K. Nermend and M. Łatuszyńska (eds.), *Problems, Methods and Tools in Experimental and Behavioral Economics*, Springer Proceedings in Business and Economics, https://doi.org/10.1007/978-3-319-99187-0_14

is more, the result of the systemic changes implemented in the Polish healthcare sector is that physicians, subjected to new rules, regulations and pressures of various types (related to employment policy, financial management of healthcare entities), no longer devote sufficient time and attention to patients. That is the reason why expressive personality characteristics, such as kindness, compassion, respect, interest in patient as a human being demonstrated through the style of communication, are listed as the attributes that patients value the most nowadays. Treating physicians and the remaining medical personnel as the service provider's fundamental capital is founded on the theory of commitment and trust (Morgan and Hunt 1994, p. 24). Satisfactory interpersonal communication leads to the development and strengthening of trust relationship between the patient and the treating physician (Cant 2009, p. 114). Trust is a multidimensional construct. Hence, the suggestion that this multidimensional aspect ought to be analysed (Svensson 2005). Although the influence of communication on trust in the objective relationship has been the focus of scientific study on multiple occasions (Northouse and Northouse 1985; Thorne and Robinson 1988; Davies 1999; Dibben et al. 2000; Mechanic and Meyer 2000; Vivian and Wilcox 2000; Hall et al. 2001; Dibben and Lean 2003; Gabay 2015), the influence of communication on individual trust dimensions has not yet been sufficiently researched. Therefore, the objective of this chapter is to verify empirically the dependence between communication in the patient–physician relationship and trust in competence, benevolence and integrity. The study was conducted within the scope of an NCN grant (No. 2011/01/D/HS4/05664).

14.2 Interpersonal Communication in the Physician–Patient Relationship

Health services belong to a group of services based on information exchange. Framing a physician–patient relationship into informational context enables its perception as a sequence in the stream of information. Exchange of information in the vast majority of cases (save for the situations in which a patient has lost the ability of receiving verbal and non-verbal stimuli as a result of illness) determines the quality of the relationship that this chapter focuses on. Moreover, it has significant consequences for the efficiency of health care understood as the achievement of the intended therapeutic result. The grounds for such a claim are provided by the results of empirical studies confirming the hypothesis that a significant part of therapeutic effect is owed to constructive communication between a physician and a patient (Korsch and Harding 1997, p. 100). The quality of communication in a physician-patient relationship is expressed in the patients' confidence to articulate their own needs, and their participation in defining and solving health problems. There by, it can affect the number of diagnostic tests ordered, frequency of appointments or length of hospitalization. Hence it influences not only purely economic sphere (Charles et al. 2000, p. 1220). In turn, from the patient's perspective, the quality of communication is determined by the physician's ability to listen to them, the physician's honesty in contacts with the patient, empathy and genuine interest in the patient's situation (Gabay 2015, p. 1552). On the other hand, the patient–physician interactions that result in the patient's annoyance, irritation, ones that inspire the sense of fear, threat or doubt become the source of erosion of the quality of communication (Epstein et al. 2007, p. 24; Fletcher et al. 2007, p. 123). Therefore, it is the professional, being the chief service provider's representative, who acts as the main communication moderator, while the interpersonal information exchange assumes the proportions of a fundamental marketing instrument of communication.

A physician, thanks to the possessed professional knowledge, professional prestige, as well as the position occupied in an organization hierarchy, becomes responsible for effective communication (Graber 2001, p. 44). The patient, when selecting a given physician, entrusts the physician with their health and hence expects some stimuli ensuring them of having made the right choice. In situations excluding freedom to choose, patient's anxiety increases, frequently causing emotional tension that they may be unaware of. In such circumstances, communication plays an even greater role, since apart from the purpose of convincing a patient, it additionally builds trust in the service provider.

A physician's professional standard, expressed in a Latin maxim "salus segroti suprema lex esto", dictates that the professional does its utmost in the interest of patient's welfare. Taking into consideration the scantiness of healthcare resources, a physician is obligated to be aware of the value of tests and medication ordered as well as their probable economic consequences for the patient. Inept communication or its lack (failure to inform the patient, ignoring the need to prepare the patient psychologically to the diagnostics and therapy awaiting them) may contribute to the exacerbation of their somatic disease (Kliszcz 2000, p. 75). Therefore, empathy is the desired form of communication (Trzebińska 1985, p. 11). By participating in patient's experience, a physician becomes more sensitive and alert to the patient's needs, thus facilitating the physician's response to those. On the other hand, a patient seeing their physician's commitment (evaluated on the basis of verbal and non-verbal data) finds it easier to open up and articulate their problems. Thus, an empathic relationship provides a patient with the sense of security, trust and support from their physician.

The patient, when entering into an interaction with the service provider, deals primarily with people. Therefore, the distinguishing characteristics of a service relationship do not limit just to an individual, but it extends to the personality of a service provider's representative, typically a physician. The issue is emphasized by the Nordic school of relationship marketing (Grönroos 1994, p. 7). As the patient's status changes and they transfer to inpatient care services, the role of mid-level medical personnel increases, chiefly that of nurses (Carman 2000, p. 94), who are tasked with the expressive role evening out the balance of a patient's "system" that has been disturbed by instrumental activities. That role involves showing compassion, interest, empathy, care.

At the level of primary health care, combing the expressive and instrumental role of a physician is desirable not only due to the significance of this type of interaction, which derives from the "gatekeeping" system existing in Poland, but mainly owing to the costs of health care. They are growing along with the increasing degree of technicality and specialization of health services, i.e. when the patient moves to the higher levels of health care. According to F. Carp: "[…] the main task of a general practitioner, when meeting a patient for the first time, aside from providing immediate assistance, is to explain the nature and meaning of an illness as well as teaching the patient what options they have of changing those circumstances in their life that have led to the illness" (Capra 1987, p. 50). Transferring those pertinent observations onto the sphere of marketing it can be concluded that a professional, apart from obvious distributive functions, fulfils a communicative role combined with the performance of marketing research, the focus of which is the client's surroundings, attitude and conduct. Therefore, a correct diagnosis depends not just on the accurate recognition of illness symptoms and interpretation of data from the clinical tests carried out, but also on the skill of acquiring knowledge and synthetizing information that may seemingly be unrelated to medicine (Tyszka 2000, p. 113). This in turn affects the number and type of diagnostic tests and medication prescribed by a physician, which need to be qualified as strictly economic decisions determining healthcare costs.

The specificity of health services allows one to define the nature of the patient–physician communication as highly individualized and intimate. A number of studies conducted both in Poland and abroad demonstrate that it is the patient's relationship with a physician, described with expressive, communicative attributes that constitute the main point of reference in building a relationship based on trust (Dibben and Lean 2003; Leisen and Hymanb 2004; Cant 2009; Lee and Lin 2010; Tarrant et al. 2010; Gabay 2015). Hence, a relationship based on trust, commitment and reliability is a decisive source of satisfaction from the relationship with a service provider. The invoked results come from studies either on a selected group of services, or they refer to medical services as such. They were conducted at different geographic locations and on various groups of respondents. Despite these differences, all the studies emphasized the expressive role of physicians, which dominates over their instrumental role in developing a relationship of trust.

The above-mentioned empirical reports justify a claim that interpersonal communication ought to be treated as one of the crucial skills of medical professionals. To a large extend, it also concerns the other side of the relationship—the patient. Depersonalization of contemporary health care, manifested by a physician identifying an individual patient as one of many cases they encounter, makes it the patient's task to attract the professional's interest in their person through an apt presentation of their medical problem (Tobiasz-Adamczyk et al. 1996, p. 40). During interaction, both the physician and the patient influence one another by sending verbal and non-verbal signals. Under that influence, both parties modify their behaviour. Mutually satisfactory communication brings about a series of beneficial effects going beyond medical categories, including also economic and psychological aspects.

14.3 Research Methodology

The relations between trust and communication have been researched on multiple occasions (Leisen and Hymanb 2004; Cant 2009; Lee and Lin 2010; Tarrant et al. 2010; Gabay 2015). In order for trust between the doctor and the patient to be built up, an appropriate communication process is necessary. It seems, however, that there is an inverse relationship, i.e. trust in the doctor may affect the nature of the conversation between the doctor and the patient. In addition, it is worth looking at these relationships, assuming that trust is a multidimensional construct. Therefore, the purpose of this chapter was to determine the relationship between doctor–patient communication and the three main dimensions of trust: the competence, integrity and benevolence of doctors.

In order to isolate the "communication" factor, a factor analysis was conducted with the use of the main component technique with Varimax rotation. Variables assignment was determined on the basis of the value of factor loading. A threshold value of the factor loading selecting variables was assumed to be at the level of 0.55. Following that, Alpha Cronbach reliability analysis was conducted on the obtained construct. The indicator reached a satisfactory value of 0.92 (Table 14.1).

The isolated construct comprises the category of behavioural patterns representing a physician's active attitude in the process of communication with the patient. Above all, it contained statements concerning informing patients about everything that was happening during a visit, but also about alternative treatment methods, as well as treatment options and effects and illness causes. Moreover, it contained the statements regarding the ways of imparting that knowledge.

On the other hand, within the scope of the factor there are physicians' behavioural patterns enabling the establishment of conditions that allow patients a greater involvement in the course of a visit, namely openness, willingness to listen

Table 14.1 Factor loading of "communication" construct

	Factor loadings
Q5.2	0.55
Q5.3	0.60
Q5.9	0.60
Q5.12	0.56
Q5.20	0.59
Q5.24	0.65
Q5.26	0.66
Q5.30	0.62
Q5.33	0.63
Q5.34	0.61
Q5.35	0.72
Q5.36	0.65
Q5.37	0.58

Source Own work on the basis of research results

Table 14.2 Structure of a research sample

Income			Gender		
	Number	Percent		Number	Percent
From 1000 PLN	84	8.6	Female	572	58.2
1001 PLN to 1400 PLN	95	9.6	Male	411	41.8
1401 PLN to 1800 PLN	108	11.0	Age		
1801 PLN to 2000 PLN	113	11.5	18–24	103	10.5
2001 PLN to 2500 PLN	76	7.7	25–34	182	18.5
2501 PLN to 3000 PLN	120	12.2	35–44	163	16.6
3001 PLN to 5000 PLN	139	14.1	45–59	252	25.7
Over 5000 PLN	118	12.0	Over 60	283	28.8
Hard to say	49	5.0			
Place of residence			Education		
Countryside	356	36.2	Primary	148	15.0
Up to 100 thou.	335	34.1	Vocational	213	21.7
100–499 thou.	164	16.7	Secondary	345	35.2
500+ thou.	127	13.0	University	276	28.1

Source Own work on the basis of research results

to a patient, encouraging the patient to articulate their needs. Patients may, thus, talk about their personal problems, they inform about their expectations and suggest preferences regarding treatment methods. Such activity of both parties in the relationship gives the communication a bilateral character and makes it more balanced.

Trust in physicians was examined in three dimensions: trust in physicians' competence, benevolence and their integrity. The level of trust was measured with single questions.

The study was carried out in 2015 with CATI method on an all-Poland representative sample of 982 respondents, who had declared that they had been using health care within the previous six months. In Tables 14.2 and 14.3, the research sample characteristics were presented.

14.4 Research Results

Descriptive statistics concerning all the variables were compiled in Table 14.4. Research results demonstrate that the surveyed individuals declared the highest trust in physicians' competences (2.94), while the lowest trust in their integrity (2.90).

In order to verify the strength of communication influence on trust, i.e. communication significance in a patient–physician relationship, in building trust to physicians in three dimensions, a regression analysis was conducted. On account of that, three regression models were developed, in which individual types of trust

Table 14.3 Place of respondents' residence by voivodeship

	Number	Percent
Lower Silesia	73	7.4
Kuyavian-Pomerania	47	4.8
Lublin	51	5.2
Lubusz	27	2.8
Łódź	68	6.9
Lesser Poland	76	7.8
Masovia	143	14.6
Opole	27	2.7
Subcarpathia	58	5.9
Podlasie	34	3.5
Pomerania	61	6.2
Silesia	132	13.4
Świętokrzyskie	31	3.1
Warmian-Masuria	30	3.0
Greater Poland	80	8.2
West Pomerania	43	4.4
Total	982	100.0

Source Own work on the basis of research results

Table 14.4 Descriptive statistics of variables

	Average	Standard deviation	Correlation			
			Trust in benevolence	Trust in integrity	Trust in competence	Communication
Trust in benevolence	2.91	1.06	1.00			
Trust in integrity	2.90	1.04	0.54	1.00		
Trust in competence	2.94	0.99	0.35	0.42	1.00	
Communication	40.75	9.56	0.58	0.52	0.45	1.00

Source Own work on the basis of research results

(in physicians' competences, benevolence and integrity) constituted the dependent variables, whereas "communication" was the explanatory variable. In each of the three models, communication occurred to be a statistically significant predictor of institutional trust in physicians (Table 14.5).

It means that along with the improvement of "communication quality" trust in each of the examined types grows as well, although communication has the greatest impact on trust in benevolence ($b^* = 0.67$, $p = 0.00$), it has an equally strong

Table 14.5 Influence of communication on three types of institutional trust—a regression model

	b^*	Standard error—with b^*	$t(866)$	p
Trust in competences $R^2 = 0.34$, $F(1.866) = 445.55$, $p < 0.00$ Standard estimation error: 0.59				
Absolute term			12.20	0.00
Communication	0.58	0.03	21.11	0.00
Trust in integrity $R^2 = 0.43$, $F(1.866) = 654.79$, $p < 0.00$ Standard estimation error: 0.57				
	b^*	Standard error—with b^*	$t(866)$	p
Absolute term			8.92	0.00
Communication	0.66	0.03	25.59	0.00
Trust in benevolence $R^2 = 0.44$, $F(1.868) = 688.51$, $p < 0.00$ Standard estimation error: 0.58				
	b^*	Standard error—with b^*	$t(868)$	p
Absolute term			7.88	0.00
Communication	0.67	0.03	26.24	0.00

Source Own work on the basis of research results

impact on trust in integrity ($b^* = 0.66$, $p = 0.00$) and the lowest on trust in physicians' competences ($b^* = 0.58$, $p = 0.00$).

The next step was to answer the question of how three dimensions of doctor trust impact the communication with patients. This time, in the multiple regression models, instead of one explanatory variable, three variables were used to measure the level of trust in the competence, integrity and benevolence of the physician. "Communication" was an explanatory variable.

As a result of the analysis, it turned out that all dimensions of trust significantly affect the course and quality of the doctor–patient communication with the determination coefficient $R^2 = 0.44$ and $p = 0.00$ (Table 14.6).

Among the analysed dimensions of trust, trust in benevolence has the strongest influence on the process of communication with the patient.

The other two dimensions of trust, i.e. trust in competence and trust in integrity, are slightly less decisive for the quality of doctor–patient communication. It is worth noting that the impact of these two dimensions of trust is comparable.

Table 14.6 Dimensions of trust and the communication process—the regression model

	b^*	Standard error—with b^*	$t(879)$	p
			12.96	0.00
Trust in benevolence	0.38	0.03	12.63	0.00
Trust in competence	0.22	0.02	7.82	0.00
Trust in integrity	0.22	0.03	7.00	0.00
$R = 0.66$, $R^2 = 0.439$, $F(3.879) = 228.27$, $p < 0.00$ Standard estimation error: 7.18				

Source Own work on the basis of research results

14.5 Conclusions

Constructive communication between a patient and a physician, a communication that focuses on the needs of both partners in the relationship, contributes to the improvement of treatment effects (Korsch and Harding 1997, p. 100), but it additionally brings about economic and psychological benefits.

According to the previous studies, the proper communication quality builds trust in the patient–physician relationship (Dibben and Lean 2003; Leisen and Hymanb 2004; Cant 2009; Lee and Lin 2010; Tarrant et al. 2010; Gabay 2015). The results were confirmed in a smaller study, but communication has the greatest impact on trust in physicians' benevolence, and the lowest impact on trust in their competences.

High quality of communication is a rather broad concept, especially in the patient–physician relationship. That is why, it was attempted to define which types of physician's behavioural patterns are the most expected and desirable in building a relationship based on trust. In literature, it is emphasized that it is a physician who has the decisive impact on the course of a communication process (Graber 2001, p. 44). Since it is the physician who informs, explains, shows openness and interest to the patient, the one who listens, but also creates conditions supporting a patient's involvement, enabling them to verbalize their needs, allows cooperation in solving health problems, ensures a wider outlook on the patient's health situation (Gabay 2015, p. 1552).

Therefore, this chapter attempts to determine which dimensions of trust in the doctor affect the quality of communication the most. It turned out that trust in benevolence makes it easier for patients to communicate with the doctor: inform about their health condition, ask questions, dispel doubts. Patients trusting in benevolence also make the doctor more involved in the communication process: he/she is more likely to inform the patient about the options and effects of treatment, to explain all the complexities associated with the treatment and also encourage the patient to active communication.

Trust in competence and trust in integrity affect the communication process to the same extent, although their impact is slightly weaker. If patients trust in competence and integrity, they are more willing to provide detailed information; they consult their suspicions with the professional knowledge of the doctor.

It can therefore be said that there is a feedback between trust in the doctor and communication (Fig. 14.1).

Communication between the doctor and the patient affects trust, which in turn strengthens the communication process. As it turns out in these interdependencies, trust in benevolence is particularly important, although other trust dimensions also play a significant role.

The limitation of this research is the declarative nature of the study. The respondents' opinions were collected after the expiration of a few months after the doctor's visit; hence, some respondents may not have remembered the impression the doctor had on them and have a problem in assessing the level of trust. In the

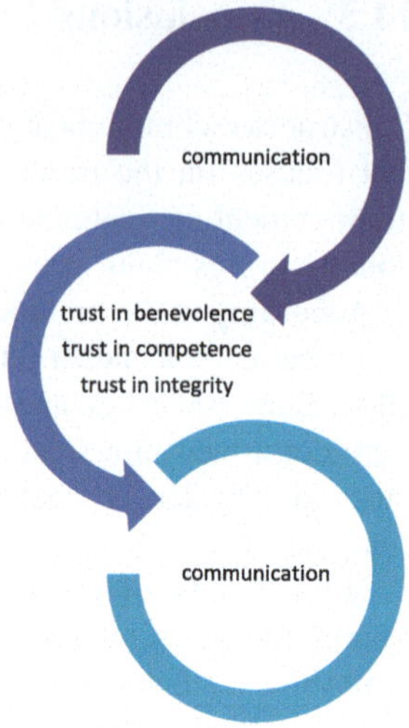

Fig. 14.1 Relationship between trust in the doctor and the communication process. *Source* Own work on the basis of research results

future, it would be worth to monitor and measure trust levels and differences among 16 Polish regions. More work could also be done to perfect existing trust measures. It refers especially to the validity of the measures and reliability assessment.

References

Cant R (2009) Constructions of competence within dietetics: trust, professionalism and communications with individual clients. Nutr Diet 66:113–118

Capra F (1987) Punkt zwrotny. PIW, Warszawa

Carman JM (2000) Patient perceptions of service quality: combining the dimensions. J Serv Mark 14(4/5):94

Charles C, Gafni A, Whelan T (2000) How to improve communication between doctors and patients. BMJ 320:1220–1221

Davies H (1999) Failing public trust in health services: implications for accountability. J Health Serv Res Policy 4:193–194

Dibben MR, Lean ME (2003) Achieving compliance in chronic illness management: illustrations of trust relationships between physicians and nutrition clinic patients. Health Risk Soc 5(3): 241–252

Dibben MR, Morris SE, Lean ME (2000) Situational trust and co-operative partnerships between physicians and their patients: a theoretical explanation transferable from business practice. Q J Med 93:55–61

Epstein RM, Shields CG, Franks P, Meldrum SC, Feldman M, Kravitz R (2007) Exploring and validating patient concerns: relation to prescribing for depression. Ann Fam Med 5:21–28

Fletcher KE, Scott LF, David TS (2007) Patients speak: what's really important about bedside interactions with physician teams. Teach Learn Med 19(2):120–127

Gabay G (2015) Perceived control over health, communication and patient-physician trust. Patient Educ Couns 98:1550–1557

Graber DR (2001) Spirituality and healthcare organizations. J Healthc Manag 46(1):44

Grönroos C (1994) From marketing mix to relationship marketing: towards a paradigm shift in marketing. Manag Decis 32(2):4–20

Hall MA, Dugan E, Zheg B, Mishra AK (2001) Trust in physicians and medical institutions: what is it, can it be measured, and does it matter? Milbank Q 79:613–639

Kliszcz J (2000) Psychologiczne aspekty jatropatogenii (Psychological aspects of jatropatogeny). In: Barański J, Waszyński E, Steciwka A (eds) Komunikowanie się lekarza za pacjentem (Communication between the doctor and the patient). Astrum, Warszawa

Korsch BM, Harding C (1997) The intelligent patient's guide to the doctor-patient relationship. Oxford University Press Inc., London

Lee Y, Lin JL (2010) The effects of trust in physician on self-efficacy, adherence and diabetes outcomes. Soc Sci Med 68:1060–1068

Leisen B, Hymanb MR (2004) Antecedents and consequences of trust in a service provider: the case of primary care physicians. J Bus Res 57:990–999

Mechanic D, Meyer S (2000) Concepts of trust among patients with serious illness. Soc Sci Med 51:657–668

Morgan RM, Hunt SD (1994) The commitment-trust theory of relationship marketing. J Mark 58(3):24

Northouse PG, Northouse LL (1985) Health communication: a handbook for professionals. Prentice Hall, New Jersey

Svensson G (2005) Mutual and interactive trust in business dyads: condition and process. Eur Bus Rev 17(5):411–427

Tarrant C, Dixon-Woods M, Colman AM, Stokes T (2010) Continuity and trust in primary care: a qualitative study informed by game theory. Ann Fam Med 8:440–446

Thorne SE, Robinson CA (1988) Reciprocal trust in healthcare relationships. J Adv Nurs 13: 782–789

Tobiasz-Adamczyk B, Bajka J, Marmon G (1996) Wybrane elementy socjologii zawodów medycznych (Selected issues of sociology of medical professions). Collegium Medicum Uniwersytetu Jagiellońskiego, Kraków

Trzebińska E (1985) Empatia jako forma komunikacji interpersonalnej (Empathy as a form of interpersonal communication). Przegląd Psychologiczny 2:11

Tyszka T (2000) Psychologiczne pułapki oceniania i podejmowania decyzji (Psychological pitfalls of assessing and making decisions). Gdańskie Wydawnictwo Psychologiczne, Gdańsk

Vivian B, Wilcox J (2000) Compliance communication in home health care: a mutually reciprocal process. Qual Health Res 10:103–116

Chapter 15
Wine Tasting: How Much Is the Contribution of the Olfaction?

Patrizia Cherubino, Giulia Cartocci, Enrica Modica, Dario Rossi, Marco Mancini, Arianna Trettel and Fabio Babiloni

Abstract Neuromarketing predicts that multiple factors contribute to the choice of a product, among them, the perceived value, pleasantness, and emotion related to the use of it. In this framework, a particular field is constituted by luxury items, such as wine. Wine is particularly suitable to marketing effects, both extrinsic (label) and intrinsic features (volatile composition and color) lead to the constitution of the experienced value, and the analysis of the contribution of olfaction to the process of tasting is fundamental in order to study flavor perception. Scope of the present study was to investigate the reaction to the smell and the gustation of the wine, with and without the olfactory contribution, through an

---

Patrizia Cherubino and Giulia Cartocci—equally contributed to the present chapter.

P. Cherubino (✉) · G. Cartocci · E. Modica · D. Rossi · F. Babiloni
Department of Molecular Medicine, Sapienza University,
Viale Regina Elena 291, 00161 Rome, Italy
e-mail: patrizia.cherubino@brainsigns.com

G. Cartocci
e-mail: giulia.cartocci@uniroma1.it

E. Modica
e-mail: enrica.modica@uniroma1.it

D. Rossi
e-mail: dario.rossi@uniroma1.it

P. Cherubino · G. Cartocci · E. Modica · D. Rossi · M. Mancini
A. Trettel · F. Babiloni
BrainSigns srl, Via Sesto Celere 7/C, 00152 Rome, Italy
e-mail: marco.mancini@brainsigns.com

A. Trettel
e-mail: arianna.trettel@brainsigns.com

F. Babiloni
Department of Computer Science and Technology,
Hangzhou Dianzi University, Hangzhou, China
e-mail: fabio.babiloni@uniroma1.it

K. Nermend and M. Łatuszyńska (eds.), *Problems, Methods and Tools in Experimental and Behavioral Economics*, Springer Proceedings in Business and Economics, https://doi.org/10.1007/978-3-319-99187-0_15

electroencephalographic index, assumed as an indicator of approach or withdrawal (AW) motivation, and an autonomic index (emotional index—EI), deriving from the matching of heart rate and galvanic skin response activity. Results of this pilot research showed a statistically significant increase of the EI values in correspondence with wine-smelling phase in comparison with the other two phases ($p < 0.01$) and a trend of major avoidance attitude in correspondence with wine tasting with the olfactory component in comparison with the other two conditions. This result could be explained by the lack of specific subjects' expertise. Present data suggest a synergic action exerted by olfaction and gustation sensory modalities, where manipulation could be further studied so to investigate emotional and cognitive aspects of wine tasting experience.

Keywords EEG · Emotion · Interest · Pleasantness · Neuromarketing
Wine

15.1 Introduction

Agricultural companies and wine manufacturers are operating in the environment with a high level of competition, and therefore it is essential for them to retain and even improve their market position to reach high production process efficiency (Raz et al. 2008; Bielik and Hupková 2011). This led some manufacturers and retailers to try creating a positive emotional connection to their brand, product, and point of sale (Malär et al. 2011). The most challenge of marketing discipline is to understand the consumer behavior, and marketers are constantly trying to find new tactics and new methodologies to influence and to evaluate the behavior. In this context, neuromarketing is a new discipline that allows as to view what is happening in the human brain and which is the perception about the product or the customer experience (Horská et al. 2016).

A number of scientific studies have focused on the relationship between emotion and odor. The connections between the two have been used by many authors in the classical and contemporary literature (Kohler et al. 2007). Physiologically, olfactory stimuli are processed according to their emotional content, even when any emotional context is lacking. Like emotions, odors may be given positive (appetitive), negative (aversive), or neutral valence. These close connections, which all of us encounter in everyday life, are related to cerebral substrates common to the two.

In the sensory processing, the idea of the multidimensional integration has long been used to frame a range of questions about the cross-modal interactions in the physiological and behavioral responses (Stein et al. 1996; Wallace and Stein 1997; Armony and Dolan 2001; Laurienti et al. 2003). In the last year, this phenomenon (cross-modality) has been receiving growing interest, and it has been defined as sensory–sensory connectivity and influences of one modality over primary sensory cortex of another (Driver and Noesselt 2008). The importance of studying the interaction among sensory modalities becomes of immediate clarity when applied to the study of a daily experience for humans: food and wine perception. In fact, in the case of food, cross-modal interactions occur between aroma, taste, and texture (Poinot et al. 2013). Furthermore, "flavor is perhaps the most multimodal of all of our sensory experiences" (Small 2012), where flavor has been defined as a perception including gustatory, oral somatosensory, and retronasal olfactory signals, arising from the mouth during foods and beverages consumption. Moreover, typically, for the wine tasting, sommeliers in addition to the use of the gustation, by the introduction of the wine into the mouth, employ the stimulation of the olfactory system both through a direct olfactory stimulation (by the nose) and through a retronasal pathway (accomplished by air inhalation while whirling the wine around in the mouth). The distinction between these two olfactory stimulation modalities is worthy, since evidences showed that in correspondence with congruent taste–odor pairs using the orthonasal route (implying subject to sniff), neural suppression occurred in chemosensory regions. The convergence of taste and odor, firstly thought to occur only at the level of the orbitofrontal cortex, has been showed already at the insula (Small et al. 2004) and piriform cortex (Maier et al. 2012; Small et al. 2013) levels. Therefore, analysis of the contribution of olfaction to the process of wine tasting is fundamental in order to study the product perception by potential users.

There is no doubt that wine marketing is an area where not only the economic but also the noneconomic factors, such as emotions and hidden reactions of a customer, play a decisive role. Even in the current era when it seems that the economic indicators are of a great importance and affect both the business and consumer decisions (Bielik et al. 2014), there are also hedonistic values that can affect choosing a bottle of wine for special occasions or demonstrating some specific, noneconomic values, e.g., the environmental ones (Olsen et al. 2012). The affect that the consumers experience also cannot be adequately measured by the self-reported verbal indicators due its complexity (Zajonc 1980; Panksepp 1998; Davidson 2004). Therefore, the neuromarketing methods are proposed to measure the hidden consumer reactions at the process of buying but also consuming certain products. They can also help with identifying proper retail solutions and specific in-store parameters (Nagyová et al. 2014).

Aim of the present study was to investigate the reaction to the wine gustation with and without the direct olfactory contribution, through an electroencephalographic index, assumed as an indicator of approach or withdrawal (AW) motivation (Davidson et al. 1990), and deriving from the matching of heart rate and galvanic skin response activity, considered an indicator of emotional involvement (Vecchiato et al. 2014).

The AW index has been already applied to food taste (Di Flumeri et al. 2017) and odor (Henkin and Levy 2001; Kim and Watanuki 2003; Di Flumeri et al. 2016). Concerning the emotional index, a list of 16 emotional words has been defined by a behavioral categorization study using the model of circumplex affect (Russell and Barrett 1999); the words were in fact classified on the basis of pleasantness/unpleasantness and arousal (high/low) describing the wine tasting (Ferrarini et al. 2010). The IE has been already applied to neuromarketing studies on advertising

(Cherubino et al. 2016a, b) and antismoking public service announcement (Cartocci et al. 2017), supporting the suitability of its use to product testing.

15.2 Methodology and Sample

The test, which has been conducted in the last September (2017), measured the brain activity and the emotional engagement of individuals during a degustation of the two types of the Italian wines: *Sangiovese* and *Morellino di Scansano*. The experiments have been conducted in the Industrial Neuroscience Laboratory of Sapienza University in Rome. Participant were naïve wine-taster subjects, balanced for gender, with an average age of 37.5 ± 15.52 (Fig. 15.1). The experimental procedure consisted, after smelling two types of the wine, in the tasting of two Italian wines once in the open nose and after that in a closed nose condition, resulting in a total of four wine testing. The closed nose condition was performed with the participants wearing a nose clip (Fig. 15.2). Wines were randomly assigned to participants and served at room temperature in order to avoid undesired temperature-related effects (Craig et al. 2000). After smelling the wine for 10 s, participants were asked to drink from the glass and to keep the wine into the mouth for 10 s before swallowing (Fig. 15.2). The quantity was 20 ml for each wine trial, and before each trial participants were instructed to drink a glass of water.

15.2.1 EEG Recording and Signal Processing

The EEG signal recorded Hz by the BrainVision LiveAmp amplifier (Brain Products GmbH), with a sampling frequency of 250 by 8 EEG electrodes (Fp1, Fpz,

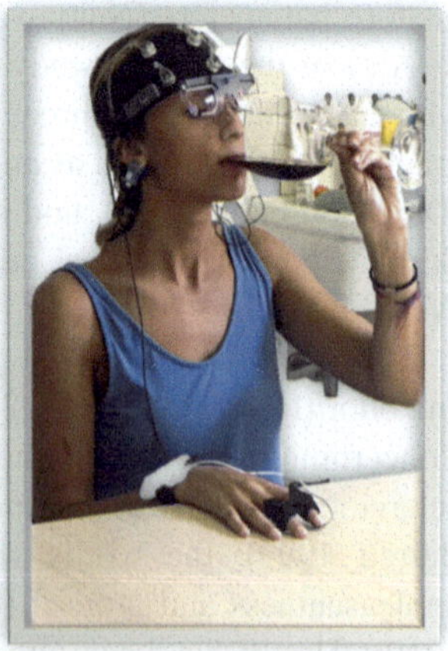

Fig. 15.1 One of the participants equipped with the EEG band on the forehead and the autonomic sensors on the fingers during one of the wine tasting trials

Fig. 15.2 The picture shows the three phases about the experimental conditions

Fp2, AF3, AFz, AF4, ground, and reference), following the 10–20 international system, and the impedance was kept below 10 kΩ. Each EEG trace was then converted into the EEG laboratory format in order to perform signal preprocessing such as artifacts detection filtering and segmentation. The EEG signals have been pass filtered at 2–30 Hz and depurated of ocular artifacts by using the independent component analysis (ICA). Individual alpha frequency (IAF) has been calculated for each subject in order to define four bands of interest according to the method suggested in the literature (Klimesch 1999). Such bands were reported in the following as IAF+, where IAF is the individual alpha frequency, in Hertz, and is an integer displacement in the frequency domain which is employed to define the band ranges. In particular, we focused the present analysis on the alpha bands (IAF-4, IAF+2).

To summarize the activity from all these electrodes, the global field power (GFP) was computed. This is a measurement introduced by Lehmann and Skrandies (1980) to summarize the overall activity over the scalp surface. GFP is computed from the entire set of electrodes by performing the sum of the squared values of the EEG potential at each electrode, resulting in a time-varying waveform related to the increase or decrease of the global power in the analyzed EEG.

The cerebral appreciation has been monitored in the target population by using the approach-withdrawal index, according to the theory related to the EEG frontal asymmetry theory (Davidson 2004). The AW index is correlated with the unbalance of the right and left prefrontal activity. The formula used is the following:

$$AW = GFP\alpha\_right - GFP\alpha\_left$$

where the GFPα_right and GFPα_left stand for the GFP calculated among right (Fp2, AF4) and left (Fp1, AF3) electrodes, in the alpha band, respectively. The waveform of AW cerebral index has been estimated for each second and then averaged for all the duration of the stimuli. The AW index was then standardized according to the baseline EEG activity acquired at the beginning of the experiment. Positive AW values mean an approach motivation toward the stimulus expressed by the subject, while negative AW values a withdrawal tendency. The AW index was in fact normalized returning a z-score values across all the experiments for each subject. In fact, such index has been defined by taking into account the frontal EEG asymmetry's theory by Davidson and coworkers (1990).

15.2.2 The Autonomic Data Recordings and Signal Processing

The blood volume pulse (BVP) and galvanic skin response (GSR) have been recorded with the Shimmer system (Shimmer Sensing, Ireland) with a sampling rate of 52 Hz. For the recording of these signals, three were placed to the palmar side of the middle phalanges of the second and third fingers, on the nondominant hand of the participant, according to the published procedures (Roth et al. 2012). In order to obtain the heart rate signal from the BVP, it used the Pan–Tompkins algorithm (Pan and Tompkins 1985). The constant voltage method (0.5 V) was employed for the acquisition of the skin conductance, and by using the Ledalab software (Benedek and Kaernbach 2010), the tonic component of the skin conductance (skin conductance level, SCL) was estimated.

In order to match GSR and HR signals producing a monodimensional variable which returns the emotional state of subjects, the emotional index has been defined by taking into account the GSR and HR signals (Vecchiato et al. 2014). We refer to effects plane (Russell and Barrett 1999; Posner et al. 2005) where the coordinates of a point in this space are defined by the HR (horizontal axis) and the GSR (vertical axis). Several studies have highlighted that these two autonomic parameters correlate with valence and arousal, respectively (see Mauss and Robinson 2009 for a review). The interpretation of the EI implies that the higher the value the more positive the emotion experienced by the subject and vice versa.

15.3 Results

15.3.1 Approach-Withdrawal Index

The first evidence of the analysis is that there is not statistical significance due the relative high variance of the estimates. The approach-withdrawal index results provided evidence of a trend characterized by approach tendency in the condition in which people taste the wine with open nose, while a tendency of withdrawal in the condition without the olfactory contribution to the wine tasting (nose closed) and during the smell phase (F (2.12) = 1.4499, p = 0.27291) (Fig. 15.3).

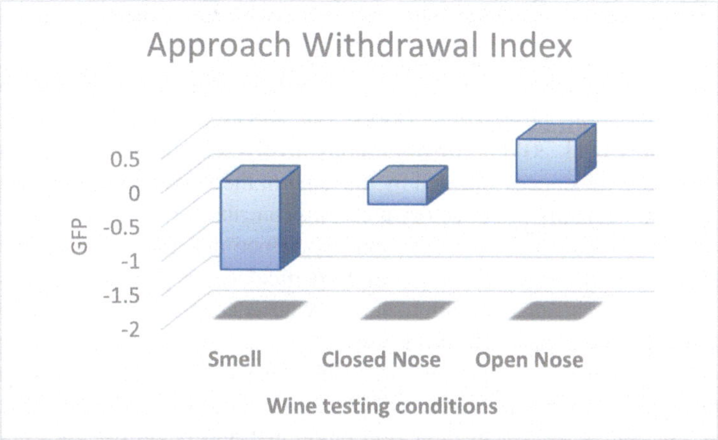

Fig. 15.3 The graph shows the average AW values reported by the experimental group in the three wine tasting conditions (smell, closed nose, and open nose)

15.3.2 Emotional Index

Emotional index results showed a statistically significant effect of the testing phase ($F = 9.678$; $p = 0.005$), in particular, the post hoc comparison showed a decrease of the closed nose condition in comparison with the smell condition ($p = 0.002$) and the open nose condition ($p = 0.010$) (Fig. 15.4).

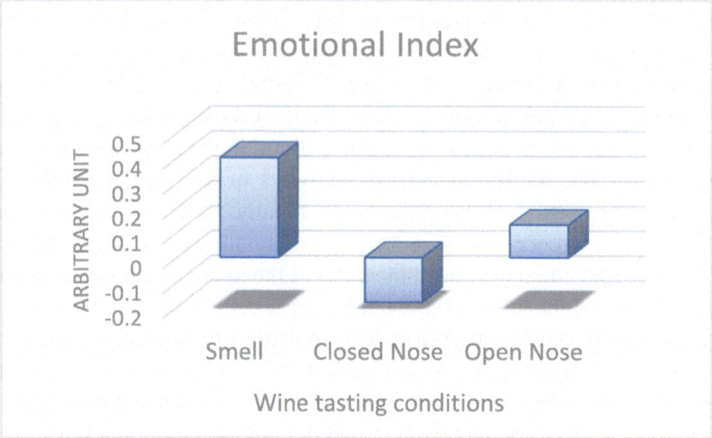

Fig. 15.4 The graph shows the average EI values reported by the experimental group in the three wine tasting conditions (smell, closed nose, and open nose)

15.4 Discussion: Perception, Action, and Emotion

A large number of studies suggest a close relationship between olfactory and affective information processing. Odors can modulate mood, cognition, and behavior (Soudry et al. 2011). The physiology involved in the wine tasting suggests the wine volatile substances warmed by the hand in the glass before the degustation could target immediately the olfactory areas, by contributing to the formation of the taste sensation. However, it is a common experience that the wine tasting experience will be poor if the subject has a cold. In particular, it is generally suggested not to drink costly wine in such condition, since the absence of olfaction modality could decrease greatly the pleasure to drink wine.

Present data numerically support such old heuristic observation for experts. In fact, data suggest a clear interaction between the two sensory modalities of taste and olfaction, since it observed an increased emotional and cognitive appreciation of wine tasting experience with the open nose when compared to the closed nose condition.

Thus, both emotional and cognitive appreciations were increased on average by allowing to the volatile substances of the wine to properly target the olfactory areas. The increased emotional appreciation was obtained in naïve subjects also by using functional magnetic resonance imaging in previous study (Castriota-Scanderbeg et al. 2005). Taken together, these results suggest the modulation of the smell and the open nose conditions is important in the wine degustation when compared to the closed nose (or cold) condition. For all concern, the fact that the cognitive (AW) increased appreciation for the open nose condition was not significantly different from change and although it demonstrated an increase in the average value, we hypothesize that this could be due to the high variance estimated for the AW index. However, it is not possible to disentangle such result from also the fact that the result was not obtained in professional wine taster, e.g., sommelier. In fact, it was found in previous research (Castriota-Scanderbeg et al. 2005) that sommelier showed a bilateral activation in the prefrontal cortex during wine tasting. This could suggest that the lack of statistical significance found in the AW index (i.e., based on the unbalance of the prefrontal cortices activity) in the present study could be influenced by the expertise of the participants. Finally, as showed in the Pazart et al. study (2014) a difference exists in brain activity in wine experts compared to novices testers. This could also be at the basis of the avoidance tendency (suggested by a greater frontal right activity) showed by our testers in the smell condition. Also probably caused by the fact that they were not used to approach wine by Smell, therefore possibly adversing the action itself. On the other hand, it is interesting to note that indeed the smell condition produced in the participants the higher emotional involvement (EI), so suggesting a parallel intense emotional reaction to such condition.

15.5 Conclusion

It has been shown that the "experienced emotion" for the wine smell tasting results from intrinsic properties (such as the molecular composition of a drink) and the state of the individual (such as being thirsty) (Allison and Uhl 1964), together with extrinsic properties (such as price) of products (Plassmann et al. 2008). Plassmann and colleagues provided evidence that varying the price of wine affects the BOLD activity in the medial orbitofrontal cortex, an area associated with primary taste. Therefore, it would be interesting to further investigate also extrinsic properties of the wine by such neurophysiological indicators. Finally, due to the possible influence of the expertise of participants it could be worthy to investigate also this contribution to the neurophysiological response.

Acknowledgements This work was partially done under a grant agreement by the Fondazione Banfi, Montalcino, Italy, accorded to F.B. for the study of the neurometric signature of the wine tasting.

References

Allison RI, Uhl KP (1964) Influence of beer brand identification on taste perception. J Mark Res 1:36–39

Armony JL, Dolan RJ (2001) Modulation of auditory neural responses by a visual context in human fear conditioning. NeuroReport 12(15):3407–3411

Benedek M, Kaernbach C (2010) A continuous measure of phasic electrodermal activity. J Neurosci Methods 190(1):80–91

Bielik P, Hupková D (2011) The technical efficiency analysis—case of agricultural basic industry in Slovakia. AGRIS On-line Papers Econ Inf 3(1):3

Bielik P, Bellérová B, Prokeinová RB et al (2014) Agribusiness and commerce. Slovak University of Agriculture

Cartocci G, Caratù M, Modica E et al (2017) Electroencephalographic, heart rate, and galvanic skin response assessment for an advertising perception study: application to antismoking public service announcements. J Vis Exp JoVE (126)

Castriota-Scanderbeg A, Hagberg GE, Cerasa A et al (2005) The appreciation of wine by sommeliers: a functional magnetic resonance study of sensory integration. Neuroimage 25 (2):570–578

Cherubino P, Cartocci G, Trettel A et al (2016a) Marketing meets neuroscience: useful insights for gender subgroups during the observation of TV ads. In: Applying neuroscience to business practice, p 163

Cherubino P, Trettel A, Cartocci G et al (2016b) Neuroelectrical indexes for the study of the efficacy of TV advertising stimuli. In: Selected issues in experimental economics. Springer, Cham, pp 355–371

Craig AD, Chen K, Bandy D et al (2000) Thermosensory activation of insular cortex. Nat Neurosci 3(2):184

Davidson RJ (2004) What does the prefrontal cortex "do" in affect: perspectives on frontal EEG asymmetry research. Biol Psychol 67(1–2):219–234

Davidson RJ, Ekman P, Saron CD et al (1990) Approach-withdrawal and cerebral asymmetry: emotional expression and brain physiology: I. J Pers Soc Psychol 58(2):330

Di Flumeri G, Herrero MT, Trettel A et al (2016) EEG frontal asymmetry related to pleasantness of olfactory stimuli in young subjects. In: Selected issues in experimental economics. Springer, Cham, pp 373–381

Di Flumeri G, Aricò P, Borghini G et al (2017) EEG-based approach-withdrawal index for the pleasantness evaluation during taste experience in realistic settings. In: 2017 39th annual international conference of the IEEE engineering in medicine and biology society (EMBC), pp 3228–3231

Driver J, Noesselt T (2008) Multisensory interplay reveals crossmodal influences on 'sensory-specific' brain regions, neural responses, and judgments. Neuron 57(1):11–23

Ferrarini R, Carbognin C, Casarotti EM et al (2010) The emotional response to wine consumption. Food Qual Prefer 21(7):720–725

Henkin RI, Levy LM (2001) Lateralization of brain activation to imagination and smell of odors using functional magnetic resonance imaging (fMRI): left hemispheric localization of pleasant and right hemispheric localization of unpleasant odors. J Comput Assist Tomogr 25(4): 493–514

Horská E, Bercik J, Krasnodębski A et al (2016) Innovative approaches to examining consumer preferences when choosing wines. Agric Econ-Zemed Ekon 62:124–133

Kim YK, Watanuki S (2003) Characteristics of electroencephalographic responses induced by a pleasant and an unpleasant odor. J Physiol Anthropol Appl Hum Sci 22(6):285–291

Klimesch W (1999) EEG alpha and theta oscillations reflect cognitive and memory performance: a review and analysis. Brain Res Rev 29(2–3):169–195

Kohler CG, Barrett FS, Gur RC et al (2007) Association between facial emotion recognition and odor identification in schizophrenia. J Neuropsychiatry Clin Neurosci 19(2):128–131

Laurienti PJ, Wallace MT, Maldjian JA et al (2003) Cross-modal sensory processing in the anterior cingulate and medial prefrontal cortices. Hum Brain Mapp 19(4):213–223

Lehmann D, Skrandies W (1980) Reference-free identification of components of checkerboard-evoked multichannel potential fields. Electroencephalogr Clin Neurophysiol 48 (6):609–621

Maier JX, Wachowiak M, Katz DB (2012) Chemosensory convergence on primary olfactory cortex. J Neurosci 32(48):17037–17047

Malär L, Krohmer H, Hoyer WD et al (2011) Emotional brand attachment and brand personality: the relative importance of the actual and the ideal self. J Mark 75(4):35–52

Mauss IB, Robinson MD (2009) Measures of emotion: a review. Cogn Emot 23(2):209–237

Nagyová Ľ, Berčík J, Horská E (2014) The efficiency, energy intensity and visual impact of the accent lighting in the retail grocery stores. Potravin Slovak J Food Sci 8(1):296–305

Olsen J, Thach L, Hemphill L (2012) The impact of environmental protection and hedonistic values on organic wine purchases in the US. Int J Wine Bus Res 24(1):47–67

Pan J, Tompkins WJ (1985) A real-time QRS detection algorithm. IEEE Trans Biomed Eng 3:230–236

Panksepp J (1998) The periconscious substrates of consciousness: affective states and the evolutionary origins of the SELF. J Consciousness Stud 5(5–6):566–582

Pazart L, Comte A, Magnin E et al (2014) An fMRI study on the influence of sommeliers' expertise on the integration of flavor. Front Behav Neurosci 8:358

Plassmann H, O'Doherty J, Shiv B et al (2008) Marketing actions can modulate neural representations of experienced pleasantness. Proc Natl Acad Sci 105(3):1050–1054

Plassmann H, Ramsøy TZ, Milosavljevic M (2012) Branding the brain: a critical review and outlook. J Consum Psychol 22(1):18–36

Poinot P, Arvisenet G, Ledauphin J et al (2013) How can aroma–related cross–modal interactions be analysed? A review of current methodologies. Food Qual Prefer 28(1):304–316

Posner J, Russell JA, Peterson BS (2005) The circumplex model of affect: an integrative approach to affective neuroscience, cognitive development, and psychopathology. Dev Psychopathol 17 (3):715–734

Raz C, Piper D, Haller R et al (2008) From sensory marketing to sensory design: how to drive formulation using consumers' input? Food Qual Prefer 19(8):719–726

Roth WT, Dawson ME, Filion DL (2012) Publication recommendations for electrodermal measurements. Psychophysiology 49(8):1017–1034

Russell JA, Barrett LF (1999) Core affect, prototypical emotional episodes, and other things called emotion: dissecting the elephant. J Pers Soc Psychol 76(5):805

Small DM (2012) Flavor is in the brain. Physiol Behav 107(4):540–552

Small DM, Voss J, Mak YE et al (2004) Experience-dependent neural integration of taste and smell in the human brain. J Neurophysiol 92(3):1892–1903

Small DM, Veldhuizen MG, Green B (2013) Sensory neuroscience: taste responses in primary olfactory cortex. Curr Biol 23(4):R157–R159

Soudry Y, Lemogne C, Malinvaud D et al (2011) Olfactory system and emotion: common substrates. Eur Ann Otorhinolaryngol Head Neck Dis 128(1):18–23

Stein EA, Fuller SA, Edgemond WS et al (1996) Physiological and behavioural effects of the endogenous cannabinoid, arachidonylethanolamide (anandamide), in the rat. Br J Pharmacol 119(1):107–114

Vecchiato G, Cherubino P, Maglione AG et al (2014) How to measure cerebral correlates of emotions in marketing relevant tasks. Cogn Comput 6(4):856–871

Wallace MT, Stein BE (1997) Development of multisensory neurons and multisensory integration in cat superior colliculus. J Neurosci 17(7):2429–2444

Zajonc RB (1980) Feeling and thinking: preferences need no inferences. Am Psychol 35(2):151

Chapter 16
Information Assimilation as a Decisive Factor About Website User's Behaviors

Michał Nowakowski

Abstract The twenty-first century is the time of unlimited inflow of the huge amount of information, which the average person is no longer able to fully receive. That is why it becomes so important that the provided information have not only relevant content, but also be presented in a suitable and easy-to-interpret way. This aspect has influence on information assimilation among recipients, which is also one of the factors of useful information and besides it is explaining what work or costs must be borne by the user, to be able to take full advantage from provided information. This chapter presents analysis and methodology of information assimilation evaluation on websites, which is one of the factors determining the behavior of recipients and further use of the acquired information for decision-making, consumption, or informative purposes. Furthermore, the study describes the basic methodological assumptions, the research procedure of information assimilation evaluation, and the results of data analysis from the study conducted on a group of respondents. In order to determine the factors that have the greatest impact on information assimilation and learning newly learned content, the data obtained from the study were analyzed using cognitive walkthrough method, methodology for testing respondents before and after the research, and knowledge growth evaluation indicator. Results of research presented in the chapter can be useful in creating assumptions for ways of content presentation for the needs of websites.

Keywords Information assimilation · Forms of information presentation and informative content · Customers' behaviors of Internet services Cognitive walkthrough method · Methodology for testing respondents before and after the research · Knowledge growth evaluation indicator

M. Nowakowski (✉)
Department of IT System Engineering, Faculty of Economics and Management, Institute of IT in Management, University of Szczecin, Mickiewicza 64, 71-101 Szczecin, Poland
e-mail: michal.nowakowski@wneiz.pl

K. Nermend and M. Łatuszyńska (eds.), *Problems, Methods and Tools in Experimental and Behavioral Economics*, Springer Proceedings in Business and Economics, https://doi.org/10.1007/978-3-319-99187-0_16

16.1 Introduction

The twenty-first century is a time of great technological progress, in particular the rapid development of information and communication technologies, which the main purpose is easy access to information. That is why it becomes so important that the provided information have not only relevant content, but also be presented in a suitable and easy-to-interpret way. This aspect has influence on information assimilation among recipients, which is also one of the factors of useful information and besides it is explaining what work or costs must be borne by the user, to be able to take full advantage from provided information.

Although the information assimilation aspect refers to the most forms of media messages, it is particularly important in the case of content provided by websites. Internet network, like no other currently available form of transmission, enables not only browsing information on all possible topics, but also access to a wide range of interactive services and supporting all of the forms of human activity. That is why various forms of presenting information on websites should be understandable and accessible to all users, regardless of age or acquaintance of technology. The following forms of multimedia content are the most frequently used forms of presenting information and informational content on websites for years: texts, images, photographs, animations, sounds, music, or movies. For some time on the Internet, modern forms of data and information visualization have become more and more popular and one example of them are information graphics, also known as infographics. The main task of the infographics is to catch the attention of the potential recipient and enable him to get acquainted with its content quickly using the transparency of the information message (Nowakowski 2014). Certainly, the tendency to increase the content assimilation and information messages is in line with the widely developed and implemented methodology of improving the usability of websites (Nowakowski 2016).

The chapter describes application of cognitive walkthrough method, methodology for testing respondents before and after the research, and knowledge growth evaluation indicator for analysis and evaluation of information assimilation and the process of learning newly learned content with particular emphasis on text, graphics, infographics, and shopping content. The research problem of the chapter is analysis and evaluation of information assimilation applied in selected information and shopping websites. The purpose of the study is assimilation evaluation of text and graphics information, presented in these types of websites, in terms of the intelligibility and general usability of content for end users. The additional purpose of the study is cognitive analysis of the influence of the form of presentation and information content, browsed and read by the respondents, on the quantity and scope of new information adopted by them, as a result of familiarizing themselves with the services being the subject of the study.

16.2 Information Concept

In the literature, there are many different definitions and meanings of the information concept. Moreover, it is often associated with such terms as data and knowledge, which is often used interchangeably. Hierarchical relationships between these cognitive terms represent so-called **the pyramid of knowledge**, which at the base contains the concept of data, the concept of information is placed higher in the hierarchy, and the concepts of knowledge and wisdom appear on the top (Zeleny 1987). The last two concepts are basically the highest level that can be achieved in the context of the interpretation of data and information for the purpose of making any decisions.

The infologic approach by infologic theory of Langefors explicitly distinguishes the information from the data and puts the emphasis on taking into account the requirements of information users (Langefors 1973). The information in this approach is a meaning which is given to the data, taking into account factors like psychological, sociological, linguistic, semantic, etc. The meaning of information (the sense and importance) is strictly related to the user's person (information sender or recipient), which implies that the same information can lead different people to a completely different conclusions. Information in this approach is subjective and describes the meaning, which a sender or recipient gives to the data (Pettersson 1993); therefore, from specific data different people can extract different information (Langefors 1973). Whereas the knowledge in this context is interpreted as information enriched by the experience, moreover it is a human resource with significantly personal and subjective nature, and it should not be the objective truth (Stefanowicz 2004). Meanwhile, wisdom is the ability to take prudent and appropriate actions in a specific situation that are based on ethical resolution of problems in accordance with the belief system (Jashpara 2011).

The subjective aspect of information affects also the value of information, which results from the fact that it is taken into account factors depending on the evaluation from the person and conditions in which the information is utilized. For these reasons, a subjective assessment should be given the most attention in the searching for the problem solution of correct estimation of the information value. The attitude subjectivity in information evaluation has also an impact on decision making, where even in the case of the same information, it may bring different effects in dependence on the specifics of individual decision-makers. Moreover, it is said that accuracy and pragmatics of information evaluation is a critical economic factor in the information society (Meyer 2005; Morrison and Cohen 2005).

16.3 Information Assimilation Concept in the Context of Different Approaches

The information assimilation aspect can be treated by recipients in various ways, depending on the attitude. The following approaches of information assimilation can be considered to be the most popular in the literature on the subject: cognitive, qualitative, knowledge-based, and technological.

According to cognitive approach, in the theory of cognitive development of Jean Piaget, the information assimilation is acceptance of new information and experiences by the human mind and including them in the resources of his knowledge. This process is usually subjective and relatively easy to implement, because it does not require too much correction of the owned knowledge. Through this process, people add new information to their existing knowledge base, sometimes re-interpreting these new experiences to fit to the information they already have. This theory is also called the Piaget's learning model, where in the absorption process, new information is combined with existing structures of knowledge, without changing these structures (Miller 2011).

The Piaget's theory mainly refers to different stages of children's development and focuses on how the child develops his cognitive structure on the subject of the surrounding reality, depending on the level of its understanding and interpretation skills. And so in early childhood, children constantly assimilate new information and experiences for their current knowledge about the world. However, this process does not end only at this stage and also in a more mature age, when people encounter new situations, make small and big changes in their existing experiences about the surrounding world (Piaget and Cook 1952; Wadsworth 2004).

However, the process of information assimilation is more complex and plays an important role in learning about the surrounding world, because people tend not only to supplement knowledge about new facts, but also to modify owned information. In this case, the process of information accommodation takes place, which relies on changing existing schemes or creating new schemes and ideas as a result of access to new information and experiences. That is why, the Piaget's cognitive development theory can be applied not only to different stages of development of children, but also to the processes of learning new things by adults, because the processes of assimilation and accommodation usually work together as part of the learning process. Some information are simply attached into existing schemes through the assimilation process, while other information leads to the development of new schemes or the complete transformations of existing ideas through the accommodation process (Miller 2011). Tuckman and Monetti also notice that other important elements in the learning process are also different types of behaviors, such as imitation, play, and developing a stable sense of self (Tuckman and Monetti 2011).

According to qualitative approach, the information assimilation is one of the factors of useful information, which is defined as persisting within the permissible norm, by the user, additional work or costs to be borne, to be able to take full advantage from provided information (Jashpara 2011). Other qualitative features of useful information that affect on assimilation can be included such information features like: intelligibility, availability, readability, currency, suitability, or appropriateness of the form of information visualization (Dudycz 1998; IT Governance Institute 2005; Miller 1996; Mazur and Nowakowski 2017; Prussak 1995; Stefanowicz 2004).

According to knowledge-based approach, knowledge management is a process in which organizations collect, restore, transform, and use various types of data and information in order to transform them into knowledge that can be later shared into strategic goals (Drucker 2003). A knowledge management system is a system that uses collective knowledge in the organization and is most often used to compete, introduce innovations, and respond to appearing business opportunities. The information assimilation in a knowledge-based approach is associated with the use of knowledge management IT systems by people to better adopting information and knowledge provided by such systems (Alavi and Leidner 2001). According to Brown and Duguid, the differences between information and knowledge are significant, and among others rely on the fact that knowledge, requires an expert, is much more difficult to detach, transmit or make available than information, and it is much more difficult to assimilate and understand it than information (Small and Sage 2006). For these reasons, the assimilation of content and information provided by knowledge management systems is so important for users of these systems and whole organizations.

In turn according to technological approach, assimilation can be seen as the appropriate technological adaptation of electronic devices and information made available to them for learning of easy reading and writing in a manner consistent with existing teaching programs, pedagogical goals, or instructional activities (Stokes 1997; Wartella and Reeves 1983). In addition, the computer as a digital device offers new and increased possibilities that can improve the conventional approach to reading, such as increasing the ability to understand, building vocabulary, stimulating interest in reading books, or improving spelling (Reitsma 1988; Roth and Beck 1987). On the other hand, the information assimilation in the technological aspect can also be used in multimedia systems and, for example, refers to the process of detecting events and joining acquired sensory and non-sensory information from a variety of data sources, using appropriate context and past experience (Atrey et al. 2006).

In the following part of the chapter, the author concentrates on two of the above-mentioned approaches to the information assimilation, that is the cognitive and qualitative approaches.

16.4 The Research Assumptions of Information Assimilation Evaluation

The research problem of the chapter is analysis and evaluation of information assimilation applied in selected information and shopping websites with the use of selected methods. The evaluation of information assimilation was focused mainly on available informational content and various forms of information presentation and visualization, such as text, graphics, images, charts, and infographics. The selected research problem was prepared and developed on the basis of quantitative research (internet survey) and qualitative research. Analysis of the results was carried out with the use of cognitive walkthrough method, methodology for testing respondents before and after the research, and knowledge growth evaluation indicator.

The research entity survey conducted in January 2018 was 44-person group of respondents, which was selected for the study by the targeted selection method and represented various forms of education, from secondary education, and higher ending. The sample size was considered as statistically representative due to the specificity of the study related to the websites' usability evaluation. Most of the respondents were citizens of Polish nationality (68%), and the others (32%) were citizens of countries such as Italy, Spain, Portugal, and Turkey. Respondents represented different age-groups, a large majority (91%) were young people (18-26 years old), while the rest of them (9%) were the representatives of a few older people (27-35 years old). Among the respondents, the majority were men (57%), and the remainder of women (43%). From the answers obtained from respondents, it can be concluded that exactly everyone (100%) use the Internet several times a day. The most popular forms of communication with the Internet among respondents were mobile devices (98%) and stationary devices like laptops (73%) and to use the desktop computers (20%) and tablets devices (20%) admitted a significant minority of them.

Therefore, it can be said that the group of surveyed respondents had a minimum sufficient knowledge and skills, for the purpose of research, in using various information and shopping websites. This aspect is particularly important in the context of learning support of Internet services as seen sometimes for the first time during the study, as well as the credibility of the results of the subjective evaluation of various criteria of information assimilation.

The research object were four Polish-language (for respondents of Polish nationality) and four English-language (for respondents of a non-Polish nationality) Internet services with the possibility of content reading and browsing and online shopping. To the study there were selected the services based on the first search results obtained in the Google search engine (https://www.google.pl), where the range of search pages related to one selected topic. Selected websites were characterized by various forms of information content presentation on a selected topic, such as text content, text and graphic content, text and infographics content as well as text and graphic content with the possibility of shopping. The different forms of information presentation on websites were additionally associated with various types of information about the selected product category. Selected services are also representatives of modern, powerful, and highly advanced solutions both in terms of technical, quality, and marketing aspects.

The research thematic scope there was a group of electronic devices like electronic book readers (so-called e-book readers), which can be an alternative to other devices used to read documents and electronic books. Electronic book readers are devices more and more popular and dedicated primarily for displaying and convenient reading of texts stored in digital form, e.g., e-books or e-newspapers. These types of devices are equipped with a display, usually made in the technology of electronic paper and internal memory. Thanks to the technology of electronic paper, these devices allow, among others, creating electronic notes or reading content like classic paper, which largely minimizes computer-specific eye fatigue. In addition, e-readers not only allow reading e-books, but also popular formats of text and graphics files, in at least one of the following formats: TXT, EPUB, Mobipocket (PRC/MOBI/AZW), FB2, HTML, PDF, RTF, DOC, PDB, DjVu, JPG, and others (https://en.wikipedia.org/wiki/E-reader).

During the research among informational content, for both Polish-language and English-language services, there were pages describing the following characteristics of e-book readers: general information and the purpose of such devices, practical recommendations on choosing such devices, statistics on the use of such devices, and current prices in online stores for various manufacturers of this type of equipment.

As a curiosity, it should be recognized the fact that in the entire examined group, only one person (2% of the population) admitted to use the electronic book reader earlier. This information is so important because from the point of view of the objectives of the study, practically all respondents did not have too much knowledge about this type of devices or this knowledge was small.

The main objective of the research (subject of research) of selected information and shopping websites was evaluation of text and graphics information assimilation presented in these services, in terms of intelligibility and content general usefulness for end users. Main objective of the study was analyzed and evaluated on the basis of the electronic survey (quantitative analysis) and results of the activities and behaviors of respondents (qualitative analysis) within the selected websites. Among the activities that respondents performed were such operations as: reading comprehension descriptions and characteristics about the products (textual content), browsing selected information articles about the products (the content of text and graphics), browsing the additional materials associated with the products (the content of text, graphics and infographics), and moving within the information structure of selected websites.

In the context of study it was assumed, that information assimilation is understood as a set of several selected characteristics of the information quality. Content intelligibility, content suitability in the future, availability of all text and graphics content, information completeness of all textual and graphic content, ease and convenience of reading content, visual attractiveness of text and graphic content as well as intelligibility and visual attractiveness of infographics included in the chapter.

The additional objective of the research was a cognitive analysis of the impact of the form of presentation and information content, browsed and read information by the respondents, on the quantity and scope of new information adopted by them as a result of familiarization with the services, which were the subject of the study. The final result of the scope and quantity of newly acquired knowledge, by respondents, about electronic devices such as e-book readers and thus its increase or not, was to show the degree of influence of the form of presentation and information content on the amount of memorized and newly learned information. As is known, any increase in the resources of knowledge held by the respondents, as a result of familiarization with the given content, could have a major impact on their future decisions regarding the use of electronic documents or interest in the purchase of such devices.

16.5 Evaluation Methodology of Information Assimilation on Internet Services

The research procedure of information assimilation evaluation in websites was based on performing the following actions:

(1) creation of survey and collecting data from respondents,
(2) construction of structure of criteria, which contain a list of criteria and obtained values of final results,
(3) creation of sample scenario of browsing and reading of selected websites in order to collect a minimal range of knowledge about devices such as e-book readers using the cognitive walkthrough method,
(4) analysis of the obtained research data for an example scenario in terms of information assimilation evaluation of text, graphics, infographics, and purchasing information,
(5) cognitive analysis of the obtained research data in terms of the impact of the form of presentation and information content on the quantity and scope of new information adopted by respondents,
(6) drawing out final conclusions from analysis.

In the first stage, in order to collect data from respondents, electronic survey was created using free of charge *Google Forms* online survey system (https://www.google.pl/intl/pl/forms/about). Survey study was based on evaluation of selected criteria and performing simple successive tasks, which were done in network environment using Internet browser application and selected Internet information and shopping services. All of the tasks were evaluated by respondents on a slightly extended Likert scale for values from 0 (lack or lowest rating) to 5 (highest rating),

Table 16.1 Structure of each main criteria and values obtained from the survey. *Source* Self study

Symbol	Short name of criterion	Data from survey study			
		Thematic websites			
	Information and presentation aspects of the content	Site-1	Site-2	Site-3	Site-4
MC-1	Content intelligibility	4/5	3/5	3/5	4/5
MC-2	Content suitability in the future	3/5	4/5	4/5	4/5
MC-3	Availability of all text and graphics content in the Internet service	4/5	3/5	3/5	3/5
MC-4	Information completeness of all textual and graphic content in the Internet service	3/5	4/5	4/5	3/5
MC-5	Ease and convenience of reading content	4/5	4/5	3/5	4/5
MC-6	Visual attractiveness of textual content in the article	2/5	3/5	3/5	4/5
MC-7	Visual attractiveness of graphic content in the article	3/5	3/5	3/5	3/5
MC-8	Intelligibility and visual attractiveness of infographics included in the article	–	–	4/5	–

based on the level of satisfaction and usability fulfillment of specific quality criteria by selected Internet services (Likert 1932).

In the second stage, one-level structure of eight main criteria was created, which concerned information and presentation aspects of the content. The selected criteria were the tasks actually performed and evaluated by the respondents, from the point of view of the main objective of the study.

Symbols of the main criteria (*MC-1, MC-2, ..., MC-8*), a list of individual main criteria and values obtained from the survey for four analyzed websites (*Site-1, Site-2, Site-3, and Site-4*), are presented in Table 16.1.

The third stage of the research procedure relied on creation of sample scenario of browsing and reading selected websites in order to collect by respondents a minimal range of knowledge about devices such as e-book readers. This scenario used the cognitive walkthrough method and depended on loading, in the right order to the web browser, four different websites that were previously selected by the author of the chapter. Due to the different language needs of the respondents, two analogical page groups were created, where four different pages in each group were selected in Polish and English. Each of the sites has been selected for the presence of various types of information on the selected product category, various forms of information content presentation, and various positions in the Google search engine (https://www.google.pl). The order of loaded websites by the surveyed was not accidental and was related to the forms of information content presentation, starting from typically textual content and ending with graphic, infographics, and shopping content. This was to show the participants, how different forms of content presentation from more difficult textual to easier visual ones can affect the comfort and efficiency of their cognitive assimilation.

During the questionnaire survey, each of loaded pages was browsed and read by the respondent's ongoing basis and then evaluated for selected qualitative features that affect the total information assimilation. For all sites, the respondents also assessed the scope of the knowledge they had learned about, which they obtained thanks to the information available there. As the information content available on individual pages related to various aspects of e-book readers, the respondents were able to compare different (usually new) information content with their previous (achieved so far) knowledge on the subject each time. This aspect presents the way of acquiring new information and learning, using the properly selected content on the Internet, in order to expand the range of its own knowledge and based on the current, individual for everyone, experience.

As the analysis of the above-described scenario also took into account the behaviors of the respondents during browsing and reading websites, the way in which they moved and navigated within selected websites was also important. This aspect was included in the survey by adding tasks using the cognitive walkthrough method. Cognitive walkthrough method is one of the popular methods of expert usability evaluation, which based on website testing by a chosen expert from the potential tasks point of view (e.g., browsing information on the website using navigation systems) performed by users. The main assumption of using this method in the field of websites research is to focus on usefulness aspects related to ease of learning to navigate on the service. As a result, this method allows to detect errors that hinder the implementation of the tasks, during the first users contact with service (Nielsen and Mack 1994; Rieman et al. 1995; Wharton et al. 1994). As follows from the above definition and description of cognitive walkthrough method, using it for usefulness evaluation of content presentation, learning of newly learned content and related to them information assimilation, and not only to aspects of websites information architecture, was justifiable in the context of the main objective of the study.

The fourth stage of the research procedure relied on data analysis for an example scenario of expanding knowledge on a given topic, in terms of information assimilation evaluation of text, graphics, infographics, and purchasing information. Therefore, first of all, the result data from the survey were collected for the main criteria values. In order to determine one resulting value for every criterion, there was primarily used a value of arithmetical mean for data. In situation, when the results largely pointed to only one specific resulting value, there was used a value of dominant.

The next step as part of this stage was analysis of the resulting data in terms of selected scenario, with emphasis on various forms of information presentation, in order to determine the level of information assimilation among the respondents. Different forms of information presentation were represented by individual selected websites, which were also the subject of the study. The following website symbols, reflected the specific forms of information presentation assigned to them: *Site-1* (mostly textual content), *Site-2* (textual and graphic content), *Site-3* (textual and infographics content), and *Site-4* (textual content with graphic elements and shopping functions).

Information assimilation evaluation for individual forms of presentation was made using the authoring method on the assumption the same level of significance for all the main criteria taken into account. The level of significance for the criteria was determined at the same level, because during browsing and reading information content presented on websites, various forms of presentation overlap each other and it is difficult to clearly determine, which ones are more important than others. The applied method consisted in determining four partial ratings of the assimilation level (*PRA-1, PRA-2, PRA-3, and PRA-4*), which were calculated for all main criteria (*MC-1, MC-2, ..., MC-8*) within four selected websites (*Site-1, Site-2, Site-3, and Site-4*). Selected partial ratings were calculated as the sum of the results obtained in the study, compared to the maximum sums values possible to obtain and then converted to percentages. It is worth to add that a similar way of analyzing individual criteria using their aggregate value is also used by another known method of usability evaluation of IT products, which is the SUM method (*Single Usability Metric*). This method is based on a quantitative model and focuses on three standard aspects of usability, such as efficiency, effectiveness, and satisfaction (Sauro and Kindlund 2005).

The role of main criteria fulfilled the following qualitative information features:

(1) content intelligibility (evaluation made four times for each form of information presentation),
(2) content suitability in the future (evaluation made four times for each form of information presentation),
(3) availability of all text and graphics content in the Internet service (evaluation made four times for each form of information presentation),
(4) information completeness of all textual and graphic content in the Internet service (evaluation made four times for each form of information presentation),
(5) ease and convenience of reading content (evaluation made four times for each form of information presentation),
(6) visual attractiveness of textual content in the article (evaluation made four times for each form of information presentation),
(7) visual attractiveness of graphic content in the article (evaluation made four times for each form of information presentation),
(8) intelligibility and visual attractiveness of infographics included in the article (evaluation made one time for infographics forms of information presentation).

On the basis of such partial ratings, it was possible to conclude about the level of information assimilation of selected presentation forms of text, graphics, infographics, and shopping content.

All values calculated, in accordance with the above assumptions, are presented in Table 16.2.

The fifth stage of the research procedure relied on cognitive analysis of the obtained research data in terms of the impact of the form of presentation and information content on the quantity and scope of new information adopted by respondents. Therefore, a list of six additional criteria was created that referred to

Table 16.2 Final results from the study after analysis in terms of assimilation evaluation of text and graphics information. *Source* Self study

Data from survey study after analysis in terms of the information assimilation evaluation				
Thematic websites	Site-1	Site-2	Site-3	Site-4
Applied forms of information presentation	Mostly textual content	Textual and graphic content	Textual and infographics content	Textual content with graphic elements and shopping functions
Partial rating symbol	PRA-1	PRA-2	PRA-3	PRA-4
Partial rating values	23/35	24/35	27/40	25/35
Partial rating values in percentage	65.71	68.57	67.00	71.43
Position in the ranking in terms of the information assimilation	4	2	3	1

the cognitive aspects of the browsed and read content. The selected criteria complemented the tasks actually performed and evaluated by the respondents, from the point of view the additional objective of the research.

The role of additional criteria fulfilled the following cognitive aspects:

(1) the assessment of the knowledge degree of what is and what is it for an e-book reader device (evaluation made one time before study),
(2) feelings/emotions accompanying the respondent while reading the article (evaluation made four times for each form of information presentation),
(3) feedback whether the respondent learned something new while reading the article (evaluation made four times for each form of information presentation),
(4) the level of remembered information by the respondents from the whole article (evaluation made four times for each form of information presentation),
(5) the assessment of the knowledge degree of what is and what can it be used for an e-book reader device (evaluation made one time after study),
(6) the level of knowledge about e-book reader devices (evaluation made one time after study).

Cognitive evaluation of the impact of the form of presentation and information content on the quantity and scope of new information adopted by respondents was made using knowledge growth evaluation indicator, which the application source are various assessing models of education effectiveness and trainings conducting. In the literature on the subject, the concept of education effectiveness is, on the one hand, the achievement degree of the assumed didactic goals, and on the other hand, it is the improvement of the action results, obtained as a result of the conducted training. The changes taking place in people as a result of education process can be such effects as: learning new content and better assimilation of knowledge, mastering new skills or changing them attitudes. Another understanding of the effectiveness and trainings efficiency assessment is the approach based on the objectives that should be achieved during the training, after its completion and after returning to work in the long-term perspective (Bramley 2007). One of the most popular and most useful models of this type is the Kirkpatrick model, based on the assumption, that the training goals should be formulated and evaluated at the following four levels: assessment of reaction to training, assessment of learning, assessment of changes in behavior, and assessment of results (Kirkpatrick 1996; Pocztowski 2008).

From the point of view of the additional objective set in the chapter, the most adequate approach to the cognitive evaluation of the impact of the form of presentation and information content on the quantity and scope of new information is using the second level of the Kirkpatrick model, relating to the process and assessment of learning. On this level, information is obtained about: what and how much participants of the training/research have learned, what kind of knowledge they have gain, what skills they have acquired and what extent their attitudes have evolved. The degree of new content capture can be measured by means of various tests and touchstones, known from educational practice, which are most often used before the training/research and after its completion (Bramley 2007; Kirkpatrick 1996; Molina et al. 2014).

In the cognitive analysis of the impact of the form of presentation and information content on the quantity and scope of new information adopted by the respondents, the methodology for testing respondents before and after the research and the knowledge growth evaluation indicator was used. According to Bramley, a knowledge growth indicator (*KGI*) depends on the test results before a study (*ResultBeforeStudy*), after a study (*ResultAfterStudy*), and results that can be achieved in a study (*PossibleResults*), and it has the following mathematical structure (Bramley 2007):

$$KGI = \frac{ResultAfterStudy - ResultBeforeStudy}{PossibleResults - ResultBeforeStudy} \times 100\%$$

The applied methodology consisted at the beginning in collecting the result data from the questionnaire for the values of additional criteria. In order to determine one resulting value for every criterion, there was primarily used a value of arithmetical mean for data. In situation, when the results largely pointed to only one specific resulting value there was used a value of dominant.

Symbols of the additional criteria (*AC-1, AC-2, ..., AC-6*), a list of individual additional criteria and values obtained from the survey for four analyzed websites (*Site-1, Site-2, Site-3, Site-4*), are presented in Table 16.3.

Then four partial ratings were determined for the quantity and scope of the newly adopted information (*PRC-1, PRC-2, PRC-3, and PRC-4*), which were calculated for all additional criteria (*AC-1, AC-2, ..., AC-6*) within four selected websites (*Site-1, Site-2, Site-3, and Site-4*). All of the partial ratings were calculated on the basis of the knowledge growth indicator described earlier, and then presented in the form of numerical and percentage values.

Table 16.3 Structure of each additional criteria and values obtained from the survey. *Source* Self study

Symbol	Short name of criterion	Data from survey study			
		Thematic websites			
	Form of presentation and information content cognitive aspects	Site-1	Site-2	Site-3	Site-4
AC-1	The assessment of the knowledge degree of what is and what is it for an e-book reader device	4/5 (80%)			
AC-2	Feelings/emotions accompanying the respondent while reading the article	3/5	3/5	3/5	3/5
AC-3	Feedback whether the respondent learned something new while reading the article	3/3	2/3	2/3	2/3
AC-4	The level of remembered information by the respondents from the whole article	3/5	3/5	3/5	3/5
AC-5	The assessment of the knowledge degree of what is and what can it be used for an e-book reader device	4/5 (80%)			
AC-6	The level of knowledge about e-book reader devices	2/5 (40%)			

On the basis of such partial ratings, it was possible to conclude about the scope and quantity of the new knowledge adopted by respondents, what was to show the impact of the form of presentation (textual, graphic, infographics, and shopping content) and information content on quantity of remembered and newly learned information by them.

All values calculated, in accordance with the above assumptions, are presented in Table 16.4.

The last sixth stage of the research procedure relied on developing conclusions from the performed study. The final results were analyzed in terms of the following two aspects:

- analysis of an example scenario in terms of information assimilation evaluation of various forms of information presentation on websites,
- cognitive analysis in terms of the impact of various forms of information presentation and information content of websites on the quantity and scope of new information adopted in this way by respondents.

The first of the analyzed areas was assimilation evaluation of various forms of information presentation occurred on websites. The study scenario involved the evaluation of various forms of information presentation for four selected pages in the following order: textual, graphic, infographics, and shopping information. This aspect was the main objective of the research and was analyzed on the basis of the results, obtained from the respondents, related to browsing and reading various forms of content presentation about devices such as electronic book readers. The information assimilation was understood, in this context, as the usefulness of access to multimedia thematic content from the selected websites and the ease of its

Table 16.4 Final results from the study after analysis in terms of cognitive evaluation of the impact of the form of presentation and information content on the quantity and scope of adopted new information. *Source* self study

Data from survey study after analysis in terms of the cognitive evaluation				
Thematic websites	Site-1	Site-2	Site-3	Site-4
Applied forms of information presentation	Mostly textual content	Textual and graphic content	Textual and infographics content	Textual content with graphic elements and shopping functions
Partial rating symbol	PRC-1	PRC-2	PRC-3	PRC-4
Test result before study	$4/5 = \frac{4}{5}$			
Test result during study	9/13	8/13	8/13	8/13
Test result after study	$4/5 + 2/5 = \frac{4}{5} + \frac{2}{5} = \frac{6}{5} = 1\frac{1}{5}$			
Results possible to achieve after study	$5/5 + 5/5 = \frac{5}{5} + \frac{5}{5} = 1 + 1 = 2$			
Knowledge growth evaluation indicator	$\text{WPW} = \frac{\frac{6}{5} - \frac{4}{5}}{2 - \frac{4}{5}} * 100\% = \frac{\frac{2}{5}}{\frac{6}{5}} * 100\% = \frac{1}{3} * 100\% = 30\%$			
Partial ratings values	9/13	8/13	8/13	8/13
Partial ratings values in percentage	69.23	61.53	61.53	61.53
Position in the ranking in terms of the cognitive evaluation	1	2	2	2

acceptance by the minds of respondents. In addition, in order to evaluate the level of information assimilation, different qualitative features of information that were contained in it were used.

As follows from the obtained data, the values of assessments for the assimilation of all analyzed forms of information presentation are relatively high (average value approx. 68%) and on very similar level (values from approx. 65 to 71%). The highest assessment of the information assimilation obtained the textual contents with graphic elements and shopping functions (71.43%), which were also the last of the analyzed areas. This result could have been influenced, on the one hand, by the way of perceiving by respondents the various media content and thus more attractive, and on the other hand, the previous experience in operating this type of shopping websites. The second position in the ranking took the textual and graphic contents (68.57%), which were evaluated by the respondents as the second in order. As content of this type is one of the most popular forms of information presentation in all kinds of electronic information articles, it may mean that respondents had proficiency in using such types of websites. The third place in terms of information assimilation was taken by the textual and infographics contents (67.00%), which were evaluated as third in order. Although supplementing a textual content with infographics is an increasingly frequent phenomenon on the Internet, it seems to the author of the chapter that their visual and aesthetic message is still not completely understandable to everyone. The last fourth place in the ranking were taken by the mostly textual contents (65.71%), which were evaluated in the survey as the first. On the one hand, for this reason, they could be the least accepted and understandable by the respondents, because they had to learn from the very beginning with purely textual content, which are certainly much more difficult to acquire than their graphic and visual equivalents. On the other hand, these contents described relatively new devices for the respondents, which as they declared they had not used so far, and therefore they had to paid more cognitive attention to understanding their purpose.

The second of the analyzed areas was cognitive evaluation of various forms of information presentation and information content occurred on websites. This aspect was the additional objective of the research and was analyzed on the basis of the additional results, obtained from the respondents, related to cognitive feelings while reading information content and various forms of information presentation about devices such as electronic book readers. The impact of the form of presentation and information content on the quantity and scope of new information adopted by respondents was understood in this context, as the usefulness of multimedia information presentation forms and the intelligibility of thematic content, from the selected websites, by the minds of the respondents in order to assimilate new information as quickly and easily as possible. Moreover, to the evaluation of the impact of the form of presentation and information content on the quantity and scope of newly learned information, the methodology for testing respondents before and after the research and knowledge growth evaluation indicator was used.

As follows from the obtained data, the values of cognitive assessments of all analyzed forms of information presentation, just like in the analysis of the information assimilation, are relatively high (average value approx. 65%) and on very similar level (values from approx. 61 to 69%). The highest cognitive assessment obtained the mostly textual contents (69.23%), which were also the first of the analyzed areas. This result could have been influenced, on the one hand, by the order in which the respondents read this form of content and assimilate it relatively much, due to a significant information deficit on this subject. On the other hand, despite the fact, that textual content is relatively more difficult to receive by the human brain, it carries much more content and information transfer than the image content at the same time. The other three forms of information presentation obtained the same cognitive assessments, which were a view percent lower than the highest level (61.53%). This can be interpreted in such a way that the information contents of the other three websites, despite the use of more graphic and visual forms of content presentation, were for the respondents rather a supplement of information and knowledge about recognized devices.

The second part of the cognitive assessment of various forms of information presentation and information content was the value determination of the knowledge growth evaluation indicator for respondents. For this purpose, the additional results from the questionnaire were analyzed, of which the respondents were asked just before the beginning of the main part of the study and immediately after its completion. The question asked before the study concerned the assessment of the knowledge level of what is and what for is an e-book reader device. An interesting fact is that as many as 80% of respondents answered that this concept, to a greater or lesser extent, is known to them, what at the very beginning of the research could mean that it will be difficult to learn something new for respondents. The questions asked after the study concerned the assessment of the acquaintance degree of what is and what can an e-book reader device be used for and the knowledge level about e-book readers. These questions were aimed at verifying the level of new knowledge gained about the readers, as a result of familiarizing with the information content about them and thanks to the participation in the research. As it turned out, after the survey, the same number of respondents (80%) confirmed their level of knowledge of e-book reader devices, what could mean that they practically failed to broaden their knowledge about them. Fortunately, the second question, about the level of new gained knowledge, has shown that 40% of respondents has experienced a cognitive effect and it can be concluded that they have expanded the scope of current knowledge with new information. This is also confirmed by the result of the knowledge growth indicator, which reached 30%. It means that this percentage value of respondents increased the scope of their knowledge about electronic devices such as electronic books readers, thanks to the information available on the selected websites and various forms of presentation of this information.

16.6 Conclusions

Making research on the influence of information assimilation on the users' behaviors of Internet services is fully justified from the theoretical and practical point of view, because they have an impact on satisfying their information needs, and consequently on increasing the resources of their knowledge. This element is one of the most frequently used, in recent years by organizations, ways of attracting recipients to their websites, which offer apart from encouraging information content, also other commercial services. Moreover, in the era of the enormous popularity of information services and interactive services, access to highly assimilable and quickly available information is a key factor for the development of the information society. As the subject of the information assimilation is particularly important and present in the electronic means of information transfer, it would be worth to consider in the future the study of its impact on various fields of science or the applicability assessment of various research methods.

The research of the information assimilation of selected websites has shown that the assimilation level of various forms of information presentation among users of these websites is at a relatively high and similar level, what means, that these websites are characterized by high quality of presentation of placed information content. In the second issue, concerning the cognitive assessment of various forms of information presentation and information content occurred in the studied websites, the results were similar at a respectively high and very similar level. It means that the feelings and cognitive experiences of the respondents about the forms of content presentation and the information content available on the websites can be considered as coherent and satisfying. Moreover, as shown the results of the analysis, thanks to selected information about devices such as e-book readers, the respondents broadened their scope of new information about these devices by 30%, in relation to the level of knowledge before the study.

Summing up, it can be concluded that more and more websites use the principles of easy readability of textual content and various graphic and multimedia forms of information presentation, what positively affects on their assimilation and usability among recipients. As a result, more and more people with different individual cognitive abilities use and will use electronic media every day for personal and professional purposes.

References

Alavi M, Leidner DE (2001) Knowledge management and knowledge management systems: conceptual foundations and research issues. MIS Q 25(1):107–136

Atrey PK, Kankanhalli MS, Jain R (2006) Information assimilation framework for event detection in multimedia surveillance systems. Multimed Syst 12:239–253

Bramley P (2007) Ocena efektywności szkoleń. Wolters Kluwer, Kraków

Drucker PF (2003) New trends in management. Exec Excell 20(8):16–23

Dudycz H (1998) Wizualizacja danych jako narzędzie wspomagania zarządzania przedsiębiorstwem. Wydawnictwo Akademii Ekonomicznej, Wrocław

IT Governance Institute (2005) Control objectives for information and related technology (COBIT) 4.0. IT Governance Institute Rolling Meadows, IL

Jashpara A (2011) Knowledge management: an integrated approach, 2nd edn. Pearson Education

Kirkpatrick DL (1996) Evaluating training programs. The four levels. Berret-Koehler Publishers Inc., San Francisco

Langefors B (1973) Theoretical analysis of information systems, 4th edn. Studentlitteratur. Uerbach Publishers Inc., Philadelphia

Likert R (1932) A technique for the measurement of attitudes. Arch Psychol 140:5–55

Meyer HWJ (2005) The nature of information and the effective use of information in rural development. Inf Res 10(2)

Miller H (1996) The multiple dimensions of information quality. Inf Syst Manag 13(2):79–82

Miller PH (2011) Piaget's theory: past, present, and future. The Wiley-Blackwell handbook of childhood cognitive development. Wiley, New York

Molina AI, Redondo MA, Lacave C, Ortega M (2014) Assessing the effectiveness of new devices for accessing learning materials: an empirical analysis based on eye tracking and learner subjective perception. Comput Hum Behav 31:475–490

Morrison CT, Cohen PR (2005) Noisy information value in utility-based decision making. In: Proceedings of workshop on utility-based data mining, Chicago

Nielsen J, Mack RL (1994) Usability inspection methods. Wiley, New York

Nowakowski M (2014) Infografika jako nowoczesna forma prezentacji danych biznesowych. Zeszyty Naukowe Uniwersytetu Szczecińskiego (829) STUDIA. INFORMATICA 35:125–137

Nowakowski M (2016) Użyteczność informacji w serwisach internetowych uczelni wyższych. Stud Proc Polish Assoc Knowl Manag 81:34–46

Nowakowski M, Mazur M (2017) The impact of information usefulness of e-commerce services on users behaviors. Springer proceedings in business and economic: neuroeconomic and behavioral aspects of decision making, Cham, Switzerland

Pettersson R (1993) Visual information. Educational Technology Publications, Englewood Cliffs, NJ

Piaget J, Cook MT (1952) The origins of intelligence in children. International University Press, New York

Pocztowski A (2008) Zarządzanie zasobami ludzkimi. Strategie - procesy - metody. Polskie Wydawnictwo Ekonomiczne, Warszawa

Prussak W (1995) Ergonomiczne kształtowanie projekcyjnych wizualnych materiałów dydaktycznych. In: Materiały XII Międzynarodowego Seminarium Wykładowców Ergonomii

Reitsma P (1988) Reading practice for beginners: effects of guided reading, reading-while-listening, and independent reading with computer-based speech feedback. Read Res Q 23

Rieman J, Franzke M, Redmiles D (1995) Usability evaluation with the cognitive walkthrough. In: CHI 95 conference companion

Roth SF, Beck IL (1987) Theoretical and instructional implications of assessment of two microcomputer word recognition programs. Read Res Q 22(2):197–218

Sauro J, Kindlund E (2005) A method to standardize usability metrics into a single score. In: Proceedings of the SIGCHI conference on human factors in computing systems, ACM Press, USA, pp 401–409

Small CT, Sage AP (2006) Knowledge management and knowledge sharing: a review. Inf Knowl Syst Manag 5(3):153–169

Stefanowicz B (2004) Informacja. SGH - Oficyna Wydawnicza, Warszawa

Stokes DE (1997) Pasteur's quadrant: basic science and technological innovation. Brookings Institution Press, Washington

Tuckman B, Monetti D (2011) Educational psychology. Wadsworth Cengage Learning

Wadsworth BJ (2004) Piaget's theory of cognitive and affective development: foundations of constructivism. Longman Publishing

Wartella E, Reeves B (1983) Recurring issues in research on children and media. Educ Technol 23:5–9

Wharton C, Rieman J, Lewis C, Polson P (1994) The cognitive walkthrough method: a practitioner's guide. In: Nielsen J, Mack RL (eds) Usability inspection Methods. Wiley, New York, pp 105–140

Zeleny M (1987) Management support systems: towards integrated knowledge management. Hum Syst Manag 7:59–70

Chapter 17
Participatory Budgeting as Example of Behavioural Impact of Public Policies

Beata Zofia Filipiak and Marek Dylewski

Abstract Particular importance in the public sector takes on framing theory, indicating that 'the way in which the problem is shown to the decision-makers will have an impact on its performance'. The purpose of this study is to present the application of behavioural methods (the framing theory in particular) in shaping local communities' public funding decisions with the use of participatory budgeting. The following problems are discussed in the chapter: (1) Theoretical assumptions of the application of behavioural theories in shaping the decisions of local communities; (2) The participatory budget theory as the subject of behavioural economics influence (theoretical approach); (3) A practical example of using a behavioural approach in public policies of local communities—an example of the City of Szczecin and the Police commune. To realise the purpose, the authors have analysed of competitions announced as part of the procedure of preparing the budget of the local government unit for the selection of projects covered by the participatory budget, projects submitted to participatory budgets in the form of civic projects, types of behaviour of local communities as part of the adopted procedure for selecting projects for inclusion in the participatory budget.

Keywords Behavioural economics · Public policies · Participatory budgeting Finance

B. Z. Filipiak (✉)
Department of Finance, Faculty of Economics and Management, Institute of Finance, University of Szczecin, Mickiewicza 64, 71-101 Szczecin, Poland
e-mail: beata.filipiak@usz.edu.pl; bfilipiak@wneiz.pl

M. Dylewski (✉)
Faculty of Finance and Banking, Institute of Finance, WSB University of Poznań, Powstańców Wlkp 5, 61-895 Poznań, Poland
e-mail: marek.dylewski@wsb.poznan.pl

K. Nermend and M. Łatuszyńska (eds.), *Problems, Methods and Tools in Experimental and Behavioral Economics*, Springer Proceedings in Business and Economics, https://doi.org/10.1007/978-3-319-99187-0_17

17.1 Introduction

Studies on individual irrational decisions are a part of experimental economics which, from the today's perspective, has had the greatest influence on theoretical economics. However, since the 1950s many scientific observations have confirmed that deviations from rational behaviour are not only widespread, but also follow a regular pattern.

What has gained special importance for the public sector is the framing theory which refers to 'how the way in which a problem is presented to a decision-maker will affect their actions'.[1] The framing theory can be used to change people's behaviour and to influence their decisions so that they can be beneficial for individuals as well as for their families or communities. One of the major areas where the framing theory can be applied is a public policy concerning participatory budgeting.

The purpose of this study is to present the application of behavioural methods (the framing theory in particular) in shaping local communities' public funding decisions with the use of participatory budgeting.

17.2 Behavioural Approach in Public Policies

Public authorities (the national government and local governments) implement public policies with a view to solving important socio-economic problems and pursuing development opportunities emerging in their environment (Hausner 2008; Chrabąszcz and Zawicki 2014; Olejniczak and Śliwowski 2014). While creating these policies, public authorities use public policy instruments (Tucker 2005; Howlett 2011). A good example of such intervention is participatory budgeting.[2] The aim of such intervention is a particular behaviour that, depending on to the intervention authors (national or local governments passing legal acts or resolutions, respectively), will lead to desired effects that will be beneficial for social welfare and order (Datta and Mullainathan 2012; Shafir 2013; Olejniczak and Śliwowski 2014). The past experience shows that the effectiveness of an intervention depends on the understanding of human behaviour and decision-making mechanisms (Shafir 2013). The activities of public authorities will bring better

[1]For a detailed description, see Kahneman and Tversky (1984), Stocke (2002); for the description of an evolving approach, see Pluwak (2009).

[2]They cover a wide range of forms—from small local projects to significant government investment programmes, from regulations shaping the land use in our municipalities to legal acts defining our rights and obligations towards the state. Public interventions refer to various aspects of public life—from education and health service to security, labour market, economy, infrastructure and the protection of cultural and natural resources.

effects when the form and logic of their intervention are better aligned with the ways in which people make their decisions.

The process of constructing actions under public policies consists of eight stages, one of which is evaluation (Tsoukias et al. 2013). Consultation with stakeholders, i.e. the society, is one of the methods recommended in the stage of evaluation (Brugha and Varvasovsky 2000; Reed et al. 2009). There is much evidence in the literature that the primary purpose of consultation in the process of evaluating public decisions is to find out about the stakeholders' preferences and expectations, which in turn is vital, e.g. for assessing the impact of the implemented decisions on specific aspects of the functioning of society or for determining the utility of adopted solutions. Secondly, they allow for identifying common positions or differences in the stakeholders' opinions in reference to individual aspects of the decision, thus making it possible to define inter-dependencies among stakeholders and contributing to shared positions. Finally, they help determine the weight of diverse effects of the decision implementation (Brugha and Varvasovsky 2000). As it is pointed out in the literature, the method of consultation with stakeholders may be beneficial in a situation when a public intervention is controversial or political (Turowski and Zawicki 2007). Social consultation has been used as a method to prepare local government budgets. When conducting a consultation on projects proposed by groups of citizens, local authorities not only enable local communities to participate in financial decisions, but they also run a specific public policy that leads to implementing those of the actions that have gained the highest public acceptance, consequently reaching the ultimate goal of the public intervention.

When explaining differences in decision-making in various situations, H. Simon dismissed the monetary profit analysis in his studies. He believed that decision-making did not have to lead to substantial gains if they brought such benefits as satisfaction or peace (Simon 1955, 1997). He assumed that an individual often strived to maximise not just one but many goals (they do not even have to be coinciding).

Simon and other authors point out that when making decisions the society does not have full information about possible alternatives. Its attention (usually quite cursory) is only focused on the most available ones. Moreover, it predominantly lacks sufficient processing power to make comparisons. Therefore, it does not follow the rule of optimalisation (making the best choice out of all the alternatives) but seeks satisficing (making a sufficiently good choice that satisfies various requirements). It should be also noted that typical features of this theory are relative evaluation (depending on the adopted point of reference), decreasing sensitivity to additional gains (effects) and losses, as well as loss aversion (often understood as reduced quality of implemented tasks or their limitation) (Simon 1955, 1997; Kahneman and Tversky 1979; Mayer 1982; Makuch 2012; Kata 2013; Stachowiak-Kudła 2014). What is typical of reactions to public policies, particularly the stakeholders' choice of tasks, or financed projects being their part is the fact that the majority of decision-makers (stakeholders) pursue optimum solutions but limit their choice to the first satisficing alternative (Hermaszewski 2012).

When making decisions about individual public, the society encounters numerous problems resulting from incomplete information (as highlighted above) as well as limited capacity to analyse it, and the choices are burdened with subjective motivations and attitudes (e.g. the propensity to risk, openness to change) and by individual (incoherent) references (Hausner 2008; Chrabąszcz and Zawicki 2014; Olejniczak and Śliwowski 2014). The behavioural factors embrace emotions and perception and they influence cognitive and motivative aspects. The cognitive approach of a citizen towards whom the public policy is addressed represents all their existing views and knowledge about a given problem, their related judgments and expectations concerning the future course of events (Kata 2013). Moreover, 'the meaning, understood as interpretation of the reality, is not constant but negotiable by members of a given social group. The meaning is attributed with the use of generated by the community and common to its members conceptual elements such as symbols or frames which accumulate in each interpretation of public events' (Sadaba 2006).

This limitation to rationality in social decision-making should be minimised, which is possible and acceptable by way of consulting and subsequently by negotiating the solutions with the society, thus gaining its support (Floc'hlay and Plottu 1998).

Moreover, it is believed that *framing* in political and public debate concerning public policy-making allows for diverse interpretations of the same social phenomena or problems depending on the stated political objectives. However, efforts need to be made so that the interpretations of current social problems can be explained in the way that will make voters reject all other explanations. Policy-making can be successful thanks to the narrowed perspective that *framing* is accompanied by Scheufele (2003), Pluwak (2009).

17.3 Participatory Budgeting Theory as Object of Impact of Behavioural Economics

Being an expression of social participation through the process of social consultation of potential projects to be financed from public funds in a form of local government's own tasks, the participatory budgeting assumes the rationality of choices and decisions made by individual members of a local community. However, the frames of consultation, methods and the range of options are designed by local decision-making and executive authorities, i.e. not by the community members themselves but by their representatives. It is important to remember that during this process local government units obtain knowledge about the citizens' expectations about how communal financial and material resources are spent on a given project (Sintomer et al. 2013), while the consultation results do not bind local authorities (Janicka and Jędrowiak 2015). The binding character of the participatory budgeting stems from an unwritten social contract between citizens and a government and it is a result of the way how potential projects are presented to a decision-making society (citizens).

For the participatory budget to actually reflect social consultation and to be considered a public policy instrument, it should satisfy certain rules and the very process of its implementation should take adequate time and involve a local community. Its cycle follows several stages (Poniatowicz 2014):

- development of the project feasibility study in order to enable a member of a local community or civil groups to evaluate the planned investment,
- preparation, in accordance with frames and guidelines, of the project proposal by a member of a local community or by civil groups before submitting it to local authorities,
- social consultation on submitted projects,
- selection of projects to be implemented under participatory budgeting framework,
- monitoring the process of adopting the budget,
- monitoring the purchasing process—bidding, quotation and contracts,
- monitoring the quality of provided services.

The participatory budgeting can be described by several criteria that distinguish it from a traditional local government budgeting[3]:

- citizens have the opportunity to submit project proposals which, after positive verification by the local community, will be approved for implementation as the local government's own task.
- the amount allocated for projects financed from the participatory budget is clearly stated.
- if possible, the project costs are carefully estimated and presented in a unified form in feasibility studies.
- public debate and social consultation are arranged.
- projects submitted by local community members are not dismissed by local government officials of councillors for substantial reasons but solely due to formal and legal ones.
- the projects are selected by way of a poll following the presentation of project documents, public debate, public consultation or promotion campaigns prepared by project authors (e.g. information campaigns and social networks, mailing, advertisements).
- only the local residents who are entitled to vote can take part in the poll.
- projects chosen by local residents are implemented.

From the perspective of the behavioural economics, it should be noted that the participatory budgeting is based on the processes of civil participation in the decision-making system through orienting public authorities towards citizens–customers–residents as regards meeting their expectations about satisfying local

[3]See the opinion of Poniatowicz (2014).

needs by means of public goods provided in a form of local government's own tasks and by basing the process of constructing public policies on the rules of partnership and citizens' trust in local authorities (Poniatowicz 2014).

The public authority bodies, including local government units, often treat participatory budgeting as a social 'safety valve' and an instrument to placate their voters' negative emotions. A dissatisfied voter is extremely demanding, very critical of public authorities. It is in the local decision-makers' interest to pacify the emotions and to curb the ruling politicians so that they can maintain their legitimate decision-making capacity. The existing evidence confirms increased satisfaction and happiness of citizens who are involved in the process of democratic decision-making using the direct democracy instruments such as participatory budgeting (Frey 2010; Frey et al. 1999; Poniatowicz 2014).

Another essential element of the public choice process is *fiscal illusion* which refers to purposeful hiding by governments of their real cost and public expenditures (Buchanan 1960, 1997). This confirms the framing theory which states that the way in which a problem is presented to decision-makers influences their actions (Neuman et al. 1992; Entman 2004; Dahinden 2006; Matthes 2007). In this context, the use of the participatory budgeting in the system of local finances as an instrument to enforce policies respecting the citizens' needs may have a beneficial effect on shortening the distance between local residents/taxpayers and the local government (Poniatowicz 2014).

It is generally considered that framing constitutes the second level of the *agenda-setting* theory (McCombs 2008; Palczewski 2011). It is highlighted that on the first level, the agenda-setting defines the subject about which (i.e. which existing problems) the community is supposed to think, while the frames indicate how people are supposed to think about specific events, issues or problems. 'Fully developed frames typically perform four functions: problem definition, causal analysis, moral judgment and remedy promotion' (Entman 2004; Scheufele and Tewksbury 2007; McCombs 2008). Authors present a diverse approach to the definitions of frames (Neuman et al. 1992; Semetko and Valkenburg 2000; Palczewski 2011). Due to a specific nature of public policies, it seems adequate to categorise the frames as referring to conflict, human interest, attribution of responsibility, morality and economic consequences (Semetko and Valkenburg 2000).

As far as the conflict frame is concerned, it is difficult to say that it is prevalent and certain to happen, but it definitely affects the final stages of the participatory budgeting process. The frame itself does not indicate the conflict as such, but it describes a pattern, according to which the events or actions are presented, not always explicitly. This means that the way in which public consultation is carried out, how the related procedures and regulations as well as the short lists of projects are reported, can be presented in a biased way, which can significantly affect the citizens' decisions. It also concerns the future projects and the way they will be presented by the community members.

It should also be emphasised that the conflict frame can represent political competition and media interpretation of the world of politics as a series of struggles

(Neuman et al. 1992) with their winners and losers, because the final list of submitted and chosen projects divides the community into winners and losers. The impact of this frame can manifest itself by citizens' requesting public authorities to change the social consultation regulations or to strengthen social control.

In the case of the human interest frame, it is worth noting that the instrument such as the participatory budget relies on the elementary idea of the framing theory which emphasises the way a problem, in a form of a project submitted by a citizen (citizens), is presented. The project authors announce their project assumptions in such a way as to be able to evoke positive citizens' decisions and to make them reject the other projects. Thereby they influence the lives of other people or groups (the human interest frame). According to Semetko and Valkenburg (2000), this particular frame individualises the message containing the description of a specific problem and gives a human face and an emotional value to problems that will be tackled through the project implementation.

The attribution of responsibility frame indicates who is responsible for causing or resolving key problems that will be associated with the completion of a project submitted for funding from the participatory budget. The answer seems to be very simple, but it is not. Public authorities who have delegated the task to executive bodies or have outsourced it to an independent provider cannot be held fully responsible for solving a given problem. Responsibility is also an attribute of these society members who have prepared and promoted the project. The framing effect can be seen in the way a project, its implementation and effects are shown to a decision-maker and to the public. From the presentation itself, some conclusions will arise that will have an effect on further actions and on the success of the project.

According to Semetko and Valkenburg, the frame of economic consequences presents an event or a problem in terms of economic consequences for individuals, for a group or for a local community as a whole. This frame makes it possible to analyse the project in reference to the pursued values, gained benefits (profits), costs and effects, economic costs and, as a consequence, to short- and long-term effects on the budget and their consequences in case of an economic crisis, etc., 'as a process during which the community members gain influence on and, indirectly, control over the decisions of public authorities when these decisions directly or indirectly affect their own interests' (Długosz and Wygnański 2005).

The last frame of morality refers to moral judgement concerning the actions undertaken in connection with the decision made. The judgements may differ throughout the community because they are based on varying criteria, e.g. values or religious convictions.

In conclusion, it should be stressed that public bodies, particularly local governments, impact on the local communities' decisions about public funds allocation based on the participatory budgeting. Local governments choose their own ways of communicating information to the public, thus influencing decisions made by local community members. Within the outlined above frames, further actions are undertaken that determine the choices and decisions of both the public authorities and the society.

17.4 Practical Example of Behavioural Approach Applied in Local Public Policies in Szczecin and in Community of Police

17.4.1 Scientific Approach

It is believed that 'improved realism of psychological assumptions underlying economic theory leads to better predictions. Making such assumptions is an effect of observing the reality, not just seeking to create elegant and simple mathematical models of behaviour' (Camerer 2006).

Therefore, the analysis covers:

- the guidelines of calls for proposals announced under the local government budgeting procedures with a view to identify participatory budgeting projects, with a special focus on budgetary resolutions in this respect being an expression of the angle at which the problem should be presented to the decision-makers, i.e. to the local community.
- projects to be funded from the participatory budgeting submitted as civil society projects that are subject to social consultation and whose way of public presentation has impact on the community members voting decisions.
- types of local community members' behaviour in reference to formal procedures adopted to select participatory budgeting projects based on the information provided by the organizer (local authority) in Public Information Bulletins (PIBs). It should be emphasised that the basic assumption is making decisions based only on data from the PIB regarding projects included in the participatory budget.

The analysis will allow to draw conclusions concerning the settlement of the research problem: will the way, in which a problem (project) is presented to a decision-maker, influence their action (i.e. their vote)?

Considering the fact that public authorities are free to create their own public policies as well as have full decision-making autonomy, their legislature is of local nature and may differ between individual types of local government units. Due to the budget size criterion, local governments take into account current obligatory and voluntary tasks that need to be continued. Only a part of the budget can be allocated for the purpose of social participation. Therefore, it is very difficult to compare participatory budgeting funds in various local government units. Owing to the type of local government unit they represent and their budget size, the authors chose for the analysis the City of Szczecin (performing both community and poviat statutory tasks) and the Community of Police (an urban–rural unit performing only the community statutory tasks). Both the local governments are now implementing local participatory budgeting projects.

The analysis is based on public information provided by local Public Information Bulletins.

17.4.2 Findings and Discussion

The concept of the participatory budgeting is based solely on bottom-up initiative. Such a situation is not possible in practice because of numerous reasons of legal, organisational, social, psychological and mentality nature. Therefore, such initiatives are formalised to a larger or smaller extent and they are typically launched under the framework of local government policies in a form of resolutions. However, besides their purpose of encouraging civil participation in the process of making decisions about public expenditure, these initiatives are one of the elements of local government promotion as well as they serve as the public authorities' declaration (often of a facade character) of will to share their powers with their constituency members. Table 17.1 shows the draft participatory budget in two local government units: in Szczecin (a city with poviat rights) and in the Community of Police.

General characteristics of participatory budgeting objectives[4] indicate the following elements:

1. budgets are the representation of policies implemented by local government whose objective is to intervene in the areas which, according to, are impossible to be identified by the policy authors. The identification of these intervention areas enables local public authorities to reach public and political goals, which would be impossible otherwise.
2. it is a small and insignificant part of the total budgets in both local governments. Despite a considerable difference in the size of their budgets, their expenditures per capita do not differ much. In Szczecin, the amount allocated to the participatory budget is several times bigger than in Police. Yet, it can be clearly seen that in a smaller community of Police the civil participation level is relatively higher than in Szczecin. Both the quantitative share in total expenditure and the amount per capita are twice higher than in Szczecin. Nevertheless, in both local governments the decisions concerning over 99% of total budget expenditure are made in a traditional way, i.e. by elected representatives in local legislative and executive bodies.
3. in both local governments, the participatory budgeting is a decision-making process based on public engagement which is not of continuing character, but which takes place once a year. This means that citizens' participation in local governance can be of accidental nature. What is more, depending on the adopted timelines and impact instruments chosen by local public authorities, there is a risk of the intended exclusion of citizens from the decision-making process. In other words, there is a risk of the framing effect.
4. the analysis of the territorial range reveals that in the first step the allocated amount is divided between individual parts of the local government territory

[4]In both LGs, it is called 'Citizens Budget' and is implemented with the use of public consultations.

Table 17.1 Draft participatory budget based on basic information about local government units under examination

Frames of participation in participatory budgeting (PB)		Szczecin			Police		
Population (2017)		404,400			41,543		
Local government budget (2017)		2,462,868,725			212,601,832		
Expenditure per capita (2017)		6090			5118		
		PB amount	Share in municipal budget (%)	PB per capita	PB amount	Share in municipal budget	PB per capita
Amount allocated to PB and share in total budget	2016	6,000,000	0.28	14.83	1,000,000	0.57	23.8
	2017	7,000,000	0.28	17.30	1,000,000	0.48	23.8
	2018	8,000,000	0.28	19.76	1,000,000	0.47	23.8
Territorial range of PB	2016	General city projects—0 District projects (4 districts)—4 × 1,500,000			Town of Police—750,000 Sołectwo (12)—250,000		
	2017	General city projects—0 District projects (4 districts)—4 × 1,750,000			Town of Police—750,000 Sołectwo (12)—250,000		
	2018	General city projects—2,400,000 District projects (4 districts)—4 × 1,400,000 1,120,000—major district projects 140,000—minor district projects			Town of Police—750,000 Sołectwo (12)—250,000		
Expenditure limit per a PB project	2016	1,350,000			None		
	2017	2,100,000—general city projects 980,000—major district projects 122,500—minor district projects			None		
	2018	2,400,000—general city projects 1,120,000—major district projects 140,000—minor district projects			None		
Type of PB task	2016	Investments (tangible)			Current and investment (physical)		
	2017	Investments (tangible)			Current and investment (physical)		
	2018	Investments (tangible)			Current and investment (physical)		

(e.g. Sołectwo—a subdivision of a community, or city districts), which means that an artificial division is made into even smaller communities within a given local government area. Basing on previous experience, some adjustments have been made in Szczecin where besides the district projects all local residents can vote on general city projects, while in Police the decision-making process is not limited strictly to the place of residence, but all local residents can vote for any project they choose. In reference to the framing effect, it is clear that it is the local government's intention to incorporate in their public policies specific rules in order to promote particular areas as the ones which require public intervention.

5. significant differences have been found in the ceiling amounts allocated to a single project as well as in the types of projects that could be proposed. The City of Szczecin has introduced both the ceiling amounts and limited the task scope to investments. In Police, the local government has not determined the top limits (the ceiling amount of funds allocated to the participatory budgeting purposes). It has also allowed both operational (current) and investment projects. The framing effect manifests itself in such presentation of the problem to be addressed so that the residents of Szczecin can submit only the projects that will serve the community for many years as local infrastructure. The Community of Police, as a result of social consultation, promotes both the initiatives that improve the existing quality of life of its residents as well as the projects focused on infrastructure. Therefore, the local government in Police has designed its message to the local residents to convince them that every idea that enhances the local quality of life is important.

Table 17.2 shows the characteristics of the decision-making process within the framework of the participatory budgeting.

Basing on the analysis of public presentation of problems in each of the examined local governments and of the two procedures of decision-making concerning participatory budgeting projects, the following observations were made:

1. in both local governments, the legal framework of the participatory budgeting was developed by the legislative and executive bodies. That confirms the fact that local government bodies have major impact on the decision-making process and on the character of the proposed projects.
2. it is President (in Szczecin) or Mayor (in Police) who determines the amount of funding allocated to participatory budgeting. It should be added that the participatory budgeting process is always accompanied by social consultation, but it is much formalised and the actual citizens' participation is little.
3. entirely different regulations apply in the case of proposed participatory budgeting projects. In Szczecin, every resident is entitled to submit an unlimited number of projects, while in Police the proposal must be submitted by a group of at least 15 residents, which necessitates better-organised actions than in Szczecin.
4. in both local governments, the verification of submitted tasks/projects is formal and substantive. There are differences in the structure of the reviewing committees. In Szczecin, the role of administrative factors and of the local government officials is much smaller than that of the community members. In Police, it is completely opposite—the role of community representatives is marginal, while the administrative factor and local government representatives have the final say. Therefore, the framing effect appears as early as in the verification stage because the way of presenting the problem to be tackled in a way of public intervention (as a participatory budgeting project) determines the evaluating committee's judgment.

Table 17.2 Decision-making process in reference to selection of projects to be included in participatory budgeting

Szczecin	Police
Defining legal framework and personal and material scope of PB	
Legislative body resolution President's decree	Legislative body resolution Mayor's decree
Defining overall and unit ceilings to PB	
Executive body—President	Executive body—Mayor
Submitting projects to PB	
Every city resident Unlimited number of applications Mandatory application form	Minimum of 15 residents can submit one project Unlimited number of projects Mandatory application form
Verification of submitted projects	
Formal verification—appointed organisational unit Factual verification—competent organisational units Voting list of project proposals—Evaluation Committee: representatives of residents (8), city hall officials (1), councillors (4), representatives of NGOs (4).	Minimum of 15 residents can submit one project Unlimited number of projects Mandatory application form
Vote	
Electronic and paper form	Electronic and paper form
Shortlist of PB projects	
Shortlist of projects with highest score and below cost limit	Shortlist of projects with highest score and below cost limit
Inclusion of winning PB projects in budget	
Including projects in draft budget Legislative body's final decision	Including projects in draft budget Legislative body's final decision
Project implementation	
Standard procedures of budget execution	Standard procedures of budget execution
Project evaluation	
Evaluation of PB consultation process	PB execution report

5. the manner of voting is similar in both local governments. Voting in the electronic and paper form is allowed. The evidence shows that the electronic vote is more popular. A conclusion can be drawn that without the access to electronic tools the success of the participatory budgeting would be unlikely.
6. the result of the public vote determines which projects will be budgeted. Practically speaking, the way of presentation and how information is conveyed to the public will influence individual decisions. It should be remembered that the final decision belongs to the legislative local government body.
7. in reference to project implementation, standard procedures adopted by given local authorities are applicable, based on legal regulations in force.

8. the local governments under study had a different approach to the participatory budgeting evaluation. In Szczecin, the evaluation covers the whole participatory budgeting process, while in Police it is limited to a report on implementation of the participatory budget added to a standard budget implementation report.

The ways of public intervention in (or impact on) local community's decisions concerning participatory budgeting are similar in both local government units (see Table 17.3). They both launched dedicated websites providing general information about participatory budgeting. Additionally, local participatory budgeting is promoted by means of fliers, banners and online advertising. Despite the applied promotion and communication tools advertising the community members' participation in creating the local budget spending policy, the local authorities intentionally formalise the decision-making related with participatory budgeting with a view to eliminating from the process those residents who are not able to meet formal requirements. The following elements contribute to the framing effect:

- the project application form (imposing the way how information is to be presented—the human interest frame and the attribution of responsibility frame),
- the required authorisation to process personal data (expressing how information is to be presented—the attribution of responsibility frame),
- the voting process, including voting cards layout (expressing the way of communication—the attribution of responsibility frame and the morality frame).

In both Szczecin and Police, the level of formalisation and necessary information that an applicant is required to provide when submitting a project to participatory budgeting is relatively high, which contributes to the framing effect. Thereby the public authorities impose on applicants a uniform level of knowledge, skills and competence concerning the principles and regulations with regard to the decision-making process in a given local government. This method of proceeding leads to the elimination of those individuals whose knowledge and competences are

Table 17.3 Elements of mandatory participatory budgeting application form

	Szczecin	Police
Application form instructions	No	Yes
Project title	Yes	Yes
Project implementation location	Yes	Yes
Project summary	No	Yes
Project description with justification including:	Yes	Yes
Description of the problem and activities (justification)	Yes	Yes
Beneficiaries	Yes	Yes
Project objective	Yes	Yes
Estimated project costs	Yes	Yes
Contact person (project author/authors)	Yes	Yes
Authorisation to process personal data	Yes	Yes
Necessary annexes	Yes	Yes

insufficient to meet formal requirements of participatory budgeting. It is particularly striking in Szczecin where a single resident has the right to submit a participatory budgeting project provided their skills and qualifications are sufficient to submit a duly completed application. In Police, this obstacle has been indirectly compensated by the required minimum of 15 applicants supporting the project. Theoretically, such a solution facilitates the application process offering a better chance to those residents who are not competent enough to formalise their project description but can indirectly influence the success of the application by expressing their support for the project.

Moreover, the very participation in the voting process requires some knowledge and competence to ensure that a cast vote is valid, which is also connected with the framing effect. In both the local governments, a considerable number of invalid votes cast in all the participatory budgeting editions clearly indicate that the voting process was arranged in an ineffective way. It was particularly obvious in the case of paper ballots. As far as the online vote is concerned, the problem was offset by an algorithm which prevented casting invalid votes (e.g. by marking more projects than allowed or failing to give authorisation to process one's personal details).

To sum up, in both the examined local government units, the decision-making processes concerning participatory budgeting are repeated on an annual basis and are highly formalised in reference to timelines. Every stage of the process is subordinated to formal requirements. The budget principles are defined according to strict legal regulations which practically model the residents' attitudes to submitted projects and to their evaluation.

An important element of the process of selecting projects to be included in the local government budgets is the procedure of verifying the submitted applications by appointed committees. It is worth noting that in Police the committee has mainly an expert character with a minor social component, while in Szczecin there are two stages: the formal and factual. Verification is made separately from the evaluation and approval. The Evaluation Committee is in much smaller extent represented by officials and councillors than by local residents and NGOs.

17.5 Conclusions

It can be generally concluded that in both the analysed local government units the decision-making processes are supported by framing practices. By the way the local problems are presented to the public the local authorities influence the citizens' decisions. What is more, the community members who promote their projects submitted to participatory budgeting influence the voters' decisions in the same way. Despite the formalisation of the decision-making process, the public authorities exert influence on the citizens' choices in order to reach the public policy objectives (e.g. by the choice of the evaluating committee members or by setting targets which the projects have to be complacent with).

The frame of economic consequences is represented both by individual projects and by the total of funds allocated by the local government to participatory budgeting as an expenditure budget line, i.e. economic consequences of the approved projects in an annual perspective as well as over the longer period of time. This means that the decisions that have been made address the particular goals of an individual social group and the community as a whole may or may not identify themselves with these goals. Moreover, the failure of a given project to be approved may lead to the feeling of loss (the lack of acceptable effects) in these members of the community who will not benefit from the project that has been funded from the participatory budget but who could have benefitted from the rejected one.

The opinions within the community may differ (which is confirmed by the presence of the morality frame) because they are made based on diverse criteria and values. Even though the project will not improve their lives, some community members will accept it as an important contribution to their environment. On the other hand, others will feel frustrated, which may result in their disinterest in the future editions of the vote for PB projects (as revealed by the analysis).

The frame of attribution of responsibility not only represents the responsibility of public authorities for the project implementation financed from the local budget but also authorises them to identify the problem as vital for the local community, because it has been highlighted by a member of a group of members of this community, their project has been approved by an evaluating committee (in a way of verification, for which the committee is responsible), and other community members supported the project in a vote, thus taking responsibility for solving the problem the project is addressing.

The examples examined above fully confirm the research hypothesis that the way in which a problem to be settled by means of participatory budgeting projects is presented to the public influences the actions and decisions made by the community members.

References

Brugha R, Varvasovsky Z (2000) Stakeholder analysis: a review. Health Policy Plan 15(3): 241–244

Buchanan JM (1960) Fiscal theory and political economy. The University of North Carolina Press, Chapel Hill

Buchanan JM (1997) Finanse publiczne w warunkach demokracji. Wydawnictwo Naukowe PWN, Warszawa

Camerer C (2006) Behavioral economics. In: Blundell R, Newey WK, Persson T (eds) Advances in economics and econometrics: Volume 1: Theory and applications, ninth world congress (Econometric Society Monographs), Cambridge University Press, Cambridge, pp 181–214

Chrabąszcz R, Zawicki M (2014) Nauki o polityce publicznej. In: Zawicki M (ed) Wprowadzenie do nauk o polityce publicznej. PWE, Warszawa, pp 17–40

Dahinden U (2006) Framing. Eine integrative Theorie der Massenkommunikation. UVK Verlagsgesellschaft, Konstanz

Datta S, Mullainathan S (2012) Behavioral design. A new approach to development policy. CGD Policy Paper 16 (Nov), 1–33
Długosz D, Wygnański J (2005) Obywatele współdecydują. Przewodnik po partycypacji społecznej, Forum Inicjatyw Pozarządowych, Warszawa
Entman R (2004) Projections of power: framing news, public opinion and U.S. foreign policy. University of Chicago Press, Chicago
Floc'hlay B, Plottu E (1998) Participation et decision publique: de l'incantation a la mise en oeuvre d'une evaluation democratique. Can J Program Eval 13(1):39–60
Frey BS (2010) Glück. Die Sicht der Ökonomie. Rüegger Verlag, Zürich/Chur, p 86
Frey BS, Kucher M, Stutzer A (1999) Outcome, process & power in direct democracy. New econometric results. Working Paper 222, pp 1–29 http://www.cesifo-group.de/DocDL/cesifo_wp222.pdf. Accessed 19 Dec 2017
Hausner J (2008) Zarządzanie publiczne. Małopolska Szkoła Administracji Publicznej, Uniwersytet Ekonomiczny w Krakowie i Wydawnictwo Naukowe Scholar, Warszawa
Hermaszewski J (2012) Decyzje finansowe i inwestycyjne w zarządzaniu jednostką samorządu terytorialnego na przykładzie gminy Sława - praktyczne aspekty. Prace Naukowe Uniwersytetu Ekonomicznego we Wrocławiu 243:296–303
Howlett M (2011) Designing public policies. Principles and instruments. Routledge, London
Janicka R, Jędrowiak P (2015) Budżet obywatelski – chęć zwiększenia partycypacji społecznej w rozwoju miast czy narzędzie marketingu politycznego w rękach prezydentów i burmistrzów? Refleksje 11:53–68
Kahneman D, Tversky A (1979) Prospect theory: an analysis of decisions under risk. Econometrica 47(2):263–292
Kahneman D, Tversky A (1984) Choices, values and frames. Am Psychol 39:341–350
Kata R (2013) Czynniki behawioralne i demograficzne wpływające na korzystanie przez rolników z kredytów inwestycyjnych. Zeszyty Naukowe SGGW w Warszawie. Ekonomika i Organizacja Gospodarki Żywnościowej 103:53–65
Makuch MA (2012) Decyzje podmiotów gospodarczych w ujęciu ekonomii behawioralnej. Studia i Prace Wydziału Nauk Ekonomicznych i Zarządzania 27:125–148
Matthes J (2007) Framing Effekte. Zum Einfluss der Politikberichterstattung auf die Einstellungen der Rezipienten. Verlag Reinhard Fischer, München
Mayer W (1982) The research program of economics and relevance of psychology. Br J Psychol 21:81–91
McCombs M (2008) Ustanawianie agendy. Media masowe i opinia publiczna, Wydawnictwo Uniwersytetu Jagiellońskiego, Kraków
Neuman WR, Just M, Crigler AN (1992) Common knowledge. News and the construction of political meaning. University of Chicago Press, Chicago
Olejniczak K, Śliwowski P (2014) Analizy behawioralne w interwencjach publicznych. In: Haber A, Olejniczak K (eds) (R)ewaluacja 2. Wiedza w działaniu. Polska Agencja Rozwoju. Przedsiębiorczości, Warszawa, pp 13–45
Palczewski M (2011) Koncepcja framingu i jej zastosowanie w badaniach newsów w Wiadomościach TVP i Faktach TVN. Media Studies 1:31–44
Pluwak A (2009) Geneza i ewolucja pojecia framing w naukach społecznych. Glob Media J Pol Ed 1(5):49–79
Poniatowicz M (2014) Kontrowersje wokół idei budżetu partycypacyjnego jako instrumentu finansów lokalnych. Stud ekon 198:177–189
Reed MS, Graves A, Dandy N, Posthumus H, Hubacek K, Morris J, Prell C, Quinn CH, Stringer LC (2009) Who's in and why? A typology of stakeholder analysis methods for natural resource management. J Environ Manage 90(5):1933–1949
Sadaba T (2006) Framing: Una Teoria Para Los Medios de Communicacion. Ulzama, Pamplona
Scheufele B (2003) Frazes—Framing—Framing-Effekte. Springer VS, Wiesbaden, p 2003
Scheufele DA, Tewksbury D (2007) Framing, agenda setting, an priming: the evolution of three media effects models. J Commun 57:9–20

Semetko HA, Valkenburg PM (2000) Framing European politics: a content analysis of press and television news. J Commun 50(2):93–109

Shafir E (2013) Introduction. In: Shafir E (ed) The behavioral foundations of public policy. Princeton University Press, Princeton, pp 1–9

Simon H (1955) A behavioral model of national choice. Quart J Econ 69:99–118

Simon HA (1997) Administrative behavior, 4th edn. The Free Press, New York

Sintomer Y, Herzberg C, Allegretti G, in collaboration with Röcke A. (2013) Participatory budgeting worldwide—updated version, Dialog Global 25. Engagement Global/Servicestelle Kommunen in der Einen Welt, Bonn, Nov, 1–91

Stachowiak-Kudła M (2014) Wartościowanie decyzji publicznych metodą konsultacji z interesariuszami In: Opaliński B (ed) Prawo administracyjne w ujęciu interdyscyplinarnym. Oficyna Wydawnicza Uczelni Łazarskiego, Warszawa, pp 51–68

Stocke V (2002) Framing und Rationalität – Die Bedeutung der Informationsdarstellung für das Entscheidungsverhalten. Scientia Novia, Oldenburg Verlag, München

Tsoukias A, Montibeller G, Lucertini G, Belton V (2013) Policy analytics: an agenda for research and practice. EURO J Decis Process 1(1–2):115–134

Tucker J (2005) Intervention. In: Mathison S (ed) Encyclopedia of evaluation. SAGE, London, p 210

Turowski B, Zawicki M (2007) Funkcje, etapy, metody i narzędzia ewaluacji In: Mazur M (ed) Ewaluacja funduszy strukturalnych - perspektywa regionalna. Uniwersytet Ekonomiczny w Krakowie, Małopolska Szkoła Administracji Publicznej, Kraków, pp 20–58

Chapter 18
Confirmation Bias in Valuation of Footballers' Performance Rights

Sebastian Majewski

Abstract Professional sportsmen all over the world are subjects of many ratings and grades, especially when they have big contracts. Journalists try to find the best player and the spectators (fans) try to believe that their football star is proper position. But is this valuation free from external pulling power of media and sponsors? The last five years in football is dominated by two players: Cristiano Ronaldo and Lionel Messi. But the question is that is it really proper classification, reflecting their performance on the football pitch? The hypothesis raised in the research is that the market value of the player has a strong impact on the classification. The verification of the hypothesis will be based on the classification methods and a process of eliminating of diagnostic variables. The sample taken into the research will consist of series of 25 most valuable forward players from seasons 2016–2017 and 2017–2018. The final analysis will be limited to the top players and compared with the results of France Football's plebiscite called Golden Ball and FIFA's Golden Boot.

Keywords Behavioural finance · Confirmation bias · Football

18.1 Introduction

The history of the sports shows that a rivalry between athletes excites emotions of spectators. From the beginning of Greek Olympics games to the contemporary, times different sports games draw attention of ordinary people and the athletes become heroes. According to the ideology of Coubertin, sports rivalry has to switch negatively recognized nationalism for positively meant sports competition (Morgan 1995). In both cases, spectators are very closely tied to own nationality but the difference is in expressing of affiliation. Sports in its idea has to push away violence from games; unfortunately, nowadays everybody knows it went not so well. Many

S. Majewski (✉)
University of Szczecin, ul. A. Mickiewicza 64, 71-101 Szczecin, Poland
e-mail: sebastian.majewski@wneiz.pl

K. Nermend and M. Łatuszyńska (eds.), *Problems, Methods and Tools in Experimental and Behavioral Economics*, Springer Proceedings in Business and Economics, https://doi.org/10.1007/978-3-319-99187-0_18

authors write about the dark side of sports supporting (e.g. Firlej and Trzepalka 2015). But this chapter concerns commercial part of the sports games. In this chapter, author treats football clubs as companies and players as companies' assets following Sloane (1971). So the background of the research in this chapter is economic rules and laws.

European football, especially the big six leagues (English, Spanish, French, Italian and German), is a goal of every football player in the world. The attractiveness of European football is caused by huge quota of money engaged in football. Big companies realize their own policy of creating international brands entering as sponsors to the market; by the way, it is also a good occasion to present themselves as the social responsible company (creating "goodwill"). It all could not be possible without spectators–purchasers of goods and services attached to the football market, games and athletes. Many authors lead their researches taking into account the issue of spectators: commercial and traditional (Antonowicz et al. 2012). This chapter refers to values of football players and their influence on the spectators but especially on the journalist's behaviour. Every year journalists publicize information about the best players, create ratings, vote prizes, and etc. Since 1956, following the idea of Gabriel Hanot, French journal France Football has been voting "Golden Ball" prize for the best player of the year (with six years break for common prize with FIFA's Player of the World). UEFA founded in 1967 the second important prize in football—for the best scorer from European highest football leagues "Golden Boot". These two prizes are continuously the subject of discussions between sports journalists and football fans. Such deliberation could stand a scientific problem—are the prizes impartial from external pressures?

The aim of this chapter is to classify football players using variables describing their activity on the football pitch, FIFA's rating points of country of origin of the player and the value of club footballer plays for. The hypothesis raised in the research is that the market value of the player has a strong impact on the classification. It means that ratings publicized by FIFA, UEFA and France Football are effects the behavioural confirmation bias. To verify that hypothesis another one type of classification will be done—including to the diagnostic set the market value of players. The methodology of Breslavian taxonomy (SDM—synthetic development measure) will be used to classification—building a rating of the best player in the world. The results obtained from SDM will be compared with results of "Golden Boot" and "Golden Ball".

Data used to classification are taken from: the website transfermarkt.de (all characteristics of players and clubs, "Golden Boot" rankings), fifa.com (FIFA/Coca-Cola World Ranking) and www.przegladsportowy.pl ("Golden Ball" rankings).

The chapter consists of three parts: the practical background of the research, the methodology of the research and empirical results. Professional football, footballers' performance rights as the assets of football clubs, the role of media on the football market and reactions of fans for the media information and match performances will be presented in the first chapter. The multidimensional statistical analysis, particularly synthetic development measure will be described in the second part of the chapter. Results of analysis conducted in the research and conclusions are the last parts of the chapter.

18.2 Professional Football, Journalists and Spectators Reactions—The Background of Confirmation Bias

The first text about professional football in Europe was written by Sloane in (1971) but the interests of scientist in sports economics dates back as far as the mid-1950s in USA (Dobson and Goddard 2001). Sloane entered term "football industry" to the terminology of sports economics (Sloane 1971). He raised there a thesis that football industry could be treated as normal company but the assumption of profits maximization is inappropriate because where there were limits on the payment of fees to directors and the payment of dividends to shareholders (Sloane 2015). The most important part of the football market is labour market with its major element—footballers' performance rights. Frick wrote that researches on this filed growth rapidly from the 1990s (Frick 2007). Such kind of development was caused by three base causes:

- football stood an economically significant part of the entertainment industry in the last 15 years;
- football players labour market has experienced changes in its regulatory framework that are unparalleled in other labour markets;
- detailed information about footballers' salaries, contracts and fees caused that empirical analysis could be conducted by economists not only in American's Major Soccer League.

The development of professional sports, especially football (in America called soccer), caused that the difference between regular companies and sports enterprises stood more clear. In my opinion, special meaning has some of them (Sznajder 2007):

- a strong media dependency;
- untypical purchasers (buyers are loyal to the club from the one side and would like to have an influence on the club policy from the other hand);
- strong legal regulations.

The most significant part of the football economics is the player's labour market, because it concerns the major asset of this industry. Theoretically, footballers' performance rights (a contract, which gives the club rights to manage a player to achieve business goals) are quoted continuously but transfers are allowed only on certain conditions:

- a time (transfers are allowed only in transfer windows—there are only two such windows in a year: summer and winter—dates depend on regulations of national associations);

- Bosman ruling (players could move to a new club at the end of their contract without their old club receiving a fee);
- Webster ruling (it formalised the "buy-out" rules for disputed transfers of players still within their contract term).

The transfer market is active only a few months in the year—the highest number of transactions is accomplished in June (23%), January (21%), August (21%) and February (13%). Transactions without fee and first contracts dominate in the rest of the year (www.fifatms.com).

As it was underlined earlier, media have a great influence on the football market. Similarly to the research conducted by Shiller (2000), media plays important role in creation of prices not only on the Stock Exchange but also on the football transfers market. The relation between sports and media has a symbiotic character. The television rights are the main source of income for many sports, and sports has a big significance for media because of events attracting television audience (Jeanrenaud and Kesenne 2006). The network of symbiotic relationships formed between right owners, broadcasters, advertisers, sports event managers and audience. The rules of the game could change for the needs of television transmission (e.g. entering Video Assistant Referee VAR system in football or challenge system in volleyball), but commentators and experts have the strongest influence—they could change an image of a player or a club, they also could make the transfer of the player faster or cancel it.

The group coming under the pressure of media are spectators. They could be divided into two basic parts: commercial spectators and traditional fans (Antonowicz et al. 2012). Both of these groups have its different characteristics. Commercial spectators are people who treat a football match as an every social event—a place where people could spend free time, where it is "well" to be seen. The second group is team supporters following by the footballers through all the country or the continent. There is a big gap between these two groups depending on whether the supported team is the national team or the club. Gullianotti and others divided them into three groups: fanatics, hooligans and expressive supporters (Gullianotti et al. 2005). Fanatics and hooligans are focused on their club. They are emotionally related with the history of the club, its colours and organized like paramilitary troop fighting against fans of the another club. National team supporters are not aggressive and well-organized group of fans. Different are also emotions accompanying activity of these two groups: the first one is oriented on continuous confrontation and a second one on the guaranty of rooting for the team (Majewski 2017).

We could observe confirmation bias in the light of such background. The literature gives two meanings of term confirmation bias. The first one is to preference for confirming information, and the second is defined as a way of testing hypothesis on the basis of instances that are predicted by the hypothesis while ignoring instances beyond its scope (that is why it is called as confirmatory strategy of hypothesis testing) (Lewicka 1998). According to these definitions, it could be understood that authors of every ranking are setting them up the way to confirm raised by themselves hypothesis (the player X is the best player in the world). If it is true, it means that the journalists are the strongest power on the football market.

18.3 Methodology of the Research

This research is based on quantitative taxonomy methods in particular on synthetic development measure. This measure was firstly described by Hellwig in 1968. This measure called the multidimensional comparison analysis allows for making rankings of objects in multidimensional space of objects' characteristics.

The procedure of the Hellwig's method could be presented as follow (Majewski 1998):

1. the determination of goal of the research
2. the identification of diagnostic variables—building a matrix of diagnostic variables X:

$$X = \lfloor x_{ij} \rfloor$$

$i = 1, 2, \ldots, n$
$j = 1, 2, \ldots, m$

3. the transformation of destimulants and neutral variables to stimulants using formulas (i.e.):

For destimulants	For neutral variables
$x'_{ij} = \frac{1}{x_{ij}}$ $x'_{ij} = 1 - x_{ij}$ $x'_{ij} = -x_{ij}$ $x'_{ij} = C - x_{ij}$	$x'_{ij} = \frac{\min\left\{x_{ij}^N : x_{ij}\right\}}{\max\left\{x_{ij}^N : x_{ij}\right\}}$ $x'_{ij} = -\left\|x_{ij} - x_{ij}^N\right\|$

where

x'_{ij} value of transformed variable;
C constant;
x_{ij}^N the normative value for variable.

4. the normalization of data using formulas:

– standardization—rescaling variables to normal distribution N (0, 1)

$$z_{ij} = \frac{(x_{ij} - \bar{x})}{s(x)}$$

– unitization:

$$z_{ij} = \frac{x_{ij} - \min_i x_{ij}}{\max_i x_{ij} - \min_i x_{ij}}$$

– quotient transformation:

$$z_{ij} = \frac{x_{ij}}{\bar{x}}$$

– rang normalization:

$$z_{ij} = R_i$$

where

z_{ij} standardized value;
R_i the rang for the normalized value.

Generally, the result of processes of normalization is a transformation of data set so as to have a normal distribution N (0, 1).

5. the setting parameters of pattern by the pattern object are determined on the base of the standardized matrix of observations:

$$O_0 = \lfloor z_{0j} \rfloor$$
$$z_{0j} = \max_i z_{ij}$$

where

O_0 pattern object with coordinates z_{0j}.

6. the calculation of the distance vector—many different methods could be used in this point. In the research, I choose Euclidian distance measure:

$$d_{0j} = \sqrt{\sum_{i=1}^{n} \left(z_{ij} - z_{0j}\right)^2}$$

d_{0j} the distance from the pattern to analysed object.

7. the calculation of synthetic development measure (SDM):

$$SDM_i = \frac{d_{0j}}{\bar{d} - 2S(d)}$$

8. building a ranking on the base of SDM (from the highest value to the lowest) The last step of the research is to compare obtained results with rankings presented in sports journal. The correlation coefficient is calculated to verify how strong is an influence of the market value of the player for results of journalists' ranking. It could also give an answer on the question—is it possible that the organizers of the popular ranking could control its results.

18.4 Empirical Results

The collected set of data contains two lists of TOP25 most valuable football players in 2016 and 2017 according to the website transfermarkt.de. There such diagnostic variables on the lists:

- the market value of the player (X_1);
- the age of the player (X_2);
- the number of matches played in the first squad (X_3);
- the number of goals scored (X_4);
- the number of own goals (X_5);
- the number of assists (X_6);
- the number of yellow cards (X_7);
- the number of double yellow cards (X_8);
- the number of red cards (X_9);
- the number of entrances to the football pitch from the bench of substitutions (X_{10});
- the number of exits from the football pitch to the bench of substitutions (X_{11});
- the value of club the footballer played for (X_{12});
- the place of the national team in the FIFA ranking (X_{13}).

During the research author decided to join some variables and calculated two indicators, following the research of Majewski (2016), where author showed that the country of origin (expressed indirectly by FIFA ranking of the countries) and Canadian classification (the sum of goals scored and assists) points have influence on the value of the player. So, in this way two new variables appeared in the research:

X_{14} Canadian classification points ($X_4 + X_6$);
X_{15} weighted team value:

$$X_{15} = X_{12} \cdot \frac{1}{X_{13}}$$

During the research, some variables were removed from the set of variables, because of weak cognitive value for the classification. The final set of variables includes such variables as: X_1, X_2, X_3, X_{14}, X_7, X_{15}. So, the first classification includes all variables indicated in the last sentence and the second excludes the market value of the player (X_1). The results of the classification in year 2016 are presented in Table 18.1 and the next classifications for 2017 are shown in Table 18.2.

The results of classifications were compared with popular sports rankings. The correlation coefficients between obtained classifications and popular ratings were estimated on the base of this information. The first interesting thing is that the best footballer player in 2016 and 2017 Cristiano Ronaldo did not win in any

Table 18.1 Results of footballers' classifications in 2016

Name of the player	First ranking (C1)	Second ranking (C2)
Lionel Messi	1	1
Neymar	11	15
Cristiano Ronaldo	2	4
Luis Suárez	4	8
Gareth Bale	21	25
Antoine Griezmann	6	10
Robert Lewandowski	3	3
Gonzalo Higuaín	9	11
Pierre-Emerick Aubameyang	10	9
Eden Hazard	12	13
Thomas Müller	8	7
Sergio Agüero	7	5
Karim Benzema	15	16
Alexis Sánchez	5	2
Ángel Di María	14	12
Paulo Dybala	23	22
Raheem Sterling	24	23
Mauro Icardi	18	18
Edinson Cavani	13	6
Diego Costa	16	14
Yannick Carrasco	19	19
Harry Kane	25	24
Álvaro Morata	20	20
Romelu Lukaku	17	17
Alexandre Lacazette	22	21

Table 18.2 Results of footballers' classifications in 2017

Piłkarze	First ranking (C1)	Second ranking (C2)
Neymar	3	6
Lionel Messi	1	1
Kylian Mbappé	15	20
Harry Kane	9	14
Cristiano Ronaldo	2	4
Kevin De Bruyne	7	9
Antoine Griezmann	14	16
Eden Hazard	8	7
Paul Pogba	20	22
Philippe Coutinho	4	5
Paulo Dybala	12	12
Romelu Lukaku	11	10
Luis Suárez	18	17
Ousmane Dembélé	25	25
Dele Alli	23	23
Mohamed Salah	13	11
Raheem Sterling	17	15
Sergio Busquets	24	24
Robert Lewandowski	10	8
Toni Kroos	5	2
Leroy Sané	19	18
Isco	16	13
Mauro Icardi	21	19
Gareth Bale	22	21
Sergio Agüero	6	3

Table 18.3 Correlation coefficient between results of ratings made by sports journals and obtained classifications in 2016 and 2017

	2016		2017		2016–2017	
	C1	C2	C1	C2	C1	C2
Golden ball	0.1586	0.1510	0.4136	0.2655	0.2839	0.2078
Golden boot	0.2261	−0.0633	0.4898	0.2872	0.5032	0.2652

classifications presented in Tables 18.1 and 18.2. The results of these analyses are shown in Table 18.3.

Measures of correlations between classifications and popular rankings presented in Table 18.3 are obtained with using Pearson's linear correlation coefficient. In fact, another one measure of correlation was calculated—the Spearman rank correlation coefficient, but the results were very similar. Unfortunately, both classifications made in the research and rankings do not include too many observations, so the results of correlation analysis are not statistically significant. It could be concluded that, taking into account ranking "Golden Boot", its results are not correlated with the factual performances of footballers. Table 18.3 shows that excluding the variable the market value of the player from the set of diagnostic variables causes decreasing of value of correlation coefficients. It could mean that this variable has an impact on the popular sports rankings.

18.5 Conclusion and Final Remarks

The problem drawn out in this chapter was to classify football players using variables describing their activity on the football pitch, FIFA's rating points of country of origin of the player and the value of club footballer plays for. The hypothesis raised in the research was that the market value of the player has a strong impact on the classification. Results of statistical verification of hypothesis were not confirmed it. First—correlation coefficient indicates only on the moderate relationship between classifications and results of popular rankings. Second—in every case, the number of observations was too small to generalize results of the comparison analysis.

Positive results of the research are:

- higher correlation coefficients are obtained for first classifications (C1) than for the second classification (C2);
- slightly higher correlation coefficients are obtained for the "Golden Boot" ranking than for the "Golden Ball";
- Cristiano Ronaldo, recognized by journalist as the best player in the world, did not win in any classification and in classifications C2 his position was fourth.

In my opinion, positive results confirm possibility of existing confirmation bias in sports finance but it requires definitely greater number of observations to obtain statistically significant results. We cannot argue that journalists have an influence on the results of rankings but the question stands still open.

References

Antonowicz D, Szlendak T, Kossakowski R (2012) Piłkarz jako marka i preferencyjny kibic jako aborygen. O wybranych społecznych konsekwencjach komercjalizacji sportu. Kult i Spol. Sport w kult 3:3–26 (in Polish)

Dobson S, Goddard J (2001) The economics of football. Oxford University Press

Firlej K, Trzepalka P (2015) Sports nationalism—truth or fiction in the area of football. ZN WSES w Ostrolece 19:126–137

Frick B (2007) The football players' labour market: empirical evidence from the major European leagues. Scot J Polit Econ 54(3):442–446

Global Transfer Market Report. A review of all international football transfers in 2017. FIFA/TMS. Access at www.fifatms.com on 10 Feb 2018

Gullianotti R, Bonney N, Hepworth M (eds) (2005) Football, violence and social identity. Routledge, London, New York

Hellwig Z (1968) Zastosowanie metody taksonomicznej do typologicznego podzialu krajow ze wzgledu na poziom ich rozwoju oraz zasoby i strukturę wykwalifikowanych kadr. Przeg Stat 15(4):307–326 (in Polish)

Jeanrenaud C, Kesenne S (eds) (2006) The economics of sport and the media. MPG Books LTD, Bodmin, Cornwall, UK

Lewicka M (1998) Confirmation bias. Cognitive error or adaptive strategy of action control? In: Kofta M, Weary G, Sedek G (eds) Personal control in action. Plenum Press, New York, pp 233–258

Majewski S (1998) Szeregowanie krajów przy pomocy Diagramu Czekanowskiego i Taksonomicznego Miernika Rozwoju. Przeg Stat 8:76–84 (in Polish)

Majewski S (2016) Identification of factors determining market value of the most valuable football players. J Manage Bus Adm Cent Eur 24(3):91–104

Majewski S (2017) Investors decisions in the light of exploitable predictable irrationality effect on Warsaw stock exchange. The case of UEFA EURO 2012 and 2016. In: Nermend K, Latuszynska M (eds) Neuroeconomics and behavioural aspects of decision making. Springer Proceeding in Business and Economics, pp 175–184

Morgan WJ (1995) Cosmopolitanism, olympism, and nationalism: a critical interpretation of Coubertin's ideal of international sporting life. OLY: Int J of Olym Stud IV:79–92

Shiller R (2000) Irrational exuberance. Broadway Books, New York

Sloane P (1971) The economics of professional football. Scot J Polit Econ 18(2):121–146

Sloane P (2015) The economics of professional football revisited. Scot J Polit Econ 62(1):1–7

Sznajder J (2007) Charakterystyka rynku sportu profesjonalnego. Gosp Nar 10:45–65 (in Polish)

Chapter 19
Comparison of the Order-Picking Route and Time Obtained by Using the TMAL Method with Results of Selected Take-Out Strategies

Krzysztof Dmytrów

Abstract When a company utilises the shared storage, then the selection of locations in the process of order-picking is not an easy task. In the literature of the subject, there are several take-out strategies, but none of them considers it as the multiple-criteria decision-making problem. The goal of the chapter was to compare the results of designations of the picker's route obtained by means of the two take-out strategies (priority of partial units and quantity adjustment) with the results obtained by using the Taxonomic Measure of Location's Attractiveness (polish abbreviation—TMAL) method with three decision criteria: distance from the I/O point, degree of demand satisfaction and the number of other picked products in the neighbourhood of analysed location. After selection of locations, the picker's route will be designated by means of the *s-shape* heuristics. The analysis will be performed by means of the simulation experiment, where one hundred of ten-element orders will be generated for each method and the picker's route length and time will be compared.

Keywords Order-picking · Multiple-criteria decision-making · Taxonomic Measure of Location's Attractiveness · *s-shape* · Simulation experiment

19.1 Introduction

Warehouse management is one of the most important aspects of the company management. Warehouse costs consist of about 20% of total logistic costs in the company (De Koster et al. 2007). Among the costs of warehouse management, order-picking costs consist from 55 (Bartholdi and Hackman 2016) to 65 (Miłaszewicz and Rut 2014) per cent of them. On the other hand, travelling comprises the greatest part of the order-picking time (about 55%) (Merkuryev et al. 2009).

K. Dmytrów (✉)
Institute of Econometrics and Statistics, University of Szczecin, Szczecin, Poland
e-mail: krzysztof.dmytrow@usz.edu.pl

K. Nermend and M. Łatuszyńska (eds.), *Problems, Methods and Tools in Experimental and Behavioral Economics*, Springer Proceedings in Business and Economics, https://doi.org/10.1007/978-3-319-99187-0_19

Therefore, there is a need to improve the order-picking process. There are many order-picking systems. They can be fully automatic to employ humans in the process. Among fully automatic systems, we have the automated or robotised picking systems. Among the systems that employ humans, there are the picker-to-parts, put or part-to-picker (AS/RS, miniload, VLM and other) systems. The first and the second ones are generally the least robotised, while the third one the most. Despite many possibilities, classical picker-to-parts systems are still by far the most popular ones (De Koster et al. 2007).

The order-picking process can be optimised in many ways. It can be done by designing the appropriate warehouse layout, by using the appropriate storage assignment or by utilising effective routing method.

19.2 Literature Review

The warehouse layout can decrease order-picking routes and times in many ways. Generally, in most works related to the warehouse management and order-picking it is assumed that the warehouse layout is standardised, rectangular. However, it is not always true. Very often, warehouses are placed in buildings, where the standard, rectangular layout cannot be used. For such warehouses, it is very important to place the I/O point in the most appropriate place. Among the non-standard warehouse layouts, the *L-shape* layout is the most popular (Sabo-Zielonka 2015).

The appropriate storage assignment plays very important role in optimisation of the order-picking process. The ABC class-based storage assignment is one of the most widely used ones. By using this storage assignment, the picker's distance can be decreased by more than 40%, when compared to the random (chaotic) assignment (Le-Duc 2005). Also, the storage order plays an important role. There are two types of goods storage order—fixed or free storage order (Gudehus and Kotzab 2012), also called the dedicated or shared storage systems (Bartholdi and Hackman 2016). If a company utilises the dedicated storage system, every product is assigned only to one location and every location is assigned only for single product. For the shared storage system, any product can be stored in many, sometimes very distant locations and many products can be stored in one location. The dedicated storage system is much more convenient for the pickers because they can remember location of products in a warehouse; however, its main drawback is poor storage space utilisation (on the average 50%). The shared storage, on the other hand, allows much better space utilisation; however, locations of each product change constantly, what makes it impossible for the picker to remember. Utilisation of the shared storage system also requires the usage of warehouse management system and discipline in warehouse processes. In the case of the shared storage system, other question arises—if completed product can be accessed in many locations, which one should be selected by the picker? According to Gudehus and Kotzab (2012), there are four possible strategies:

- FIFO—units will be picked accordingly to their arrival to the warehouse.
- Priority of partial units—locations, where there is the lowest content of the product, will be accessed first even if it increases labour.
- Quantity adjustment—the opposite to the previous one—the picker retrieves the product from the locations, where requested quantity is fully satisfied even if it generates additional low amounts of products in locations.
- Taking the access unit—if the amount of the product on given location exceeds or is equal requested quantity, the complete unit is taken after the excess quantity is put aside.

The first strategy is natural for the quickly expiring products, such as fresh foods or cut flowers. The second one is applied, when we want to clean the locations from small amounts of products. This strategy helps to maintain order on the shelves and, however, in exchange, increases the order-picking time. The third strategy is used, when it is desirable to visit as little locations as possible, while the last one if we want to collect the complete packages in which the ordered products are stored. Even if the decision-maker uses one of the above-listed strategies, applying just one criterion is very often not enough. For instance, if the FIFO strategy is used, there may be several locations, in which ordered products have the same storage time. Going further, if we combine the FIFO with the quantity adjustment strategy, there still may be locations in which there are products stored for the same length of time and in the same (from the given order's point of view) amount. Therefore in case of the shared storage system, selection of locations, from which the products should be picked, becomes the multiple-criteria decision-making problem. For this purpose, the discrete multiple-criteria decision-making techniques, such as the AHP, ANP, Electre, Promethee (Trzaskalik 2015), SAW, COPRAS (Podvezko 2011), TOPSIS (Hwang and Yoon 1981) or SMAA (Lahdelma and Salminen 2010), can be used. All these methods originate from the decision theory. We can also apply methods that were originally developed for purposes of the multivariate statistical analysis, such as the composite measure of the development (Hellwig 1968).

After the locations are selected, the picker's route needs to be designated. It can be done by means of the modified travelling salesman problem, first developed by Ratliff and Rosenthal (1983). Obtained by this method route will be optimal or the shortest possible. However, such route is very often not considered as the best one by the pickers (Le-Duc 2005). As a result of this consideration, the pickers tend to deviate from the route. Calculation of the optimal route is also very time-consuming for the warehouse management system (especially for larger orders, i.e. when more than 20 locations are to be visited). Also, the optimal route does not take the aisle congestion or traffic direction into account. Therefore, there are several heuristics that are used instead of the optimal method: *s-shape*, *return*, *largest gap*, *mid-point*, *combined* (Tarczyński 2013). The most popular ones are the *s-shape* and *return* heuristics—they are easy to implement and effective (Tarczyński and Jakubiak 2017).

The goal of the chapter is comparison of the results of designations of the picker's route obtained by means of the two take-out strategies (priority of partial units and quantity adjustment) with the results obtained by using the Taxonomic Measure of Location's Attractiveness (polish abbreviation—TMAL) method (Dmytrów 2015) with three decision criteria: distance from the I/O point, degree of demand satisfaction and the number of other picked products in the neighbourhood of analysed location with assumed systems of weights. This method is entirely based on Hellwig's composite measure of the development. After selection of locations, the picker's route will be designated by means of the *s-shape* heuristics. The analysis will be performed by means of the simulation experiment, where one hundred of ten-element orders will be generated for each method and the picker's route length and time will be compared. It is worth noting that locations for analysed take-out strategies will also be selected with the support of the TMAL method.

19.3 Applied Analytical Methods

There are three criteria that describe each location for each ordered product:

x_1 distance from the I/O point,
x_2 degree of demand satisfaction,
x_3 number of other picked products in the neighbourhood of the analysed location.

The first criterion, measured on the ratio scale, is the loss-type criterion. It is measured in contractual unit, which is the shelf width.

The degree of demand satisfaction is the profit- or loss-type criterion, measured on the ratio scale. It is calculated by means of the following formula:

$$x_2 = \begin{cases} \frac{l}{z}, & \text{if} \quad z > l \\ 1 & \text{if} \quad l \geq z \end{cases}, \tag{19.1}$$

where l is the number of units of the picked product in the analysed location and z the demand for picked product. The criterion x_2 is the profit-type criterion in case of the quantity adjustment strategy and the loss-type criterion in case of the priority of partial unit strategy.

The third criterion—the number of other picked products in the neighbourhood of the analysed location is the profit-type criterion. It is measured on the ratio scale. The term "neighbourhood" can be understood differently with respect to the warehouse type. For the typical, low-level warehouse, it could be the racks within the aisle and so it will be in this case.

When we use the multiple-criteria decision-making techniques, decision criteria should be weighed. The decision-maker may weigh the criteria subjectively and may use statistical and formal or expert methods. If the decision-maker sets the weights subjectively, he/she decides on the importance of each criterion. Among the statistical methods, weights can be based, for example, on the criteria's variability; however, this approach is very often criticised because it is considered as too "mechanical" (Kukuła 2000). The other, very often applied approach is based on the Shannon entropy (Lotfi and Fallahnejad 2010). The expert methods are very often based on the AHP method (Trzaskalik 2015). For the small number of criteria, setting weights subjectively is the effective method because the decision-maker can fairly easily specify which criterion is more important than the other. In the case of this analysis, nine combinations of weights were applied. They are presented in Table 19.1. The first combination is the reference one—it assumes that every criterion is the same important. The next three combinations assume that one criterion is twice as important as the other two. The next three combinations assume that two criteria are twice as much important as the remaining one. The reason for such combinations of weights was to check how assigning more weight to specific criteria influenced the picker's route and order-picking time. The eighth combination is the combination that assumes that the quantity adjustment (QA) strategy is being used; therefore, the second criterion—degree of demand satisfaction—is the most important. It was assumed that its weight was 0.95 and weights of both remaining criteria were 0.025. Small values of weights for other criteria are used to distinguish locations in case of the same values of the main criterion. The ninth, final combination assigns the same weights as the previous one with the exception that in this case the second criterion is the loss-type one—it assumes that the priority of partial unit (PPU) strategy is used. This situation is the generalisation of the strategy presented by Dmytrów (2014).

The steps of calculation of the TMAL method are the same as the steps of calculation of the composite measure of the development (Bąk 2016):

- The values of each criterion were normalised. In the chapter, the quotient inversion was used:

$$z_{ij} = \frac{x_{ij}}{\sqrt{\sum_{i=1}^{n} x_{ij}^2}}, \quad (19.2)$$

where x_{ij} is value of jth criterion in the ith alternative (location). There are much more normalisation formulas possible (Walesiak 2016). The reason for selection

Table 19.1 Analysed combinations of weights (own study)

Combinations of weights	x_1	x_2	x_3
C1	0.333	0.333	0.333
C2	0.5	0.25	0.25
C3	0.25	0.5	0.25
C4	0.25	0.25	0.5
C5	0.4	0.4	0.2
C6	0.4	0.2	0.4
C7	0.2	0.4	0.4
QA	0.025	0.95	0.025
PPU	0.025	0.95	0.025

of the above formula was to preserve the differences in the mean values and the variability.

- The normalised values created the so-called perfect alternative or the pattern by means of the following formula:

$$z_0 = \begin{cases} \max_i \{z_{ij}\} & \text{for the profit - type criteria} \\ \min_i \{z_{ij}\} & \text{for the loss - type criteria} \end{cases}$$

- Euclidean distances between the pattern and each location were calculated.
- Mean weighed Euclidean distances from the pattern for each combination of weights were calculated.
- The TMAL was calculated as the complement to unity from the ratio of mean weighed distance of each location from the maximum value obtained in the previous step.
- The TMAL values were sorted in the descending order.
- The highest ranking locations were selected, until the demand for each product was satisfied.

The above-mentioned procedure was applied for every strategy and combination of weights. The performance of every strategy and combination of weights were analysed by means of the simulation experiment with the following assumptions:

- A simple, rectangular low-level warehouse with 1000 locations, one main aisle and 20 aisles within racks was assumed. Every rack contained 25 locations.
- The warehouse utilised the ABC class-based storage system.
- Every order consisted of ten products, and each of them was stored in four locations.
- Available amounts of products in each location varied from a single unit to the amount that satisfied the demand twice.
- For all applied combination of weights, 100 orders were generated.
- For every picked product and every combination of weights, a ranking of locations was created.
- For each combination of weights, the highest ranking locations were selected until the satisfaction of demand.
- After selection of locations, the picker's route was designated by means of the *s-shape* heuristic (Le-Duc 2005).
- For each route, its length was measured, and the order-picking time was calculated.
- The order-picking time was the sum of the picker's movement and collection time. It was assumed that the time of passing the distance unit (shelf width) was 2 s and the product collection time from the location was 10 s.
- For each applied method, by means of the one-way ANOVA or the Kruskal–Wallis test it was analysed if both the route lengths and order-picking times were

significantly different (Shahbaba 2012). Homogeneity of variances was checked by means of Levene's test (Gastwirth et al. 2009).
- If the null hypothesis was to be rejected, by means of the *post hoc* Tukey's HSD test (Haynes 2013) or the Dunn test (Dinno 2015) the pairwise comparisons were performed.

19.4 Results of the Experiment

First, the analysis was performed with respect to the picker's route length. After the simulations, Levene's test was used to compare the variances of the route lengths. Obtained value of the test statistics $L = 1.055$ ($p = 0.393$) indicated that there was no basis to reject the null hypothesis stating that the variances of route lengths for each combination were not significantly different, so the parametric one-way ANOVA could be used. The ANOVA table for the route lengths is presented in Table 19.2.

The results presented in Table 19.2 indicate that mean route lengths were not equal for all combinations of weights. Mean route lengths for each combination of weights are presented in Fig. 19.1.

As seen in Fig. 19.1, the shortest route lengths can be obtained if the quantity adjustment (QA) strategy was used. On the other hand, the longest route lengths were obtained for the priority of partial unit (PPU) strategy. The results are pretty obvious because the PPU strategy assumes that we want to clean locations from small amounts of units and therefore in order to collect the products that are scattered among the warehouse much more locations should be visited in comparison with the QA or any other strategy. Quite good results could also be obtained if the combination of weights C7 (0.2; 0.4; 0.4) was used. It means that it is effective to assign high weights to the degree of demand satisfaction and the number of other ordered products in the neighbourhood of analysed location.

Because the one-way ANOVA indicated statistically significant differences between mean route lengths, Tukey's HSD test was conducted to indicate, where means were significantly different. Table 19.3 shows the results of Tukey's test for mean route lengths for each strategy and combination. Tukey's criterion was equal to 19.57.

Table 19.2 ANOVA table for route lengths (own study)

Source of variation	Sum of squares	df	Mean sum of squares	F	p-value
Combinations	288077.9	8	36009.740	9.036	0.000
Error	3550590.0	891	3984.949		
Total	3838668.0	899			

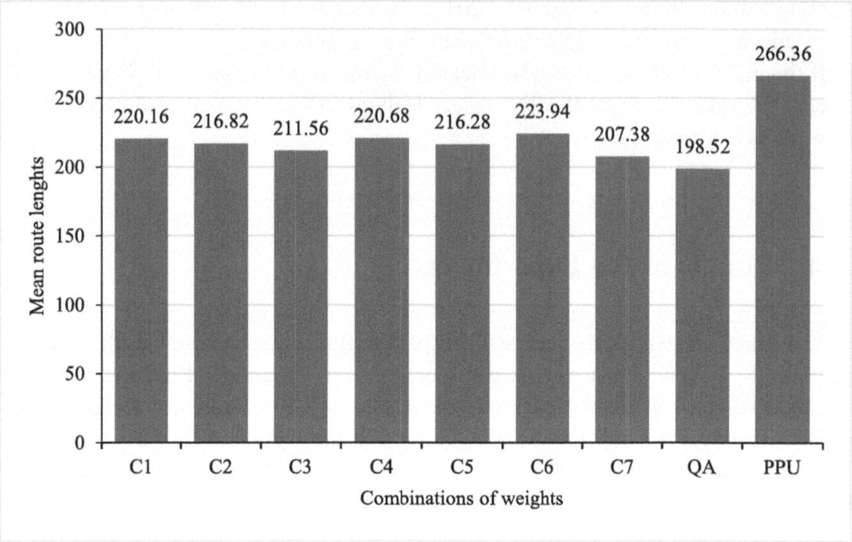

Fig. 19.1 Mean route lengths (own study)

Table 19.3 Results of Tukey's test for mean route lengths (significant differences are bolded) (own study)

	C2	C3	C4	C5	C6	C7	QA	PPU
C1	3.34	8.60	0.52	3.88	3.78	12.78	**21.64**	**46.20**
C2		5.26	3.86	0.54	7.12	9.44	18.30	**49.54**
C3			9.12	4.72	12.38	4.18	13.04	**54.80**
C4				4.40	3.26	13.30	**22.16**	**45.68**
C5					7.66	8.90	17.76	**50.08**
C6						16.56	**25.42**	**42.42**
C7							8.86	**58.98**
QA								**67.84**

Table 19.3 shows that mean route lengths obtained by means of the PPU strategy were significantly longer than these obtained by any other strategy. Additionally, application of the QA strategy yielded significantly shorter mean route lengths than reference combination C1, combination C4 (0.25, 0.25, 0.5) and C6 (0.4, 0.2, 0.4). Generally, it is advisable to assign high weight to the second criterion—degree of demand satisfaction (of course in case, when it is the profit-type criterion).

The second stage of the analysis was the comparison of the order-picking time. The application of Levene's test indicated that variances in all analysed strategies were not homogeneous; therefore, the one-way ANOVA could not be used and the

Kruskal–Wallis test was used instead. Calculated statistics *H* of the Kruskal–Wallis test was equal: $H = 74.439$ ($p = 0.0000$). Therefore, on the basis of the Kruskal–Wallis test it can be stated that analysed strategies and combinations were statistically different with respect to the mean order-picking time. Mean order-picking times for each strategy and combination of weights are presented in Fig. 19.2.

Analysing the mean order-picking times, the conclusions are virtually the same as in the case of mean route lengths. The longest order-picking times were obtained by using the PPU strategy (which is obvious, because for this strategy the picker must visit much more locations than for any other one). The shortest order-picking times were obtained by using the QA strategy. Also, good results were also obtained by using the combination of weights C7. Therefore, also for the order-picking time it is advisable to assign high weight to the criterion x_2—degree of demand satisfaction (of course, it happens in case if it is treated as the profit-type one).

Because the Kruskal–Wallis test indicated that analysed strategies were significantly different with respect to the order-picking time, the *post hoc* Dunn test was used. The criterion of the Dunn test was equal to 144.77. Table 19.4 shows the results of the Dunn test for mean order-picking times for each combination.

Table 19.4 shows that distribution of order-picking times for the PPU strategy was significantly different from all other strategies with the exception of the combination C6 (0.4; 0.2; 0.4). Also, the distribution of order-picking times for the QA strategy was significantly different from the combination C6. When we compare these results with the results obtained for route lengths, they are in most cases similar—only pairwise comparisons C6-PPU, QA-C4 and QA-C1, for mean route

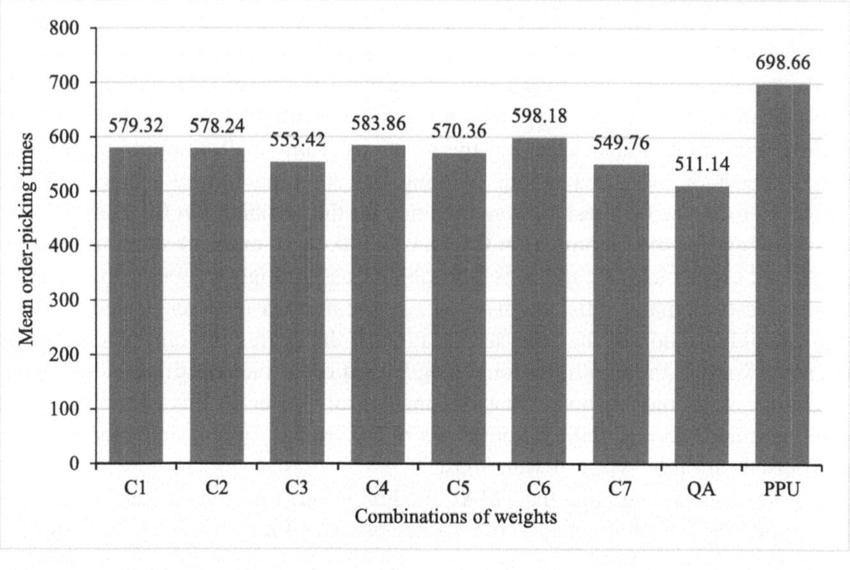

Fig. 19.2 Mean order-picking times (own study)

Table 19.4 Results of the Dunn test for mean order-picking times (significant differences are bolded) (own study)

	C2	C3	C4	C5	C6	C7	QA	PPU
C1	2.32	42.67	11.08	8.48	37.02	49.75	121.80	**175.93**
C2		40.36	13.39	6.17	39.33	47.44	119.48	**178.25**
C3			53.75	34.19	79.69	7.08	79.13	**218.60**
C4				19.56	25.94	60.83	132.87	**164.86**
C5					45.50	41.27	113.32	**184.41**
C6						86.77	**158.81**	138.92
C7							72.05	**225.68**
QA								**297.73**

lengths differences, were statistically significant, while for the order-picking times they were not.

19.5 Conclusions

The chapter presents the comparison of the order-picking route lengths and order-picking times obtained for the quantity adjustment (QA) and priority of partial unit (PPU) strategies with the results obtained for the TMAL method with various combinations of weights. The results for both these strategies were also obtained with the support of the TMAL method by assigning the highest weight (0.95) to the degree of demand satisfaction (but for the QA strategy, this criterion was the profit-type and for the PPU strategy the loss-type one). The QA strategy yielded the best results—both route lengths and order-picking times were shortest. On the other hand, the PPU strategy yielded the worst results. However, it should be noted that the PPU strategy does not aim in shortening the route length and order-picking time, but in cleaning the locations from small amounts of products with the cost of increased labour. Among the combinations of weights for the TMAL method, the best results were obtained for the combination C7 (0.2; 0.4; 0.4) and the worst for the combination C6 (0.4; 0.2; 0.4). In order to shorten the route length and order-picking time, it is advisable to assign high weight to the criterion x_2—degree of demand satisfaction—and x_3—the number of other picked products in the neighbourhood of the analysed location. If the degree of demand satisfaction had small weight, then both the route lengths and order-picking times were longer. Of course, it should be noted that obtained results refer to this specific type of warehouse and these specific assumptions of the storage system and should not be generalised on other types of warehouse.

The research showed that the TMAL method is versatile and can also be applied to support the well-known take-out strategies. The future research will include application of the TMAL or other multiple-criteria decision-making techniques, such as the TOPSIS or SMAA methods, for other take-out strategies (FIFO and taking the access unit). Especially, the latter will be interesting because it allows to analyse problems with missing or incomplete information.

References

Bąk A (2016) Porządkowanie liniowe obiektów metodą Hellwiga i TOPSIS—analiza porównawcza. Prace Naukowe Uniwersytetu Ekonomicznego we Wrocławiu 426(26):22–31. https://doi.org/10.15611/pn.2016.426.02
Bartholdi JJ, Hackman ST (2016) Warehouse & distribution science, release 0.97. The Supply Chain and Logistics Institute, School of Industrial and Systems Engineering, Georgia Institute of Technology, Atlanta, GA 30332-0205 USA
De Koster R, Le-Duc T, Roodbergen KJ (2007) Design and control of warehouse order picking: a literature review. Eur J Oper Res 182(2):481–501
Dinno A (2015) Nonparametric pairwise multiple comparisons in independent groups using Dunn's test. Stata J 15(1):292–300
Dmytrów K (2014) Procedura kompletacji zakładająca oczyszczanie lokalizacji. Studia i Prace Wydziału Nauk Ekonomicznych i Zarządzania 31(2):23–36
Dmytrów K (2015) Taksonomiczne wspomaganie wyboru lokalizacji w procesie kompletacji produktów. Studia Ekonomiczne, Zeszyty Naukowe Uniwersytetu Ekonomicznego w Katowicach 248:17–30
Gastwirth JL, Gel YR, Miao W (2009) The impact of Levene's test of equality of variances on statistical theory and practice. Stat Sci 24(3):343–360. https://doi.org/10.1214/09-STS301
Gudehus T, Kotzab H (2012) Comprehensive logistics, 2nd edn. Springer, Berlin, Heidelberg. https://doi.org/10.1007/978-3-642-24367-7
Haynes W (2013) Tukey's Test. In: Dubitzky W, Wolkenhauer O, Cho CH, Yokota H (eds) Encyclopedia of systems biology. Springer, New York, NY. https://doi.org/10.1007/978-1-4419-9863-7
Hellwig Z (1968) Zastosowanie metody taksonomicznej do typologicznego podziału krajów ze względu na poziom rozwoju oraz zasoby i strukturę wykwalifikowanych kadr. Przegląd Statystyczny 15(4):307–326
Hwang CL, Yoon K (1981) Multiple attributes decision making methods and applications. Springer, Berlin
Kukuła K (2000) Metoda unitaryzacji zerowanej. Wydawnictwo Naukowe PWN, Warszawa
Lahdelma R, Salminen P (2010) Stochastic multicriteria acceptability analysis (SMAA). In: Ehrgott M, Figueira J, Greco S (eds) Trends in multiple criteria decision analysis. international series in operations research & management science, vol 142. Springer, Boston, MA, pp 285–315. https://doi.org/10.1007/978-1-4419-5904-1_10
Le-Duc T (2005) Design and control of efficient order picking processes. PhD thesis, RSM Erasmus University
Lotfi FH, Fallahnejad R (2010) Imprecise Shannon's entropy and multi attribute decision making. Entropy 12:53–62. https://doi.org/10.3390/e12010053
Merkuryev Y, Burinskiene A, Merkuryeva G (2009) Warehouse order picking process. In: Merkuryev Y, Merkuryeva G, Piera M, Guasch A (eds) Simulation-based case studies in logistics. Springer, London, pp 147–165. https://doi.org/10.1007/978-1-84882-187-3_9
Miłaszewicz B, Rut J (2014) Nowoczesne metody kompletacji. Logistyka 6:12347–12350
Podvezko V (2011) The comparative analysis of MCDA methods SAW and COPRAS. Inz Ekon Eng Econ 22(2):134–146
Ratliff HD, Rosenthal AS (1983) Orderpicking in a rectangular warehouse: a solvable case of the traveling salesman problem. Oper Res 31(3):507–521

Sabo-Zielonka A (2015) Heurystyki wyznaczania tras w dwublokowej nieprostokątnej strefie kompletacji zamówień. Studia Ekonomiczne. Zeszyty Naukowe Uniwersytetu Ekonomicznego w Katowicach 241:125–139

Shahbaba B (2012) Analysis of variance (ANOVA). Biostatistics with R. use R!. Springer, New York, NY, pp 221–234. https://doi.org/10.1007/978-1-4614-1302-8_9

Tarczyński G (2013) Wielokryterialna ocena procesu kompletacji towarów w magazynie. Stud Ekon 163(13):221–238

Tarczyński G, Jakubiak M (2017) Wpływ kompletacji strefowej, składowania towarów i metody wyznaczania trasy magazyniera na efektywność procesu kompletacji zamówień. Optim Stud Ekon 3(87):138–152. https://doi.org/10.15290/ose.2017.03.87.10

Trzaskalik T (2015) Wprowadzenie do badań operacyjnych z komputerem. PWE, Warszawa

Walesiak M (2016) Wybór grup metod normalizacji wartości zmiennych w skalowaniu wielowymiarowym. Przegląd Statystyczny R. LXIII—Zeszyt 1:7–18

Chapter 20
Simulation Game "Step into the Future" as a Tool of Experimental Economics—Case Study

Barbara Kryk

Abstract The chapter presents a modern simulation game "Step into the future"—played using Facebook—which can be successfully used as an instrument of experimental economics. Conclusions resulting from the achieved effects of the game emphasize its suitability for economic research.

Keywords Research experiment · Didactic experiment · Simulation game
Game effects

20.1 Introduction

The purpose of the chapter is the presentation of a simulation game "Step into the future" as a tool of experimental economics. This game has been developed as a method for increasing the skills that enable youth at risk of social exclusion to function in the labor market and to support economic and social decision-making. The predefined effects that it should bring provide the opportunity for comparison with the achieved results which confirm its experimental usefulness. The elements of the game in the context of the economic experiment, as well as conclusions from the evaluation of its didactic effects, allowing determining of the possibility of using the game in economic research, were presented.

B. Kryk (✉)
University of Szczecin, WNEiZ University of Szczecin ul.
Mickiewicza 64, 71-101 Szczecin, Poland
e-mail: krykb@wneiz.pl

K. Nermend and M. Łatuszyńska (eds.), *Problems, Methods and Tools in Experimental and Behavioral Economics*, Springer Proceedings in Business and Economics, https://doi.org/10.1007/978-3-319-99187-0_20

20.2 Characteristics of the Game from the Point of View of the Experimental Elements

Smith developed the methodological basis of the experiment as a research tool in economics. He distinguished three factors defining an economic experiment: (1) environment, (2) institutions, and (3) behavior of the experiment's participants (Smith 1994). The simulation game "Step into the future" has these basic elements of an experiment (Bagozzi and Yi 2012; Harrison and List 2004; Kryk 2016; Holt 1999).

20.2.1 Environment

The **environment** consists of initial conditions, that is, young people in a specific situation (threatened by social exclusion), a system of preferences and incentives motivating rational behavior in an appropriate manner, and specific objectives of the game.

The game is intended especially for young people at risk of social exclusion,[1] particularly exclusion from the labor market. Such youth is not sufficiently prepared to start an adult and independent life, they cannot manage money rationally, there is no educated need for work, and good professional activity patterns or a well-established message that work and education are the foundation of living and a chance for a "better life." Usually, this is accompanied by a lack of social and communication skills. The majority of such young people come from professionally inactive families, marginalized poor communities with (benefit) claiming attitudes, where there is also often domestic violence. Problems that concern this group are usually cross-related, and the lack of adequate qualifications, skills, education, and professional experience as well as the ignorance of the labor market make it even more difficult to find and maintain a job. It also increases fear and anxiety of entering the labor market (Barwiński 2011; Kryk 2015), and therefore, it is so important to support such young people in the process of entering the labor market (cf. Nóżka 2011). This problem exists in all European countries, including Poland, where an innovative model for supporting young people at risk of social exclusion has been developed,[2] of which the simulation game "Step into the future" is an integral part.[3]

[1]Remaining in the system of foster care and in dysfunctional families at the ages of 15–25.

[2]The support model was developed as part of the innovative project "Adulthood, independence, work" implemented by the West Pomeranian Agency for Regional Development S.A. in Szczecin, financed by European funds under the Human Capital Operational Program 2007–2013. The description is presented in the monograph (Kryk et al. 2015).

[3]The game was developed by the author of this chapter, involved in the preparation of this innovative model of support, see detailed description (Kryk et al. 2015).

Detailed goals of the game:

- The participant in the game can move around the city based on a city plan as well as determine his or her professional predispositions; he or she knows what job they want to look for.
- The participant is aware of different forms of active job search and knows what to look for when seeking a job.
- The participant has a professionally prepared CV and knows how to prepare for the interview.
- The participant has experienced a job interview, analyzed their attitude during this interview, and drawn conclusions to work on.
- The participant is able to contact a potential employer and can submit a CV in a potential place of work.
- The participant can prepare a presentation of the analysis of the local labor market in a group (in the context of their own qualifications, experiences, opportunities, predispositions), taking into account the demand and supply sides, and present their conclusions from the analysis.
- Establishing new, supporting contacts with peers, employers, and other people in a physical and virtual space.
- Increasing skills in the field of social competences, in particular: cooperation and communication in a group, self-presentation, assessment of one's competences, resources and better planning of one's strengths, resolving conflicts in a team, responsibility for one's decisions, and estimating the consequences of one's actions.
- Strengthening a sense of self-worth and awareness of the importance of independence in undertaking activities related to job seeking.

20.2.2 Institutions

Institutions are general description of the game, rules and assumptions of the game, rules of communication between participants of the game, evaluation tools to check the effects of the game. The simulation game "Step into the future" is an integral part of the model of supporting youth at risk of social exclusion, to help participants/recipients to develop specific competences and acquire the skills needed to enter the labor market and stay in it. It can also be successfully applied in the process of economic education of students of the so-called economic studies to carry out experiments to achieve specific results because its general objective is to increase the skills that enable young people to move freely in the labor market. The game is implemented via a social network. Participants are divided into teams and go through all stages of the game, gaining experience, skills, knowledge, and information necessary in the labor market, at the same time learning competition and cooperation and joining in a supportive social network. The basic materials and resources necessary for the game are predetermined. The basic elements of the game that reflect the institutions of the economic experiment are described below.

General description of the game—the game consists of four stages:

I. "Find yourself"—duration—3 days,
II. "Search and plan"—duration—2–3 weeks,
III. "Look around and orientate"—duration—4 weeks,
IV. "Check your progress"—duration—4–5 weeks.

It is necessary to precisely determine the start time of the game, the implementation of which requires a minimum of 3 months. However, in exceptional situations—taking into account the different nature and labor intensity of individual stages of the game and the participants' abilities—a professional assistant acting as a coordinator in the game can extend the deadline for completing individual stages and the entire game accordingly.

Rules of the game:

- The game is conducted using the most popular social networking site—Facebook (FB).
- Groups of 3–8 people are formed. A professional assistant works with such a group. All groups cooperate with each other and compete in the implementation of tasks.
- Each participant of the group must pass all stages of the game.
- Tasks are assigned individual and group points (being the sum of individual points and points earned by the group for specific activities).
- Execution of a task after exceeding the time foreseen for its implementation will not be included in the points' classification.
- The maximum number of points possible to be gained by the group in individual stages: in I and II—30, in III and IV—70, and in the whole game—200. The method of division into group and individual points belongs to the professional assistant coordinating the game.
- The participants take part in the evaluation of task implementation and scoring criteria.
- Among themselves, professional assistants choose a game coordinator who will supervise the entire game (who will set up a closed group profile on FB, initiate an invitation, be responsible for coordinating what happens on the profile in connection with the implementation of the game tasks, control scoring, observe time implementation, etc.).
- A professional assistant supervises the implementation of individual tasks to which the group is subjected; he or she supports the pupils and coordinates the summary of each stage of the game.
- During the game, each recipient and professional assistant has the opportunity to follow the scoring of individual participants and groups on an ongoing basis.
- At the end, the scores of all people, groups, and benefits achieved (individual and group) are announced.

- In case of disputable issues or serious problems with the implementation of tasks (due to insufficient levels of various skills of the participants and the difficulties that may be caused by the performance of individual tasks), it is possible to renegotiate the selected game conditions—such as the time of task completion.[4] Such renegotiation is possible only at a group meeting of all participants in the game or delegated to particular groups of representatives entitled to make decisions on behalf of the group.[5]

Materials and resources necessary for the game: (1) possibility to access the Internet (using a computer during group meetings with a professional assistant or in a different manner determined by the representatives of the group), (2) mobile phone equipped for taking photographs (most people have such a phone; it is also possible to ask a colleague or career assistant to lend one to you), (3) maps of the city (can be downloaded from the Internet, collected at the tourist office, borrowed from a friend), (4) voice recorder (often a function on a mobile phone) that an employer could use during a job interview or a professional assistant during stage three of the game, (5) office supplies needed to prepare the presentation of the analysis of the local labor market.

The rules of communication between participants of the game result from its general rules, and the connection and running scheme is shown in Fig. 20.1. In the first stage, the professional assistant coordinating the game sets up a closed group profile on FB and initiates an invitation to all participants, including assistants responsible for particular groups, defining a time frame for registration. After meeting the requirements, the implementation of individual stages of the game begins. On agreed dates, consistent with the period of implementation of these stages, the assistant coordinating the game along with other assistants and participants of the game meet online to assess the achieved results. FB plays a key role in synchronizing the participants' activities, being used not only to control the course of the game but also to allow assistants to communicate among themselves, with participants of the game, in order to create a network of cooperation between members of particular groups and between groups.[6] The experiment was carried out for four groups, and there were no contraindications for the participation of more groups at the same time.[7] The problem of conducting the experiment via FB may be in the delays generated by the participants themselves, not by hardware resources.

Evaluation tools: (1) questionnaire (scale of skills' growth)—completed before and after the game, (2) summaries of individual stages of the game—discussion in

[4]The assistant coordinating the game may extend the duration of stage III and IV.

[5]Other options for the resolution of contentious issues (e.g., via online voting or debates) can only be triggered as a result of a decision taken at the above-mentioned meeting. Each of these meetings must be attended by professional assistants.

[6]Assistants can also communicate with each other directly via other tools (e.g. mobile phone, meetings).

[7]The minimum number of groups needed to play is 2, for a minimum of 4 people.

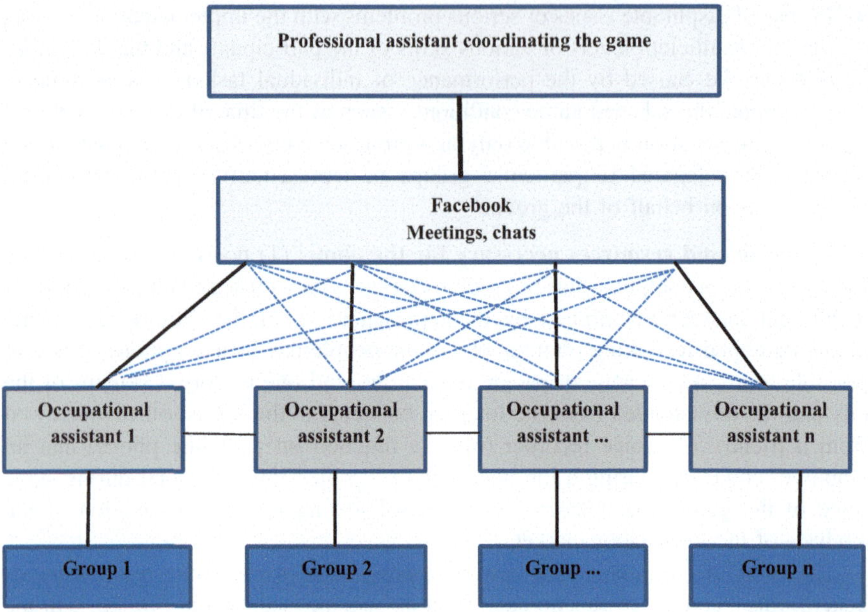

Fig. 20.1 Connection and game handling diagram. *Source* Own study

groups (questions that a professional assistant must ask to verify the effects, etc.), (3) opinion of a career assistant regarding the progress of individual participants.

20.2.3 Behaviors of the Game Participants

These are closely related to the detailed description of the game in the context of active participation of youth in all stages of the game and training, implemented as part of the model of supporting youth at risk of social exclusion, which is integrally connected with the game.

Detailed description of the game

Stage I: "Find yourself" Familiarizing group members with the assistant. To enter the game, participants must first send their e-mail to the address of the game coordinator to receive an invitation to a closed group on FB. Whoever logs in first individually and as a group gets points. If all members of the group manage to log in first, the group gets a bonus for efficiency (the number of bonus points is set by the game coordinator). The day and time of the game start (i.e., the date from which the mailbox accepts applications) must be precisely defined, and registration must be completed. Time for registration—3 days. **Effects**: After this time, the first statistic of individual and group points should be provided. It should be discussed with the group. Then, another task appears.

Stage II: "Search and plan" The group's task is to develop an attractive tour plan for a colleague who (hypothetically) comes to us from another town. The trip plan should include places: entertainment, culture, specific for the history of the village, gastronomy "for everyone" (a characteristic place or menu for the town), recreation in the field. You should:

- briefly present each place, justify the choice and—if possible—attach a photograph of the place, using, e.g., photographs posted on the Internet (the ideal situation is to take a picture of the place yourself),
- provide an estimate of such a hypothetical trip, including travel costs, meals, and attractions, taking into account promotional offers and permanent discounts, and choose the most profitable option.

The assumed amount available is 30 PLN/person. Time to complete this task: 2–3 weeks. This includes the duration of the group meeting, the purpose of which is to plan the final version of the trip, which is about 3 h (the group must develop a trip plan: START—on the map from the PKP or PKS station or the main bus terminal in the city) + 4 h for discussion. Summary of the game on FB: general assessment of the professional assistant—number of points for the task for the group + individual points granted to the group members for their contribution.

Effects Acquisition of skills in the field of resource analysis, planning, organizing, management, communication, working with a map, orientation in the field, time and money management, self-assessment, evaluation of other group members.

Stage III: "Look around and orientate" This stage consists of three elements:

(1) On the basis of the previously identified resources of the participants of the game (including skills, education), we recommend that they indicate different ways of searching for a job according to their capabilities, willingness, or personal predispositions. Everyone searches for a job for themselves, but the more ways the group presents, the more points it gets. A list of the most accessible and, at the same time, most beneficial methods for the people in the group should be established from the proposals presented.
(2) The group that obtained the highest number of points for a given task is the first to choose the way for developing "Tips for a jobseeker," based on information from the employment office (giving details of where, in what room, name of the official, telephone number, office hours, documents, requirements, etc.). The information must be available to everyone on FB so that it is possible to exchange comments and get additional information. The elements and form of the study should be determined in advance.

(3) A task complementary to the above-mentioned task is the preparation by each participant of a package of application documents suitable for the job which he or she is searching for in a determined manner.

The given stage lasts a minimum of 4 weeks. **Effects**: practical knowledge of job search methods; the participant must demonstrate and confirm that he has taken specific actions (prepare a CV and other necessary documents and take them or send them to a potential employer—he must provide a minimum of three such confirmations).

Stage IV: "Check yourself" includes four elements

(1) Preparation for a job interview.[8]
(2) Each participant must take part in a job interview.[9]
(3) On this basis and on the basis of other skills already acquired, the participant takes up the task—"Plan further work for yourself"—and tries to develop a plan of next possible actions for employment.
(4) Simultaneously with the preparation for the interview, all groups participating in the game (together) should prepare a presentation on the analysis of the labor market. This requires the meeting of all participants in one place. It is necessary to plan the event, share tasks, organize work, room, and everything else necessary to implement this project, invite participants, etc. The assistant coordinating the game can assign additional points to the group/people showing the greatest initiative and ingenuity in the task. Time for the implementation of this task is a minimum of 4–5 weeks. **Effects**: experience connected with self-presentation and joint preparation of the analysis of the labor market; participants preparing the analysis receive a certificate confirming their participation in its elaboration. The game is finished for all groups. Then, the number of points scored by all persons and groups and the benefits achieved are announced (individual and team). Winners (individual and group) should be rewarded somehow. The form of the prize should be known from the beginning of the game. The attractiveness of the prize directly influences the degree of the participants' motivation.

The assignment of individual parts of the game "Step into the future" to the appropriate elements of the experiment confirms its research usefulness.

---

[8]If the participant is invited by an independent employer for an interview, he or she will receive additional points in the game. If not, the professional assistant should arrange such an interview, so that the participant may participate.

[9]It would be advisable to record the interview so that later, the participant, along with the professional assistant, could analyze behavior, strengths and weaknesses, and determine what to improve or what steps to take in the future.

20.3 Results of Game Evaluation from a Didactic Point of View in the Context of the Experiment

It was determined that the game "Step into the future" should bring the following "hard" didactic results: (1) creation of attractive tour routes around the place of residence, (2) professional CV of each participant, (3) guide with tips for using various forms of job search, (4) an at least triplicate, in relation to the size of the group, number of participants' offers sent to potential employers, (5) training interviews conducted with the participation of each recipient (the actual number of these conversations should not depend on the number of recipients, but on their needs and abilities—there will be people who need only one such exercise and those who need more), (6) an analysis of the local labor market developed in the form of a presentation. In addition to these "hard" didactic effects, it is planned that the game:

- will raise the social and professional competences of the game's participants in obtaining and maintaining their first job,
- will help to establish contacts with employers and auxiliary institutions,
- will help half of the people participating in the game to find their first job and maintain it for a minimum of 6 months from the moment of employment, which is a very ambitious and difficult assumption taking into account the level of their skills, qualifications, and motivation to work, and the situation on the labor market,
- will change attitudes and increase overall social activity.

Thirty-two participants were recruited for the first edition of the game and divided into four groups of eight people.[10] All groups passed, according to the assumptions, the applicable stages of the game within certain time frames but, unfortunately, not all participants (a few people gave up). The evaluation showed that the game was positively assessed by participants and users from a didactic point of view (Final Report 2014; Kryk 2015). The conclusions are as follows:

- The goals of the game were properly formulated, and all its hard effects were achieved.
- Using computers/tablets and the Internet is an important didactic incentive for young people to participate in the game. However, it was indicated that among the youth at risk of social exclusion, there are people who, due to their financial situation, may not have access to a computer and the Internet. Hence, it is necessary to allow subsequent stages of the game to take place in a stationary form, e.g., during group meetings.
- According to the professional assistants, the level of difficulty of the third and fourth stage of the game is high for the examined group of young people, often characterized by a lack of independence and entrepreneurship, passivity, social

[10]Then it was used several times by other project teams.

withdrawal, and closure. Therefore, it is advisable to extend the duration of the game, if necessary, so that the changes taking place in the participants can take place parallel to the challenges they face.

– Participants in the game declared that they acquired skills defined in its objectives and changed attitudes toward their peers—mutual motivation of project participants was observed to make further efforts to fully and effectively use the support, which the specialists participating in the evaluation assessed as a very positive and significant change for this category of recipients.
– Participants established contacts with employers; however, they were not very numerous.
– Half of the participants of the game got their first job, but with a lot of help from the team by leading the game and providing support.

In the context of the above, it can be said that from the point of view of the didactic experiment, the game brought the majority of the expected effects; therefore, it is largely effective. Correcting the indicated elements should contribute to obtaining better results from its application in the future.

20.4 Conclusions

The presented text is a synthetic characteristic of the "Step into the future" simulation game and its didactic effects in the context of an economic experiment. The experience gathered during the project encourages further work on the use of this type of game in the process of education and experimentation in the field of economics.

References

Bagozzi RP, Yi Y (2012) Specification, evaluation, and interpretation of structural equation models. J Acad Market Sci 40(1):8–34

Barwiński Ł (2011) Marginalizacja społeczna młodzieży i jej przeciwdziałanie w praktyce streetworkingu—wyzwania, szanse, zagrożenia. In: Frysztacki K, Nóżka M, Smagacz-Poziemska M (eds) Dzieci ulicy—procesy marginalizacji i automarginalizacji nieletnich, Zeszyty Pracy Socjalnej (zeszyt szesnasty)". Wydawnictwo Instytutu Socjologii UJ, Kraków, pp 109–124

Harrison GW, List JA (2004) Field experiments. J Econ Lit 42:1009–1055

Holt CA (1999) Teaching economics with classroom experiments. South Econ J 65(3):603–610

Kryk B (2015) Projekt model wsparcia na rynku pracy młodzieży zagrożonej wykluczeniem społecznym—wyniki ewaluacji. Stud Oecon Posnan 3(7):190–209

Kryk B (2016) Sorts and types of experiment. In: Nermend K, Łatuszyńska M (eds) Selected issues in experimental economics. Springer proceedings in bussiness and economics. Springer International Publishing, Switzerland, pp 27–36

Kryk B, Rosińska A, Nowak J (2015) Model skutecznej metody wsparcia wychowanków domów dziecka oraz młodzieży zagrożonej wykluczeniem społecznym w wieku 15-25 lat w znalezieniu zatrudnienia i jego utrzymaniu. Zachodniopomorska Agencja Rozwoju Regionalnego S.A., Szczecin

Nóżka M (2011) Formy wsparcia MZWS w kontekście poziomu jej samooceny i motywacji do pracy. Acta Univ Lodz Folia Sociol 38

Raport końcowy z badania. Ewaluacja zewnętrzna produktu finalnego projektu innowacyjnego testującego "Dorosłość, samodzielność, praca" (2014). Szczecin. http://www.dsp.zarr.com.pl. Accessed 30 Jan 2018

Smith V (1994) Economics in the laboratory. J Econ Perspect 8(1):113–131

Chapter 21
Behavioral Economics and Rationality of Certain Economic Activities: The Case of Intra-Community Supplies

Paweł Baran and Iwona Markowicz

Abstract Behavioral aspects might be among causes of differences between the value of trade in goods shipped from Poland and acquired from Polish firms by contractors throughout EU that exist in public statistics databases. The need for profit in the short term may result in reporting unreliable data to public statistics entities. The aim of the chapter is to point out some of possible irregularities in economic activities' evidence of Polish taxpayers whose businesses depend on intra-community trade. These anomalies consist of hiding transactions by avoiding statistical declarations or late declaring which has an immediate impact on aggregated statistical data. As a result, there are huge differences between datasets containing the same data reported by both sides of transactions, i.e., as intra-community supplies (ICS), by Polish businesses and as intra-community acquisitions (ICA) from Polish businesses. At least some of such anomalies can be linked with tax fraud. Another group of anomalies includes specific schemes that can be observed in declared data. The authors have studied the above-mentioned differences and found irregularities within ICS and ICA for Combined Nomenclature chapters and positions. The structures of such differences have been compared for years 2010–2016. In the second part of the chapter, we discuss specific schemes in declared data that may indicate participation in VAT fraud. We explain the outcomes based on behavioral factors.

Keywords Behavioral economics · Missing trader intra-community fraud
Trade in goods shipped from Poland

P. Baran (✉)
Department of Operations Research and Applied Mathematics in Economics, Faculty of Economics and Management, Econometrics and Statistics Institute, University of Szczecin, Mickiewicza 64, 71-101 Szczecin, Poland
e-mail: pawel.baran@usz.edu.pl

I. Markowicz
Department of Statistics, Faculty of Economics and Management, Econometrics and Statistics Institute, University of Szczecin, Mickiewicza 64, 71-101 Szczecin, Poland
e-mail: iwona.markowicz@usz.edu.pl

K. Nermend and M. Łatuszyńska (eds.), *Problems, Methods and Tools in Experimental and Behavioral Economics*, Springer Proceedings in Business and Economics, https://doi.org/10.1007/978-3-319-99187-0_21

21.1 Introduction

Since the twentieth century, the academic discourse in economics has been dominated by neoclassical school (marginalism). However, its assumptions like full rationality of individuals or existence of perfect markets with full information processed by decision makers are often criticized. H. Simon's concept of bounded rationality gave birth to an alternative trend—behavioral economics (Simon 1972). It encompasses both social and emotional factors in human activities.

The fact that in 1978, Simon was awarded with Bank of Sweden Prize in Economic Sciences in Memory of Alfred Nobel for his pioneering research into the decision-making process within economic organizations came as a confirmation of the necessity to take into consideration numerous factors within the scope of the economic analysis (Miłaszewicz 2017). Individuals make their decisions based on incomplete information as well as on limited ability to process it. As a result, they cannot maximize their objectives so they end up with only *satisficing* level of utility (Solek 2010). Ten years later, H. Leibenstein formulated a similar concept according to which businesses do never actually reach a fully effective state.

In the twentieth century, Kahneman and Tversky (1979), and Thaler (1980) published their works that started quick development of a new scientific trend named behavioral economics. Their goal was to supplement economic theory with the psychological foundations of human behavior. To achieve this, behavioral economists loosened the strict assumptions of standard economic models to explain anomalies that remained unexplained within neoclassical economics.

A distinct characteristic of behavioral economics is its multidisciplinary nature. The observation of subjects requires psychological and sociological research, and, in order to define behavioral theories, it is necessary to integrate the knowledge developed within social sciences. Hence, economists must not only extend their area of interest, but also abandon the assumption about rational individuals (Zalega 2015).

Within behavioral economics, there exist two main trends. One developed based on behavioral science ("old behavioral economy"). It merges methodology of psychological studies on behavior with economic theories. This trend is represented in the works of such economists, as H. Simon, J. March, G. Katona, H. Leibenstein, T. Scitovsky, R. R. Nelson, and S. G. Winter (Frantz 2013). The other approach to behavioral economics is included in the works of D. Kahneman, A. Tversky, and R. Thaler. These authors represent the second generation in behavioral economics ("new behavioral economy"). Their research focuses on analyzing deviations from rational behavior (Zalega 2015).

In other words, behavioral economics is a field where economics and psychology meet. The essence of behavioral economics lies in increasing the applicability of economic theory and in enhancing its ability to explain and predict individuals' behavior (Camerer et al. 2001; Camerer 2006, 2007). Psychology and economics have their own distinct methodologies. Experiment is a typical way of research in psychology while economic research is conducted via econometric modeling.

However, nowadays economists tend to use experiment in their research as well. Behavioral economics concentrates on experiments' outcomes that reveal anomalies or deviation from neoclassical theory observed in individuals' behavior while preserving achievements of economics (Wilkinson 2008).

According to Doszyń (2017), statistical and econometric tools could be used in measuring selected aspects of behavior, but it is not always clear how to measure attitudes, tendencies, or preferences (Doszyń 2017). It is worth noting that many authors stress out the need to expand economic research with analysis concerning human factor (including emotions or propensities).

The aim of the chapter is to point out some of the possible irregularities in economic activities' evidence of Polish taxpayers whose businesses depend on intra-community trade (both supplies and acquisitions). These anomalies may be the result of hiding transactions by avoiding statistical declarations or late declaring, although there exist other possible causes of differences between intra-community trade figures. Perhaps the most important one is introducing thresholds for the obligatory declaration of foreign trade (these are different for export and for import and differ between member states). Some other are declaring fictitious transactions (VAT carousels) or simple errors in declarations (e.g., multiplying declarations, wrong CN code or wrong value of traded goods). All this has an immediate impact on aggregated statistical data. As a result, there are huge differences between datasets containing the same data reported by both sides of transactions, i.e., as intra-community supplies (ICS) by Polish firms and as intra-community acquisitions (ICA) from Polish firms. At least some of such anomalies can be linked with tax fraud. Another group of anomalies includes specific schemes that can be observed in declared data.

Our study consists of two parts. In the first part, we have studied the above-mentioned differences and found irregularities within intra-community supplies and acquisitions for Combined Nomenclature/Harmonized System chapters and positions. The structures of such differences have been compared for years 2010–2016. In the second part of the study, we discuss specific schemes in declared data that may indicate participation in tax fraud. We explain the outcomes based on behavioral factors.

21.2 Intra-community Trade Actions Consistent with Behavioral Economics Theory

One of the most important concepts invented in the field of behavioral economics is prospect theory (Solek 2010). It replaced utility function of assets (concave for risk-averse decision makers and convex for risk-loving) with a value function that connects gains and losses with their subjective value. A reference point is set (based, e.g., on one's wealth) and all the outcomes of a decision are compared with this point and then assigned a value based on possible outcomes and their respective probabilities. The value function is S-shaped and steeper for losses than for gains. A decision maker will often choose lower but certain profit. Among other significant achievements of behavioral economics, there is also theory of hyperbolic discounting according to which rewards that arrive sooner are preferred over the ones that arrive later.

Therefore, from psychological point of view we cannot judge every decision maker in the same manner. Individuals make their decisions based on incomplete information and with their own objectives in mind. It is possible that some actions are taken against the law. One example of such action is tax fraud.

Explaining illegal but profitable activities on behavioral ground seems natural; it is, however, worth mentioning that Becker (1968) previously considered utility of illegal actions on the ground of his concept of homo economicus. He had described choice between legal and criminal economic activity and concluded that calculating gains and costs, thus maximizing utility is more important than rationality itself. It is also worth noting that seeking to pay less taxes may but does not necessarily have to be illegal. According to Iwin-Garzyńska (2017) while the term tax optimization has negative connotations (often understood as tax evasion), it is not a way to avoid paying taxes but rather a form of intelligent use of regulations in order to legally decrease due payments.

Cross-border transactions within the EU have been zero-rated for value added tax (VAT) since 1992. Importers of goods are thus able to receive goods without paying VAT, but charge VAT on their resale. If the VAT they receive is not then remitted to the revenue authority, they are committing a crime: this is missing trader fraud. Should the goods be repeatedly exported and re-imported then this criminal practice can be repeated, giving the activity its more common name, Carousel Fraud. The last term represents the practice on continual import and export of the same goods in a chain of transactions (European Union Committee 2007). Basic scheme of a missing trader intra-community fraud is presented in Fig. 21.1. Table 21.1 provides a short description of all the entities and their roles in a carousel.

MTIC frauds exploit the refund of VAT to exporters to milk the VAT system of revenues through a series of contrived transactions. The two key features of the VAT that are exploited in the carousel fraud are the VAT zero-rating of exports and the system of deferred payment for VAT on imports, adopted in the EU since the removal of fiscal frontiers in 1992 (Smith 2007). According to Smith (2007), effective VAT fraud tackling would require such measures as tighter checks on firms seeking to register for VAT, requiring guarantees in dubious cases, and slowing down the payment of VAT refunds relative to the collection of VAT due. Joint liability rules by which traders can be held responsible for fraud elsewhere in the chain and establishing better and quicker information exchange between national tax authorities could help as well. Unfortunately, the above measures have strong side effects, including harming legal businesses (by affecting their liquidity) or imposing excessive bureaucratic burden on them. Later on, Smith (2007) lists several radical measures within the context of a system that preserves zero-rating:

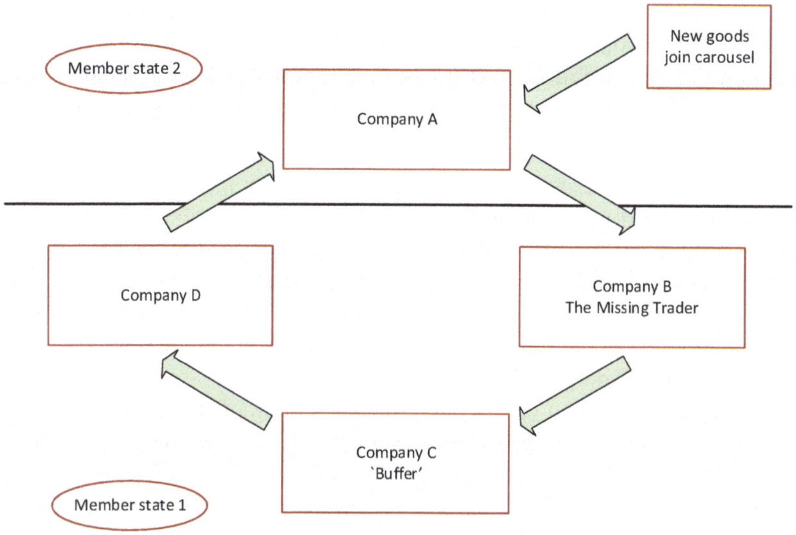

Fig. 21.1 A basic MTIC fraud (European Union Committee 2007, p. 9)

Table 21.1 Description of carousel members' activities (European Union Committee 2007, p. 9)

Company	Role in MTIC fraud
A	Purchases goods: either from company D (completing the carousel) or new goods with which to start a carousel Exports goods to company B in another member state. Export sale is VAT zero-rated
B	Purchases goods from company A in member state 2. Pays no VAT on purchase, because export by A is zero-rated Charges and receives VAT on sale to company C Disappears without remitting the VAT to the revenue authorities
C	Buys goods from B at VAT-inclusive price, and sells to D, charging VAT. Company C may be wholly unaware of the fraud (There may be multiple buffer companies between B and D, some or all of which may be honest.)
D	Pays VAT on purchase from company C Exports goods to company A, and receives a refund of VAT from the revenue authority on exported goods In effect reclaims the VAT not paid by company B, and crystallizes the revenue authority's loss

- **reverse charging** (liability in a business-to-business (B2B) transaction is placed on the buyer),
- **reverse withholding** (requires the purchaser to make a direct payment to the authorities of part or all of the VAT due on its purchase),

- a system of **VAT accounts** (traders are required to open a distinct bank account to which they would transfer the amount of VAT charged to their customers),
- the **compulsory use of a third party to guarantee VAT payments** (either in general or for particular sectors) (the idea adopted from Ainsworth (2006)).

As of 2017, some of the above-mentioned measures (mostly reverse VAT and VAT accounts) are already in use in different countries that have revenue system prone to VAT fraud but to a varying extent.

There is no doubt that VAT is susceptible to evasion and fraud, running all the way from the occasional concealed sale to sophisticated and large-scale attacks by organized crime. Certainly, non-compliance with the VAT, particularly in the form of carousel fraud, has long been on the minds of many policy makers, especially in the EU (Keen and Smith 2006).

According to Jakobsson (2013), it is the zero-rating of intra-community acquisitions in combination with the deferred payment of VAT that has made it possible to employ carousel fraud with VAT on the internal EU market. Moreover, the carousel can theoretically keep turning an infinite amount of times, and when a carousel is discovered, the people behind the company committing fraud are usually long gone. Podlipniak (2012) argues that a fault in taxing intra-community supplies with VAT enables these frauds to take place. Member states and the European Commission are aware of the fault but are unable to agree on how to change the taxation of the mentioned supplies.

VAT frauds are undoubtedly a still growing problem for EU member states. It is because fraudulent operations directly affect revenues. As of today, there exists no specific solution to eliminate the problem thoroughly. However, certain instruments are being implemented. One of such measures is reverse charging. Its implementation in a specific branch has an immediate positive impact on the scale of VAT fraud. A detailed analysis and evaluation of such a mechanism can be found in Szlęzak-Matusewicz (2015).

The European Court of Auditors audit addressed the question of whether the EU is tackling intra-community VAT fraud effectively. The Court found that the EU system is not sufficiently effective and that it is adversely affected by the lack of comparable data and indicators on intra-community VAT fraud at EU level (European Court of Auditors 2016). VAT fraud is often linked with organized crime. According to Europol's representatives, it is estimated that 40–60 billion euro of the annual VAT revenue losses of member states are caused by organized crime groups and that 2% of those groups are behind 80% of MTIC fraud (European Court of Auditors 2016). According to European Court of Auditors, there are no effective crosschecks between customs and tax data in most of the member states visited. The administrative cooperation framework allows sharing of VAT information between member states' tax authorities but there are problems with the accuracy, completeness, and timeliness of data. There is also a lack of cooperation and competences of administrative, judicial, and law enforcement authorities overlap (European Court of Auditors 2016).

21.3 Data and Methodology

We based our study on two data sources. First part of the study is based solely on aggregate data on intra-community trade provided by Eurostat (Comext database). For the second part, we provided our own examples based on our familiarity with the dataset containing raw intra-community trade data declared by businesses and collected by Polish revenue authorities. The dataset containing data from Intrastat declarations is supplemented with data from other sources and delivered to Central Statistical Office (GUS) and eventually to Eurostat. Similar procedure applies to every other member state. As a result, we obtain a database containing aggregated data on intra-community supplies (ICS) and intra-community acquisitions (ICA) for businesses in all 28 EU member states.

We downloaded Eurostat (Comext) data on all ICS dispatched by Polish businesses and on all ICA acquired by businesses throughout EU from Poland for years 2010–2016, aggregated at Combined Nomenclature/Harmonized System chapter (2-digit code) and position (4-digit code) levels. We wanted to find out what the differences between declared ICS and ICA within chapters were and what positions were accountable for them.

In order to find structural misrepresentation in Comext data, we calculated differences between ICS and ICA for all HS chapters in every year. Then for every pair of years, we compared the structure of such differences with a structural similarity index (Chomątowski and Sokołowski 1978) given by:

$$W_{ij} = \sum_{d=1}^{k} \min_{i \neq j} \left(w_{id}, w_{jd} \right) \tag{21.1}$$

where

i, j year under consideration, $i, j = 2010, \ldots, 2016$,
d number of HS chapter, $d = 1, \ldots, k$; $k = 98$,
and $w_{i,d} = \frac{n_{i,d}}{n_i}$ is a dth fraction of the total.

Because we applied the index to differences between declarations that can be either positive or negative, we had to slightly modify the procedure and the index itself. We converted all figures less than zero to their absolute values and then added up all the absolute values of differences. In order to preserve their signs (since two structures having differences of the same absolute value but different signs are not similar), we counted every chapter twice—once in the search for positive difference and then for the negative one. Formally, we calculated index given by:

$$W_{ij} = \sum_{d=1}^{2k} \min_{i \neq j} \left(w_{id}, w_{jd} \right) \tag{21.2}$$

where $w_{i,d} = \max\left(\frac{n_{i,d}}{n_i^+}, 0\right)$, for $d = 1, \ldots, k$ and $w_{i,d} = \max\left(-\frac{n_{i,d}}{n_i^+}, 0\right)$ for $d = k+1, \ldots, 2k$ are equivalent fractions of the global sum of absolute differences in year i, i.e., $n_i^+ = \sum_{d=1}^{k} \left|n_{i,d}\right|$.

21.4 Differences Between Aggregate ICS and ICA in Comext Database

First, we calculated differences between ICS and ICA for every HS chapter in 2016. The differences are huge for several HS chapters (cf. Fig. 21.2). Interestingly, these are not limited to chapters with highest turnover. We have investigated a group of chapters with huge differences that we found intriguing. List of the chapters under consideration can be found in Table 21.2.

Although differences within each chapter are caused by various HS positions, one can point out a group of goods at position level that mostly influences the difference. These groups include—in chapters where there is a positive difference between declared dispatches and acquisitions:

- in chapter 39—items classified as positions 3925 and 3917 (builders' ware of plastics),
- in chapter 85—position 8528 (TV sets and monitors),
- in chapter 27—positions 2716 (electrical energy) and 2704 (coke),
- in chapter 87—positions 8704 and 8703 (cars and trucks),
- and in chapter 89—positions 8901 (ships, huge boats, other vessels for transportation of goods).

In case of chapters with positive difference between acquisitions and dispatches:

- in chapter 84—the difference does depend mostly on difference in declarations of trade in goods classified as positions 8408 and 8409 (diesel engines and engine parts) followed by position 8407 (spark ignition engines),
- in chapter 30—position 3004 (medicaments in measured doses for retail sale),
- in chapter 82—position 8212 (razor blades),
- in chapter 24—position 2402 (cigarettes),
- and in chapter 90—position 9021 (orthopedic appliances, including crutches, surgical belts, and trusses; splints and other fracture appliances; artificial parts of the body; hearing aids and other appliances which are worn or carried, or implanted in the body).

We suspected that the differences were incidental. In order to prove the opinion, we confronted structures of differences generated for years 2010–2016 using structural similarity index. The index (21.2) is easy to compute and has a straightforward interpretation. It takes on values from the interval [0; 1] (Chomątowski and Sokołowski 1978) and reveals years for which we observe

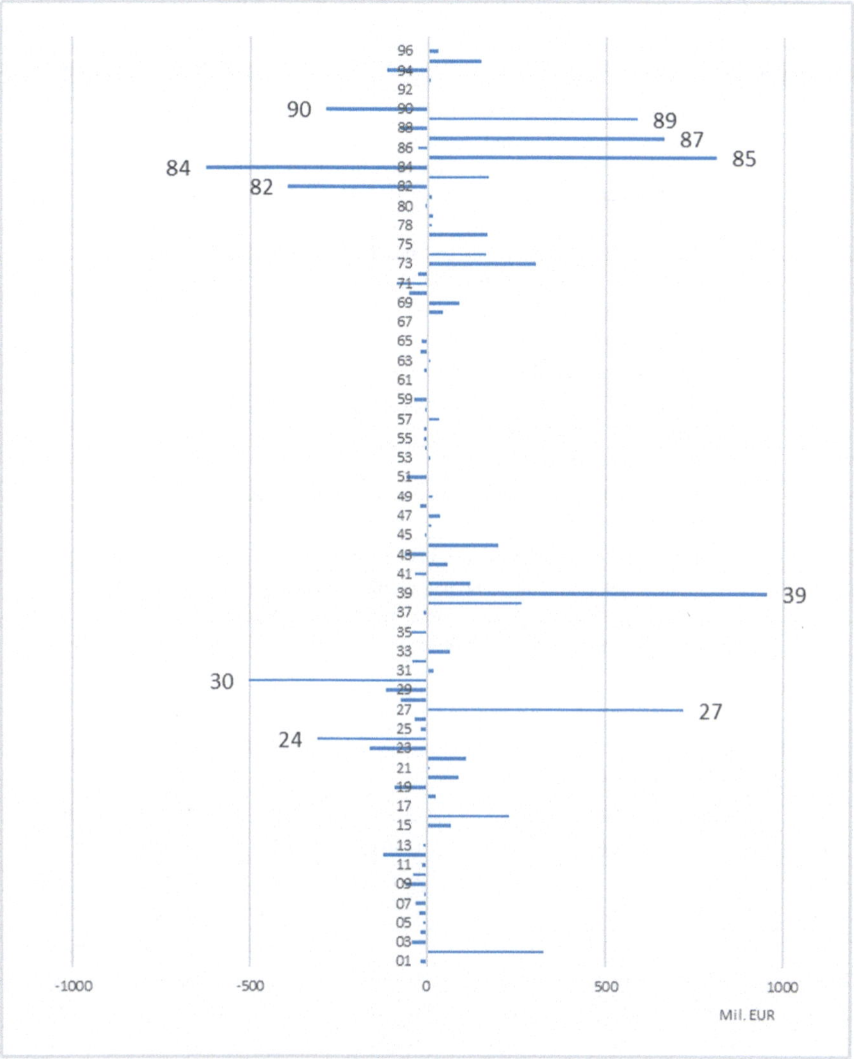

Fig. 21.2 Differences between ICS and ICA by chapter in 2016

similar structure of differences between declared dispatches and acquisitions from Poland. The greater the value, the more similar are structures for the years compared. After comparing the structures in the period 2010–2016, we found out that all of them were similar but to a varying degree. The structure was mostly stable compared year to year and has evolved with time—as we see in Table 21.3. Higher values gather along the main diagonal while lower values can be observed near top-right and bottom-left corners. Differences between dispatches and acquisitions had the most similar structure in 2014 and 2015.

Table 21.2 CN chapters with biggest differences between ICS and ICA

Number of CN chapter	Description	Difference in mil. EUR
39	Plastics and articles thereof	954
85	Electrical machinery and equipment and parts thereof; sound recorders and reproducers, television image and sound recorders and reproducers, and parts and accessories of such articles	813
27	Mineral fuels, mineral oils, and products of their distillation; bituminous substances; mineral waxes	720
87	Vehicles other than railway or tramway rolling-stock, and parts and accessories thereof	664
89	Ships, boats, and floating structures	586
84	Nuclear reactors, boilers, machinery, and mechanical appliances; parts thereof	−626
30	Pharmaceutical products	−503
82	Tools, implements, cutlery, spoons, and forks, of base metal; parts thereof of base metal	−394
24	Tobacco and manufactured tobacco substitutes	−307
90	Optical, photographic, cinematographic, measuring, checking, precision, medical or surgical instruments and apparatus; parts and accessories thereof	−285

Table 21.3 Similarity of structures of differences between declared dispatches and acquisitions from Poland by HS chapter (2010–2016)

	2010	2011	2012	2013	2014	2015	2016
2010		0.7668	0.6773	0.5640	0.6171	0.5698	0.5370
2011	0.7668		0.7836	0.6711	0.6222	0.6063	0.6021
2012	0.6773	0.7836		0.7745	0.6933	0.6617	0.6581
2013	0.5640	0.6711	0.7745		0.7604	0.7344	0.6753
2014	0.6171	0.6222	0.6933	0.7604		0.8317	0.6844
2015	0.5698	0.6063	0.6617	0.7344	0.8317		0.7422
2016	0.5370	0.6021	0.6581	0.6753	0.6844	0.7422	

We wanted to find out how stable were the differences over time for the chapters mentioned in Table 21.2. We can see the dynamics of the respective differences in Figs. 21.3 and 21.4. In Fig. 21.3, we see the differences for chapters with ICS larger than ICA in 2016. It is worth noting that all differences throughout the whole period 2010–2016 were positive. This means that in these chapters, Polish businesses have declared more goods sold to EU than other EU member state located businesses declared as bought from Poland. Level of the difference was relatively stable in chapters 89, 39 (although here difference systematically rose) or 27. For chapter 87, we observe that the difference descended throughout the period thus data are more balanced now.

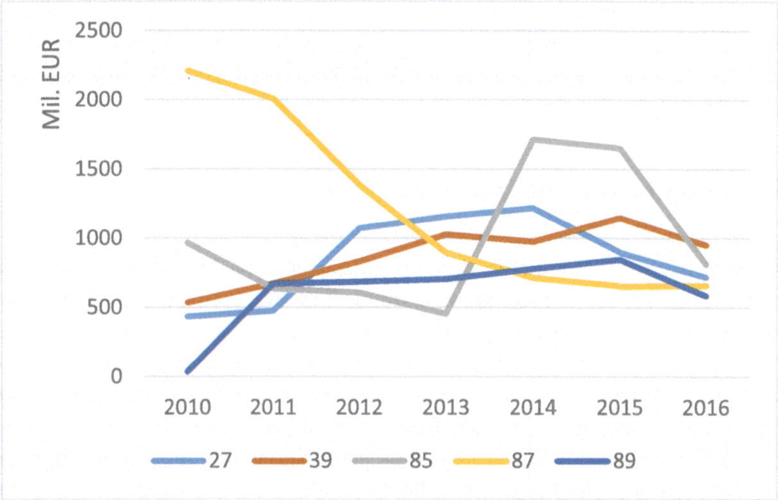

Fig. 21.3 Positive differences between ICS and ICA for selected HS chapters, 2010–2016

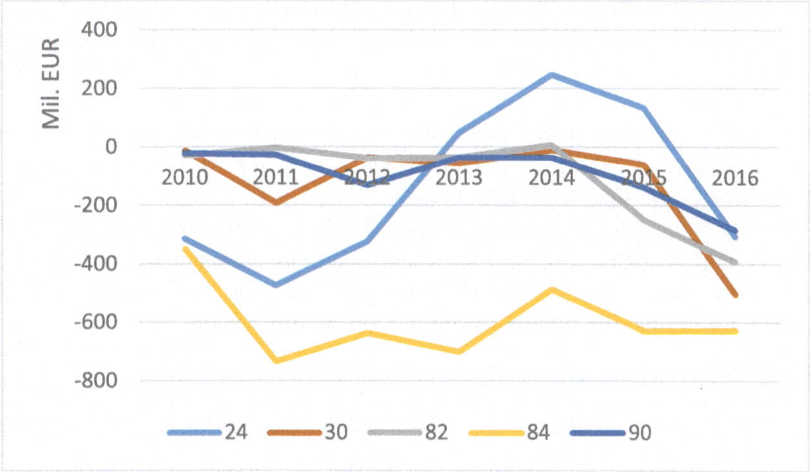

Fig. 21.4 Negative differences between ICS and ICA for selected HS chapters, 2010–2016

Similar observations hold for the second selected group of HS chapters. In Fig. 21.4, we present dynamics of the differences for those chapters with ICA much larger than ICS in 2016. Again, most of the differences remained negative (in that ICS was smaller than ICA) except for chapter 24 and one observation for chapter 82. Chapter 84 was always imbalanced and the absolute values of the difference were greatest. Interestingly, chapters 30, 83, and 90 were balanced for five consecutive years but the gap between ICA and ICS has risen in last two years under consideration. The relative stability of the differences suggests that there exist systematic causes for such differences that can be hard to eliminate. Perhaps the estimation procedure for missing data should be revised at the beginning.

21.5 Irregularities in Intrastat Data

Differences between aggregate ICS and ICA are not the only emanation of anomalies that can be connected with fraud. Not every suspicious transaction is undeclared and as such easy to spot. Often both sides of a transaction will declare it scrupulously even if the transaction itself is a part of a chain of illegal transactions. The analysts will then spot some specific patterns in Intrastat data. Unfortunately, data on intra-community trade come from Intrastat declarations and not from SADs (single administrative documents, customs declarations common in foreign trade). This means they are not only less reliable than extra-community trade data but they are also subject to statistical confidentiality.

Four of the common patterns in data are presented below. The tables contain no real data (for obvious reasons) but the schemes are real and can be observed for numerous goods that have been used in carousel frauds.

Table 21.4 presents **scheme 1** in which we observe repeated acquisition and supply of the same amount of some good. The fact that both the amount and the country of destination vary is probably just sort of a smoke screen to make the scheme unrecognizable at first sight. It is possible that within that scheme, only documents (false invoices) are traded. A common feature is a tiny margin (even well under 1%) on a pair of transactions.

Table 21.5 presents a common **scheme 2** where a business is buying and/or selling certain goods on a regular basis and beside its normal activity trades "carousel" goods (here named B and C) every now and then. The country of origin/ destination will often be different from that of the usual trade.

Table 21.4 Scheme 1—same amount of a certain good acquired then dispatched multiple times

Direction	Month	Country	Weight	Value	Description
In	1	HU	750	62,300	Item A
Out	1	SK	750	63,200	Item A
In	2	HU	550	47,200	Item A
Out	2	HU	550	47,900	Item A
In	6	HU	350	29,500	Item A
Out	6	CZ	350	30,200	Item A
In	12	HU	800	68,930	Item A
Out	12	CZ	800	69,850	Item A

Table 21.5 Scheme 2—"Carousel" goods among everyday trade

Direction	Month	Country	Weight	Value	Description
In	1	DK	3215	152,833	Item A
In	2	DE	2050	97,450	Item A
In	3	DK	2346	108,740	Item A
In	5	DK	1820	87,450	Item A
Out	5	CZ	320	31,890	Item B
In	6	DE	1250	56,470	Item A
Out	7	CZ	650	62,790	Item C
In	8	DE	1920	93,870	Item A

Table 21.6 Scheme 3—same amount and value sold for many goods and many times in a long period

Direction	Month	Country	Weight	Value	Description
Out	1	IE	320	8715	Item A
Out	2	IE	320	8715	Item A
Out	3	IE	320	8715	Item A
Out	4	IE	320	8715	Item A
Out	1	IE	215	10,525	Item B
Out	2	IE	215	10,525	Item B
Out	3	IE	215	10,525	Item B
Out	4	IE	215	10,525	Item B

Another pattern is presented in Table 21.6. This scheme (**scheme 3**) looks like a decent long-term contract with fixed prices and amounts of goods sold. But it looks unlikely to have same orders and prices for many goods and for a long time especially when exchange rates are considered. Thus, we would recommend looking into such a case, although the nature of the scheme is not yet recognized.

In Table 21.7, we can see a scheme (**scheme 4**) that may be just a result of inadvertency, omission, or mistake. However, there exist businesses that will likely declare selling the same good classified under different (even 10 or more) CN codes for a purpose and that would be avoiding too much interest from revenue authorities (if trade in good A were interesting for them).

21.6 Conclusions

In the first part of the study, we examined differences between aggregated ICS and ICA and found irregularities between them on the level of chapters and positions. The structures of such differences have been compared for years 2010–2016. The

Table 21.7 Scheme 4—one good classified under different CN codes

Direction	Month	Country	Weight	Value	Description
Out	1	CZ	325	6530	Item A (CN xxxxxxxx)
Out	2	CZ	180	4050	Item A (CN yyyyyyyy)
Out	3	SK	220	4830	Item A (CN zzzzzzzz)
Out	4	CZ	200	4250	Item A (CN vvvvvvvv)
Out	4	SK	300	6390	Item A (CN xxxxxxxx)
Out	5	IE	165	3960	Item A (CN yyyyyyyy)
Out	6	DE	340	8330	Item A (CN uuuuuuuu)
Out	6	CZ	250	5350	Item A (CN xxxxxxxx)

structure was generally stable year to year and evolved with time. That suggests the nature of the differences is not random but rather systematic. One possible explanation is that at least part of the data inconsistency can be caused by a deliberate action. We also propose revision of the algorithm used for estimation of missing data by statistical services in order to balance data that are systematically biased.

In the second part of the study, we discussed specific schemes in declared data that may indicate participation in tax fraud like selling and buying the same amounts of goods in a chain of transactions with similar characteristics or adding extra transactions on "carousel" goods to a business's everyday portfolio. We explain the outcomes based on behavioral assumptions: When there is a quick reward and virtually no chance of being caught red-handed, then the fraud is much more likely.

References

Ainsworth RT (2006) Carousel fraud in the EU: a digital VAT solution. Tax Notes International, Boston University School of Law Working Paper 06–23, pp 443–448

Becker GS (1968) Crime and punishment: an economic approach. J Polit Econ 76:169–217

Camerer CF (2006) Behavioral economics. In: Blundell R, Newey WK, Person T (eds) Advances in economics and econometrics: theory and application, ninth world congress (econometric society monographs), vol II. Cambridge University Press, Cambridge

Camerer CF (2007) Neuroeconomics: using neuroscience to make economic prediction. Econ J 117(519)

Camerer CF, Loewenstein G, Rabin M (eds) (2001) Advances in behavioral economics. Princeton University Press, Princeton New York

Chomątowski S, Sokołowski A (1978) Taksonomia struktur. Przegląd Statystyczny 2:217–226

Doszyń M (2017) Measuring Economic Propensities. In: Nermend K, Łatuszyńska M (eds) Neuroeconomic and behavioral aspects of decision making. In: Proceedings of the 2016 computational methods in experimental economics (CMEE) conference. Springer, Cham, pp 77–90

European Court of Auditors (2016) Tackling intra-community VAT fraud: more action needed. Special report 24. Publications Office of the European Union, Luxembourg

European Union Committee, House of Lords London (2007) Stopping the carousel: missing trader fraud in the EU. 20th report of session 2006–07. The Stationery Office Limited
Frantz R (2013) Frederick Hayek's behavioral economics in historical context. In: Frantz R, Leeson R (eds) Behavioral economics and Hayek. Palgrave Macmillan, New York
Iwin-Garzyńska J (2017) Granice optymalizacji podatkowej w finansach przedsiębiorstwa. In: Wieteska S, Burzyńska D (eds) Granice finansów XXI wieku. Finanse publiczne, rynek finansowy, finanse przedsiębiorstw. Wydawnictwo Uniwersytetu Łódzkiego, Łódź, pp 223–233
Jakobsson O (2013) Missing trader fraud in the EU. Faculty of Law, Lund University
Kahneman D, Tversky A (1979) Prospect theory: an analysis of decisions under risk. Econometrica 47:313–327
Keen M, Smith S (2006) VAT fraud and evasion: what do we know and what can be done? Nat Tax J LIX(4):861–887
Miłaszewicz D (2017) Neuroeconomics: genesis and essence. In: Nermend K, Łatuszyńska M (eds) Neuroeconomic and behavioral aspects of decision making. In: Proceedings of the 2016 computational methods in experimental economics (CMEE) conference. Springer, Cham, pp 63–75
Podlipnik J (2012) Missing trader intra-community and carousel VAT frauds—ECJ and ECtHR case law. Croat Yearb Eur Law Policy 8:457–472. www.cyelp.com/index.php/cyelp/article/view/135 (10.01.2017)
Simon HA (1972) Theories of bounded rationality. In: McGuire CB, Radner R (eds) Decision and organization. North Holland, pp 161–173
Smith S (2007). VAT fraud and evasion. Chapter 9. In: Chote R, Emmerson C, Leicester A, Miles D (eds) The IFS green budget 2007, pp 167–177
Solek A (2010) Ekonomia behawioralna a ekonomia neoklasyczna. Zeszyty Naukowe PTE 8: 21–34
Szlęzak-Matusewicz J (2015) Odwrotne obciążenie VAT jako mechanizm przeciwdziałający oszustwom podatkowym. Zeszyty Naukowe Uniwersytetu Szczecińskiego 864, Finanse, Rynki Finansowe, Ubezpieczenia 76(1):265–276
Thaler R (1980) Toward a positive theory of consumer choice. J Econ Behav Organ 1:39–60
Wilkinson N (2008) An introduction to behavioral economics. Palgrave Macmillan, New York
Zalega T (2015) Ekonomia behawioralna jako nowy nurt ekonomii—zarys problematyki. Studia i Materiały 1(18):7–22

Chapter 22
Cognitive Reflection Test in Predicting Rational Behavior in the Dictator Game

Monika Czerwonka, Aleksandra Staniszewska and Krzysztof Kompa

Abstract Altruism and behavioral impact on economic decisions became the center of the interest for experimental and behavioral economy. The literature widely reports the results of variety types of dictator games (DG) and cognitive reflection tests (CRT). There is a broad research on donated sum, anonymity of the receiver and dictators' position (giving vs. taking) in dictator games. Separately research on the CRT evolves from 3 questions to 7 questions variant. However, there is an evident gap in the literature for data that combines these two tools (DG and CRT) in one setup. In this study, we extend existing research on the relationship between cognitive performance on the CRT and dictator decisions taking into account such factors as donated sum, anonymity of the receiver and dictators' position (giving vs. taking). The main goal is to find out if the cognitive reflection test (CRT) helps to predict rational (or selfish) behavior in a DG. In our investigation, we asked 511 participants to respond to 6 types of dictator games and CRT test. For statistical analysis of the received results, we applied correlation, descriptive statistics, the t-student test and the Mann–Whitney test. Our results show that cognitive reflection was positively correlated with rational (selfish) behavior in DGs. Those dictators who scored high on the CRT (reflective dictators) kept more money for themselves than those who achieved lower scores on the CRT (altruistic, impulsive dictators). Our results confirm an inequity aversion attitude among altruistic, impulsive dictators and selfish, reflective dictators.

M. Czerwonka (✉) · A. Staniszewska
Warsaw School of Economics, 162, Aleja Niepodległości,
02-554 Warszawa, Poland
e-mail: monika.czerwonka@sgh.waw.pl

A. Staniszewska
e-mail: apalim@sgh.waw.pl

K. Kompa
Warsaw University of Life Sciences, 12, Skwarczynskiej Street,
91-175 Warszawa, Poland
e-mail: krzysztof_kompa@sggw.pl

K. Nermend and M. Łatuszyńska (eds.), *Problems, Methods and Tools in Experimental and Behavioral Economics*, Springer Proceedings in Business and Economics, https://doi.org/10.1007/978-3-319-99187-0_22

Keywords Cognitive reflection test · Dictator game · Rationality
Economic decision-making

JEL Classification C7 · C91 · D30 · D63

22.1 Introduction

Dual process theories assume that thought can arise as a result of two different processes. The first process (System 1) is automatic, fast and unconscious while the second one (System 2) is relatively slow, controlled and computationally expensive. The cognitive reflection test (CRT) is designed to measure the tendency to overcome intuitive but incorrect responses arising from System 1 (impulsive players) and more effortful correct responses coming from the System 2 (reflective players). Studies have shown that performance on the CRT is a good predictor of cognitive and rational thinking.

One of the simplest and most commonly used experimental games to examine an economic behavior is the dictator game (DG). In the DG, a proposer is given a sum of money to divide between him or herself and the responder. The responder has no option and must accept the offer (in contrast to ultimatum game, where he or she has the option to accept or reject the allocation).

The main goal of this study is to test the hypothesis that the cognitive reflection test (CRT) helps to predict rational (selfish) behavior in a DG. The authors aim to shed light on the relationship between rational behavior in the DG and cognitive abilities, which are measured using the CRT. Sharing in the DG is connected with emotional behavior. Therefore, more altruistic dictators (impulsive) should base their choices on intuitive and emotional thinking and share more willingly with other players. Reflective dictators (selfish), on the other hand, should behave more rationally and keep more money for themselves. The key question is whether subjects characterized by different degrees of cognitive reflection (impulsive vs. reflective players) exhibit different distributional concerns, depending on the nature of the dictatorial situation.

Our paper is organized as follows. The next section presents background information and literature review. The research data and methodology are performed in Sect. 22.3. The results and experimental evaluation are presented in Sect. 22.4. The paper is concluded and discussed in the last section.

22.2 Background

The first DG experiment in economics was introduced by Kahneman et al. (1986), who gave subjects a choice of dictating either an even split of $20 ($10 each) with another student or an uneven split ($18, $2) that favored themselves. Three-quarters of the students opted for the equal split. According to the rational framework of *homo economicus*, where agents are assumed to act in their own self-interest, proposers should maximize their profits and keep the uneven split. Studies have consistently demonstrated that most proposers share the money (although they offer less than in ultimatum games—around 15% of the stakes). The average DG allocations are above zero, typically around 20–30% of the initial gift (Engel 2011).

Thousands of participants in research laboratories around the world have been put in the role of dictator to explore the motives behind their unselfish behavior. The most popular theories explaining the dictators' behavior are altruism (Andreoni and Miller 2002), model of inequity aversion (Fehr and Schmidt 1999), and the automatic negative reciprocity hypothesis (Halali et al. 2014).

Clearly, the simplest game to elicit altruistic preferences is the DG. Andreoni and Miller (2002) conducted a series of DG experiments in which one agent could allocate "tokens" between him or herself and another agent for a series of different budgets. They found only a quarter of subjects were selfish money-maximizers, and the rest showed varying degrees of altruism. Andreoni and Miller (2002) state that participants exhibit a significant degree of rationally altruistic behavior because 98% of them made choices consistent with utility maximization. They conclude that altruism is rational, but there are many subtle influences other than the final allocation of money that are likely to influence a moral behavior such as altruism.

The model of inequity aversion leads to the hypothesis that individuals dislike outcomes that are perceived as inequitable. They experience inequity if they are worse off (in material terms) than the other players in the experiment, but they also feel inequity if they are better off (Fehr and Schmidt 1999). Therefore, dictators feel envy (i.e. aversion to inequality experienced from a disadvantaged position) or guilt (i.e. aversion to inequality experienced from an advantaged position). However, Fehr and Schmidt (1999) assume that in general, subjects suffer more from inequity related to a material disadvantage than from inequity related to a material advantage.

In general, participants make their decisions based on their tendency to favor either rational or emotional approaches. Depending on how strong one of these tendencies is, participants make different decisions. The automatic negative reciprocity hypothesis assumes that participants who behave more altruistically (in DGs) and refuse unfair offers (in ultimatum games) predominantly base their choices on intuitive and emotional thinking. Rational behavior leads participants to decisions that maximize their profits at the end of the game (Halali et al. 2014).

The reflective and impulsive approach was also investigated by Tversky and Kahneman (1974) in the domain of behavioral economy. They state that due to bounded rationality, we are unable to make decisions rationally. They state that the way we process cognitive information is conducted by System 1 or System 2. System 1 operates quickly, automatically, and intuitively without requiring a lot of time or effort while System 2 requires us to engage in effortful, demanding, and reflective mental activities, and it is slower, more deliberate and analytic (see Evans 2008). The cognitive reflection test (CRT) is designed to measure the tendency to override a predominant response alternative that is incorrect and engage in further reflection that leads to a correct response (Toplak et al. 2011). Studies have shown that the CRT predicts susceptibility to decision-making biases and heuristics (Duttle and Inukai 2015; Oechssler et al. 2009; Toplak et al. 2011, 2014), and that it is not just a mathematical test but measures something above and beyond general skills, namely cognitive reflection (Campitelli and Gerrans 2014). The CRT 3, proposed by Frederick (2005), is a 3-item task that measures the extent to which individuals form their judgments intuitively (System 1), as opposed to through reflection (System 2). The CRT 7 is an expanded 7-item task introduced by Toplak et al. (2014) that have proven to be a more potent predictor of rational thinking than the original CRT 3.

Some studies have explored the relationship between cognitive performance and dictator decisions. Chen et al. (2013) point out that subjects who perform better in math tests are more generous in the DG while subjects with higher grade point averages tend to be more selfish in dictator decisions. Ben-Ner et al. (2004) find a negative relationship between being generous in the DG and performance on cognitive tests. However, Brandstätter and Güth (2002) argue that bargaining behavior in the context of DGs or ultimatum games is less of an intellectual than a motivational and emotional problem.

To our knowledge, just a few studies have combined cognitive reflection (CTR) with experimental games (Ponti and Rodriguez-Lara 2015; Calvillo and Burgeno 2015). Ponti and Rodriguez-Lara (2015) conducted DGs and CRT 3 tests in a single research setup. The more rational players (ones who got 2 and 3 answers correct in the CRT test) behaved less altruistically compared to intuitive, impulsive players. They found that impulsive dictators showed a marked inequity aversion attitude and gave more money to responders, compared to reflective dictators, who behaved more selfishly and kept more money for themselves. They show that more rational players behave less altruistically compared to intuitive, impulsive players. Calvillo and Burgeno (2015) had similar results but with another experimental game—ultimatum game. They pointed out that reflective agents (ones who scored high on the CRT) behaved more rationally and were more willing to accept unfair offers in the game than intuitive agents (ones who scored low on the CRT).

Prompted by the paucity of evidence in this field, we want to explore the relationship between rational behavior in the DG and cognitive abilities using extended version of experiment. We extend the existing research by combining the cognitive abilities of players, tested with the CRT, with different types of dictators who have not yet been tested with the CRT. Six versions of the DG varied in the amount of money (EUR 2.5 vs. EUR 25), the anonymity of the receiver (anonymous vs. charity organization), and the position of the dictator (giving vs. taking). A recent study of Baron et al. (2015) shows that the expanded version of the CRT gives greater internal consistency than the original 3-item version. Therefore in our study, we used the expanded version of the CRT (CRT 7) with the aim of creating a more reliable measure of cognitive reflection.

To achieve the goal, we follow the design and the experimental evidence of Ponti and Rodriguez-Lara (2015) and Calvillo and Burgeno (2015).

22.3 Research Data and Methodology

22.3.1 Participants

Undergraduate and postgraduate students enrolled in finance courses at the Warsaw School of Economics participated in a survey. 511 surveys were completed in 12 random student groups. After removing the unfinished surveys, 379 surveys were analyzed (N = 379). All data were calculated using Statistica 12 (StatSoft, Poland). In all statistical tests, the significance level is $\alpha = 0.05$. The sample contained 185 (49%) women and 193 (51%) men. The age of the participants ranged from 21 to 24 years old (M = 21.74, SD = 2.33).[1] As all of the students were Polish, there were no issues with racial/ethnic background or social class in the survey.

22.3.2 Materials and Procedure

In the study participants, participated in a set of DGs, completed the CRT 7 (Toplak et al. 2014), and completed (for further research) three demographic questions on gender, religion, and age. Participants completed 6 variants of the game (A, B, C, D, E, and F), which varied by the amount of money available for sharing (Table 22.1). Dictators A and B played with PLN 10 (approximately EUR 2.5). Dictators C and D played with PLN 100 (approximately EUR 25). The games also varied in terms of the anonymity of the receiver. Dictators A and C shared their stakes with random, anonymous players from the next student group. Dictators B and D were told that they would share the stake with a well-known Polish charity organization, Polska Akcja Humanitarna.[2] The last two dictators were reversed, which means that the players had the right to claim any share from the stake of PLN 10 (Dictator E) and PLN 100 (Dictator F) from another random player. To ensure that participants took the decision seriously, they were informed that a subset of participants chosen randomly would be paid according to the decisions they had made.

After completing the dictator decisions, participants provided answers to the CRT. According to their CRT scores, the participants were categorized into reflective and impulsive dictators. Reflective players where the ones who answered 4–7 questions correctly in the CRT 7. Impulsive players were those who answered fewer than 4 questions correctly in the CRT 7.[3] High scores on CRT tests suggest that a responder uses a more cognitive rather than intuitive method of making

[1]For whole paper, n denotes number of participants; M denotes average; SD denotes standard deviation; and Me denotes median.

[2]Polish Humanitarian Action.

[3]We followed Ponti and Rodriguez-Lara's (2015) methodology, where reflective players are those who answer 2–3 questions correctly on the CRT 3, and impulsive players are those who score fewer than 2 questions correctly.

Table 22.1 Types of dictators used in the study

Game	Amount [PLN]	Interaction object	Possible action
Dictator A	10	Anonymous person	Donate money
Dictator B	10	Well-known charity organization	Donate money
Dictator C	100	Anonymous person	Donate money
Dictator D	100	Well-known charity organization	Donate money
Dictator E	10	Anonymous person	Request money
Dictator F	100	Anonymous person	Request money

Source Own assumptions

decisions. Using the Kahneman (2011) approach, system 1 induces a low score on the CRT while system 2 encourages a more effortful high score on the CRT.

All tasks were completed on paper. Most participants took about 15 min to complete the study.

22.3.3 *Hypothesis*

Altruism is connected with emotional behavior. The automatic negative reciprocity hypothesis leads to the prediction that more altruistic dictators (impulsive) base their choices on intuitive and emotional thinking and share more willingly with other players. Reflective dictators behave more rationally and keep more money for themselves. Therefore, the key question we want to investigate is whether subjects characterized by different degrees of cognitive reflection (impulsive vs. reflective players) exhibit different distributional concerns, depending on the nature of the dictatorial situation. The main research hypothesis we want to test can be framed as follows:

H_0: *In all situations, the behavior of reflective and impulsive dictators is the same.*

Apart from the main hypothesis, we formed also three additional hypotheses:

H_1: The altruistic behavior of reflective and impulsive dictators is not related to the knowledge of the receiver.
H_2: The altruistic behavior of reflective and impulsive dictators is not related to the amount of the donation.
H_3: The altruistic behavior of reflective and impulsive dictators is not related to their giving versus taking position.

22.4 Results

We begin by summarizing our data on CRT 7 performance. Table 22.2 reports our dictators' CRT 7 score frequencies and partitions our dataset by relying on our definition of reflective (dictator answered four and more questions correctly) and

Table 22.2 CRT 7 score frequencies and dictator types

CRT 7	Score								Dictator type	
Responses	0	1	2	3	4	5	6	7	Impulsive	Reflective
n	14	31	38	39	50	73	85	49	122	257
[%]	3.7	8.2	10.0	10.3	13.2	19.3	22.4	12.9	32.2	67.8

Source Own calculations

impulsive (dictator answered less than four questions correctly) dictators. We observe that 122 of our 379 dictators (32.2%) are impulsive, whereas 257 dictators (67.8%) are reflective.

22.4.1 CRT and Dictators

Table 22.3 reports the correlation coefficients for the relationship between the dictators' behavior in each type of game and their cognitive abilities (their score on the CRT 7 test). The results in Table 22.3 indicate that for the regular games (A, B, C, and D), correlation with the CRT 7 was positive. Correlation reached statistical significance with dictators A (0.23), C (0.20), and D (0.16). In the reverse games, the correlation was negative and became statistically significant for dictator F (−0.11). The direction of correlation for all types of giving DGs indicates that dictators who achieve low scores on the CRT test (impulsive types) ended games with lower scores (a smaller portion of the initial sum) than dictators who achieved high scores on the CRT test (reflective types), which is in line with the automatic negative reciprocity hypothesis (Halali et al. 2014). Impulsive players make more

Table 22.3 Descriptive statistics for DGs and Pearson correlation between CRT 7 score frequencies and DGs scores

Game	M	SD	Dictator A	Dictator B	Dictator C	Dictator D	Reversed dictator E	Reversed dictator F
Dictator A	0.76	0.30	x					
Dictator B	0.40	0.38	0.33*	x				
Dictator C	0.84	0.24	0.64*	0.23*	x			
Dictator D	0.54	0.35	0.33*	0.74*	0.34*	x		
Reversed dictator E	0.36	0.39	0.01	−0.12*	0.02	−0.11*	x	
Reversed dictator F	0.36	0.39	0.04	−0.08	0.05	−0.03	0.83*	x
CRT 7			0.23*	0.08	0.20*	0.16*	−0.05	−0.11*

Source Own calculations
Note *Means significance at the 5%

Table 22.4 Average scores of impulsive and reflective dictators in each variant of the game

	Impulsive		Reflective		Mann–Whitney *U* test		
	n = 122		n = 257				
	M	SD	M	SD	Z	*p* value	r
Dictator A	0.69	0.33	0.80	0.28	3.56	< 0.001	0.18
Dictator B	0.39	0.35	0.41	0.39	0.31	0.758	0.02
Dictator C	0.79	0.27	0.87	0.23	3.68	< 0.001	0.19
Dictator D	0.49	0.34	0.56	0.35	1.95	0.051	0.10
Dictator E	0.40	0.39	0.34	0.39	1.69	0.092	0.09
Dictator F	0.44	0.40	0.32	0.38	2.95	0.003	0.15

Source Own calculations

altruistic decisions than reflective ones. As a result, they finish the DG with a lower score (a smaller share of the initial sum).

Surprising findings arise from the correlation results for reversed DGs. In these cases, reflective dictators claim less than impulsive ones, which means that they finish the game with lower amounts of money. Nevertheless, the correlation is very weak, which may suggest that some impulsive players did not fully understand the task in the reversed DGs and behaved the same as in regular games.

The Mann–Whitney nonparametric statistics are also used to test our main research (null) hypothesis that there is no difference in behavior between reflective and impulsive dictators. Again, the results in Table 22.4 indicate that a higher score on the CRT (reflective dictators) will result in less generous behavior in dictator situations. This, in turn, implies that reflective subjects end the game with more money than impulsive subjects in dictator situations (A [0.80 vs. 0.69, MW-test 3.56, $p < 0.001$], C [0.87 vs. 0.79, MW-test: 3.68, $p < 0.001$], and D [0.56 vs. 0.49, MW-test: 1.95, $p = 0.05$]).

A different pattern emerged in situations of reversed dictators. In these cases, impulsive subjects tended to be more selfish and ended the game with higher scores (F: 0.44 vs. 0.32, MW-test: 2.95, $p = 0.003$), which is inconsistent with our assumptions. Such scores might result from a situation in which highly impulsive players did not understand last two games. After playing 4 regular dictators, they answered as reversed dictators (situations E and F) according to the regular rules of giving (not taking).

22.4.2 *Anonymity of the Dictator*

The influence of the anonymity factor (Table 22.5) was noticed in DG types where participants were informed about the particular purpose of the donation. When participants did not know the receiver (games A and C), they ended games with 76% and 84% of the initial sum, respectively. In the situation where they knew that

Table 22.5 Scores of dictators grouped by anonymity of the receiver and position of the dictator (giving vs. taking position)

	EUR 2.5 for distribution		EUR 25 for distribution		t-student test (n = 378)		
	M	SD	M	SD	t	*p* value	r
Anonymous receiver (games A and C)	0.76	0.02	0.84	0.01	6.51	<0.001	0.32
Well-known receiver (charity organization – games B and D)	0.40	0.02	0.54	0.02	10.30	<0.001	0.47
Dictator game (giving position – games A and C)	0.76	0.02	0.84	0.01	6.51	<0.001	0.32
Reversed dictator game (taking position – games E and F)	0.36	0.02	0.36	0.02	0.04	0.969	0.00

Source Own elaboration

their philanthropic decision would support a well-known charity organization (games B and D) and they ended games with an average of 40% and 54% of the initial sum, respectively. As indicated, dictators shared different amounts of the initial sum in the cases of EUR 2.5 and EUR 25. The share was smaller in the case of EUR 25. However, the nominal amount of the donation was greater.

22.4.3 Position of the Dictator

In our study, in games A and C), dictators shared the initial sum while in the last two games E and F, dictators claimed a share of the initial sum from a random player (in case of anonymous dictators). From a rational point of view, dictators should always end with the same amount of money they started with, regardless of whether they share or claim. In fact, their decisions and final scores were different depending on their position. As shown in Table 22.5, the average score in regular dictator games amounted to 76% and 84% of the initial sum (EUR 2.5 and EUR 25, respectively). At the same time, the same dictators in reversed games scored only 36%. This means that changing the position of dictators influences their rationality. They seem to feel uncomfortable or unauthorized to claim money in reverse games.

According to prior studies, the decisions of the dictators are influenced by position of the players, regardless of whether they are giving or taking. In fact, all games may give the same outcome for the player; however, require opposite decision (giving or taking). From an economic point of view, both decisions should have the same outcome because the dictator is the one who decides about the distribution of the money. However, a negative action (taking) creates a distinct emotion during the decision. It is notable that a "taking" decision initiates a less altruistic choice than a "giving" decision. Our dictators found it much easier to share than to claim from the initial sum. Levitt and List (2007) point out that "social norms" are among the factors that influence the decisions of the dictators. This is why the result of the game may change depending on the environment of the game (who is playing and where). Social norms might be predominant to such an extent that decisions change from rational into emotional. As indicated in Table 22.5, participants (impulsive and reflective together) ended reversed games (E and F) with much lower sums than regular games (A, B, C, and D). Such behavior might be explained in two ways. First, there is player confusion. The rules of the reversed games could be not fully understood, especially by impulsive dictators. Second, and what we believe is more realistic, all dictators were overwhelmed by social norms. These norms give a lower status to people who take that to people who donate. This is why, even in such experimental conditions, dictators were still influenced by social norms and made variant choices depending on their position in the game.

22.5 Discussion and Conclusion

This paper and the experimental evidence reported herein offers detailed knowledge about how cognitive and intuitive thinking influence the subjects' decision-making process. The main finding repeated the results reported in (Calvillo and Burgeno 2015) and (Ponti and Rodriguez-Lara 2015). Impulsive players (the ones who scored low on the CRT) have a proclivity toward more altruistic decisions in experimental situations such as the DG. Reflective subjects (ones who scored high in CRT) tend to finish games with higher profits than impulsive agents. Such findings reject the hypothesis that in all situations, the behavior of reflective and impulsive dictators is the same. The miscellaneous types of DGs used in this study brought to light other factors that influence decisions. When participants did not know the receiver, they kept more money for themselves when compared to the situation where they knew that their philanthropic decision would support a well-known charity organization. The position of the dictator appeared in the matter. Our study is contrary to the findings of List (2007) and Bardsley (2007). In reversed games, dictators ended games with much lower scores than in regular games. This suggests that the social norms in this sample mitigate players' claiming more money.

The main limitation of the study was financial constraints. The agents were told that only a subset of participants would have an actual payoff. This means that players might make different decisions about sharing and claiming if they are certain about being paid. Furthermore, hypothetical choices in the laboratory environment may result in decisions unlike those in the real life. However, in this field of research, we are not aware of any study with an experimental game such as the DG or ultimatum game where participants' choices were fully paid. Additionally, revision of the instructions might mitigate the issue of not understanding the rules in reversed games.

This paper expands the field of research at the edge of behavioral and experimental economies. Such issues from "the edge" require nonstandard and innovative methods. Although the results of this paper are still theoretical, this kind of approach may help charity sector to position donators better in the future.

Further development of the study should evolve toward a more diversified sample. This study is based on students with a homogenous age group (20–24 years old) and study major (finance). A more strongly diversified sample in terms of age will present changes in decision-making over players' lifetimes. In most situations, young people have low incomes and limited assets. During their lifetimes, their level of income and assets increases, which will probably result in a transformation of altruistic preferences.

References

Andreoni J, Miller J (2002) Giving according to GARP: an experimental test of the consistency of preferences for altruism. Econometrica 70(2):737–753

Bardsley N (2007) Dictator game giving: altruism or artefact? Exp Econ 11(2):122–133

Baron J, Scott S, Fincher K et al (2015) Why does the cognitive reflection test (sometimes) predict utilitarian moral judgment (and other things)? J Appl Res Mem Cogn 4(3):265–284

Ben-Ner A, Kong F, Putterman L (2004) Share and share alike? Gender-pairing, personality, and cognitive ability as determinants of giving. J Econ Psychol 25(5):581–589

Brandstätter H, Güth W (2002) Personality in dictator and ultimatum games. Cent Eur J Oper Res 10(3):191–215

Calvillo D, Burgeno JN (2015) Cognitive reflection predicts the acceptance of unfair ultimatum game offers. Judgm Decis Mak 10(4):332–341

Campitelli G, Gerrans P (2014) Does the cognitive reflection test measure cognitive reflection? A mathematical modelling approach. Mem Cogn 42(3):434–447. https://doi.org/10.3758/s13421-013-0367-9

Chen C, Chiu I, Smith J et al (2013) Too smart to be selfish? Measures of cognitive ability, social preferences, and consistency. J Econ Behav Organ 90:112–122. https://doi.org/10.1016/j.jebo.2013.03.032

Duttle K, Inukai K (2015) Complexity aversion: influences of cognitive abilities, culture and system of thought. Econ Bull Access Econ 35(2):846–855

Engel C (2011) Dictator games: a meta-study. Exp Econ 14(4):583–610

Evans J (2008) Dual processing accounts of reasoning, judgment, and social cognition. Annu Rev Psychol 59:255–278. https://doi.org/10.1146/annurev.psych.59.103006.093629

Fehr E, Schmidt K (1999) A theory of fairness, competition and cooperation. Q J Econ 114 (3):817–868

Frederick S (2005) Cognitive reflection and decision making. J Econ Perspect 19(4):25–42

Halali E, Bareby-Meyer Y, Meiran N (2014) Between self-interest and reciprocity: the social bright side of self-control failure. J Exp Psychol Gen 143(2):745–754. https://doi.org/10.1037/a0033824

Kahneman D (2011) Thinking, fast and slow. Farrar, Strauss, Giroux, New York

Kahneman D, Knetsch JL, Thaler R (1986) Fairness and the assumptions of economics. J Bus 59 (4):285–300

Levitt S, List J (2007) What do laboratory experiments measuring social preferences reveal about the real world? J Econ Perspect 21(2):153–174. https://doi.org/10.1257/jep.21.2.153

List J (2007) On the interpretation of giving in dictator games. J Political Econ 115(3):482–493. https://doi.org/10.1086/519249

Oechssler J, Roider A, Schmitz PW (2009) Cognitive abilities and behavioral biases. J Econ Behav Organ 72(1):147–152. https://doi.org/10.1016/j.jebo.2009.04.018

Ponti G, Rodriguez-Lara I (2015) Social preferences and cognitive reflection: evidence from a dictator game experiment. Front Behav Neurosci 9:1–8. https://doi.org/10.3389/fnbeh.2015.00146

Toplak ME, West RF, Stanovich KE (2011) The cognitive reflection test as a predictor of performance on heuristics and biases tasks. Mem Cogn 39(7):1275–1289. https://doi.org/10.3758/s13421-011-0104-1

Toplak ME, West RF, Stanovich KE (2014) Assessing miserly information processing: an expansion of the Cognitive Reflection Test. Think Reason 20(2):147–168. https://doi.org/10.1080/13546783.2013.844729

Tversky A, Kahneman D (1974) Judgment under uncertainty: heuristics and biases. Science 185 (4157):1124–1131

Chapter 23
A Scientific Experiment as a Research Method in the Tourism Sector in the Context of Increased Terrorism Risks

Rafał Nagaj and Brigita Žuromskaitė

Abstract The aim of this chapter is to present a proposal for a research model that will be used to examine the impact of security measures and travel costs on the decision of a tourist when choosing a tourist destination, in the context of increased terrorism risks. The increase in terrorist attacks in the world, migration problems in Europe and the more frequent targeting of tourist destinations has meant that the inhabitants of the European Union becoming more aware of terrorist threats in the tourism sector. For some people this may be the reason for avoiding tourist destinations that are considered dangerous, traveling rather to "generally considered more secure places," while for others it is an opportunity to travel cheaper as prices to these less secure destinations are often discounted. The pilot survey, which was used to determine the declared preferences of tourists in Lithuania and Poland, indicated that they are different. In the context of the emerging new field of science, which is neurotourism, it was decided to use a scientific experiment using cognitive neuroscience methods to assess the preferences of tourists at the subconscious level. In addition, the chapter will indicate the reasons why such methods are recommended for this type of study (supported by the results of pilot surveys).

Keywords Neurotourism · Tourist · Terrorism threat · Economic factors of outbound tourism

---

R. Nagaj (✉)
University of Szczecin, Mickiewicza 64, 71-101 Szczecin, Poland
e-mail: rafal.nagaj@usz.edu.pl

B. Žuromskaitė
Mykolas Romeris University, Ateities 20, LT-08303 Vilnius, Lithuania
e-mail: brigitaz@mruni.eu

K. Nermend and M. Łatuszyńska (eds.), *Problems, Methods and Tools in Experimental and Behavioral Economics*, Springer Proceedings in Business and Economics, https://doi.org/10.1007/978-3-319-99187-0_23

23.1 Introduction

High-level and improving security is one of the necessary conditions for travel and tourism development. Because, "surety in tourism, and security, reputation and respectability together" (Tan et al. 2017, p. 472). The increasing number of natural disasters, terrorist attacks, local wars, and epidemics has revealed the vulnerability of the tourism sector to security issues. After the events of September 11, 2001, the issue of security began to be more often emphasized by societies, politicians, and scientists, and the literature began to conduct research on safety in tourism (Kôvári and Zimányi 2011). Particular attention and sensitivity of society, to terrorism began to become more important depending on the country. However, as Tarlow (2011, p. 19) remarked, the phenomenon of the impact of terrorism on tourism is quite difficult to study. Horner and Swarbrooke (2009, p. 359) indicate that there may be four situations when terrorism and tourism come together/clash. First, when the terrorist attack is directed to a tourist destination or a tourist facility, secondly, when tourists are the main target (e.g., attacks at airports and airplanes), thirdly, when tourists are accidental victims (in dangerous tourist regions that are rarely visited by tourists), and fourthly, when the media creates an "atmosphere of fear" that discourages tourists from traveling to a particular region.

Panic, which appears after terrorist attacks, has a direct impact on a tourist economy (Pareek 2016), especially such "in the periods of affliction" (Albu 2016, p. 16). The increasing sensitivity of tourists to security issues will force tourist enterprises to pay more attention to this problem (Tarlow 2006). It is worth noting that the more dangerous a tourist destination/region becomes due to the threat of (e.g. terrorist attacks) it is likely that more financial losses will be borne by tourism enterprises (Matthem 2014). This phenomenon is also reinforced by the fact that tourists want to be more often informed about security measures that are used in tourist infrastructure (Tarlow 2006, 2008, 2011, 2014).

There is considerable regional variation in the world in terms of the level of terrorist threat (red24's Global Terrorism Risk Map 2017). There are regions with a high level of risk and those where the risk is very low. However, it is worth noting that despite the fact that Europe has a lower level of terrorist threat than in Africa or the Middle East, it is still higher than a dozen or so years ago. In addition, in the context of the terrorist issue and tourists' sensitivity to the level of security, attention should also be paid to the problem of tourists traveling around Europe, usually staying in less secure places, with fewer security measures than, e.g., Egypt or Turkey (Teoman 2017).

The decline in the sense of security in the world forces the tourism sector to reduce prices, improve the quality of services, or use other economic incentives, which some tourists may use to travel cheaper. It may turn out that in some countries, economic factors may start to play a growing role in such a situation. The increase in terrorist threats in the world means that tourism preferences and tourists' decisions regarding destinations can change. Hence, there is a need to adapt to the changing realities and apply new research techniques so as to assess outbound tourists' preferences.

The aim of the work is to present a proposal for a research model that will be used during a scientific experiment to examine the impact of security measures and economic factors on the decision of a tourist when choosing a tourist destination, in the context of increased terrorist risk. In the first stage of the research, the authors carried out pilot studies among students in Poland and Lithuania regarding the role of security measures and tourist preferences to use them in tourist destinations. In these studies, the role of security measures and travel price in the selection of tourist destinations in the context of terrorist threats in the world was also assessed. These studies indicated the susceptibility of subjects (respondents) to emotions and the suspicion that the declared choices may differ from those subconsciously made by the respondents. Hence, in the context of the development of a new field of science, which is neurotourism, apart from pilot surveys carried out by the authors, it was decided to further explore tourists' thoughts/decisions using an electrocardiograph to study galvanic skin reflexes. This type of methodology will be used in this experiment and will be presented in this chapter.

23.2 Outbound Tourism—Determinants of Development and Outbound Tourists' Preferences

In the era of globalization, the development of transport techniques and decreasing travel costs, the tourism sector is one of those areas whose share in generating the GDP of many economies in the world is significant and will probably grow in the future.

Tourism development forecasts are very optimistic (Alejziak 2012), and every year the number of tourists and tourism revenues in the world increase (Fig. 23.1). As indicated by the United Nations World Tourism Organization (later—UNWTO), the number of international tourists amounted to over 1.2 billion in 2016 (UNWTO 2017, p. 13). What's more, in general, since the 1950s, the growing trend in the number of international tourist arrivals has been observed (Fig. 23.2).

It is also worth remembering that tourism not only has optimistic prospects in the context of development and thus an impact on the creation of a global product, but also has a positive impact on eliminating the adverse effects of economic crises, quickly undergoing "cyclical normalization." The recent global financial and economic crisis indicated that the recession affected this sector to a small extent. Data on global international tourism revenue (Fig. 23.1) indicates that only in 2009 a decrease of 9.4% was recorded. What's more after the so-called debt crisis and during the migration crisis, there was only a 4.5% drop in revenues in 2015.

Similar conclusions are provided by data on the contribution of travel and tourism to the global economy (Fig. 23.3). This data confirms that the deterioration of the economic situation in tourism (2009 and 2015) due to economic crises was

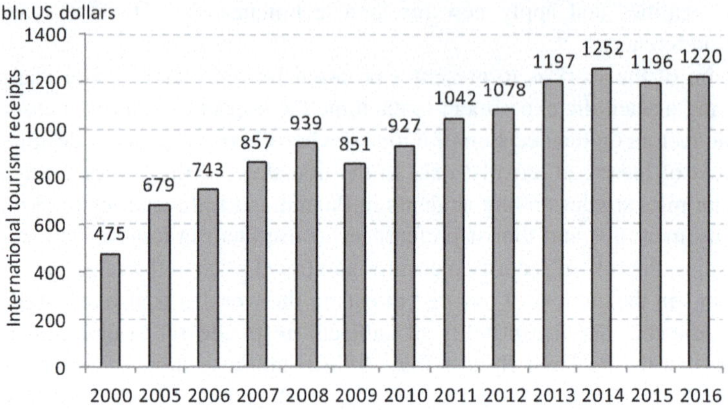

Fig. 23.1 Global international tourism revenue from 2000 to 2016. *Source* Based on Statista (2018b)

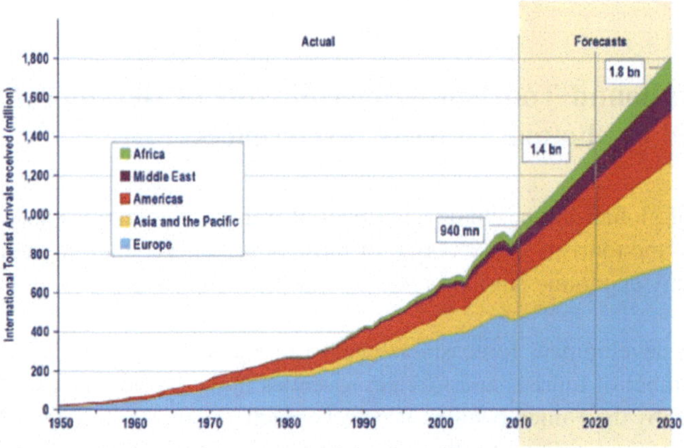

Fig. 23.2 Number of international tourist arrivals received in the world since 1950 and forecasts until 2030. *Source* Based on UNWTO (2017, p. 14)

only short-term, and the long-term contribution of this sector to the global economy is growing.

The impact of the tourist sector on the global economy is much broader and is not limited only to international visitors' expenditure, supporting the export sector and creating GDP, but also includes job creation (in 2016, it was about 10% of all jobs in the world), supporting investments. In 2017, the total contribution of travel and tourism was 3.6% (World Travel & Tourism Council 2017, pp. 2–3).

The tourism industry exerts not only a purely economic contribution, but also enables the satisfaction of human needs and lifestyle changes. World research shows that even tourist preferences change over time as well as the style of

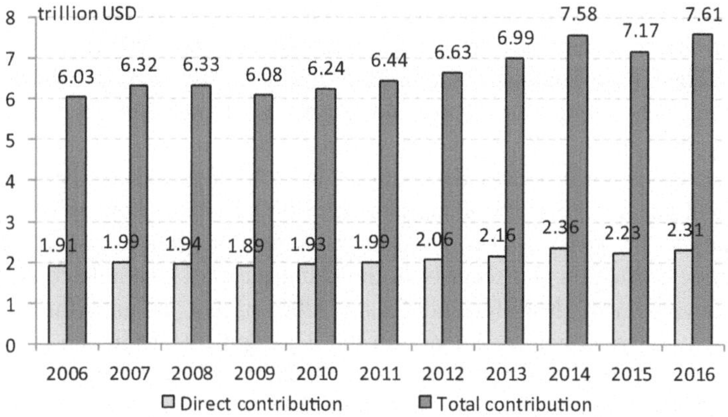

Fig. 23.3 Direct and total contribution of travel and tourism to the global economy from 2006 to 2016. *Source* Based on WTTC, in: Statista (2018a). https://www.statista.com/statistics/233223/travel-and-tourism–total-economic-contribution-worldwide/ (07.01.2018)

traveling. More and more tourists are choosing individual journeys that provide a higher quality of cognitive experiences (MacCannell 2005; Holloway and Taylor 2006). As pointed out by Niezgoda (2012, p. 22), "*Motivations should be treated as a dynamic process in the behavior of the buyer, which fills the gap between perceived needs and the decision to take action or make a purchase.*" Boniface and Cooper (2005) emphasize that today people travel to discover new and rarely visited tourist places, experience unforgettable adventures, learn about new traditions and cultures, observe and explore nature, look for new places of entertainment (visit clubs, festivals, and other entertainment places) or spend time in active pursuits/hobbies. Of course, the price and quality of services and tourist products (Tosun et al. 2016) have a considerable impact on its preferences.

Changing tourist preferences shape the needs and lifestyle of people. For this reason, it seems important to study the determinants of tourism demand and tourist preferences. Literature distinguishes many such factors. Middleton, focusing on tourist demand in the twentieth century, distinguished determinants: economic, demographic, geographic, legal and political, media influence and psychosocial factors (cit. Niezgoda 2012). Alejziak (2012), stressing the megatrends in society in the twenty-first century, considers the most important factors: demographic, political, social, cultural, economic, technological, and ecological.

Considering the purpose of the research, the authors' attention will be focused on two of them: economic and political. Economic factors include the globalization of economic activity, increasing differences between rich countries, economic conditions, especially financial and economic crises that are more and more frequent, uniformity of the currency (e.g., creation of the euro area), the cost of accommodation or, more broadly, cost of travel, income level, and standard of living.

Economic factors are often considered the most important and having the greatest impact on the development of modern tourism (Kaczmarska 2014).

The second most important factor is political factors that take into account political changes, emigration, wars, and terrorism. Taking into account the contemporary challenges facing the world, especially Europe, i.e., migration problems, the situation existing in tourist destinations and the threat of terrorist attacks, the authors will call it "the level of tourism security." Tourist safety is an important factor that can be decisive when choosing a destination (Bernaś and Pujer 2014). Good political situation and security in the country create favorable conditions for tourism development (Mansfel and Pizam 2006, p. 16). In turn, threats in this element may have a negative impact on the development of tourism at the local, regional, and international levels (Santana 2005, p. 231). Pennington-Gray and Schroeder (2013) indicate in their research that the majority of tourists give priority to their safety and are willing to give up visits to dangerous tourist regions. This problem in tourist destinations seems particularly timely in the current context of the fact that terrorist attacks are one of the most important problems with which tourists are increasingly faced (Karwacka 2014, pp. 45–46). A dangerous country will not arouse interest among tourists. In addition, terrorist attacks in a certain country may have a negative impact on other neighboring regions. Because a tourist is not always well-informed about specific threats in a given country, it can rather persuade them to travel to countries where such problems are not or are to a much lesser extent. This is due to the fact that tourists are not fully aware of the terrorist risk, because for a long period tourists were not targeted by terrorists (Marczak 2012). Also, many travelers come from countries where there is a low risk of terrorism (red24's Global Terrorism Risk Map 2017). Unfortunately, as the events of recent years indicate, terrorists choose places often visited by tourists (museums, hotels, airports, etc.) (Tarlow 2014) and more popular tourist destinations (e.g., Paris, Barcelona, Istanbul, London).

It seems, therefore, that a high terrorist threat will likely affect recession in the tourism sector. Meanwhile, despite this threat, the number of tourists traveling is high, even to more dangerous tourist regions. Representatives of different countries often treat the dangers with which they may face during their travels in various ways. According to studies, tourists distinguish risks when traveling to be mainly diseases, terrorist attacks, natural disasters and crime (Baker 2014; Pennington-Gray and Schroeder 2013). However, tourists are often willing to downplay some threats and may be more afraid of robbery than terrorist attacks (Teoman 2017).

The question arises why is this so? Maybe, it is not security and economic factors that are the dominant factor for tourists? It should be remembered that the decline in the level of security in some regions of the world has resulted in a reduction in the prices of these tourist destinations, which, together with the fall in travel prices, mainly in the air, has had a positive impact on the cost of tourist trips with lower prices. Such research questions can be provided by research carried out in Bangkok, Lithuania, and others. Rittichainuwat and Chakraborty (2009) surveyed tourists at the airport in Bangkok (mainly tourists from Europe, Australia, and America). They pointed out that 63% of respondents' value their own safety more than the price (only 13% indicated the price as a decisive factor). It was also stated that if a planned terrorist attack were to take place in chosen tourist destination, 38% of respondents would abandon the trip altogether, and 63% would choose a safer choice of destination (Rittichainuwat and Chakraborty 2009, p. 13). These were results from research at a time when the frequency of terrorist attacks in tourist destinations was still relatively low (lower than in the last decade). However, research carried out by International SOS and Ipsos MORI in October 2016 (Fig. 23.4) showed that the attitude of tourists to the terrorist risk have changed (1119 tourists from 75 countries were examined). Eighty percent of respondents said that they changed their travel destinations, and 51% did so due to the terrorist threat (Ipsos MORI & International SOS 2016).

The conclusions from the preliminary studies in Lithuania (Survila et al. 2017) are different. Lithuanians, seeing lower prices, sometimes forget about their own safety when making a decision to travel to high-risk regions. Possibly, the decision of tourists from Lithuania is influenced by the fact that they only have basic knowledge about terrorism and about security measures that are used in tourist infrastructure facilities. Lithuania belongs to countries where the level of terrorist risk is low (red24's Global Terrorism Risk Map 2017), which creates an atmosphere of "artificial peace" in Europe.

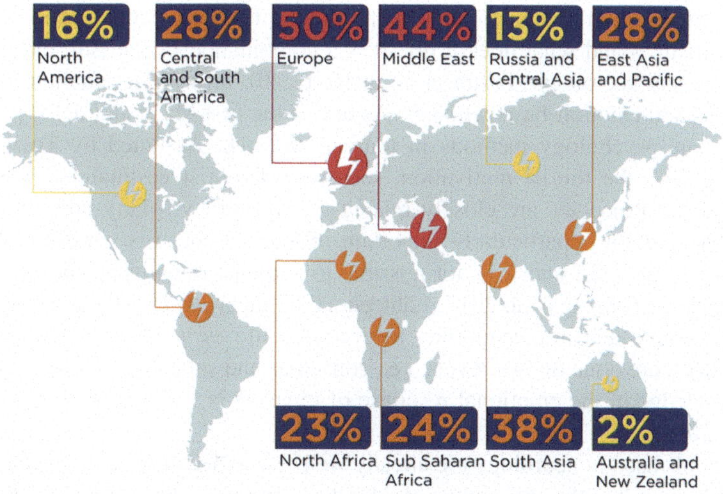

Fig. 23.4 Share of respondents who say that risks have increased for tourists to this region. *Source* Based on Ipsos MORI, International SOS (2016)

23.3 Neurotourism—Cognitive Neurology Research Methods in Tourism

In research on the behavior of tourists, various research methods are used, the main purpose of which is to understand the behavior and motives of consumers. One of these methods is used in neurology. In economic sciences, tools such as electroencephalography (EEG), electromyography (EMG), positron emission tomography (PET), functional magnetic resonance imaging (fMRI) (Šerić et al. 2015) have been able to use this type of research and functional near-infrared spectroscopy (fNIRS) (Giudici et al. 2017) are used.

In research in the field of tourism, two types of research are most often used, namely those relating to body reactions and those showing how the brain responds to received stimuli (Giudici et al. 2017). Literature analysis indicated that the following methods are most often used: facial expressions, eye tracking, electrodermal activity, breathing and heart rate, and response time. In addition, positron emission tomography (PET), functional magnetic resonance imaging (fMRI), electroencephalography (EEG), and magnetoencephalography (MEG) (Giudici et al. 2017) are used. Although these techniques are still a novelty in social sciences, they are considered innovative and useful in the field of tourism market research (Markgraf et al. 2012).

The development of a new field of research—neurotourism—confirms the scientific attractiveness of this topic. It is still a very young field of scientific research on the phenomenon of tourism (Parrinello 2012). This raises the question of what neurotourism is and what does it do? It is a combination of tourism, psychology, medicine, and sociology (Tosun et al. 2016, p. 20), in order to examine the subconscious and emotion-based choices. As one of the first Ma et al. (2014) proposed to use neuropsychology methods in tourism research. As noted by Tosun et al. (2016, p. 20), the tourist motivation, selection of tourist destinations, and other travel-related processes are closely related to psychology. Many authors emphasized that tourism is particularly important in tourism and it is worth considering them in the analysis, and it is not possible to examine them using the main paradigm methods (Prayag et al. 2017; Lähteenmäki-Uutela 2017). All choices made by man, economic and non-economic, in everyday life as well as related to tourist experiences, are done on two levels, i.e., conscious and subconscious. Nevertheless, our knowledge of the emotional response of travelers is still very limited (Lee and Gerard 2012).

The tools used in neurology are already well researched and the brain structure is so well known that the techniques of cognitive neurology have wide potential and possibilities to study social phenomena. There are already interesting results due to research, which includes the area of tourism economics.

Some studies of this type were carried out by Kim and Fesenmaier (2015). They used the individual's electrodermal activity (EDA) method, which was designed to test the emotions of tourists through skin reactions (the emotions of two people visiting Philadelphia in the USA within four days were studied). Another interesting research in this field of science was an experiment conducted by Ma et al. (2014). During it, an electroencephalography (EEG) was used and participants' reactions to the photographs of the Jiuzhaigou National Park in China which were examined. Within the framework of neurotourism and the use of psychology methods, including cognitive neurology, for the study of social phenomena in tourism, an interesting study was also conducted by Tosun et al. (2016). They used electroencephalography (EEG) for research on hospitality management, the aim of which was to determine the most important criteria taken into account by tourists when choosing a hotel.

Neurotourism allows us to explore decisions, emotions, fears, and other experiences while traveling, choosing a destination or a tourist product. It also allows us to study subconscious reactions of people to perceived stimuli and to obtain objective and more reliable results. These research techniques allow what traditional research methods, i.e., surveys, interviews (Ma et al. 2014) do not allow. Sometimes people are not fully aware of the reasons for their decisions and choices. They can be identified, including in the field of tourist experience, by methods of cognitive neurology. In short, using neurological research we can reach the subconscious motives and intentions; that is, we can obtain more reliable research results (Giudici et al. 2017). Moreover, these methods can be used to avoid or significantly reduce the risk of manipulation of results by respondents.

Such research methods can also be successfully used to investigate the real preferences of tourists. Both take into account emotions connected with taking care of one's own safety and making choices based on economic rationality. These research techniques are intended to be used by the authors to determine what role travel costs and security considerations play in choosing a tourist destination, i.e., what we are willing to choose: security or an attractive price offer, in the context of increased terrorism risks in the world.

23.4 Methodology

The aim of this chapter is to present the research model, which will be used during a scientific experiment to examine the influence of security measures and travel costs on the tourist's decision to choose a tourist destination in the context of increased terrorist risk. The proposed methodology is one of the elements of methodology for the research that is planned to be carried out as part of an international research grant, which will cover tourists leaving Lithuania and Poland (Nagaj 2017). The aim of this future research project, proposed by the Polish-Lithuanian team, under the leadership of Nagaj is to assess the tourist tendencies of tourists from Poland and Lithuania and the impact of security measures and economic factors on the choice of tourist destinations in the context of increased terrorist risk.

The methodology in this chapter can be divided into two parts. The first part is the results of pilot surveys, which indicate that people sometimes choose conflicting answers to questions in surveys. This confirms Ma et al. (2014) that in surveys, respondents sometimes manipulate answers or are not aware of their choice. We have seen this discrepancy in our research. This discernible phenomenon requires researchers to search for other, modern methods of research, such as those used in neurotouristics.

The survey tool was used for the first part of the survey. The questionnaire consists of a questionnaire that characterizes the respondent from a socio-demographic point of view, a section describing tourism preferences and a section that examines the impact of security and economic factors on tourist tendencies. This research was conducted by the authors of the study, among 130 students at the Faculty of Economics and Management University of Szczecin in Poland and 130 students of the Faculty of Public Governance at Mykolas Romeris University in Lithuania. The choice of these universities to make the comparison resulted from the fact that both faculties have a similar number of students at the time of the survey (1554 persons and 1545 persons, respectively) and both universities educate people in the field of social sciences. The research was conducted in November 2017 and the researched research samples accounted for 8.4% of the total number of students studying at each of these faculties. The authors of the chapter would like to emphasize that the data and the conclusions from the survey refer only to the surveyed group of students and not the entire population in Poland and Lithuania. The aim of this research was to determine the declared differences in preferences of tourists in Lithuania and Poland, as well as arguments for the purpose of conducting a scientific experiment (including susceptibility to emotions) (Table 23.1).

The circumstantial research sample was similar in both countries. Two third of the respondent groups in Poland and Lithuania consisted of women (slightly larger percentage of women in Lithuania; in Poland 66.2 and 68.5% in Lithuania). The respondent groups were in ages approximately 22–26 years old (the students in Lithuania were on average 4 years older) and mostly single (72.3%). The expenses of the surveyed students per 1 trip were usually between 200 and 1200 €; however, the Lithuanians spent on travel and accommodation on average about 200 € more.

Table 23.1 Description of the research sample

Itemization	Poland	Lithuania
Sample size	130	130
The percentage of the respondents in the total number of students at the given academic year	8.4	8.4
Age (average)	21.6	25.8
Percentage of respondents being single in marital status	72.3	72.3
Involvement of women	66.2	68.5
Involvement of men	33.8	31.5
Average total budget for traveling per person (expenses per 1 trip in euro)	431.9	640.5

The results of the pilot studies have been used in this chapter. Three of these were used. The first question relates to travel expenses. Assessing the significance of this economic factor in the decision-making process of tourists concerning the choice of tourism destination, the authors did not assess the role of disposable income of the respondent. This is due to the fact that the aim of the chapter was not to assess the impact of all factors on the preference decisions of tourists, but only assess what is more important for tourists, i.e., the safety or cost of travel. In addition, it should be noted that the level of GDP per capita in both countries is similar [in 2017, in Lithuania was 12,700 €, and in Poland 11,800 € (Eurostat)]. The purpose of this question was to examine how much the target group spent on their trips. The other two questions used in the work concerned the conscious choice of tourists. The question was to determine which factor is more important in choosing the trip (the respondents answered on a scale from 1 to 5, where 1—completely unnecessary and I do not want them, while 5—they are very important and necessary for me): travel cost (economic factor) or safety level (political factor). The next question was whether tourists are willing to pay more for a safe tourist destination.

In the analysis of the results of the responses, statistical methods of statistical changes in time and *Mann–Whitney U test* were used, which will be used to verify the hypothesis of statistically significant difference between the response structures of the surveyed groups of respondents from Poland and Lithuania. At the *P*-value below 0.05 for both questions used in the questionnaire, it was assumed:

- H0—a null hypothesis: There are no differences in the "distributions" of the responses of students from Poland and Lithuania,
- H1—an alternative hypothesis: There are differences in the "distributions" of the responses of students from Poland and Lithuania.

In the context of the growing new field of science, which is neurotourism and discrepancies in survey results, the preferences of tourists at subconscious level should be examined. Since tourists' preferences regarding their safety are linked to their emotions and subconscious choices, the authors decided that a scientific experiment should be conducted using cognitive neurology methods. To this end, a proposal for the conduct of a scientific experiment will be made. We propose the use of an electroencephalograph (EEG) method for investigating brain waves, which is recommended as an effective tool for assessing human behavior (Ma et al. 2014; Wolf 2015; Tosun et al. 2016) and the method of a galvanic skin response (GSR). EEG and GSR are noninvasive ways of studying the body's reaction to external stimuli (e.g., images in a computer or television) (Fortunato et al. 2014; Grigaliūnaitė and Pilelienė 2015).

23.5 Results

According to the survey results, the level of tourist travel expenses for respondents in both countries differed (Fig. 23.5).

Lithuanians spend more on travel, i.e., the percentage of tourists from Lithuania surveyed spent higher amounts on travel. Moreover, in Poland the majority of respondents (40.8%) spent up to 200 €, the higher the amount of expenditure, the lower the percentage of respondents do so. In Lithuania, meanwhile, the majority of people (30.8%) spend 401–800 € on tourist trips, and about 1/5 of the surveyed spend over 800 €. This may indicate that Lithuanian respondents are less concerned about travel costs and pay more attention to the quality of such a trip. Perhaps it is also affected by the higher number of air connections from Poland than from Lithuania, which may have resulted in slightly lower prices of transport connections in Poland than in Lithuania.

A stochastic analysis confirmed the differences in travel expenses between students from the examined countries. Analysis by *Mann–Whitney U test* indicated that there is a significant statistical difference in the amount of expenses incurred by students from Poland and Lithuania for tourist trips $p = 0.0000001$ ($Z = -5.4430329$).

Figure 23.6 shows how the respondents assess the importance of factors such as travel costs and security levels when deciding on a tourist trip and the direction of the trip.

The results indicate that both analyzed factors play a very important or important role in the decision to travel. However, what is characteristic of the Lithuanians (86.2%) is that they pay more attention to the issue of price, travel expenses than

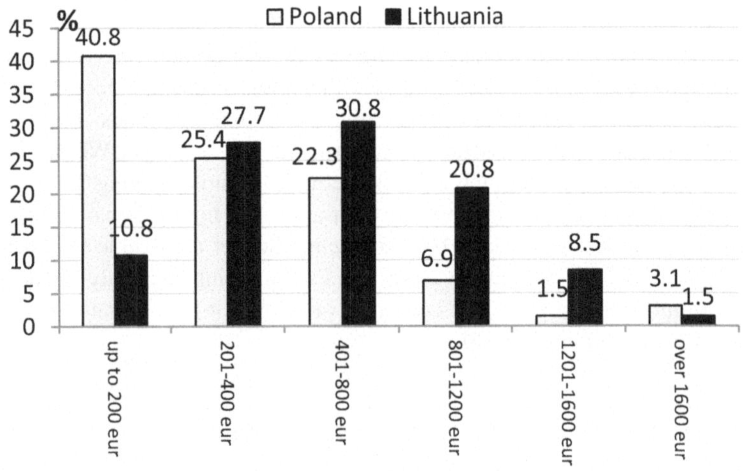

Fig. 23.5 Total budget of Polish and Lithuanian respondents for a trip per person. *Source* Survey data

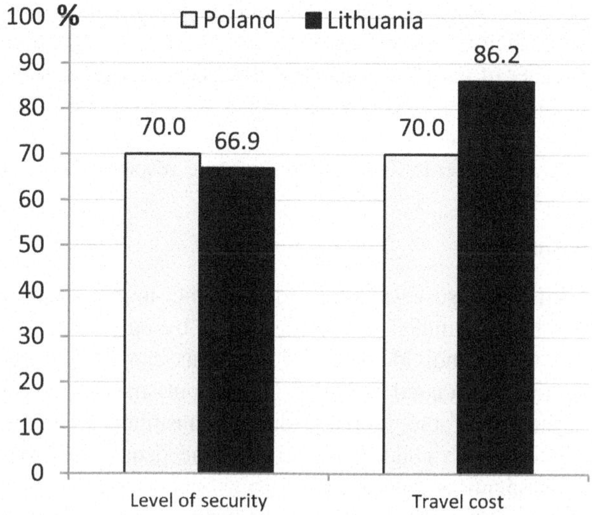

Fig. 23.6 Factors determining the trip of respondents in Poland and Lithuania. *Source* Survey data

Poles (it is important or very important for 70%). For only 30% of respondents from Poland, the cost of travel is "very important" and for 40% of them "important," while among people from Lithuania, this percentage is 50 and 36.2% respectively. What is also characteristic, even though Poles spend much less on travel than Lithuanians, safety is more important for the former (70% of them, of which 44.6% is very important) than for those surveyed in Lithuania (66.9%, of which 40.8% is very important).

The statistical analysis partially confirms the conclusion that there is a difference between student groups in both countries in assessing the determinants of mobility. Analysis by *Mann–Whitney U test* indicated that there is no significant statistical difference in the assessment of safety level by students from Poland and Lithuania as a significant factor determining the choice of tourist destination $p = 0.5587407$ ($Z = 0.6186766$). However, results of analysis by *Mann–Whitney U test* indicated that there is a significant statistical difference in the assessment of travel costs by students from Poland and Lithuania as an important factor determining the choice of tourist destination $p = 0.0005595$ ($Z = -3.6844610$).

Conclusions presented above may prove that either the declared preferences of the respondents differ significantly from each other, or the respondents are strongly susceptible to emotions. An analysis of whether the students surveyed would be willing to pay more and go to a country with a low risk (high level of safety) contradictory to the above results. The results showed that in both countries around 70% of people would be willing to do so. The lack of a statistically significant difference in assessment between Polish and Lithuanian students confirmed the analysis by *Mann–Whitney U test*, where $p = 0.915272757$ ($Z = -0.1345319$).

These conclusions are somewhat contradictory to the answers obtained from the questions about the factors determining the choice of tourist destination (Fig. 23.4), where a large number of people, especially Lithuanians, pay attention mainly to the cost of travel. Such a discrepancy in preferences may be indicative of the respondents' vulnerability to emotions and differences in declared and subconscious choices, or of the respondents' lack of given a true response to the questionnaire survey.

Proposed experiment

The conducted pilot surveys revealed that the tourist inclinations of the respondents may be determined to a large extent by emotions. This means that the conditions in which individuals make decisions can influence their choices. Moreover, consumers' declared attitudes in the tourism sector may differ from subconscious attitudes of the tourist industry consumers. Therefore, it seems appropriate to initiate such conditions and examine people who decide to travel with the help of a scientific experiment.

Taking into account the development of neurotourism and the results of a pilot study, we propose the use of cognitive neurology methods, in the form of recording brain waves with electroencephalograph (EEG) and studies of galvanic skin reflexes (GSR). For both studies, it is proposed to use an additional audiovisual technique. For this purpose, a video will be created by the authors to illustrate certain life situations and to create specific emotions among the respondents. For this purpose, the course/scenario of the experiment, which was already used by Tosun et al. (2016), will be used. Each image will be displayed on the computer screen for up to 10 s. The authors will select images that reflect security measures in tourism infrastructure, tourist destinations in the context of the increased terrorist risks and economic factors. In this way, the subconscious selection of tourists coming from Poland and Lithuania will be examined (graphic illustration of the course of the experiment is shown in Fig. 23.7).

As mentioned above, it is proposed to use audiovisual technology in the form of creating a video that would create specific emotions for the researcher. The person watching the film would have a head cap for measuring brain waves attached to the

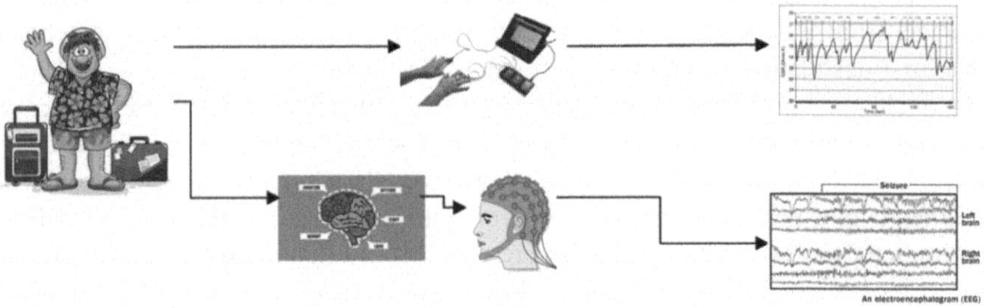

Fig. 23.7 Diagram of the research using a scientific experiment *Source* Own elaboration based on photographs on the Google search Web site

computer. The study would also use a galvanometer with electrodes attached to the fingers of their hand, which would be connected to the next computer.

Different images (external stimuli) would be displayed on the computer monitor, the purpose of which would be to induce various emotions in the subjects (negative emotions: anxiety, fear, disgust; positive emotions: joy, peace, delight). With the computer, researchers, on the other hand, would register the recording of waves of different frequencies emitted by the brain of the researched person. In addition, a record of skin and palliative reactions and the test pulse would be recorded. After the end of the experiment, we would analyze the recorded waves, which would consist in determining how strong their emotions are and at what point during watching the film the examined person emitted waves of higher amplitude (higher emotions) and when lower.

The results obtained would make it possible to examine the response to this:

- tourist destination and tourist infrastructure, with various levels of visible safety measures,
- the possibility of traveling to tourist destinations at different travel costs.

In order to ensure the representativeness of the survey, it is proposed to survey at least 30 persons in both countries according to different gender and age groups. The experiment conducted in this way should provide an answer to the question of how tourists in Poland and Lithuania react subconsciously. Experienced persons will be assessed for the same decision-making situations as during the survey.

23.6 Conclusions

This work has focused on new ways of analyzing social phenomena in the tourism sector. The object of the research consists of tourist preferences of tourists from Poland and Lithuania, while the research problem was how to examine the influence of economic and security factors on these preferences when choosing a tourist destination, in the context of increased terrorist risk.

Although the results of the questionnaire survey referred only to the students in both universities, not the entire population, however, some differences could be observed between the respondent groups. To this end, the authors conducted a pilot survey which indicated that respondents from Lithuania spend more on their travels than their Polish counterparts. Moreover, it has been stated that for Polish respondents, their safety is more important than the cost of traveling, and vice versa, for Lithuanians who pay more attention to travel costs. The significance of the differences was statistically confirmed by *Mann–Whitney U test*.

However, surveys have shown that there are discrepancies in respondents' replies. Based on these conclusions and analysis of the subject literature, the authors have proved that it is appropriate to examine the preferences of subconscious tourists. It was pointed out that the future analysis of these phenomena has created a new field of research, which is termed neurotourism and uses cognitive neurology methods. These are the methods proposed by the authors in the experiment, who intend to carry out an experiment among tourists from Poland and Lithuania. Undoubtedly, the potential results obtained will indicate sufficient evidence that further such tests/research is necessary.

However, in order to be scientifically objective, it is also necessary to stress the risks arising from such research. As was pointed by Fortunato et al. (2014, p. 211), it "*concerns the measurement of deeper brain structures; it can only record more superficial electrical signals.*" Besides research is conducted in unnatural, i.e., laboratory, conditions, which may affect the test results. In addition, there are moral, social, and ethical issues concerning the use of neuroscience devices used for neurotourism research. Such studies would be better conducted on larger research groups, the reason being that the results would be more representative.

References

Albu CE (2016) Tourism and terrorism a worldwide perspective. CES Work Pap VIII(1):1–19

Alejziak W (2012) Sekwencyjna analiza trendów turystycznych (SATT) jako instrument diagnozowania zmian w popycie turystycznym. Zeszyty Naukowe Uniwersytetu Szczecińskiego 697:27–42

Baker D, Mc A (2014) The effects of terrorism on the travel and tourism industry. Int J Relig Tour Pilgr 2(1):58–67

Bernaś B, Pujer K (2014) Bezpieczeństwo i zagrożenia w turystyce. Wroclaw Sch Bank Res J 15(2):223–243

Boniface B, Cooper C (2005) The geography of travel and tourism. Butterworth-Heinemann

Eurostat, http://ec.europa.eu/eurostat/tgm/table.do?tab=table&init=1&language=en&pcode=sdg_08_10&plugin=1. Accessed 17 Mar 2018

Fortunato VCR, de Giraldi JME, de Oliveira JH Caldeira (2014) A review of studies on neuromarketing: practical results, techniques, contributions and limitations. J Manag Res 6 (2):201–220

Giudici E, Dettori A, Caboni F (2017) Neurotourism: futuristic perspective or today's reality? In: 20th excellence in services international conference, pp 335–345

Grigaliūnaitė V, Pilelienė L (2015) Neinvazinių galvos smegenų elektrinio aktyvumo tyrimų metodų ir žvilgsnio sekimo sistemos taikymo galimybės reklamos efektyvumo vertinimui. Manag Theory Stud Rural Bus Infrastruct Dev 37(2):212–220

Holloway C J, Taylor N (2006) The Business of Tourism. FT Prentice Hall

Horner S, Swarbrooke J (2009) International cases in tourism management. Elsevier

Ipsos MORI, International SOS (2016) Travel risk and reality: The new normal for business. https://www.ipsos.com/sites/default/files/migrations/en-uk/files/Assets/Docs/Infographics/travel-risks-and-reality-infographic.pdf. Accessed 6 Jan 2018

Kaczmarska A (2014) Wybrane czynniki rozwoju turystyki. Studia Ekonomiczne. Zeszyty Naukowe Uniwersytetu Ekonomicznego w Katowicach 176:202–215

Karwacka D (2014) Ocena zagrożeń terrorystycznych i ich wpływ na bezpieczeństwo Polski. Rozprawy Społeczne 1(VIII):42–50

Kim J, Fesenmaier DR (2015) Measuring emotions in real time: implications for tourism experience design. J Travel Res 54(4):419–429

Kôvári I, Zimányi K (2011) Safety and security in the age of global tourism. APSTRACT Appl Stud Agribus Commer 5:59–61

Lähteenmäki-Uutela A (2017) Psychophysiological methods for measuring tourism experiences by the sea: case Bothnian Sea. In: Proceedings of the heritage, tourism and hospitality international conference HTHIC. Pori, Finland, 27–29 Sept 2017, pp 139–142
Lee JJ, Gerard TK (2012) Recollection consistency of festival consumption emotions. J Travel Res 51(2):178–190
Ma QG, Hu LF, Pei GX et al (2014) Applying neuroscience to tourism management: a primary exploration of neurotourism. Appl Mech Mater 670–671:1637–1640
MacCannell D (2005) Turysta. Nowa teoria klasy próżniaczej. Wydawnictwo Literackie MUZA SA
Mansfel Y, Pizam A (2006) Tourism, security and safety: from theory to practice. Elsevier
Marczak M (2012) Wpływ terroryzmu na rozwój turystyki Międzynarodowej. Zeszyty Naukowe Uniwersytetu Szczecińskiego. Ekonomiczne Problemy Turystyki 20:89–102
Markgraf I, Scheffer D, Pulkenat J (2012) The needs of package tourists and travel agents—neuromarketing in the tourism sector. In: Conrady R, Buck M (eds) Trends and issues in global tourism. Springer, Berlin, pp 79–91
Matthem A (2014) Examining the indispensability of safety and security for tourism and travel trade in Nigeria. In: Proceedings of the IIER international conference, Dubai, UAE, 14 Dec 2014, pp 48–51
Nagaj R (2017) Application for a grant to the National Science Centre in Poland No. 395674 in the DAINA (Polish-Lithuanian Funding initiative) for financing a research project entitled "Security measures in tourism infrastructure and the cost of travel in the context of terrorism threat: Lithuanian and Polish tourists' preferences"
Niezgoda A (2012) Popyt turystyczny – uwarunkowania i perspektywy rozwoju. Zeszyty Naukowe Uniwersytety Szczecińskiego 697:11–25
Pareek R (2016) Terrorism and its psycho-social impact on society. Pune Res Int J English 2(3):1–5
Parrinello GL (2012) Tourism and neuroscience: a preliminary approach. Tourismos Int Multidiscip J Tour 7(2):39–54
Pennington-Gray L, Schroeder A (2013) International tourist's perceptions of safety & security: the role of social media. Matkailututkimus Finnish J Tour Res 9(1):7–23. https://www.researchgate.net/publication/263009819_International_tourist%27s_perceptions_of_safety_security_The_role_of_social_media. Accessed 8 Jan 2018
Prayag G, Hosany S, Muskat B et al (2017) Understanding the relationships between tourists' emotional experiences, perceived overall image, satisfaction, and intention to recommend. J Travel Res 56:41–54
red24's Global Terrorism Risk Map 2017. https://opinion.red24.com/2017/01/10/red24s-global-terrorism-risk-map-2017/. Accessed 5 Jan 2016
Rittichainuwat BN, Chakraborty G (2009) Perceived travel risks regarding terrorism and disease: the case of Thailand. Tour Manag 30(3):410–418
Santana G (2005) Globalisation, safety and national security. In: Cooper C, Wahab S (eds) Tourism in the age of globalisation. Routledge, London, pp 213–241
Šerić N, Jurišić M, Petričević D (2015) Neuromarketing potential for tourist destination brand positioning. In: Tourism in Southern and Eastern Europe, 3rd International Scientific Conference Tourism in Southern and Eastern Europe, vol 3, pp 429–439
Statista (2018a) Direct and total contribution of travel and tourism to the global economy from 2006 to 2016 (in trillion U.S. dollars). https://www.statista.com/statistics/233223/travel-and-tourism–total-economic-contribution-worldwide/. Accessed 7 Jan 2018
Statista (2018b) Global international tourism revenue from 2000 to 2016 (in billion U.S. dollars). https://www.statista.com/statistics/273123/total-international-tourism-receipts/. Accessed 7 Jan 2018
Survila A, Mikėnas E, Žuromskaitė B (2017) The impact of terrorism on the tourism sector of Lithuania. Montenegrin J Econ 13(3):101–118
Tan CH, Chong XW, Ho SB (2017) Significance of safety and security issues on tourism industry in Malaysia. Sci Int 29(2):471–475

Tarlow P (2006) A social theory of terrorism and tourism. In: Yoel M, Pizam A (eds) Tourism, security and safety: from theory to practice. Amsterdam, pp 33–48
Tarlow P (2008) The changing face of tourism security in times of terrorism and crime. EPICC Forum Canada, pp 1–20
Tarlow P (2011) Tourism risk management in an age of terrorism. Econ Autónoma 4(7):18–30
Tarlow P (2014) Reflective epilogue: concerns in tourism safety. Int J Relig Tour Pilgrim 2(1): 68–70
Teoman DC (2017) Terrorism and tourism in Europe, new partners? European J Geogr 8(2): 132–142
Tosun C, Ozdemir S, Cubuk F (2016) Usage of neuro-tourism methods in hotel preferences of the consumers. In: The 2016 WEI international academic conference proceedings, Boston, pp 19–26
UNWTO (2017) Tourism highlights, 2017 edition. https://www.e-unwto.org/doi/pdf/10.18111/9789284419029. Accessed 8 Jan 2018
Wolf K (2015) Measuring facial expression of emotion. Dialogues Clin Neurosci 17(4):457–462
World Travel & Tourism Council (2017) Travel & Tourism. In: Global economic impact & issues 2017. https://www.wttc.org/-/media/files/reports/economic-impact-research/2017-documents/global-economic-impact-and-issues-2017.pdf. Accessed 6 Jan 2018

Chapter 24
The Role of Behavioral Methods Used in Research on Tourism Development

Rafał Nagaj and Brigita Žuromskaitė

Abstract The aim of the paper is to identify the role of emotional factors in the analysis of socioeconomic phenomena in tourism and the resulting distortions of test results obtained with the help of the questionnaire tool. The authors also tried to show the usefulness of the application of new, non-standard research methods to study socioeconomic phenomena in tourism. In accomplishing this goal, a critical analysis of professional literature and empirical studies based on primary sources of data from pilot surveys conducted by the authors of the paper among students of one of the universities in Vilnius (Lithuania) and in Szczecin (Poland) was carried out. To pilot survey research, simple elements of descriptive statistics research and testing of the difference between two population proportions were used in the paper. The results of the research indicated that the above phenomena also occur among tourists. The imperfection of the methods used in this new field of science, neuro-tourism, is also presented, which requires further research on this issue.

Keywords Behavioral methods · Tourism · Neuro-tourism

24.1 Introduction

Economic practice and decisions made by people in social life prove that people are not always driven by rationality when making decisions. The classic economics precursor Smith (2005) stressed out that even though humans are egoists and are guided by rationality while making choices, trust is important to them as well. It happens because people wish to live in a society they feel happy in.

R. Nagaj (✉)
University of Szczecin, Mickiewicza 64, 71-101 Szczecin, Poland
e-mail: rafal.nagaj@usz.edu.pl

B. Žuromskaitė
Mykolas Romeris University, Ateities 20, 08303 Vilnius, Lithuania
e-mail: brigitaz@mruni.eu

K. Nermend and M. Łatuszyńska (eds.), *Problems, Methods and Tools in Experimental and Behavioral Economics*, Springer Proceedings in Business and Economics, https://doi.org/10.1007/978-3-319-99187-0_24

The neoclassical paradigm reveals that life is dominated by *homo economicus* rule. There are at least a few more conditions for a man to follow to be completely reasonable though (Solek 2010, p. 22). These include: acting on the basis of a full and exact information, having unlimited possibilities of processing information, maximizing the expected usability and acting strictly in their own interest which means excluding any possible benefits for others, as consumers should present consistent behaviors.

Although, as pointed out by i.a. Ellsberg (1961), Kahneman and Tversky (1974) or Thaler (1980), humans are not able to act completely rationally on a daily basis —probably due to psychological barriers they may encounter. As indicated in Knight's theory (2012), everything that happens in our lives bears some uncertainty and risk. This, in turn, causes that every human deed in both social and economic aspects of life should not only be based on rationality as determined by the main paradigm of economics, but on behavioral preferences as well. This is why the professional literature underlines that due to emotional side of every human being, people experience many cognitive disruptions. These may include:

- Certainty effect which causes people to make choices that are certain to happen at the expense of decisions which may be more profitable but are subject to even the smallest level of risk;
- Rebound effect which causes people to avoid risky decisions when there is profit to be obtained and choose risky when the loss is possible;
- Von Restorff effect, also known as the isolation effect, which may lead to inconsistency of preferences. It assumes meticulous analysis of alternatives and ignoring of traits that are common for those alternatives, focusing on differences instead;
- Framing effect which causes contextual or formulative changes of a determined issue and which are seemingly irrelevant and result in significant differences in choices made by people;
- Endowment effect according to which people demand more money for a certain thing if they already possess it;
- Bandwagon effect which causes a man to make the same choices as the choices made by people they want to identify with;
- Availability bias which makes economic entities to pay more attention to things that have already been memorized and are easy to be reminded of;
- Fear of the unknown which makes people avoid choices when they lack full information which, as a result, may lead to irrational decisions (Nagaj 2015, p. 26).

Additionally, neuro-economics points out those human behaviors which are consistent with cognitive disruptions should actually be assessed rational as it helps people minimize any potential losses, e.g., when deciding on certain, even more expensive options, people tend to minimize any unpleasant feelings which may occur with the loss for a braver choice (Fox and Poldrack 2009).

The paper explores research that has examined tourists and their tendencies to change their minds once they are surveyed which is the most common study method. Therefore, using alternative methods, such as behavioral, is intentional in research on tourism. Identification of this phenomenon in the field, determining of its extent and purposefulness of applying new, untraditional approaches for examining social and economic phenomena within the tourism industry is the goal of the following study. This aim of the paper will be achieved by critical analysis of professional literature and empirical research based on original sources of data from surveys conducted by authors among respondents in their alma maters.

24.2 The Role of Emotions in Tourism

When traveling people make their decisions based on a number of aspects, among them—on emotions. In general, tourists experience a wide range of different emotions that can influence their preferences and traveling plans from the very beginning of each journey. Emotions are actually present at every stage of the trip, including preparation, leaving, and staying away from home, coming back and for a certain period after the trip as well. Their condition is also influenced by other aspects such as psychological, social, cultural, and even natural factors (Fratu 2011).

Consideration shall be also taken of the reasons why tourists go on a journey as it may be found out that they might be burdened emotionally. Fratu (2011) points out two different reasons for traveling: conscious (which are directly linked to one's previous experiences) and unconscious (which can be identified using indirect psychological examination methods). Both of them influence tourists' comfort during the trip and after coming back home.

However, people can experience both positive and negative emotions during the trip. They can be caused by the result of the trip, but also be dependent on the quality of tourist services (Hosany et al. 2015) and perception of the destination which, in turn, may be influenced by crowds, queues, tackiness of places visited and overpricing among others. Circumstances such as natural disasters or terrorist attacks may affect the time spent out of the home as well. Other factors impacting emotional assessment of the trip include cultural shock and tourists' psychological syndromes such as Paris syndrome, Stendhal syndrome, Rubens syndrome which may cause psychological (hallucinations, déjà vu, depression, nervous breakdown, aggression, etc.), and physical (increased heart rate, dizziness, confusion, unconditional sex drive, etc.) disorders.

The question is how to examine tourists' emotions to obtain their most realistic image as such a wide range of feelings can be experienced by each and every tourist during every journey. Science underlines that there are many types of research on emotions experienced by tourists; however, they were all conducted after coming back home in an "artificial" environment. Therefore, emotions described by the authors of these publications were not authentic enough since most of the research had been conducted in laboratories, applying methods that are not always suitable for examining tourist behaviors. As a result, Hosany and Gilbert (2010) created an emotional scale—Destination Emotion Scale (DES), which aims to measure the emotional experience of tourists (Measuring Tourists' Emotional Experiences). The Destination Emotion Scale (DES) consists of 15 items, representing three emotional dimensions: joy (cheerfulness, pleasure, joy, enthusiasm, and delight), love (tenderness, love, caring, affection, and warm-heartedness), and positive surprise (amazement, astonishment, fascination, inspiration, and surprise) (Hosany et al. 2015).

However, the scale of this research lacks a very important group of emotions related to safety, fear, anxiety, and panic issues. These are emotions which begin to be felt by tourists subject to the increased risk of terrorist attacks in their travel destinations. Fortunately, they are covered in different studies where researchers apply interesting methods. One of them is the experiment (on the basis of appraisal tendency theory) conducted by Lerner et al. (2003), which concluded that "fear increased risk estimates and plans for precautionary measures; anger did the opposite" (Table 24.1).

An alternative approach to measuring tourists' emotions may be observation of neurophysiological reactions, including facial expressions, eye tracking, functional magnetic resonance, and galvanic skin response (Wilhelm and Grossman 2010).

Emotions and traveling (tourism) are directly connected with each other; however, nowadays we are lacking efficient methods for examining emotional states in real time which would be very helpful in understanding tourists and matching them with products meeting their requirements.

24.3 Neurocognitive Studies and Tourism

The studies on tourism increasingly exploit neuro-scientific practice (Tosun et al. 2016). According to researchers, traditional methods do not guarantee reliable results as people tend to manipulate their responses when being surveyed (Ma et al. 2014). This, in turn, forces tourism researchers to seek for alternative, more efficient ways of examining the phenomena. As a result, they lean toward exploiting neuroscience in research on tourism (Giudici et al. 2017). According to Giudici et al. (2017, p. 340), neurocognitive examination helps examine tourists' subconscious and unconscious choices, which is not possible while applying traditional research methods.

According to Karremans et al. (2006, p. 792), results of neurocognitive examination are much more reliable and unprejudiced because they are obtained subconsciously. A similar opinion is also expressed by Giudici et al. (2017), who state that "it allows us to focus on the deep mechanism regarding social behaviors that come directly from the brain without interference using the neuroscience tools" (p. 339).

Table 24.1 Key approaches to measuring emotions (Kim and Fesenmaier 2015, p. 422)

Measure	Response system	Modality	Advantages	Disadvantages
Self-report	Subjective experience	Diary, interview, questionnaire	Unobtrusive, straightforward, and simple	Assuming that people are aware of and willing to report their emotions; subject to the respondent's bias; results of different studies might not be directly comparable
Observation	Behavior	Facial expressions, speech, gestures	Use of unobtrusive techniques for measuring emotion	Cannot perform context-dependent interpretation of sensory data, highly dependent on environmental conditions, and some responses can be faked
Neuro-/ physiological response	Peripheral and central physiology, affect-modulated startle, fMRI	Skin conductance, body responses: pulse rate, blood pressure, brain activity	Can detect short-term changes; cannot be easily faked	Reliance on non-transparent, invasive sensors; can reduce people's mobility, causing distraction of emotional reactions; inability to map data to specific emotions; require expertise and special equipment

Tosun et al. (2016) have a similar approach to this issue, who claim that "neuro-tourism investigates neural mechanisms of the behavior of tourists for tourism research" (Tosun et al., p. 20). According to these scientists, the brain is a black box that conceals emotions and preferences, and neurocognitive research acts like a window that reveals and gives access to these emotions (Fortunato et al. 2014, p. 205). As Giudici et al. (2017, p. 341) note "Neuro-tourism (and neuro-marketing) research instruments and procedures are divided into two general classes: tools that measure reactions of the body to tourism, and tools that measure reactions of the brain." The most commonly used are functional magnetic resonance imaging (fMRI), electroencephalography (EEG), positron emission tomography (PET), magnetoencephalography (MEG), eye tracking, facial recognition (or electromyography), cardiovascular parameters, and the galvanic skin response (Fortunato et al. 2014).

Table 24.2 Limitations/opportunities and implications of techniques and neurological tools (Giudici et al. 2017, pp. 342–343)

Limitations	Implications
– Development of high-priced and short-time neuroimaging experiments – Development of experiments confined to artificial laboratory environments – Use of a single neuroimaging technology at the time: fMRI – Use of a single non-neuroimaging device – Moral, social, and ethical abuses of neurosciences devices used for neuro-tourism	– Limited sampling – Inadequate evaluation of neurophysiological variations – Experimental distortion – Incomplete comprehension of subjects' emotional states – Incomplete map of brain functions – Over interpretation of results – Scarce integration of neurological and physiological signals – Over interpretation of results – Inadequate protection of vulnerable populations – Manipulation of consumers' minds
Opportunities	**Implications**
– Employment of nanotechnologies to measure emotional states in real time – Use of unobtrusive and portable nanotechnologies devices – Application of multifunctional nanotechnology devices – Combination of laboratory experiments and testing of daily life through miniaturized nanotechnology devices – Balance of nanotechnology techniques applied in the neuro-tourism field with moral, social and ethical requirements	– Continuous and real-time monitoring of subjects' emotional states and purchasing experiences – Eliminating generalizations of limited laboratory studies – Increased reliability and validity of findings – Eliminating perception of intrusiveness and distortions of conventional laboratory devices – Monitoring different neurophysiological signals in a natural, continuous and comfortable way – Co-measuring of different neurological and physiological signals – Increased reliability and validity of findings – Co-measuring of different neurological, biological and physiological signals – Increased reliability and validity of findings – Defense of consumers' privacy and autonomy – Protection of vulnerable population groups – Comprehension of compulsive behaviors and pathologies and consumer buying habits

There are still many limitations imposed on a wide use of neurocognitive methods in tourism (see Table 24.2). One of the main flaws includes conducting examination in an unnatural environment and using really expensive equipment; however, many problems have been solved by nanotechnology. Plus, there is a wide range of wireless devices that can be used remotely in the field.

Increased exploitation of neurological methods in tourism studies has resulted in the emergence of neuro-tourism. It mainly analyses the nervous system which is an essence of tourists' behaviors during their journeys (Ma et al. 2014). It helps attach to the tourists' sub-consciousness and an understanding of the emotional basis of their choices and motives.

Literary sources of neuro-tourism provide a lot of interesting and quality research. One of the first experiments of this type was conducted by Ma et al. (2014) and was focused on beauty perception. It exploited an electroencephalograph (EEG). During the experiment, people were shown pictures of Jiuzhaigou nature reserve and national park in China. Twenty photographs showcased the place in different perspectives—both beautiful and less delightful landscapes. The study was conducted on bachelor students. The results of the experiment indicated that it is possible to investigate and access such factors as happiness, tourist satisfaction, and possible intention to revisit location in relation to the tourism experience.

Another interesting experiment in this field was conducted by Kim and Fesenmaier (2015). They exploited an individual's electrodermal activity (EDA) which was supposed to examine tourists' emotions through their skin responses in order to obtain information on feelings experienced by a tourist in real-time and natural environment. Two 23-year-old female students were chosen for this experiment. They were sightseeing Philadelphia for four days, visited popular destinations, tourist attractions and used different means of transportation. They had to wear the Affectiva Q-sensor wrist bands during the whole journey. They were also asked to take pictures, record videos, and note their feelings. Afterward, the girls were thoroughly interviewed. The experiment helped understand better the emotions experienced by tourists in real time, on every stage of the journey.

A number of interesting research which applied psychological methods, including cognitive neurology so as to study the occurring social phenomena in tourism, were also conducted by Tosun et al. (2016). They used 16-channeled electroencephalography (EEG) to study hospitality management. Their goal was to distinguish the most important criteria tourists take into consideration when booking their hotels. In contrast, in the qualitative part of the study open-ended questions were used and "'content analysis' method applied for the solution of qualitative surveys was used for the analysis of the data collected by considering the participant opinions" (Tosun et al. 2016, p. 21). The study (the experiment) was carried out on 15 participants aged 18–55, all living in Ankara. Pictures, which were shown to them, were chosen randomly and displayed for 10 s. The analysis showcased pictures regarding: price, location, quality, service, and comfort. Later on, the study's results were compared. Having used statistical instruments, researchers compared whether the criteria were chosen consciously or subconsciously and whether they were selected in the same manner. The majority of the results were similar, with a small statistical difference (more significant differences were spotted in price and quality criteria).

Professional literature analysis has proved that cognitive neurology, just like other behavioral methods, is increasingly practiced in studying tourism which has caused a new field of science—neuro-tourism—to emerge. Moreover, those methods came out to be very efficient in examining tourists' tendencies, especially those of a subconscious character, where traditional methods applied in social and economic sciences are much less effective. The analysis has pointed out that there are still many research gaps to be examined in this field though. These include tourists' preferences and emotions when exposed to safety-related circumstances.

24.4 Methodology and Results

It was decided to explore pilot surveys' research results conducted among students, who declared to travel a lot, so as to determine whether tourists tend to act emotionally and behaviorally. The research was supposed to point out that tourism consumers tend to change their minds, even in cases of the same subject. The purpose of this research is to confirm the results of the research carried out by Ma et al. (2014) stating that in surveys, respondents–tourists sometimes manipulate answers or are not aware of their choice. The aim is to confirm that in the tourism industry, there are also emotional/behavioral considerations and tourists are not always rational. For this purpose, a method research survey was carried out which describes tourism preferences and examines the impact of security and economic factors on tourist trends. This survey research was conducted in November 2017 by the authors of the study, among 130 students at the Faculty of Economics and Management University of Szczecin in Poland and 130 students of the Faculty of Public Governance at Mykolas Romeris University in Lithuania. The research samples accounted for 8.4% of the total number of students studying at each of these faculties. Three questions were used from this survey questionnaire:

- which factor is more important in choosing the trip (all the variables were measured using Likert scale with 5 response levels (from 1 = of no importance to 5 = very important): travel cost or safety level;
- at what price reduction of the total cost of the tourist trip, the respondent would be willing to choose to travel to a country that has lower level of security (a tourist destination with a higher risk rating);
- would the respondent be willing to pay more and go to a country with a low level of risk (high level of security).

First, the research determined two groups of people on the basis of the first question:

- those who consider safety level significant (i.e., important or very important), at the same time assessing economic factor (travel cost) as having little significance (indifferent, of little significance or insignificant);
- and those who consider economic factor—travel cost—significant (i.e., important or very important), at the same time assessing the level of safety as having little significance.

Furthermore, the research determined a percentage of people excluded on the basis of the first question who changed their minds when answering the second and the third question.

In the second question, the fact of changing one's mind was identified based on:

- the number of people who consider the price a factor determining their tourist trip (at the same time stating that the safety level is insignificant) who responded that they would not choose a traveling destination with a low level of safety no matter the price;
- the number of people who consider the level of safety a factor determining their tourist trip (at the same time stating that the travel cost is insignificant) who responded that they would choose a traveling destination with a low level of safety provided the price reduction by 20 or 30%.

The third question—"Would you be willing to pay more and go to a country with a low level of risk (high level of security)"—determined:

- a percentage of people responding negatively, at the same time having answered that safety level is an important factor in choosing the trip in the first question;
- a percentage of people responding positively, at the same time having answered that safety level is not important factor in choosing the trip in the first question.

In order to verify the statistical significance of changes in answers during the survey, the authors will additionally do testing of the difference between two population proportions (separately for question 2 and for question 3). At the significance level of 0.05, it is assumed that:

null hypothesis: $p_1 = p_2$, i.e., in question 1, the percentage of people stating that the level of safety is insignificant is the same as in question 2 (or in question 3);
alternative hypothesis: $p_1 \neq p_2$, i.e., in question 1, the percentage of people stating that the level of safety is insignificant is different from that in question 2 (or in question 3).

Results and findings

Figures 24.1 and 24.2 represent a percentage of people who change their minds while responding to the given questions:

- and who claim that there is only one factor determining their decision on going for a trip (which is either safety or travel cost—Fig. 24.1);
- compared to the total number of people surveyed (Fig. 24.2).

The research results reveal that both in Poland and in Lithuania part of people surveyed tended to change their minds while responding to different questions of the same tourism matters. About 10% of the surveyed Lithuanians compared to the total number of people examined and 30% of people who were certain of their responses changed their minds. The percentage of people who were not certain of their responses and changed their minds was slightly lower among Poles and,

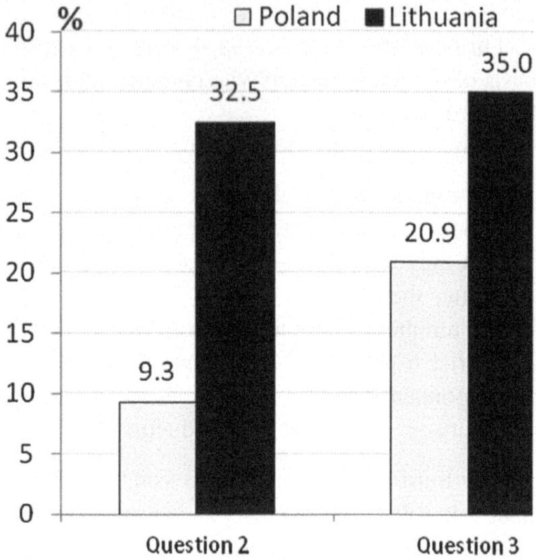

Fig. 24.1 Percentage of people who change their minds while responding to the questions and who claim that there is only one factor determining their decision on going for a trip (measured in relation to people who consider only one factor as significant)

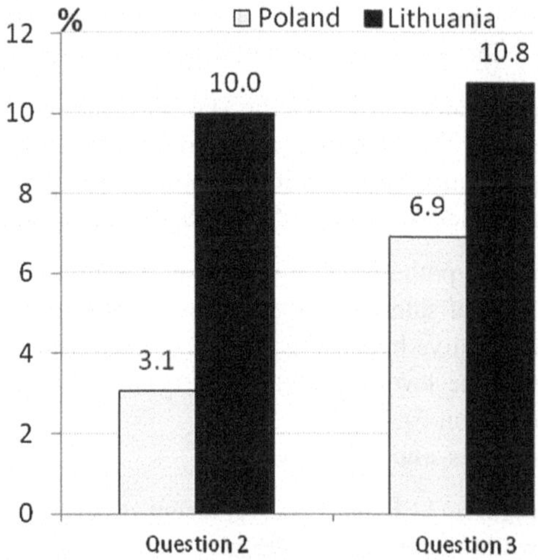

Fig. 24.2 Percentage of people who change their minds while responding to the questions measured in relation to the total number of people surveyed

depending on the question, varied from 3.1 to 9.1% which, in the context of people who were initially certain of their responses, amounted to 9.3 and 20.9%, respectively. Such results prove that in the tourism industry, people either tend to rely on their emotions and change their minds or are eager to manipulate their responses during surveys (Table 24.3).

According to the results of statistical verification which used a test to determine the difference between two population proportions with independent samples, in Poland, in terms of the third question, the percentage of responses differed statistically significantly from the answers in the first question, while in Lithuania,

Table 24.3 Results for testing the difference between two population proportions (test statistics)

Factor	Importance of level of security		Importance of travel of cost	
Studied proportions	Question 1/ question 2	Question 1/ question 3	Question 1/ question 2	Question 1/ question 3
Poland	−0.2687	0.1358	−10.1613	−6.5740
Lithuania	−0.6501	0.5339	−12.4167	−9.1750

with regard to question 2 and question 3, there was a difference between the two population proportions. Thus, the statistical analysis confirms the research conclusions that both in Poland and in Lithuania part of people surveyed tended to change their minds while responding to different questions of the same tourism matters.

24.5 Conclusions

The study explores tourism and research methods applied in conducting studies in this field. The goal of this article was to point out the flaws of traditional methods of research applied in tourism development, to identify this phenomenon and stress the purposefulness of applying behavioral methods of research of social and economic phenomena in the tourism industry. The study was carried out on a small, 130-person research group; however, the results of the research have yielded some important conclusions. It was discovered that emotional factors highly influence tourists' perception of reality. The studies on tourists showed that people tend to respond contradictorily when being surveyed. Therefore, the theses found in the literature were confirmed in this paper. Studies conducted by the authors during their pilot pioneer surveys on tourism preferences in Poland and Lithuania showcased that no matter the origin, manipulation of results occurs when using traditional methods of research; however, their level was slightly higher in Lithuania.

Theoretical and empirical analysis of this study also helps point out the fact that behavioral methods, including those applied in neurology and psychology, are not flawless either. It was found that there are several weaknesses of conducting such research using cognitive neuro-scientific methods and conducting the research in an environment which is "artificial." Emotions experienced in the laboratory are not always exact when showcasing pictures and videos, especially when it comes to the feelings of fear, panic, etc. Therefore, it is important to continue neuro-tourism examinations in order to develop a workshop tool, to provide results and enhance the efficiency of behavioral research methods in examining the phenomena regarding tourists and contributing to further development of tourism.

References

Ellsberg M (1961) Risk, ambiguity, and the savage axioms. Q J Econ 75(4):643–669

Fortunato VCR, de Giraldi JME, de Oliveira JH Caldeira (2014) A review of studies on neuromarketing: practical results, techniques, contributions and limitations. J Manag Res 6(2): 201–220

Fox CR, Poldrack RA (2009) Prospect theory and the brain. In: Glimcher PW, Camerer CF, Fehr E et al (eds) Neuroeconomics: decision making in the brain. Elsevier Academic Press, London, pp 145–173

Fratu D (2011) Factors of influence and changes in the tourism consumer behavior. Bull Transilvania Univ Braşov 4(53):119–126

Giudici E, Dettori A, Caboni F (2017) Neurotourism: futuristic perspective or today's reality? In: 20th excellence in services international conference, pp 335–345

Hosany S, Gilbert D (2010) Measuring tourists' emotional experiences toward hedonic holiday destinations. J Travel Res 49(4):513–526

Hosany S, Prayag G, Deesilatham S et al (2015) Measuring tourists' emotional experiences: further validation of the destination emotion scale. J Travel Res 54(4):482–495

Kahneman D, Tversky A (1974) Judgment under uncertainty: heuristics and biases. Sci New Ser 185(4157):1124–1131

Karremans JK, Stroebe W, Claus I (2006) Beyond Vicary's fantasies: the impact of subliminal priming and brand choice. J Exp Soc Psychol 42:792–798

Kim J, Fesenmaier DR (2015) Measuring emotions in real time: implications for tourism experience design. J Travel Res 54(4):419–429

Knight FH (2012) Risk, uncertainty and profit (1921). Courier Dover Publications, New York

Lerner JS, Gonzalez RM, Small AA et al (2003) Effects of fear and anger on perceived risks of terrorism: a national field experiment. Psychol Sci 14(2):144–150

Ma QG, Hu LF, Pei GX et al (2014) Applying neuroscience to tourism management: a primary exploration of neurotourism. Appl Mech Mater 670–671:1637–1640

Nagaj R (2015) Zniekształcenia poznawcze gospodarstw domowych na rynku detalicznym energii elektrycznej w Polsce (Cognitive biases of households on the retail Electricity Market in Poland). Rynek Energii 2:25–31

Smith A (2005) Theory of moral sentiments, 6th edn (1790), Sao Paulo, Metalibri. Retrieved 13 Feb 2018, from https://www.ibiblio.org/ml/libri/s/SmithA_MoralSentiments_p.pdf

Solek A (2010) Ekonomia behawioralna a ekonomia neoklasyczna (Behavioral Economics vs Neoclassical Economics). ZN PTE 8:21–34

Thaler RH (1980) Towards a positive theory of consumer choice. J Econ Behav Org 1(1):39–60

Tosun C, Ozdemir S, Cubuk F (2016) Usage of neuro-tourism methods in hotel preferences of the consumers. In: The 2016 WEI international academic conference proceedings, Boston, pp 19–26

Wilhelm FH, Grossman P (2010) Emotions beyond the laboratory: theoretical fundaments, study design, and analytic strategies for advanced ambulatory assessment. Biol Psychol 84(3): 552–569

The manufacturer's authorised representative in the EU is Springer Nature Customer Service Centre GmbH, Europaplatz 3, 69115 Heidelberg, Germany. If you have any concerns regarding our products, please contact ProductSafety@springernature.com

Printed and bound by CPI Group (UK) Ltd, Croydon, CR0 4YY
05/10/2026
02228139-0014